NOT BAD
FOR
DELANCEY
STREET

BRANDEIS SERIES IN AMERICAN JEWISH HISTORY,
CULTURE, AND LIFE

Jonathan D. Sarna, EDITOR | *Sylvia Barack Fishman,* ASSOCIATE EDITOR

─────

For a complete list of books that are available in the series,
visit www.upne.com

─────

Mark Cohen

Not Bad for Delancey Street

THE RISE

OF BILLY ROSE

Brandeis University Press   Waltham, Massachusetts

Brandeis University Press

An imprint of University Press of New England

www.upne.com

© 2018 Mark Cohen

All rights reserved

Manufactured in the United States of America

Designed by Mindy Basinger Hill

Typeset in Garamond Premier Pro

For permission to reproduce any of the material in this book, contact
Permissions, University Press of New England, One Court Street, Suite 250,
Lebanon NH 03766; or visit www.upne.com

For credits see p. 317, which constitutes a continuation of the copyright page.

Library of Congress Cataloging-in-Publication Data

Names: Cohen, Mark, 1956– author.

Title: Not bad for Delancey Street: the rise of Billy Rose / Mark Cohen.

Description: Waltham, Massachusetts: Brandeis University Press, 2018. |

Series: Brandeis series in American Jewish history, culture, and life | Includes
bibliographical references and index.

Identifiers: LCCN 2018017992 (print) | LCCN 2018020360 (ebook) | ISBN
9781512603132 (epub) | ISBN 9781611688900 (cloth)

Subjects: LCSH: Rose, Billy, 1899–1966. | Theatrical producers and directors—
United States—Biography.

Classification: LCC PN2287.R756 (ebook) | LCC PN2287.R756 C55 2018 (print)

DDC 792.02/33092 [B] —dc23

LC record available at https://lccn.loc.gov/2018017992

5 4 3 2 1

FOR

Danielle,

Ilana,

and Rebecca

Row out over that great ocean of material,

and lower down into it, here and there,

a little bucket, which will bring up to the light

of day some characteristic specimen . . .

LYTTON STRACHEY | *Eminent Victorians*

contents

Illustrations follow pages 70, 152, and 226.

introduction

On March 28, 1939, a young woman complained to the authorities that she did not get a chance to show her legs to Billy Rose.[1] The objection was comical, but not trivial. Rose was hiring, and as the woman explained in a letter to the president of the upcoming New York World's Fair, she and "many pretty girls in N.Y." had missed the beautiful legs contest Rose had held the previous day in a Times Square shop window. Its ostensible purpose was to find a Miss World's Fair before the great event opened in April and, not incidentally, draw attention to Rose's much-anticipated fair attraction. Billy Rose's Aquacade would feature two hundred young women in bathing suits performing a synchronized water ballet. It would also earn him millions, as it built on the branding formula that had won him national fame with entertainments dubbed Billy Rose's Music Hall, Billy Rose's *Jumbo,* Billy Rose's Frontier Fiesta, Billy Rose's Show of Shows, Billy Rose's Casa Mañana, and Billy Rose's Diamond Horseshoe. During the 1930s, as one-third of the nation sat unemployed, waiting for the Depression to end, Rose graduated from obscurity to fame to being practically unavoidable. "A little man with a Napoleonic penchant for the colossal and magnificent, Billy Rose is the country's No. 1 purveyor of mass entertainment," announced *Life* magazine.[2] With 1,400 people on his payroll, he ran a larger organization than any other producer in the country, reported the *New York Times.*[3] "It is likely that no more dynamic combination of artist, psychologist, businessman and salesman has ever struck Broadway," asserted the *Saturday Evening Post.*[4]

His popular appeal also got a boost from his self-assured defiance. A wiseguy attitude smacked of that older American archetype, the capable loner. "I'm in a racket," he told the columnist Mark Hellinger. "I'm not supposed to have any friends."[5]

So it is not surprising that the would-be contestant was upset that she had missed an opportunity to strut her stuff before the celebrated showman, but in truth she had missed nothing. Rose's March 27 legs contest was a fake. Its true purpose was to camouflage a major break with his cynical, no-attachments creed. The Nazi threat against the Jews had lately brought to the surface the code instilled by Rose's mother to respond to the needs of the Jewish community, and that day a Jewish refugee he had secretly rescued from Europe petitioned immigration officials on Ellis Island to let him stay in New York and not force him to sail on to Cuba, which was the destination noted on the visa Rose had paid for and arranged. This was something Rose had not anticipated. It would be a disaster if on the eve of the World's Fair the public learned he was becoming more political and more Jewish. Most Americans wanted no part of the looming bloodbath in Europe and were suspicious of Jewish agitation for intervention. Rose had to quiet his noisy refugee.

The legs contest did the trick. With his usual flair for publicity, Rose arranged for a WMCA radio announcer to join him in the window of the Ansonia Bootery at Forty-Seventh Street and Broadway and broadcast the competition, as half-naked women displayed their charms. "The leg display precipitated a near riot in the street outside," reported *Variety,* and nobody learned of the refugee's arrival, petition, or deportation to Cuba.[6] Rose's reputation as the smartest and toughest s.o.b. on Broadway was secure.

That reputation was so solidly constructed that it forever obscured his transformation from hardheaded American businessman to generous Jewish philanthropist. As the American-born son of poor immigrants, he eagerly embraced success in business as his worldly salvation. It was the American way. In 1906, when Rose was a schoolboy, the philosopher William James had diagnosed America's "exclusive worship of the bitch-goddess SUCCESS ... with the squalid cash interpretation put on the word success" as the "national disease."[7] Rose welcomed the contagion and went on to write hit songs, run nightclubs, produce plays, mastermind spectacles, own Broadway theaters, make a fortune, screw competitors, marry beautiful young women, and buy mansions, art, a Rolls-Royce, and even his own island. He flaunted contempt for anything that did not contribute to the bottom line. "He was cruel and cold," said his secretary Helen Schrank. "If you said anything sentimental, he would say, 'What are we, back on Second Avenue?'"[8] That was where Yiddish theaters, with their often-maudlin plays, once thrived. Rose also aimed his blunt brutality at women. Harsh treatment was not unusual at the time, but even then, some men were notably rough. In Billy Wilder's 1951 film, *Ace in the Hole,* the female lead tells the character played by Kirk Douglas, "I met a lot of hard-boiled eggs in my life, but you—you're twenty minutes." Rose could be twenty-five.

But the Jewish catastrophe posed by the Nazis forced Rose to make an exception to his hardboiled outlook. Ruthless individualism had its limits. The mutual assistance of peoplehood turned out to be as crucial as ever. This realization was as unwelcome as it was widespread. As Saul Bellow observed, many Jews were in the process of shedding the bonds of Jewish brotherhood, a "special phenomenon" of their existence. But when Western civilization collapsed, it "collapsed on top of them, and the divestiture could not continue."[9]

What started with saving one refugee continued and grew, and during the war Rose produced *We Will Never Die,* a spectacular pageant that urged the American government to save European Jews marked for death. After the war he visited Jews stranded in Europe's displaced-persons camps, worked behind the scenes to secure them better conditions, hatched a plan to adopt twenty-five refugee children, and when that failed, funded an orphanage for survivors. No category could hold him. He took on an important fundraising position for the mainstream United Jewish Appeal and at the same time worked with militant right-wing Zionists and financed the drama *A Flag Is Born,* which funded efforts to break the British blockade and bring Holocaust survivors to Palestine. With the birth of Israel, he became a public supporter and benefactor of the Jewish state and received letters of introduction to President Chaim Weizman and Prime Minister David Ben-Gurion, who during a personal meeting practically ordered Rose to help Israel. Rose was the first to conceive of and publicize the idea that Israel should raise money through the issuance of bonds. He chaired an Israel Independence Day bond rally, played murky roles in an Israeli arms deal and a plan to free Jews imprisoned in Romania, and in 1961 volunteered to head worldwide fundraising—and the solicitation of gifts of artworks—for Jerusalem's planned Israel Museum. He had already promised to fund the design and construction there of a sculpture garden and donate his art collection to fill it. It is still known today as the Billy Rose Art Garden.

By the time he died in 1966, Rose had achieved a hard-won balance between his American pursuits and his Jewish passions, to become a marvelously exaggerated example of the Jewish American experience. Like his community, Rose was successful, affluent, often intermarried, in love with Israel, and wed to

America. He is also a prime example of how during his lifetime the American dream expanded to include the freedom to inhabit a rich identity, and not just possess riches. That even the wealthy Rose desired such an identity makes him an imperfect hero for our time.

One

ILLUSTRIOUS ANCESTORS

"All my grandiose strains stem right from my mother. She was a completely fantastic person," said Billy Rose. "Her name was Fannie. The word Fannie in Jewish means a bird, a little bird. That's how she was, small, fluttering around; you couldn't keep her still or tied down. She was one of the great desperadoes I have known in my life, and I have known plenty of desperadoes."[1]

UNSTOPPABLE

Fannie Wernick was twenty years old in 1895 when she became the first of her eight siblings to emigrate from Odessa to America. Her older and unmarried brother Abraham would have been the more conventional choice as the family's New World pioneer, but Fannie's personality resembled that of a famed Hasidic rabbi her parents followed, and that likely made all the difference.[2] In November 1860, Rabbi Duvid Twersky left his village of Talne in Ukraine to visit the Jews of Odessa, and according to an observer "was triumphantly conducted through the streets" to speak at the Russian port city's central synagogue. Twersky was "witty, appreciative of music, and elegantly dressed." He sat on a throne made of silver that signified his assumption of a royal station, a king in the house of Israel.[3] These were not his only dramatic effects. He also addressed audiences using at first a very low voice. After listeners strained to hear, he turned up the volume. Fannie employed the same technique. "She was a terrific super-salesman," Rose said. "She would start off talking in a quiet voice, very low, and staring at you with intense sharp blue eyes. She had brown hair, a high forehead, a large nose, and an imperious stare in her eyes."[4] Her energy and ambition drove her to industry, invention, and gatecrashing. Washquick was her idea for a laundry detergent. "The house was filled with barrels of borax and potash and mama stirred up her mixtures and packed them in a liquid form in quart bottles," Rose said. "She placed cards in East Side grocery stores and even in snow and rain would take out a satchel full of Washquick bottles and lug them around." Incorporation and tax records show that Fannie founded the business in June 1908.[5] It survived until 1915, and its eventual failure did not blunt her drive. "She always told the children, 'You want to do something—go ahead and do it. Don't be afraid for nothing nor nobody,'" said Rose's sister Polly Rose Gottlieb.[6] Fannie made fearlessness look easy. In the only portrait photograph of her, a scarf around her neck is her only adornment, and it softens but does not obscure her determined demeanor. Without makeup or jewelry, what stands out is her healthy glossy dark hair, cut short to frame her uplifted, attractive, somewhat mannish face, which expresses both boldness and impatience.

Business was just one arena for the exercise of these traits. The other was the welfare of her fellow Jews. Like many followers of Twersky, Fannie was dedicated to Jewish brotherhood.[7] "Her constant project was with bringing greenhorns to America out of the pogrom areas of Russia," Rose said, using a slang term for new immigrants. "It cost $300 to bring a greenhorn over and she was always whipping around trying to raise money. She was a one-woman collection agency. Nobody and nothing could stop her. She once walked into Kuhn, Loeb & Company and hit Jacob Schiff for $1,500" to help her bring over Russian Jews.[8] There was, however, a downside for the people this overwhelming powerhouse rescued, said Rose's first wife, the comedienne Fanny Brice. She "wanted to run the lives of the people she brought over and they wished they were back in Europe."[9]

THE GREAT VICTORY

Rose's mother was not the only larger-than-life old-world influence that made predictable Rose's success as a producer and showman. Another was Fannie's uncle, Solomon Rosenthal, who preceded her arrival in New York and sponsored her immigration. For both, self-promotion and exaggerated claims bordering on the comic were as central to their lives as their Jewish identity. The two passions often overlapped, and tales of their adventures surrounded Rose in childhood. Rosenthal was Fannie's partner in the Washquick business, and Rose grew up also hearing about Rosenthal's victory over Anthony Comstock, founder of the New York Society for the Suppression of Vice. The event took place two years before Rose was born, but he recounted it with pride fifty years later.[10]

Comstock's typical enemies were purveyors of racy postcards and contraceptive devices. Armed with police powers, between 1872 and 1915 he arrested more than three thousand New Yorkers on vice charges.[11] In 1897, however, Comstock strayed from prosecuting sexual liberties to go after two Jewish books that treated Jesus and his origins as anything but immaculate. *Yeshu ha-notsri* (Jesus the Nazarene) and *Maʻaseh talui* (The story of the crucified) originated in the first centuries of the Common Era and were written down in the ninth. Both attack core beliefs of Christianity, such as the virginity of Jesus's mother, in language direct and indelicate. "*Mamzer ben ha-nidoh,* the bastard son of an unclean woman," was the bottom line on Jesus.[12] Converted Jews at New York's Hebrew Missionary Union informed Comstock that these books were for sale on the Lower East Side, and he arrested Meyer Chinsky for selling the works from his shop at 19 Ludlow Street. Chinsky hired prominent defense attorney Elias Rosenthal, who tapped Fannie's uncle Solomon as the expert witness for the defense. A Talmudic scholar of no relation to the attorney but probably known to Chinsky, Solomon Rosenthal took the stand on September 29, 1897, at the New York Court of Special Sessions and rebutted the testimony of Comstock's informants with a combination of erudition and mendacity. Uncle Solomon lied like a rug. "The 'Yishu' mentioned in the book sold by Bookseller Chinsky did not refer to the Jesus of the Christians, and was not intended to be derogatory to Christ," he said. Instead, Yishu referred to an early Jewish reformer "hanged by his countrymen for having abandoned their faith."[13]

Comstock lost his case, and Chinsky returned to his book business. But Solomon Rosenthal was not ready to put the event behind him. Instead, he published a Yiddish pamphlet that in its title purged the bookseller and attorney from the trial and transformed it into a historic showdown between himself and Comstock. *The Victory: The Great Victory of Judaism over Christianity at the Astonishing Religious Trial between the Leading Jewish Expert, S. Rozenthal against the Christian, A Kamfstok* is carnival barker brio. The come-on is a foretaste of classic Billy Rose. Its fanfare defies the customer's disbelief with a sales pitch that overwhelms. The apparent redundancy in the title is due to its claim on a Jewish literary tradition. Its opening words are the Hebrew *ha-Nitsahon* (the victory), which since the Middle Ages have begun Jewish accounts of the debates Christian authorities forced upon the Jews to defend the validity of their faith. "Victory" is then repeated in the Yiddish subtitle that explains the event at hand. The sixty-six-page booklet sold for twelve cents.[14]

Rose did not know all these details of the case, but he knew that Solomon Rosenthal, a relation, had fought as a Jew against a Christian enemy and "outbested" his foe.[15] It was a story he liked.

PASSAMENTERIES

These influences were formative, but Rose's father, David Rosenberg, contributed the humiliations of poverty and the example of failure that outfitted Rose with what the American billionaire Larry Ellison called "all the disadvantages required for success."[16] Rose came to detest his father and throughout his life sought to amass riches to prove he was not his father's son.

Rosenberg landed in Philadelphia on September 22, 1895, and traveled to New York to meet his brother Jacob, who was already living on the Lower East Side at 145 Forsyth Street with their cousin, Ben Halperin. His hometown was the tiny Russian shtetl of Dzhurin, home to fewer than 1,500 Jews and the opposite in size and importance of the vital Black Sea port of Odessa. Still, Rosenberg identified himself on his ship passenger manifest as a clerk, a position that suggests some education, and according to Rose, in Russia his father studied Morse code, a system for fast communication that hints at Rose's future mastery of shorthand.[17] Rosenberg also played the piano and possessed the elegant handwriting necessary to succeed as a "public letter-writer and transcriber of documents." This manual dexterity and musical ability also played a role in Rose's early successes. And like Rose's mother, Rosenberg possessed a sense of Jewish distinction. He "boasted that he traced himself from a long line of rabbis, scholars and wise men," Rose said.[18] In this way Fannie and David resembled each other and also the sociologist Max Weber's characterization of the Jews as "aristocratic pariahs," outcasts with an attitude.[19] Unfortunately for his wife and children, Rosenberg decided that his heritage was incompatible with the demands of the American marketplace. "He complained of having to work for a living," and preferred ludicrous business schemes such as raising silkworms, Rose said. David became a bitter failure. Fannie always charged forward but was equally incapable of successfully managing worldly matters, Rose recalled. "She lived in a crazy never-never land. She had her two feet planted firmly in the clouds."[20]

Fannie's Uncle Solomon brought these two dreamers together with the promise of a practical plan. He told David he would help the young man study pharmacy at City College if he married Fannie.[21] The pair would have been unlikely to meet if not for Uncle Solomon. According to their November 13, 1896, marriage certificate, David lived on the Lower East Side at 713 East 6th Street, while Fannie was uptown in East Harlem at 216 East 102nd Street.[22] But pressures were building on both parties. David had been in America more than a year and was twenty-five years old. He clearly needed help finding a bride. And Fannie apparently had to move out of her lodgings, which either belonged to or were coveted by Joseph L. Sossnitz, the rabbi who performed the marriage ceremony. After Fannie moved out, Sossnitz moved in.[23]

Uncle Solomon reneged on the bargain he had made with his niece's new husband. David Rosenberg never received the money he needed to attend pharmacy school. Instead, like twenty-five thousand others in New York, he worked as a peddler, and surely like many others, he failed at it.[24] But the camaraderie of failure was no consolation to his wife. "Mama was continually annoyed and irritated by Papa's butterfingered attitude to life," Rose said. "Mama used to berate him: 'When they're buying passamenteries, you're selling trimmings and when they're buying trimmings you got a satchel full of passamenteries.'" Rose took his mother's side with a more damning assessment of his father's abilities. It was not a matter of lacking the right product. His father "would have difficulty selling a famished dog a bone."[25] The issue was salesmanship, which for Rose was akin to showmanship. This was something his mother Fannie with her imperious stare, her Uncle Solomon with his self-congratulatory pamphlet, and certainly Rabbi Twerksy with his silver throne understood instinctively and that his father never learned. The contempt of son for father may have bred the same in the father for the son, but in Rose's unlikely version it was his father who started the feud. At Rose's birth his mother exclaimed, "Ain't he pretty," while his father supposedly replied, "Yeah, but what we really needed was an icebox."[26]

ROSE IN LOVE

Samuel Wolf Rosenberg was born on September 6, 1899, which that year was the second day of Rosh Hashanah, the Jewish New Year.[27] It was an auspicious beginning for any Jew and especially for one with a mother loyal to Twersky, whose rabbinical court in Russia during Rosh Hashanah had attracted Hasidim "rejoicing in song and all of them clapped their hands without pause and hundreds of them danced on the table."[28] Rose's mother claimed her son for this festive legacy and the energetic engagement with the Jewish world that accompanied it and that she personified. Though her husband named the boy Samuel for his deceased male ancestor and only his middle name, Wolf, referred to Fanny's deceased grandfather, Velvel (Wolf), Fannie immediately waged a campaign against this traditional order.[29] She called her son Velvel, and by the time Rose was five, she had prevailed. The New York State census of 1905 lists her son as William Rosenberg. By 1908, Rose's school records reveal that the name Samuel was not merely deposed from its first position; it did not even survive as a middle initial. Still, in high school Rose was William S.[30] By then Fannie had apparently acquiesced to the vestigial remnant of Samuel that, after all, helped distinguish her son from the many William Rosenbergs of early twentieth-century New York. And distinguished he would be, because, his mother insisted, "Billy is a genius."[31] His preciousness to Fannie was surely enhanced by her disappointment with her husband, and perhaps also by the failure of earlier pregnancies or the death of an earlier child. Fannie and David had been married nearly three years when their son was born, and in 1910 Fannie told the census taker she had given birth to four children but was the mother of only three still living.

Rose was born on the Lower East Side in a tenement at 129 Clinton Street, near the corner of Delancey Street and on the border of Manhattan's Tenth Ward, the most densely populated in the city and one of the most crowded in the world, with more than 700 people per acre.[32] In June 1900, the census taker found the family six blocks south at 227 Clinton Street. In the less-congested Seventh Ward there were 290 people per acre, but the Rosenberg tenement was still an excellent example of how, for the visiting Englishman Arnold Bennett, the Jewish ghetto "seemed to sweat humanity at every window and door."[33] The family's building preexisted the 1901 Tenement House Law that improved the city's housing stock, so a three-room apartment was only 340 square feet and lacked its own bathroom. Bennett rightly guessed that the tenements' "hidden interiors would not bear thinking about." On each floor four apartments, or about twenty people, shared two bathrooms in the hall. To pay the rent of about fifteen dollars a month, Fannie Rosenberg rented out a sleeping space—it was Jewish women who handled these domestic transactions—to a boarder named Jacob Kigulsky, a forty-year-old widower who worked in a laundry.[34]

Despite Rose's later vilification of his father's business ineptitude, the family's initial poverty was typical of the Jewish immigrant experience at the turn of the twentieth century and not a sign of extraordinary incompetence. To make ends meet, Russian Jews survived thanks to the income earned by working-age children.[35] David Rosenberg had no working-age children. Worse, his wife spent money to bring over her family. On July 18, 1900, the first one arrived. Fannie's brother Abraham, twenty-seven, landed in New York that day and headed to the Rosenberg apartment. It is not clear whether the boarder moved out or if the tiny apartment now held four adults and an infant, but less than a year later, on April 22, 1901, room had to be made for Rose's sister Miriam.[36] Six months later Fannie's brother Schmuel, twenty-one, and sister Lierel, nineteen, arrived in New York. They stayed with Abraham, who lived nearby at 222 Clinton Street.[37] Then in September 1903 a fresh example of Jewish family unity occurred when Fannie's father, Israel Wernick, and his three youngest children—Schloime, seventeen, Chane, sixteen, and Moishe, thirteen—arrived from Odessa.[38] The Wernick clan was reunited, a milestone apparently spurred by the April 1903 Russian pogrom at Kishinev, less than a hundred miles inland from Odessa. In New York, Fannie Rosenberg joined the thousands of Jews who flooded the streets in mass demonstrations against the Kishinev violence that killed fifty, injured five hundred, and left thousands of Jews homeless.[39] Billy Rose fell in love. "One of my earliest memories is of my mother standing on a soapbox on Henry Street and giving an oration about the Kishinev massacres," he said. "A carbon lamp on a nearby pushcart lit up her face, the hair falling over it. She passed the hat after the appeal."[40]

At the time of the Kishinev pogrom Rose was three and a half years old. That might be old enough for a first memory, though there was no shortage of pogroms in the early 1900s and the scene he described might have been tied to a later demonstration, perhaps in response to the October 1905 violence against the Jews of Odessa. And it is clear that Rose's description of the scene benefits anachronistically from his adult experience staging theatrical productions, arranging lighting or an actress's hair, and placing key props on the set. Yet even so, the evidence of Rose's lifelong obsessions with his mother, the theater, and the Jews is persuasive. The historical moment preceded and informed the later theatrical work. Rose was inspired and even transported by his mother's theatricality and disheveled beauty, which could not be separated from the Jewish people.

His father's family also contributed to the Jewish network of mutual aid. In 1900, David's married sister, Ida Ginsberg, lived nearby on Rivington Street with her husband Charles and their eight children.[41] "Ida nursed Billy Rose as a child. She partly raised him," said Ida's granddaughter Shirley Gatsik.[42] Even at age sixty Rose remembered Ida's loving help and wrote Gatsik, "I was very much moved when I saw your dad's mother again."[43] Rose certainly needed some conventional mothering, and Fannie needed someone to provide it to. She was not a natural homemaker and "kept house in a helter-skelter fashion, leaving the dirty dishes piled around," Rose said. She was too busy helping Jews come to America. "We were always going to Ellis Island. She was always travelling down to Washington to get visas."[44]

His mother's example of good works, of acts of *mitzvah* and the Talmudic teaching that all Jews are responsible for each other, was something Rose never forgot, but it was at odds with the values of business success that, as the only son of a poor family, he was desperate to master. Life in the slums was brutal, his family's poverty was dire, and the ecstatic possibilities of American life beckoned.

Two

CLEVER ISAAC

"Hey, fellers," said one of a gang that tormented the young Billy Rose. "What say we dig a hole and bury the little shrimp?"[1]

In 1905 the Rosenbergs lived on the Lower East Side at 268 East Broadway, this time with David Rosenberg's brother Morris as a boarder. Morris was a druggist's clerk, and so he worked at least peripherally in the field David had once hoped to pursue. In fact, druggists soon surrounded Rose's father, as Fannie's brothers Solomon and Maurice (formerly Schloime and Moishe) both entered the trade.[2] This probably pained Rosenberg, but emotional wounds were not the worst the slums could dish out. As Jacob Riis reported in his 1890 book *How the Other Half Lives,* "every corner has its gang," and terrible violence was not unusual. One group that attacked a Jew tried "to saw his head off."[3] Rose was also the victim of savagery as a child, when some kids threatened to put him underground. He escaped and soon armed himself with a heavy lock tied to a leather strap that he learned to swing at enemies. He told the story of his prowess with this weapon many times. He told the story of nearly being buried alive only once and then prevented the journalist from publishing the book that contained the tale. The episode remained traumatic and apparently left him with a lifelong fear of small spaces. "There may be something in Rose's claustrophobia complex," said a normally skeptical Rose publicity man. "He functions best out of doors."[4] Rose remained forever alert to danger and as an adult carried a gun. He called it his "six-shot equalizer."[5]

The Rosenbergs left the raucous and violent Lower East Side for Manhattan's Washington Heights neighborhood by the time the family's last child, Polly, was born on October 12, 1906.[6] By renting from the Geoghan family at 511 West 185th Street, the Rosenbergs enjoyed an environment that was suburban, even rural, and non-Jewish. Rose always remembered the Irish landlady who treated him kindly when his family had no money. She gave him meals of milk, fresh eggs, and meat.[7] Immigrant Jews frequently viewed Irish youths as antisemitic troublemakers, but Irish women were another story. In 1922 the hit play *Abie's Irish Rose,* and in 1925 the less successful *Kosher Kitty Kelly,* confirmed the sociological facts of Jewish-Irish attraction. Rose also would be drawn to Irish women.[8]

After their respite uptown the Rosenbergs moved to Brooklyn in 1908, and then in 1909 they went back to the Lower East Side, at 98 East Broadway, where the bills were again paid with the aid of a boarder, and then in 1910 they returned to Brooklyn, so between the Septembers of 1908 and 1910 Rose attended three primary schools. Stability was something the family could not afford. "We were always just beating the gun with the butcher or the landlord," Rose said.[9] Still, his school records reveal that he and his family took his education seriously. During the 1909–10 school year he was never absent or even late for class, and despite the disruptions, he did well, winning four As and two Bs in the fourth and fifth grades.[10] Most important for his future, in September 1910 his family's practice of hopping from place to place like a marble bouncing on a roulette wheel paused long enough to land on a winning number.

THRILL OF APPLAUSE

On October 18, 1910, a hydrogen-gas airship named the *America* lost engine power northwest of Bermuda as it attempted to be the first to fly across the Atlantic Ocean. The *America* was about 150 miles off the coast of Maryland when it established with a nearby ship the first wireless distress radio contact issued from an aircraft.[11] The signal was received by a wireless operator on the steamship *Trent* who turned out to be Rose's first cousin Louis Ginsberg.

Just a month prior, the Rosenbergs had relocated to 146 Jackson Street, Brooklyn, to live around the corner from Ida Ginsberg and her family at 338 Graham Avenue. The move promised to be at best uneventful and at worst humiliating. The 1910 census found Rose's father without an occupation, while Rose's uncle, Charles Ginsberg, had a dry goods store.[12] It was during this sojourn in Brooklyn that Rose at age eleven became aware he was the poor relation in need of charity, and he later cited this as the moment when he came to "despise his own father for not being able to own a store and make money so they wouldn't have to beg," reported an early biographer.[13] Fannie had "to go around pawning a lot of her things to get money for food. . . . Because the father never worked," said one relative. By the time he was twelve, Billy ran errands for nickel tips to earn money.[14]

So the news of Louis Ginsberg's role in the rescue at sea was a welcome distraction, an exciting diversion, a moment of celebration, and a study in journalistic ballyhoo at a time when newspapers were the greatest and most ubiquitous media in the world, the maker of careers and fortunes from Hearst to Pulitzer. The story of the rescue hit the local papers on October 19, 1910, and Ginsberg's name appeared on the front pages of the *Brooklyn Daily Eagle,* the *Brooklyn Daily Times,* and the borough's *Standard Union,* which noted Ginsberg's name in the subhead of its double-column story: "Wireless Operator Ginsberg a Brooklynite."[15] But the *Daily Eagle* scooped the competition with a wireless message Ginsberg sent from the *Trent.* The four-paragraph report on the rescue of the airship ended, "(Signed) 'LOUIS GINSBERG,' Wireless Operator, Steamer Trent.'"[16] What's more, the *Standard Union* reported that friends and neighbors "planned a surprise for [Ginsberg] in the shape of a banquet . . . for his part in the rescue of the crew of the dirigible." In a later remembrance Louis Ginsberg said Rose helped arrange the October 20 festivities, which according to a press report were quite elaborate. Ginsberg's ship docked that day in Manhattan, and he was "brought in an automobile"—a noteworthy treat in 1910—to Brooklyn, where he was applauded by an alderman, before being "escorted to his home at 338 Graham avenue by about 5,000 enthusiastic people and a band."[17]

Rose did not play a part in the planning of these celebrations. He was too young and too marginal to the events and the players. The *Standard Union* reported that a Ginsberg friend and neighbor was the impresario of Graham Avenue. But Rose was not too young to be impressed by the excitement of fame and the satisfaction of being noticed. "It was the first time I heard applause and the sound of it thrilled me," he recalled. "I reveled in the reflected glory. I felt as if I had arranged Ginsberg's stunt and everybody I knew shared in the glory."[18]

The fanfare and Rose's vicarious participation seem a symptom and extension of the extraordinary possibilities New York itself then trumpeted. The city's first skyscrapers were being born. "The entire town has felt the inspiring power of this prosperity," proclaimed *Harper's Weekly* as early as 1902. "It is as if some mighty force were astir beneath the ground, hour by hour pushing up structures that a dozen years ago would have been inconceivable."[19] The novelist Henry James in 1904 detected in New York "the power of the most extravagant of cities, rejoicing, as with the voice of the morning, in its might, its fortune, its unsurpassable conditions."[20] By 1909, the skyscrapers expressed the "cry of the individual in brick and stone and steel, this strain for novelty or peculiarity or mere 'loudness,'" and in 1913 the 792-foot Woolworth Building became the crowning achievement of Manhattan's new sky-piercing profile. It was the tallest building in the world and a model of the kind of astounding achievement immigrants might dream of in America. The president of the construction company that built it was the Russian-Jewish immigrant Louis J. Horowitz, and in accord with the increasingly nativist mood that mass immigration sparked, the *Magazine of Wall Street* credited him with the "American quality of 'push.'"[21] The more thoughtful *Literary Digest,* however, understood that Horowitz's so-called American qualities "are often, as in this case, imported products."[22]

Public amusements such as Luna Park and Dreamland at Brooklyn's Coney Island added to the spirited cacophony. During Rose's childhood these attractions drew millions of visitors to a fantasy world that historian David Nasaw terms a mad hodgepodge "where all was artifice, extravagance, and excess." There were "camels to ride, diving horses, and elephants that slid down their own 'Shoot the Chutes' ride," set in what a journalist in 1904 called an "enchanted, story-book land of trelleses [*sic*], columns, domes, minarets, lagoons, and lofty aerial flights."[23] These were direct ancestors to Rose's multimedia nightclubs that offered dance, music, and films projected on the walls, and the mixture of circus acts and musical theater in his 1935 *Jumbo.* Gondolas gliding on an artificial lake and a buffalo stampede emerging from a man-made mountain at his 1936 Texas *Frontier Centennial* can also be seen as products of the Coney Island spirit that embodied in dream form the New York ideal that the architect Rem Koolhaas calls Manhattanism.[24] In *Delirious New York,* Koolhass interprets the idea as the wish to live in a fantastical invented world, "to live *inside* fantasy," and Jewish New Yorkers were the most intoxicated imbibers of Manhattanism. "All your children love you, New York, but the Jews among them love you even more," wrote the author Shimon Halkin, and the Yiddish writer Shmuel Margoshes recognized that his brethren belonged to a new hybrid category. They were not Jewish. That was not accurate. They were "*New Yorkish.*"[25] This refashioning was a reflection of the Jews' own reworking of the city in their image, which Henry James realized made it a place more hospitable to the alien than to the native. "We, not they, must make the surrender and accept the orientation . . . which is all the difference between possession and dispossession."[26] Rose partook of this Jewish infatuation with New York. "Billy loved many things, but the deepest of his loves was the city of New York," wrote Ben Hecht, his journalist and screenwriter friend.[27] The radio host Tex McCrary called Rose "a Manhattan primitive," and Abe Burrows, the writer of the musical *Guys and Dolls*, clearly knew what made New York tick, as he "couldn't bear the thought of a New York City without Billy Rose."[28]

The city made sure that its schools, too, in their more earnest way, contributed to the spirit of uplift. In February 1911, Rose attended Manhattan's Public School 64 on East Ninth Street, which dominated its Lower East Side surroundings as Gothic cathedrals did the humble residences of medieval Europe. The school was only five years old when Rose registered, and its French Renaissance Revival architecture, large light-filled courtyards, and auditorium that opened directly to the street served the community as a sanctuary of culture and beauty among the tenements.[29]

Schools also sought to instill a code of American uprightness and square dealing. These Rose filtered through a Jewish—or New Yorkish—sense of irony. He was in his last weeks of eighth grade at Community School 44 in the Bronx when the Public Schools Athletic League, on January 16, 1914, congratulated itself on transforming thousands of "Russian or Polish Hebrews" through athletics, which they and their parents formerly considered "a waste of time." Not only were these young Jews now equipped for success, thanks to the experience of "endurance and self-reliance under the strain of competition," but they played "with absolute fairness and strictly according to the rules of the game."[30] The implicit suggestion was that Jews could be expected to cheat.

As an adult, Rose set out to prove that the PSAL had failed to transform him. In 1935 he bragged to the *New Yorker* that in 1914 he won a PSAL competition through skilled cheating. "I won the 50 yard dash for 85 pound boys . . . and committed my first larceny through acquainting myself with the mannerisms of the starter and thus being able to beat the gun."[31] This false assertion, and another that he was a poor student, was among the many Rose offered to build his credentials as a charming rule-breaker. The truth is even more delightful: Rose did not win the race at all. When the 1914 athletic events were held outdoors in October, and indoors at Madison Square Garden in December, Rose was a student at the High School of Commerce and as a graduate from elementary school he was no longer a possible participant.[32] In 1913, when Rose was at PS 44, the fifty-yard dash for eighty-five-pounders was won by a student at his school, but not by him, and if he did participate, he was not among the top four finishers recorded in the PSAL yearbook.[33] Still, the PSAL may have had an inadvertent effect on Rose. On June 6, 1913, the league organized an event that brought ten thousand boys to Central Park to perform athletic exercises. The "spectacle which was presented of this great mass of boys . . . bending, swinging, sitting down and rising simultaneously was not only remarkable but beautiful," said its organizer.[34] Twenty-five years later, Rose's synchronized-swimming Aquacade spectacle may have owed a debt to that day in Central Park.

CLEVER ISAAC

When Manhattan's High School of Commerce for boys opened in September 1902 it was among the first in New York City, which only began opening high schools in 1897. Its charter was to prepare boys for business, not university, and it was meant to serve "pupils who are not fitted by aptitude, or permitted by circumstance" to pursue an academic route.[35] The number not permitted by circumstance was easy to measure. In 1910, only 2 percent of high school–age Jews received a diploma in four years. The recent immigrants and their children were too poor to afford to stay in school and not work.[36]

Rose was one of those who could not afford to finish high school, even a business-oriented school such as Commerce. But the bigger surprise is that he attended high school at all. When he graduated eighth grade in January 1914 he was fourteen and eligible for working papers. The family could have used any income he could generate. In 1915, his father claimed to be a traveling salesman, an unpromising position at best and likely a face-saving way of saying he was without steady work.[37] Yet despite the family's need, Rose entered Commerce in February 1914. He was a good student in grades six, seven, and eight, winning As and B-pluses despite attending four schools during those years, and it is safe to assume that Rose's mother pushed for her son the genius to stay in school. In fidelity to the family's pattern of mobility his enrollment at Commerce was accompanied by another move.[38] The family left the Bronx and returned to Washington Heights at 500 West 172nd Street, a five-story walk-up that was also home to Fannie's father, Israel, her brother Abraham and his wife and three children, and her sister, Annie Taffel, and her husband and three children.[39] Rose's home life was a Jewish and Yiddish-speaking one, and while at Commerce he also received a Jewish education at the Uptown Talmud Torah on 111th Street near Lexington Avenue.[40] The imprint of his Jewish childhood and youth never left him. "He felt very Jewish always," said his secretary, Helen Schrank.[41] A host of friends and associates agreed. "He was thoroughly Jewish," said one. "About Jewishness he was fanatical," said another. "He was extremely proud of his Jewish heritage," agreed a third.[42] Rose, predictably, avoided such humorless declarations. "He said he was all bad, all Jew, and all bastard," reported the Broadway actress Mercedes McCambridge.[43]

The other lasting influence was poverty. Rose's grandfather Israel lived with his family, but the money for his support likely came from Fannie's brother Maurice, who by 1915 was a pharmacist in Jersey City. Maurice's stipend also probably helped support Rose and his parents and sisters. The success of several of Fannie's brothers, combined with her husband's inability to make a living, caused Fannie to lose her role as the Wernick family linchpin. In 1920, two young women relatives of Fannie's mother roomed with Fannie's brother Abraham.[44] Fannie could not accommodate them. She did not regain her family prominence until the early 1920s, when her son began making money.

What good would it do him if he "got 100 in Biology? Or became the brightest student in History or Geography?" Rose rhetorically asked about his high school career.[45] Those attainments would not lead to money. That need made Commerce High a natural fit. The emphasis on the practical payoff of an education was so hardheaded there that even excellence in mathematics was mocked. "Remember Paul Pinhead?" begins an autumn 1916 episode of the "Crippled Careers" comic strip that ran in the *Commerce Caravel*, the student publication. Pinhead was a Commerce High whiz at advanced algebra, but "Crippled Careers" depicts him five years later sitting unemployed on a park bench and using his computational skills to figure out if he can buy a meal.[46] Typical articles in the *Caravel*—named for the type of ships Columbus sailed to America—introduced students to the business world through interviews with executives, including those at New York's great retailers Gimbels and Macy's. The *Caravel* also offered advice columns such as "Six Dont's [*sic*] in Speaking to Business Men," "Learning to Sell," and "The Business of Getting a Job." The school's curriculum included "Salesmanship" classes in its English Department, and math courses stressed practical skills such as commercial algebra and business arithmetic.[47] The liberal arts were sternly reminded of their humble place. In a poem called "Poetry vs. Business," poetry sings,

"Few are the pleasures,
A business life brings,
I stride the ages,
Companion of kings."
Said Business to Poetry,
"You'd best be discreet,
If it weren't for me—
You—couldn't eat."[48]

The goal of the school's 3,840 pupils was success, and in April 1915 the *Caravel* published "Success Formula," which encouraged students but also warned them about what they were up against. "How much discouragement can you stand? How much bruising can you take? How long can you hang on in the face of obstacles?"[49] However, on the next page a comic article taught a very different lesson. "Isaac Cleverly Turns a Loss into Profit" relates how the fictional Isaac Rabinowitz sold a secondhand coat for eight dollars only to learn in the next day's Jewish paper that in the coat's pocket was one thousand dollars. Isaac was sorely grieved until he was reminded of the advantage to be found in exploiting men's greed. His store soon filled with customers hoping to find the same good fortune they read about in the paper, and to keep the customers coming Isaac planted five-dollar bills in a few of the coats. "That evening Isaac looked at his empty shelves and smiled to himself. 'Vell,' he said, 'he got von tausend dollars, but,' and he tapped the cash drawer. 'I got an empty store.'"[50]

Rose absorbed both lessons and applied the Success Formula and Isaac's example as necessary in his climb to fame and great wealth. He was genuinely impressed by businessmen and respected and appreciated their intelligence and great capacity for work. "The American businessman as I came to know him is not a jerk or a schnook as he is frequently painted," he said. "He's a damn smart guy who knows his job and works harder than anybody on his payroll."[51] Rose made it his business to know his job better than anyone. When he produced theater, "a certain kind of curtain cost a certain amount a yard. [Theater producer Jed] Harris didn't know. Others didn't know. He knew."[52] But Rose also knew that the Success Formula made no allowances for the corners that were liable to be cut if you were poor and, like Isaac, a Jew with no training in or respect for Victorian rules of propriety. In high school Rose forged paper subway tickets. He simply could not afford to buy them.[53] And in his career as a showman he shared Clever Isaac's cynical attitude toward attracting customers. "My line's full of hullabaloo, ballyhoo and razzle-dazzle," he said. "You've got to bang the drum."[54] In fact, it was a source of amusement among the school's Jewish students that their community offered few poster boys for the wholesome creed of Horatio Alger. It was they who invented the Clever Isaac character. After all, prostitutes lived as neighbors in their tenement buildings, and with the beginning of American involvement in World War I soldiers and girls had sexual intercourse outdoors, in parks, or against the walls of city streets in plain view.[55] Lofty ideals of human behavior faced a barrage of contrary evidence.

More realistic was another Clever Isaac story called "Isaac's Scheme," in which the hero's shrewdness backfires. After insuring his inventory of secondhand clothes far above their value, Isaac hopes for a robbery and gets his wish, but when he appears at the insurance company, he finds he has been swindled. The company never employed the man who sold him the policy.[56] In another story, Jake Cohen sells the prominent Morris Rosenberg a machine that appears to churn out counterfeit dollar bills. When Rosenberg learns that Cohen seeded the machine with real bills to trick him into buying it, Rosenberg wants to sue, but desists to spare himself the embarrassment of having everyone learn that he fell for the ruse. (Real-life con man "Count" Victor Lustig made the money-box famous.[57]) At the story's end Rosenberg is said to have learned that honesty is the best policy. Cohen clearly learned the opposite.[58] The 1916 story was part of a cultural moment that in the previous year yielded Irving Berlin's "Cohen Owes Me Ninety-Seven Dollars," a song about a comically conscientious Jewish businessman who on his deathbed tells his son to collect Cohen's debt and also reminds him, "Levi brothers don't get any credit."[59]

Such shrewdness was mother's milk to Rose. With a father he viewed as a failure, a desperado mother, and the example of his uncle Solomon he was raised on a school of thought akin to the Isaac stories, one that prized financial security and viewed cutting corners as no great sin. At the same time, he also took to heart the Success Formula's admonition about work and persistence. At Commerce High, Rose found one subject that responded to both cultural credos. He made himself its master.

"Hats off to Mr. William S. Rosenberg, Shorthand School Champion of Manhattan," announced the April 1916 *Caravel*. "He lives on shorthand and never lets an opportunity to use it slip past him. Notebook and pencil are always ready to be whipped out. No one's conversation is safe from him."[60]

If Rose's later enemies in the songwriting game had ever seen this quote, they would have smirked at the observation that he cribbed words at every opportunity. They always charged that his real skill was thievery, not lyricism. But for the students at Commerce the acclaim was merely deserved recognition of Rose's devotion to the Gregg system of shorthand introduced at the school in February 1915.[61] In addition to classroom instruction, Rose practiced at home with the help of his sister Polly, with whom he had a warm relationship his entire life. She read him the day's newspapers, and he took down the stories in shorthand at increasing speeds. (His sister Miriam demanded payment for the job and she and Rose never shared anything but enmity.)[62] Rose was vice president and then president of the school's Gregg Shorthand Club and wore its "Do You Gregg?" button. "To the outsider, this has absolutely no meaning," reported the *Caravel*, but to members it signified affiliation with an elite and somewhat mysterious society.[63] "I completely and maniacally fell in love with shorthand," Rose said. "I was as crazy about shorthand as a guy would be about sex."[64]

The appeal was partly instinctual. He inherited his father's manual dexterity and interest in the mechanics of communication. It is also clear—and surprising, given his poverty and his school's pragmatism—that Rose's passion for shorthand was not purely mercenary. If it had been, articles in the *Caravel* would have scared him off. Women already dominated shorthand and, the publication warned, had the insurmountable edge of working for lower pay than men. "Business is cruel, and there is no philanthropy about it," an April 1915 article cautioned. "So long as the woman continues to work at a lower price . . . the man cannot compete." The author relented briefly to give hope to the "higher grade of stenographer" and to recognize that "some of our most eminent business men were once stenographers." Then the assault resumed. "I would advise the boy who thinks seriously of becoming a stenographer to pause and reflect, and then to pause again, and to continue to reflect, for several days or weeks, before entering a profession which has comparatively few prizes to offer, and has very little substantial reward even for those who draw a prize."[65]

The New York–based Gregg Publishing Company fought this sentiment with *Caravel* advertisements that resembled the hard-sell approach of Rose's uncle Solomon. One ad featured a photograph of President Woodrow Wilson standing next to his personal stenographer, Charles Swem, a Gregg man, with a quote from the *New York Herald* that shorthand's "real importance and significance lies in the opportunities which the position holds for rapid and practically unlimited advancement."[66]

Rose was not discouraged by the warnings against shorthand, and his attraction to it does not seem to have been spurred by the Gregg ads. In addition to his natural inclinations, shorthand offered a shortcut, a quick way around the laborious straightforward path, and was thus a kind of Clever Isaac–approved, Jewish-style alternative to the deadly grind advocated by the Success Formula. Through the use of this strange written language Rose could gain an advantage, attain goals more quickly, and establish society with other inductees. In these ways it resembled aspects of the Yiddish-speaking world he was raised in, and also the Hebrew language instruction he received at the Uptown Talmud Torah. Both Hebrew and Yiddish, obscure to outsiders, denoted membership in a group that considered itself, though often with a heavy dose of irony, a people of great merit.

Gregg practitioners were similarly a proud underdog group. They sought to overthrow the reign of the well-established Pitman method and gave hints of sympathy with the Jews. In July 1915 the company's magazine, the *Gregg Writer*, printed a tribute to the recently deceased rabbi Solomon Schindler of Boston, who was memorialized as the "first member of a School Board to advocate the introduction of Gregg Shorthand in the public schools." In addition, "a better informed, well-read and scholarly gentleman than the Rabbi it would have been difficult to find."[67] The champion Gregg practitioner Fred Gurtler was a passionate Zionist who took Gregg to a Zionist meeting, apparently at the time of the 1917 Balfour Declaration that committed England to a Jewish homeland in Palestine. This philosemitism allowed Rose to view the Gregg founder as his first substitute father. Gregg even shared characteristics with the great financier Bernard Baruch, who would become Rose's most beloved alternate patriarch. Gregg was "the acme of democracy," "easygoing," and also "a dignified man," Swem said. "Bernie Baruch is a dignified man, but you wouldn't call him very formal, would you? Well, Mr. Gregg was the same type."[68] It was a type that amazed and captivated the young Rose. "By comparison with the groin-kicking, ill mannered, loud shouting boors I had known all my life," he said, "Gregg was like somebody from another planet."[69]

The combined effect of all these factors drove Rose to become an extraordinary shorthand writer and win for himself the fame he had seen showered on his Brooklyn cousin. In March 1916, the *Gregg Writer* put Rose's photograph at the center of a feature about his becoming in January the Manhattan champion: "Opportunity didn't get a chance to knock at his door. He saw it first—and had it lassoed, tied and branded before it got the chance."[70] The article's author neglected to record Rose's shorthand speed, but in January 1917 Rose won a contest attended by students from all the high schools in New York City, an event that in "the number of contestants competing . . . exceeded all previous all-system shorthand contests ever held in this country."[71] Rose's winning speed was 157.8 words per minute, a performance that put him so far ahead of the second-place finisher's speed of 118.8 that he seemed an interloper from an unfairly advantaged realm. In a photograph of the winning Commerce team Rose is at the center of the group of eleven students, serious and unsmiling. The seventeen-year-old is small, almost delicate, with a finely shaped head that tapers nearly to a point at his chin. His hair is dark and thick and his ears prominent, as if straining outward to hear, but it is his demeanor that demands attention. He outdoes his mother's determined look with a poise that commands respect without her fanfare. His intelligent face is a study in formidable assurance, challenging, free of fear, forceful. As a later acquaintance put it, "Billy Rose's face in repose was not exactly conducive to laughter."[72]

By this time, the Gregg organization viewed Rose as a star and worked to make him shine. In December 1916, the *Gregg Writer* ran a story about his extraordinary typing skills and his medal from the Remington Typewriter Company, and the article contains what appears to be Rose's first press interview:

"'What book were you taught [typing] from?'"

"'I know SoRelle's book backward and forward,'" Rose answered without false modesty.[73] The Gregg company touted his shorthand achievements in advertisements that appeared in trade publications across the country, including the *American School Board Journal,* the *California Teachers Association Journal, Midland Schools: Official Organ of the Iowa State Education Association,* and the *Stenographer and Phonographic World.* "Mr. William Rosenberg wrote at a higher speed than that made in the International Contests a few years ago," crowed the widely placed ad.[74] His name had become a brand, a lesson he later applied to his producing career by affixing his name to all his creations. His wins were good for the Gregg brand, and the company paid him fifty dollars a week to practice. Rose's wins were also good for Rose. "He was good-natured because he was always winning," said Gregg executive Louis Leslie. "I have never been in the presence of anybody who sparkled so consistently. Talking to Rose was like listening to an Oscar Wilde play. Same sparkle, same wisecrack. Always twisting a sentence or word. Looking at it from a different angle." Leslie dictated, Rose wrote, and during breaks "we would sit there and laugh and laugh and laugh."[75]

In February 1918, Rose displayed his extraordinary skill for the third time at New York's Fifth Annual Metropolitan Shorthand Contest. That year, two Commerce students recorded speeds of 156 words per minute, nearly matching Rose's 1917 performance, but Rose had also improved and registered the contest's top speed of 178.4 words per minute—while writing with a damaged right hand. "It is interesting to note in connection with Mr. Rosenberg's success," reported the *New York Globe*, "that because of a fall on the ice a few days before the contest his right arm was so sprained that he could not close his fingers." To compensate, "he stuck his pen through a potato."[76] This was an early example of Rose showmanship. "The Idaho potato appealed to the spectacular and fraudulent in me," he said.[77] His hand was adorned with more bandages than absolutely necessary.

AN AMERICAN IS BORN

Rose competed in 1918 as an amateur, not a student. He had left Commerce High on May 2, 1917, about four months shy of his eighteenth birthday and a semester short of graduation, to work for the Thompson-Starrett Company, celebrated builder of the Woolworth skyscraper, whose president was so famous among New York's Jews that the novelist Abraham Cahan could allude to him as the "Russian Jew" who built the Woolworth Building and be certain that readers of *The Rise of David Levinsky* would know the man was Louis Horowitz.[78] The United States government, in its preparations for fighting in World War I, charged Thompson-Starrett with the task of building Camp Upton, a military training camp at Yaphank, Long Island, and Rose worked there for the construction superintendent. Rose's salary of $3,000 a year was enough to support his family, which is what he did during his eight months of employment from June 1917 to February 1918.[79]

Camp Upton filled him with admiration for the productivity of business and also with flag-waving patriotism. The war had the latter effect on most Americans. But in an article Rose wrote about his experience for the *Caravel,* another strain in his character surfaced. His search for alternative father figures and more inspiring models of masculinity found an example in the top military men at Upton. "The officers are certainly a trim-looking, clean-cut body of men," he wrote. "There is a something, a whizz, a concentrated go about their commands. Men who a few months ago literally didn't know they were alive now respond with alacrity and 'pep' to orders fired at them with machine gun rapidity."[80] This impression left its mark on Rose's mind and in his bones. Near the end of his life he had the comic perspective to see himself as "the kind of dunderhead" who believes he is not one of "the ordinary people," but while clawing his way to the top—"and he did plenty of clawing," said one associate—he had no ambivalence about his superiority.[81] "He always informs you how grateful you should be when you're working for him," said a former nightclub employee.[82] And the commanding posture of the officers influenced his physical presence. Rose developed a distinctive stride, a way of walking that announced him as a person of note and rank. "He would just walk into a restaurant, not rudely or arrogantly, but as if he owned it," said Judy Goetz Sanger, who knew Rose through his friendship with her parents, the playwrights Ruth and Augustus Goetz. "It was a way of moving that was heavenly to watch, just heaven."[83]

By early 1918, Rose had assembled an impressive collection of shorthand trophies, a modicum of attendant fame, the mentorship of John Robert Gregg, work experience at Thompson-Starrett, and a worldview that valued the role played by men of vigor and discipline, a group he believed included himself. His natural arena was his hometown of New York. The city was the national capital of industry and finance and retail and entertainment. It was also home to his family and the country's greatest Jewish community. But World War I raised the profile of Washington, DC. In October 1917, the *Gregg Writer* reported on the jobs its shorthand stars had landed in the capital as secretaries to cabinet members, generals, and, in the case of Swem, President Wilson. The article also alluded to the newly formed War Industries Board (WIB), when it explained that shorthand writers were crucial to offices that "select, mobilize and control food, equipment, munition [*sic*] and men."[84] A year later, Rose wangled a position at the WIB, and in the nationalist spirit spurred by the war the Gregg magazine attributed his success to his Americanism: "He 'got by' all the preliminaries" thanks to his "American enterprise, American courage and sound salesmanship."[85]

Years would pass before Rose and America acknowledged the influence of Rabbi Twersky, Uncle Solomon, Clever Isaac, and Rose's mother, Fannie.

Three

NOT BAD FOR DELANCEY STREET

The organizational chart for the War Industries Board resembles a large family tree that in place of descendants offers more than twenty divisions, commissions, committees, bureaus, and sections that all flowed from and answered to their one patriarch and leader, Bernard Baruch. All the resources of American industry crucial to fighting Germany and its allies in World War I were overseen by the WIB, which President Woodrow Wilson created in May 1917, one month after the country entered the war. But the WIB was unable to coordinate or settle the demands and conflicts between the needs of the government's War Department and private industry's profit motive until Wilson, on March 4, 1918, named Baruch the WIB chairman. During his tenure Baruch "came closer to achieving an absolute dictatorship of US industry than any man has ever done before or since."[1]

Baruch's august position seemed natural justice itself. He was a compendium of gifts, inherited and acquired. Bernard Mannes Baruch, at six feet four inches tall, possessed a "well-honed charm" and good looks too striking for him to pretend to ignore, and was slim and athletic and good enough with his fists in his youth to win a compliment from prizefighter Bob Fitzsimmons. He was a self-made multimillionaire and, emphasizes a biographer, his generation's example of "the American dream come true. He was the American success story, the aspiration fulfilled of every young man off the farms, or out of the little towns and villages, who dreamed of conquering the city and of amassing wealth and fame and power."[2] Born in South Carolina on August 19, 1870, to Simon Baruch, a Jewish immigrant from Germany who became a respected physician, and his wife, Isabelle Wolfe, who traced her Jewish roots to colonial America, Baruch attended high school and college in New York, found work in the city as a stockbroker, and by 1900 was a legend for his ability to prosper on Wall

Street in good times and bad, betting long that stocks would rise and betting short that the value of an investment would tumble.[3] He became known as the Wizard, and Doctor Facts, but Baruch was no bloodless monument to Commerce High's Success Formula and its ideal of self-denial. He loved the theater, actresses, and publicity and sought coverage in newspapers and newsreels. He was also a ladies' man with a healthy libido.[4] At age sixty-eight, Baruch vigorously pursued the singer Kitty Carlisle Hart, then the twenty-eight-year-old Kitty Carlisle. He "chased me considerably around the bedroom in his long winter underwear," Hart recalled. This was in the summer of 1938, when she accepted his invitation to shoot game at the apparently chilly ten-thousand-acre hunting estate and lodge Baruch rented in Scotland during grouse season. Because of their forty-year age difference, Hart said, "I thought he was so old that I kept saying to him, 'Bernie, get into bed.'"[5]

Any young man working in proximity to such a successful and robust figure might understandably come to admire and even idolize him, but to Billy Rose, Baruch's gifts seemed the antidote to his—and his father's—every deficiency. Where Rose was short, just five feet two inches, and an athlete manqué, Baruch was tall and strong, features that always impressed Rose. In 1940, he wrote to the columnist Walter Winchell that his new press agent was "six foot, all man."[6] That ideal intensified Rose's appreciation of Baruch: "He was the best looking man in North America, as far as I was concerned. He wore the quietest and best fitting clothes, he was pink skinned, premature[ly] gray."[7] Baruch's sartorial example informed Rose that his own style was off base. "My shoes, ties, were wrong. I was talking too loud. I lowered my face. I knew the legend, he was a living legend."[8]

Just as crucial as Baruch's success was his identity as an American Jew, born not in Russia but in the American South. Rose's father was saddled with the immigrant Jewish speech that was viewed as comical. He "talked with a terrible Jewish accent," said Rose's secretary. "He was unwittingly funny." Baruch, by contrast, apparently recognizing the value of his South Carolina speech as an authentic American credential, retained "a trace of a southern accent" even after seventy years in New York.[9] When Rose in the mid-1920s found himself among New York's Jewish songwriters he mocked the pretensions of their "back-to-Dixie" tunes and shrewdly demanded, "What Tennessee? More likely it's Odessa or Riga."[10] Baruch, on the other hand, was a real Southerner and also a prominent Jew, one who intermarried but at crucial moments aided Jewish causes, an approach Rose would follow as closely as he did the older man's financial advice.[11]

Baruch inspired Rose but also humbled him. "I would like to think I was a pale carbon copy of Bernard Baruch. I don't think it would be correct to say that I was even a pale carbon copy."[12]

That note of modesty was not, however, Rose's characteristic key, and it is not how people remembered him at the WIB. "In the office was an undersized stenographer, who distinguished himself by taking dictation at an infernally rapid rate and who, in leisure moments, amused himself and the rest of us by his uncanny skill in drawing fascinating pictures of strange beasts and birds on his typewriter," said the three-time Pulitzer Prize–winning reporter and Algonquin Round Table wit Herbert Bayard Swope, who worked with Baruch at the WIB and who, in his mention of Rose's sketches of "strange beasts," left a clue to Rose's later interest in the art of Salvador Dalí. "Rose, I am willing to wager, secretly believes that he won the World War."[13] Baruch was more restrained but affectionate when he wrote in his autobiography, "We had one particularly bright young lad—a crackerjack stenographer—named Billy Rose, who has since earned fame and fortune."[14] Neither man verified a story that Rose organized and headed a team of shorthand reporters and typists that delivered to Baruch daily verbatim reports of WIB activities. Rose succeeded in getting the tale accepted as fact elsewhere, but he did not share it with a Baruch biographer whose book appeared while her subject was alive. Here Rose was careful to claim only that part of his "job was to carry chocolate sodas to Baruch at three in the afternoon."[15] This circumspection supports the truth of a story he did share with Baruch's biographer: while at the WIB, Rose met the president of the United States. In November 1918, with the war at an end, President Wilson relaxed for a few minutes with the young office worker to talk shorthand. "I understand you're quite a shorthand writer," Wilson said, and then a low-key shorthand showdown took place between the young man and the president, who practiced the Pitman method. "I walked out of the White House and floated back to my office via the rooftops," Rose said, as he thought to himself, "Not bad for Delancey Street."[16]

The six months Rose worked in Washington began on July 24, 1918, and ended on January 8, 1919. That was not what he had hoped for. On his "Application For Employment" Rose sought a permanent job, not a temporary one. It was a curious request. Though it was impossible to predict the war's duration, it was unlikely to last forever, and unsurprisingly Rose's job and the WIB itself disappeared soon after the war ended on November 11, 1918. Baruch and Swope returned to New York, and it was not until the 1930s that Rose achieved the success that enabled him to transform his youthful acquaintance with Baruch into a friendship. What's more, at the WIB Rose's salary of $1,800 a year was just a little more than half the $3,000 he made in New York at Thompson-Starrett. John Robert Gregg, Rose's primary professional reference—and the one that allowed Rose to get the WIB job without taking the civil service exam—was also in New York. So the goal of permanent employment in the nation's capital is confounding, except that a return to New York meant a return to his unreliable father and relentless mother.[17]

THE GETAWAY

In early 1919, the National Shorthand Reporters' Association was preparing its first convention since 1917 and its first shorthand speedwriting contest since 1916. The 1918 convention was called off because of the war, and the 1917 speed contest was canceled because so many prospective contestants had enlisted in the army. In 1919, with the war at an end, the NSRA brought back the convention, revived the speed competition, and rekindled Rose's quest for a national victory his mother could relish.[18] "He desperately wanted to be champion. He wanted to be the world champion," Louis Leslie said. "He used to bring the medals home to his mother. . . . He had this medal complex for Mama." The Gregg company shared Rose's dream of glory and upon his return to New York put him on the payroll so he could afford to prepare for the August convention in Detroit. "Training in any physical or neuro-muscular skill is the same. You have to have a sparring partner. We took Albert Schneider. . . . He was miles below [Rose] but at least he was close enough. . . . We simply paid two salaries in order to have the pacer for [Rose]," Leslie said. He tested Rose every week, while Gregg himself "was upstairs chewing his finger nails."[19]

Two days of convention proceedings took place before the speed contest was held at ten o'clock on Thursday morning, August 21. According to the NSRA Bulletin, "The great event, which has its attraction for the oldest as well as the youngest reporter," confirmed that "the Speed Contest has come to stay, and it is now an admitted fact that the shelving of this important feature of our annual gathering was a mistake."[20] Then comes silence. Rose apparently fainted during the contest, but the Gregg organization declined to discuss it. Its official reports offer no explanation of what happened to its star, though Leslie said Gregg believed Rose and Schneider got drunk the night before in nearby Windsor,

Ontario, where the liquor that was recently outlawed in America was available. But that does not explain Schneider's adequate performance. Rose claimed he did poorly owing to "fatigue, exhaustion, brain-fever."[21]

A more suggestive explanation is that Rose buckled under the stress of winning the contest to please his mother. He experienced another disabling moment years later when courting his first wife, vaudeville star Fanny Brice, whose resemblance to Rose's mother included not just her Jewishness and first name but also her superior position over him, signified by her fame, her height advantage, and her being eight years his senior. As the junior partner in the future marital union sat down to dinner at Brice's home, he was struck by "a terrific and sudden nosebleed." Brice responded with calm competence and tact and took care of him in "her big happy-looking kitchen."[22] She was a benevolent Fanny, not an overbearing one, but it seems that eagerness to please his mother, or a symbol of her, made Rose vulnerable to collapse. Her expectations were enormous. "She was a doer," said a niece. "Did things on a very large scale. Thought big." Brice agreed that Rose's mother demanded "big, big everything big."[23] She set a high bar for her short son.

In August 1919, Rose had good reason to feel anxiety over what he might have to render to Fannie Rosenberg. Big changes in the works surfaced on December 4 when Fannie spent $15,000 on a four-story Manhattan row house at 767 St. Nicholas Avenue, in the so-called Sugar Hill neighborhood, where residents lived the sweet life.[24] The home had the commanding presence that suited Fannie's yearnings for splendor, and in later years Rose referred to anything great, rich, and fine as a "real Fannie Rosenberg."[25] The home was one of ten Italian Renaissance–style townhouses on the west side of St. Nicholas Avenue between 148th and 149th streets, a row that is "one of the most impressive" in the now-historic district. Designed by the prominent architect Frederick P. Dinkelberg, the lavish single-family houses completed in 1895 offered master bedroom suites outfitted with "octagonal dressing room[s] . . . with full-height plate-glass mirrors" and adjoining bathrooms with fireplaces.[26] When the Rosenbergs arrived the neighborhood still hosted remnants of an earlier elite. Though many homes had been remodeled to accommodate multiple families, one block south at 747, 749, and 751 St. Nicholas the homes still each served one family and a live-in servant. The Rosenbergs' building could accommodate several families, and the idea was to rent out the extra space to pay the monthly expenses.[27]

There was, however, a catch. Rose was supposed to be Fannie's silent partner in the deal. Five weeks after Fannie bought the house she began to mortgage it, probably to repay whoever loaned her the $15,000 purchase price (likely her brothers Abraham and Maurice). So on January 16, 1920, she committed herself to an $11,000 mortgage from Emigrant Industrial Savings Bank and another for $3,700 from one Abram Libman. She closed both transactions without her husband. Though husband and wife still lived together, Fannie had clearly decided to make her way without his help. When she signed her name, in Hebrew characters, to the mortgage agreement with Libman, the only witness was her son, William Rosenberg. On March 8, 1920, Fannie further mortgaged the property to a Sadie Wolper for $1,200, bringing the total obligation to $15,900, more than she had paid for the house three months before. Rose did not witness this third mortgage.[28] He had likely already left town. In the winter of 1920, Rose made his getaway.

Since January 1919, Rose had weathered a series of setbacks. He lost his job at the WIB and the company of outstanding men such as Baruch. That was nobody's fault, and there was nothing to be done about it. Then he returned to New York and the practice of shorthand, drilled regularly to win the national speed contest, and failed spectacularly, spoiling his deserved reputation for excellence. "Don't let anybody derogate Billy . . . about being a reporter," Charles Swem told an interviewer. "He was never world champion, but he was a grand reporter."[29] But Fannie's decision to make her son her business partner may have signaled to Rose that he might now suffer a much greater failure. He could become another emasculated David Rosenberg. Rose witnessed the dynamics of his parents' marriage. Fannie "overpowered papa. She dominated him," said his sister Polly.[30] Probably to escape that fate, and also to see the country beyond New York—accounts of American journeys were featured in the Commerce High *Caravel* when he attended school there—Rose for the first time in his young life made a move without regard for professional fame or monetary gain.[31] He set out on a four-month travel excursion to Ohio, Kentucky, Tennessee, Texas, and New Orleans.[32] His apparent goal was freedom, independence, and a chance to test his resilience.

Rose bought his first gun, a .32 Smith & Wesson pistol, in an assertion of manliness that emphasized independence from his mother and also reflected his realist view of the world and its dangers, and lit out alone, starting in Ohio. There, the *Caravel* reports, he worked as a stenographer for the state's governor, James Cox, who was seeking the Democratic Party's nomination for president.[33]

According to Rose's account of his wanderings, he next found a shorthand job in Memphis, Tennessee, working for Clarence Saunders, founder of the Piggly Wiggly grocery store chain, and visited Bowling Green, Kentucky, to see the Mammoth Caves, which in 1917 had installed electric lights to facilitate tourism. The trip also gave him his first look at Texas. Rose worked in the oil boomtown of Wichita Falls as a stenographer for attorney Fred Weeks.[34]

His next stop was San Antonio, where election-year politics created demand for his shorthand skills. The Texas state Republican convention there soon turned into two conventions as three hundred African American delegates boycotted it and staged their own convention. Rose said he covered the breakaway group, transcribed the delegates' speeches, and had typists create copies he sold to the protesting delegates, a tale supported by a newspaper report that the African American delegates had "stenographic reports" of their convention. "I was a specialist and I quickly learned that my specialty was a marketable commodity wherever I went," Rose said.[35]

Another specialty came in handy when Rose needed money between shorthand gigs: he hustled pool. The game was at the height of its popularity, with forty-two thousand pool halls across America, so there was no shortage of opportunities.[36] "He was a great pool player," said the art dealer Gilbert Lloyd, who in the 1940s helped Rose amass his collection of paintings and sculptures, "He was superb." With less admiration a press agent confirmed his skill. "He was a shark. Would take every penny from you."[37] In the early 1920s, future movie actor George Raft tried to hustle Rose but got taken by him at Crenshaw's, a well-known New York hangout at Broadway and 166th Street.[38]

Crenshaw's and places like it formed a lasting part of Rose's education; they were where the proper English taught in school was undermined by the slang of those whom linguist James Sledd terms "gentlemen who are not gentlemen and dislike gentility."[39] That was the place for Rose, and when his travels up the social ladder delivered him into environments that lacked the desired conversational color he supplied it himself. "He didn't talk like someone who had gone to a good school. . . . He talked like an East Side Jewish kid," said a longtime acquaintance.[40] Examples abound. In a letter to Winchell, Rose wondered of their fanatical devotion to work, "Can it be we're both nuts?"[41] When he was rich enough to live in a home with a private elevator that sometimes stalled between floors he complained to his butler, "See who the hell is caught in the gimmick."[42] And when it was time for dinner he commanded the help, "Give me the works."[43]

He liked to use Jewish locutions, too, and said of avoiding sunshine, "I should get wrinkled. What am I, a prune?"[44] The style charmed Alistair Cooke, the British-born journalist and America enthusiast who saw how much Rose loved the underdog persona this language signaled, that of "a little, cocky, bright boy from the east side."[45] The approach paid off when he became a songwriter. As lyricist Chester Conn explained—an explanation that itself required slang—the title of Rose's "I Found a Million Dollar Baby (In a Five and Ten Cent Store)" leveraged Rose's "lingo. He used that same language."[46]

Rose's 1920 excursion ended with a conveniently dramatic return to New York. Though he never let the truth interfere with a good story, it seems he really was a passenger on the steamship *Comus* that sailed from New Orleans to New York, which, on July 12 in a fog off New Jersey, rammed into and sank another ship, the *Lake Frampton*. In the panic, *Comus* passengers clutched their belongings, which "if our boat was going to sink was of no use," Rose said.[47] This derision of others' character and incompetence was fundamental with Rose, and decades later he would remind the director of Jerusalem's Israel Museum to inspect the lamps that illuminated the sculptures he donated. "The screw which keeps the [lamp] hood firm sometimes gets loose and the hood falls. In that event, the light, instead of focusing on the sculpture, merely spills on the ground."[48] Rose's kingdom would not be lost for want of a nail, or screw, while he was on the job.

Rose was back in New York when Fannie's dream of home ownership ended on August 10, 1920. She had been a homeowner only eight months when she signed over to one Will N. Clurman all three mortgages to 767 St. Nicholas Avenue.[49] Rose was an official signatory to this failure, which he later hid with a lighthearted story that his mother grew tired of the property and sold it for a $7,000 profit, a sum she spent on "bringing over greenhorns."[50] This white lie protected his mother's reputation as a businesswoman. A $7,000 profit represented a gain of nearly 50 percent in eight months. This was impossible, especially because Fannie had the bad luck to buy her home on the eve of the 1920 recession. After her purchase, real estate prices fell.[51] The true story of his headstrong mother's fiasco was too humiliating. He had already aligned himself with her against his father the failure. She had to be, if not a success, at least bold and indefatigable, not overbearing and foolhardy. Before the end of the decade, in addition to a substitute father Rose found a replacement mother.

On January 15, 1920, just before Rose began his American excursion, a New York census taker found him living in a rooming house on West Fifty-Fifth Street. It was the last time Rose identified himself as William Rosenberg and the first time he announced his new vocation as an "artist" in the "theatrical" industry.[52] He was determined to be a songwriter, and upon his return to New York in July he picked up where he had left off, which was at the bottom. The songwriting idea was not completely out of left field. Rose had played piano in his high school orchestra, where he shared musical duties with fellow student Harold Warren. "I was designated the piano player for the classical pieces and Rosenberg the piano player for the popular music," Warren said.[53] Rose's interest in popular music was revived when he and Albert Schneider prepared for the 1919 shorthand contest. "He told me himself how he got into the song business," Louis Leslie said. "The two boys went to all those shows, took down the lyrics of all the songs in shorthand. Just to be writing."[54] Acquaintanceships with songwriters followed and familiarity bred contempt. "I wasn't at all impressed by these characters. . . . [They were] shoddy and second rate compared to the industrial giants I met in Washington. . . . All they talked about was how stupid the music publishers were and how they wouldn't recognize a hit song if you shoved it down their throats." But he could not dismiss the money the songwriters made: "It just struck me that here was a two-penny world where people were earning $50,000 a year." Rose decided that if "these men who write infantile mush can make six times as much as a man who writes shorthand at the rate of 280 words a minute this is the life for me."[55]

He was hardly the only one with this notion. "It gets into the newspapers that a chauffeur has written a tune which has made thousands of dollars," and this attracts "gullible hopefuls and ignoramuses," wrote Isaac Goldberg in his 1930 book *Tin Pan Alley: A Chronicle of the American Popular Music Racket,* a title appropriate to its jaded participants. But Rose was neither innocent nor dumb, and few were better suited to a business where inspiration, wrote Goldberg, "punches a time clock."[56] First, songwriting was a largely Jewish pursuit, and this allowed Rose to join the general trend of greatly diminished, if not wholly abandoned, Jewish practice, while remaining within the Jewish community. Sales of kosher meat in New York, for example, dropped 30 percent between 1914 and 1924, and "Jewish identity began to be defined partly as . . . association with other Jews."[57] Such association was unavoidable on Tin Pan Alley. As Goldberg noted, from the onset of the twentieth century, "Of a sudden, it seemed, the business took on a Jewish complexion."[58] This was widely understood, and when in the 1920s Rose pestered a press agent to win him a *New Yorker* profile, the magazine's editor Harold Ross replied, "One more profile about a Jewish songwriter and we will go out of business."[59] Some of the greatest entertainers of the time, including Al Jolson, Sophie Tucker, Fanny Brice, Eddie Cantor, and George Jessel, were Jews who won over audiences with Jewish songs and comedy, such as Brice's "Second Hand Rose," Tucker's "My Yiddishe Mama," Cantor's parody version, "My Yiddisha Mammy," and Jessel's comedy routine about taking his mother to a Broadway play, where she behaves as she would in the Yiddish theater, eating fruit and yelling at the actors. Rose soon wrote a similar sketch for Brice called "Mrs. Cohen at the Beach." Unlike in the nation's capital, where Rose's clothes and speech were all wrong, in the New York songwriting game he needed no alterations.

Songwriting also took advantage of what a fellow writer called Rose's "perfect ear for speech."[60] A love for the everyday language of American life was key, because slang had a "revivifying influence" on popular song, Goldberg said.[61] But his greatest advantage was not being a typical songwriting type. "The personality of songwriters is emotional and sentimental," said Rose's writing partner Edward Eliscu. "They don't think much about the future. They act much more impulsively."[62] That was not Billy Rose. "He was very methodical and conscientious," said Ray Henderson. "All I can say is by sheer determination and studying he learned the modus operandi of songwriting."[63] That drive to succeed was so seldom seen among songwriters that a biographer of Irving Berlin wrote that it was Berlin's emphasis on "work and *work,* and then WORK . . . that set Berlin apart."[64] With far less talent than the master, Rose nevertheless had an edge over the songwriters he disparaged as "spontaneous grasshopper types."[65] Rose was the hardworking ant.

NASTY, JEWISH, AND SHORT

During the summer of 1920, Rose lived on money borrowed from songwriter Walter Hirsch and others, survived on Automat doughnuts, and lingered at restaurants "until he was sure somebody would pay the check."[66] To make money he hustled, and a sign of his desperation is an August 18, 1920, review of a dismal act at the Harlem Opera House by "Billy Rose, blackface comedian," which is notable for his rare work as a performer and for the first report of his new name.[67] That same summer Rose visited Camp Lake Brant in New York's Adirondack Mountains, four hours' distance from the city, to buy lyrics from then virtually unknown songwriter Lorenz Hart. "Their system was to go out in a boat at ten or eleven o'clock in the morning" and write there all day. Rose paid Hart one hundred dollars for each day's work and then sold the songs for a profit back in New York.[68]

By the fall Rose's efforts to write and sell songs made him a regular visitor to the offices of song publishers Leo Feist; Shapiro, Bernstein; and Irving Berlin, Inc., where Saul Bornstein was the business partner who went on to cheat Berlin and the kind of guy who liked to tell people, "My first name is Saul. . . . My last name is Bornstein, and my middle name is Oscar. You know what my initials spell."[69] His true middle initial was H., but it was part of the 1920s code of big-city Jewish masculinity to boast of bad qualities. It warded off potential enemies. Rose was cut from the same rawhide, and years later in a letter to acting coach Lee Strasberg he referred to "what I laughingly call my heart."[70] Insiders understood that this kind of talk was (partly) ironic. When actress Mercedes McCambridge told Rose she "thought Jewish guys insulted each other too much," he explained that it was "how they showed their love for one another."[71] Rose understood the community. It was often, like him, nasty, Jewish, and short.

In 1921, Rose had his first successful song. When the Ziegfeld Follies opened in New York in June of that year, one of the acts in the variety show famous for its beautiful girls in extravagant costumes was the male singing duo of Van and Schenck performing "I Hold Her Hand and She Holds Mine: Ain't Nature Grand?" The lyric was credited to the newly minted Billy Rose, and it reports on a boy's nights in the park with his girlfriend. She is "not too bad and not too good," a perfect mixture for the amorous male, who cheerfully admits he is one of nature's more uncouth creations: "With me it did the best it could." The song also touts a streetwise contempt for education. The boy did not go to college and does not care for "the knowledge found in books." Rose's first notable song reveals that its creator was made of coarse material. How much sanding down and smoothing over he would stand for was a battle he waged with himself, his friends, and his several wives for the rest of his life.

"Most of my songs were written without distinction or merit," Rose admitted. But he would not take a put-down from those who claimed they adhered to higher standards. "Guys who never saw their mothers were writing about mother," he said. "Their songs had nothing to do with their actual experiences," including their Jewish immigrant experience, which as he observed was often obscured with songs of longing for the Old South. Rose played the same game with "That Old Gang of Mine," a 1923 hit he wrote with Henderson. It expresses a yearning "for that old gang that has drifted apart," which was nonsense, Rose said. "I did not in the least want to get back to my old East Side gang of chiselers and muzzlers."[72]

Another Rose hit from 1923, written with Con Conrad, was based on experience. "You've Got to See Mamma Ev'ry Night (Or You Can't See Mamma at All)" was perfect for Sophie Tucker, the powerhouse Jewish vaudeville singer who made it a hit. The so-called "last of the red-hot mamas," Tucker was always happy to toss over respectability in favor of the less refined facts of life, and in "Mamma" she found a song about an earthy and love-hungry woman that suited both her sexually frank persona and also the new woman of the 1920s, who engaged in premarital sex at "astounding" rates. In the twenties, half of all "young white women of courting age" engaged in premarital sexual intercourse.[73] This female sexual liberty, however, was mainly restricted to their fiancés, and the complaint of the aggrieved woman in the song reflects this reality. A sexual relationship required commitment and allegiance. Tucker sings to her part-time lover, "Now I'm not showing you the door / I'm just laying down the law," which is spelled out in the song's title. "Laying down the law" signals an improvement in Rose's lyric ability. The colloquialism connects the song to the actual spoken language of the audience and the reality of their lives. The song also may have reflected the reality of Rose's life. In January 1923, he apparently folded in the face of a similar ultimatum when he married an actress named Betty Weston in Tijuana. There is no evidence the relationship lasted long or ended with a stateside divorce, but Rose seems to have paid off his sexual debt to Weston the following year by helping her land a part in *The Melody Man,* the first Broadway play he backed.[74]

"That Old Gang of Mine," "You've Got to See Mamma," and a song called "You Tell Her—I Stutter" made 1923 the year Rose emerged as an important player on Tin Pan Alley, but all those numbers were eclipsed by "Barney Google," a novelty song based on a popular comic strip character of the same name. "That song wasn't a hit, it was a disease," Rose said.[75] It certainly spread like one. The character was a lovable loser overpowered by his wife who found solace in "the male fantasies of his loyal readers," including the alluring Ziegfeld girls, wrote the biographer of Billy DeBeck, Barney's creator. Barney Google was a "reflection of their hopes, dreams and failures."[76] That was one interpretation. The cultural critic Gilbert Seldes, in his 1924 book *The 7 Lively Arts,* took popular culture more seriously and saw Barney Google as part of a lively insurgency that desecrated what society venerated. Barney had "so little respect for law, order, the rights of property, the sanctity of money, the romance of marriage, and all the other foundations of American life" that if he had appeared as a character in a more respectable art form, such as a novel, "the Society for the Suppression of Everything" would drag him into court.[77] Rose's song anticipated Seldes's view. It comically celebrates the loser as a great man, a hero. "Who's the most important man this country ever knew?" asks the song's opening line. It is Barney Google, who is never respectable but always finds a way to survive. "Women take him out to dine, then he steals the waiter's dime." The song sold a million copies of sheet music and three million records. DeBeck received one-third of the royalties, but Rose's take was still an impressive $25,000, and his 1923 income was $60,000, a figure that surpassed the amount he dreamed of making three years before.[78] Rose was a success.

His growing prominence owed as much to his guts as to his hits. Rose was fearless toward song publishers. His "Gang" was a big hit for Irving Berlin's publishing company at a moment when Berlin himself suffered a creative drought, so when Berlin one day ignored Rose's greeting of "Good morning," Rose set him straight. "When I say good morning, answer me, because my tune is paying for your flops." Rose later reflected, "I was a pretty fresh punk."[79] Such bravado made him a songwriter's hero. "He upset all the traditions, as almost all the other writers came into the publishers and kowtowed," said Walter Hirsch. "He used to fight them."[80] "We were all anxious to write with Billy because he was a pugnacious guy," Dave Dreyer said. "He was the first song writer to stand up to the publishers and tell them off. He made beautiful deals, pulled advances. Therefore we wanted to work with him. . . . He was ruthless."[81] Exactly what he did and how he did it Rose kept to himself. "He'd go in and make a deal, come out, hand you some money, that was it!" remembered Harry Warren. "You never found out what he sold it for till the statement came. Then you'd find you'd been rigged, he'd taken the biggest bite. And on the one hand you hated him, and on the other hand you knew you wouldn't have gotten any deal without him."[82]

The same calculus applied among publishers. "Publishers told me later on [that] in spite of all the antagonism he showed . . . they liked him," Hirsch said.[83] Rose got deals done, and that was the name of the game. Publishers also appreciated that Rose made sure his partners actually delivered product. "He kept you on the thing," Henderson said. "If you started to talk about the World Series he would listen for a half second and say, 'Let's get back to the songs.'"[84] The approach was a relief to many. "He was 100 percent business," Eliscu recalled, "and I enjoyed that after [Eliscu's regular partner Vincent] Youmans' chaotic work habits."[85] "He was a great feeder," Warren said. "He'd sit with the boys, and he'd say something like, 'Come on, gimme another line, nah, nah, you can do better than that, come on, gimme something like . . . ' then he'd come up with a phrase or a line, something. Somehow, a song would come out of all this, somehow. And nobody knew what Billy had done, but he'd done something."[86] Rose's magic touch later led to accusations that he did not write his song repertoire but was instead "cut in," given credit he did not deserve. According to popular song authority Michael Feinstein, the assertion is almost wholly untrue. Ira Gershwin and Harry Warren "told me personally that Billy did in fact write many lyrics," Feinstein wrote.[87] It was a case of Rose's self-created reputation for larceny shaping his story more powerfully than the facts. He did not let it bother him. Rose could not be insulted, said one. He "had a skin like a crocodile."[88]

IMPORTED BRIDEGROOM

That skin was, however, sensitive to his mother's touch, and in the year of his great success she put the touch on him. Now that Rose had money he could solve some family problems, one of which was his sister Miriam, who in 1923 was twenty-two years old and single. "Miriam was plain and frumpy. Polly was the golden girl," said Vicki Walton, daughter of Rose's third wife, Joyce Mathews.[89] To fix the Miriam situation, Fannie visited her son at his room in the Princeton Hotel, a residence on West Forty-Fifth Street popular among entertainers such as the Marx Brothers, and made a pitch that could have been booked as a vaudeville sketch about Jewish mothers.[90] Miriam is not married, began Fannie. "It's a catastrophe! The shame is on the whole family already." Rose was not ashamed, he told his mother, who replied, "You should feel ashamed if you got a spark of feeling in your blood, for your own flesh and blood, your own poor sister, what is crying day and night because her heart is breaking she is not living a normal life." Rose admitted defeat and mother and son became coconspirators. According to Rose, the scene went like this:

"'What's the notion, mama?'

"She leaned forward confidentially. 'I have arranged a husband for her!'

"'Fine! I'm glad to hear. I'd like to meet him.'

"'That's a little difficult,' she says. 'He's in Russia.'"[91]

Fannie had discovered a Jewish doctor in Russia she decided would make a good husband for her daughter. A fictional story about a similar Jewish parental plot, Abraham Cahan's "The Imported Bridegroom," was published a quarter century before, in 1898, and even at that time the American-born daughter in the tale objects to the arrangement. In fact, in 1898 a Jewish matchmaker in New York complained that young people today "believe in love and all that rot. They are making their own marriages."[92] By 1923, Fannie's plan was truly archaic. But Rose became his mother's partner in the plan, and he spent $500 to bring over from Russia one Joseph Berenstein, who arrived in Boston on November 1, 1923. The ship arrival passenger list shows his age as thirty-three and confirms Fannie's story that he was a doctor.[93]

Berenstein's arrival overlapped with another of Fannie's Jewish projects. At the same time that she arranged a husband for Miriam she planned with her brothers Maurice and Abraham to found a synagogue in the small town of Park Ridge, New Jersey, where the two men lived with their wives and children. Maurice was the first to leave New York and by 1923 had a successful dentistry practice in Park Ridge.[94] Abraham was in the dry goods business and arrived in the northern New Jersey town between 1920 and 1923. Rose's parents joined the Wernick brothers there in 1923, and on October 10 of that year, the three Wernick siblings and their spouses joined fifteen other Jews to found the Park Ridge Hebrew Community Center. The congregation's English name, as opposed to a Hebrew one, and its designation as a community center instead of a synagogue, is evidence that the project had to serve a variety of needs and, as the town's only Jewish community, be comprehensible to its non-Jewish neighbors. Fannie and her brothers were prime movers of the project. Of the twenty-one founders only eleven sat on the board of trustees, and more than one-quarter of this small group consisted of the Wernick clan, including Abraham Wernick, Maurice Wernick, and Fannie Rosenberg.[95] Rose's mother had found another opportunity to rule.

Fannie's parallel ventures of importing a bridegroom and founding a synagogue converged after Miriam married Joseph Berenstein in New York on September 21, 1924.[96] The union was followed by a celebration at the Park Ridge synagogue on a field that "was turned into a carnival playground, with Japanese lanterns, tables, a band playing *freilichs,* Jewish wedding music, a nervous gyrating string music with a single clarinet, single trumpet and some fiddles and a piano," Rose said. The uproarious scene got a little out of hand. "It was a completely unreal wedding—nearly a thousand guests, children roaming around, chasing chickens, men getting drunk and falling into a lake. The crowd and the noise so loud you couldn't hear the rabbi."[97]

It was the Jewish source of the mad entertainments Rose later produced in his nightclubs and theatrical shows, as well as an example of the Jewish gift for enjoyment that some felt did not get enough publicity. "It pleased me enormously to find that back where I came from there were hundreds of thousands of Jews who stuffed themselves with highly flavored food, got pie-eyed, sang dirty songs and occasionally punched each other on the nose," wrote A. J. Liebling in his 1938 book *Back Where I Came From.* "A saloon-keeper I know on Delancey Street once made me a proposition that would have delighted [the ribald French poet François] Villon. 'We'll eat good,' he said, 'then we'll get shikker, go upstairs and see the girls, and then we'll go to a Turkish bath and have a good sweat.'"[98] Other visitors were also struck by Jewish spiritedness. Despite the poverty of the Lower East Side, "the impression given by the inhabitants is one of intense vitality," noted the fashion photographer Cecil Beaton.[99] Rose translated this into the American vernacular but kept his distance from the original. Despite his later embrace of Jewish causes, he could not integrate Jewish customs into his personal life. Regardless of the kick he got out of recalling his sister's wedding, Rose would never have one remotely like it.

four

"SINCE HENRY FORD APOLOGIZED TO ME"

Whether getting drafted into his mother's machinations awakened Rose to his true nature or convinced him he had a lot to do in order to outdo her, after Fannie pushed him to bring over Miriam's husband, Rose began his lifelong pattern of cooking up several projects at once and minding each so diligently that none seemed banished to the back burner. Everyone who met him during the twenties and early thirties agreed on the essentials. "Billy had a seven track mind," said Fanny Brice. "He could talk to seven people on different subjects and remember everything—never forget anything."[1] The civil rights attorney Arthur Garfield Hays called Rose "five feet two of dynamic activity. He is persistent, impatient, energetic, and tireless."[2] "Rose seemed to be possessed of unbounded courage, energy and enthusiasm," agreed the theater and film director John Murray Anderson.[3] The composer Richard Rodgers remembered him as a "very shrewd, highly complex and oddly likable character," who was "forever churning up new ideas, each more adventurous than the last. Even when one of his schemes fell through, it was never for want of boldness or imagination."[4] Rose's own take is the most acute and predictive: "I was groping around. I was seeking something big and grandiose, something strange and wonderful."[5]

That search became apparent in 1924, when Rose moved out of the Princeton Hotel and into his own apartment one floor above the street in a brownstone building at 64 West Fifty-Second Street. Rose gave the apartment a "Turkish harem" look with a living room comprising several couches, "deeply upholstered chairs, heavy wine colored drapes.... A carved Morris chair. Deep oriental rugs." The furnishings were "fake rich, heavy," Rose said later. "If you were furnishing an apartment out of a bad auction that's what you'd wind up with."[6] That was a stock line from Rose's self-disparagement routine. It lent him charm. But Rose's interest in design, style, art, and furniture was and remained genuine and keen. In the 1960s, when he hired the New York interior decorator Melanie Kahane to furnish his villa in Montego Bay, Jamaica, he surprised and impressed her when he spoke of a black, white, and pumpkin bedroom she had once designed. "Can you imagine his remembering that room for 25 years," she said. "And for a man to be that interested in decorating was even more astounding to me."[7] In 1924, Rose was already a producer at heart, striving to realize a theatrical effect, look, and mood.

ARMS RACE

New York in the twenties was booming, and "nightlife was one of the most colorful and well-known service industries in the metropolitan colossus." Between 1924 and 1929, twenty-six new theaters opened in the city, the total reached ninety, together they hosted more than two hundred new shows a year, and after those theaters closed for the night at eleven, New Yorkers continued their revelries at the city's more than one thousand nightclubs, which stayed open until four or even five in the morning. This nighttime world employed thirty thousand musicians and entertainers performing numbers that might feature "near-naked girls" singing a "song about cherries," while hand-feeding the fruit into the mouths of male patrons.[8] The twenties purred as well as roared. Nightclub customers ran the gamut from the easy out-of-town marks known as "butter-and-egg men" to big shots such as New York's so-called "night club mayor," Jimmy Walker; William Rhinelander Stewart, aristocrat of old New York; the columnist Walter Winchell, who could plug a place and create a stir; and the gangsters Owney Madden, Dutch Schultz, Waxey Gordon, and others drawn from "the raffish battalions of gyps, ex-holdup men, clip joint experts, towel-swingers and cheap thugs who handled illegal liquor" after the Volstead Act instituted Prohibition on January 16, 1920.[9]

Rose's neighborhood was fertile ground for this after-hours world, and shoots from the surrounding festivities sprouted in his apartment. Parties were continual, gin was plentiful, someone was always playing Rose's grand piano, and guests included the young songwriting team of Richard Rodgers and Lorenz Hart and the singing star Helen Morgan, who liked to feed grapes to "a large green macaw, chained to a perch, which croaked at everyone."[10] There were also some real Broadway characters. In the article "I'm a Sucker for Screwballs," Rose explained, "All my life I've been intrigued by the Daffy Dans who were almost, but not quite, ready for the long white shirt with the starch."[11] One was Solly Violinsky, who played the piano and violin simultaneously and when glum explained, "I'm under the care of a doctor that doesn't care." Sammy Levy was another zany, lost soul, and the butt of jokes. He publicized songs for the music publisher Henry Waterson and "once strode angrily into [the] Waterson [office] and said, 'I'm entitled to a raise or more respect.' Waterson gave him $5 more a week."[12] When Rose was not hosting a gathering he was probably at the Congress apartment building on West Fifty-Fourth Street, where composer, pianist, and depressive Oscar Levant lived upstairs from the Ziegfeld Follies star Mary Eaton, who also had a piano and celebrity friends who liked to gather around it and sing till dawn.[13]

Presented with New York's possibilities Rose was not interested in making choices. He wanted it all. It was the right moment for such ambition: Rose was becoming a contender. In April 1924 he took a bold and publicity-grabbing stand against song publishers at the annual American Society of Composers, Authors and Publishers (ASCAP) meeting. The group's president "gave Rose the floor thinking he was going to make the usual harmless song-writer speech." Instead, Rose charged publishers with "double-crossing" songwriters through subsidiary companies that acted as broadcasters and did not pay royalties, which was against ASCAP rules. Publishers yelled out for proof. Rose said he would soon provide it, and *Billboard* editorialized that Rose's arrival meant the publishers would no longer have it so easy. "Billy Rose is one of the most successful of the young lyric writers and is said to be imbued with business acumen unusual for a song writer," the publication observed. "For this reason it is generally understood that he and publishers do not 'love' each other, in that Rose always holds out for large advance royalties and is independent in his dealings with the music houses."[14] A few weeks later Rose lived up to *Billboard*'s billing when he opened Conrose Music, a music publishing partnership with Con Conrad formed to get around ASCAP regulations that prevented composers from selling their own creations to the public.[15] It was Rose's warning to publishers that he was willing to pursue an arms race. He would fight their phony broadcast subsidiaries with his own phony publishing subsidiaries. Rose changed the rules of the game. "You see, he does not walk into a publisher's office like some panhandler looking for a favor," explained *Billboard*.[16]

By the middle of the year, publishers treated Rose with more respect. An advertisement from Irving Berlin, Inc., promoted Rose as a winning brand. He was the man behind "That Old Gang," "Barney Google," and "You've Got to See Mamma," and the ad promised that his new song, "Old Familiar Faces," "will electrify your audiences. Sure Fire."[17] Other 1924 songs kept the money coming in and his name before the public. "Does the Spearmint Lose Its Flavor on the Bedpost Over Night" was one of Rose's novelty or "nut" songs, and it highlighted the facet of his character that was anarchic, avid for the mad and offbeat, and of a piece with his affection for screwballs, the chained green macaw, and the weird drawings he created at the WIB. It was full of "wonderful nonsense"[18]: "Can't you see I'm going crazy, won't somebody put me right? / Does the Spearmint lose its flavor on the bedpost over night?"

The song captured a sensibility common among New York's immigrant Jews. They were often mystified, amused, bewildered, thrilled, and intimidated by the nonstop assault of the city's frenetic life.[19] The Russian-Jewish artist Louis Lozowick depicted this tumult of emotion in his 1925 print *Coney Island*. Its flat plane piles the amusement park's rides and diversions on top of each other to evoke the venue's mad atmosphere. The same goes for Abraham Walkowitz's 1927 *New York,* with its colliding and crashing skyscrapers that clamber over each other to reach the sky. In the same vein, Rose's madcap song suggests that the colossal "Spearmint" sign in Times Square—a "200-foot . . . dazzling display boasting 17,500 bulbs, . . . peacocks, flowing fountains, and six 'spearmen'"—had blasted its way into New York's consciousness until madness set in.[20] Izzy Yereshefsky, proprietor of Broadway's I & Y Cigars shop, got the joke; he featured the song's title verse in an advertisement for his store. In the *New Yorker,* Liebling presented Izzy as a comically honest alien trying to cope with Broadway's liars and oddballs.[21] Rose's "Spearmint" nonsense made sense to Izzy.

PSYCHOLOGICAL GAMBLE

In 1924 a reporter noted that "affluent popular songwriters are getting the production-backing bee." One of the examples was Billy Rose, who invested in *The Melody Man.* The other was Rose's writing and business partner Con Conrad, who took a stake in a revival of *The Fatal Wedding.* In fact, Rose played a role in both productions.[22] He was one of the first songwriters to branch into producing.

Rose's opportunity came when Max Hart, father to the lyricist Lorenz Hart, approached him for the additional money needed to bring his son's *The Melody Man* from Chicago to New York in time to capitalize on patronage expected during the June 1924 Democratic National Convention, the first such held in New York in sixty years.[23] Rodgers and Hart had written *Melody*'s two songs and Hart's work with Rose during the summer of 1920 made him a good prospect for funds. *Melody* was so bad that Rose had to be "hoodwinked" into making the investment, Rodgers said, though it is hard to imagine Rose as a sucker, even at age twenty-four.[24] Hart and Rodgers both claimed Rose invested $1,000. The news story said he came through with $5,000.[25] It was Rose's first use of the press to inflate his credentials.

Regardless of the amount, the play's theme dispels the notion that Rose needed to be tricked into backing the production. It has elements that are easy to believe appealed to the successful young songwriter who detested his old-world father's inability to meet the challenge of the American marketplace. The play was produced by and starred Lew Fields, a vaudeville and theater stalwart born Moses Schoenfeld whose partnership with Joe Weber made the duo "the most beloved and ambitious of comedy teams," not to mention successful. In 1904, Fields opened his own Lew Fields Theatre on Forty-Second Street.[26] In *Melody Man* this veteran played a European composer of classical music forced to eke out a living as an arranger in a Tin Pan Alley song factory that "borrows" musical ideas from classical tunes. Eventually the company exploits a composition by Fields's character, turning his "Dresden Sonata" into "Moonlight Mama." On top of that, the derided and cheated and disillusioned old man sees his daughter happily corrupted by the business. She embraces its ruthlessness and marries the firm's unprincipled principal. Yet somehow everything ends happily, reported the *New York Times*: "Not to put too fine a point on it, 'The Melody Man' is about as far as possible from being a good play. Buy why should it be a good play? Isn't it enough that it is Broadway entertainment?"[27]

Melody opened on Broadway on May 13, 1924, and in its first week did only passably, bringing in $5,500, but for Rose it earned its keep as a course of instruction in everything the neophyte producer needed to learn about the theater from an old pro like Fields.[28] First, Fields tried to fix the play. The producer added a jazz combo and softened the character of the unscrupulous music publisher so his marriage to the composer's daughter would be "more plausible."[29] That had little effect, which led to step number two: cut costs. The show left the Ritz Theatre and moved to the Forty-Ninth Street Theatre, where it played through

June.[30] That was a victory, because on June 4 *Variety* tagged the show as one of the "Failures of the Season."[31] One tactic that allowed it to hang on was to make several members of the cast equity stakeholders. In expectation of shared profits, they worked without salaries.[32] Even after the show closed, the resourceful Fields found ways to make it yield a return. He sold Rodgers and Hart's "Moonlight Mama" to a song publisher and made plans to take the show to Philadelphia with new song material that would fill it out as a musical comedy. That did not work out. The theater in Philly canceled the planned date. Fields then announced "a condensed version" for New York's Palace Theatre.[33] That version never appeared, and *Melody Man* was finally silenced. But Rose had completed his first class in the hybrid art-as-business called theater, where the most fascinating action often takes place in the producer's office. As the Group Theatre founder Harold Clurman put it, "The theatre is in the very heart of the market-place, where a feverish and fabulous exchange of goods seems the essential drama."[34]

Before *Melody Man* closed, Rose's Broadway education was supplemented by *The Fatal Wedding*. It held great lessons for his future. The plot of the 1901 play by Theodore Kremer stemmed from an 1893 African American vaudeville song that tells of a wedding interrupted by the groom's abandoned wife and child. The child dies on the spot, the would-be groom commits suicide, and the wife and the intended bride leave with the latter's parents, who promise to care for both women.[35] Kremer saw the comic possibilities of the song's story and upped the ante in his *The Fatal Wedding, or, The Little Mother: A Comedy Drama in a Prologue and Three Acts.* His version includes a scheming friend of the groom, the friend's mistress, the groom's falsely disgraced first wife and their two children (including an infant cared for by an older sister who is the "Little Mother" of the title), an escape "by way of a rope over a precipitous chasm" (don't ask), the suicide by poison of the would-be second bride of the groom, and a near shoot-out at the wedding altar. It opened in New York in October 1901 and closed unreviewed after a one-week run.[36]

On May 14, 1924, *Variety* ran news of the play's revival on its front page. In fact, it was careful to point out that the new *Fatal Wedding* was not properly a revival but a "reproduction of the original play." When it opened at the Ritz on June 2—it replaced *Melody Man*—theatergoers experienced a trip back in time to the turn of the century, including "a typical gallery cop [who] rapped his stick and yelled 'Hats off,'" "old time songs between acts," and, for the departing audience, "instead of autos at the door, there was a flock of old-fashioned horse cabs to take the folks home. Many availed themselves of the horse-drawn equipages."[37] The inclusion of these antiquated effects escorted the play the short distance from melodrama to camp. The *Times* called it "excellent fun" and "frequently hilarious entertainment."[38] The audience was encouraged to see the over-the-top plot as comic, and the crowd "joined in with applause and hisses for the righteous and the villainous." Nostalgia played an important role in the fun. "The women's pompadour coiffures and big hats were a riot with the women in the audience," and a reviewer gave the producers "credit for putting their money into a venture purely speculative, an unqualified psychological gamble."[39] Rose made this gamble the foundation of his entertainment career. "He became a merchant of nostalgia and psychological escape," said one observer.[40] Rose agreed. "Nostalgia is the best commodity in show business," he said.[41] His introduction to it was *The Fatal Wedding*.

Rose remained attached to the theater for the next forty years. In 1961, when his wealth was in the tens of millions and the need to deploy capital responsibly made him a savvy investor, he told a business reporter that backing a play "was plain silly."[42] The risk was too great. Yet he could not stay away from it, and playwright Arthur Miller cited Rose as one of the exceptions to the understanding that "money rules everything." Rose was one of the "crazy people" who produced plays despite the prospect of an almost certain loss.[43] This patronage derived from a cultured and altruistic aspect of Rose's character that he was careful to hide. Even those who disliked him, such as his press agent Charles Samuels, understood this need to obscure decency and come on tough. "He was in [a] business where kindness could kill a man," Samuels said.[44]

WHAT NO MEANT

The nightclubs of the twenties "seemed to bring a wholesale reorientation of the average day for a large number of well-to-do New Yorkers, making them into entirely nocturnal creatures."[45] Rose understood the appeal of the night. "When the sun goes down people don't want to be educated," he said. "They want a drink, a bite to eat, and they want to have some fun."[46] Moralizers did not like the sound of that and protested the nightclubs as centers of sin, including "the corruption of young women, the spread of organized lawlessness, and the rise of public immorality." Clubs and their patrons retaliated with an indulgence that amounted to a "rebellion in American culture against traditional concepts of civic life."[47] The revelers' argument was attractive, and opponents were often seduced. Even the city got into the nightclub business with the New York–owned Central Park Casino.[48] The 1920s were the beginning of an age of greater freedom for less decorum.

The clubs were also a business opportunity. Like songwriting, the nightclub trade enticed many who had no chance of making it and others, such as Liebling subject Hymie Katz, who made a living bilking the deluded. "All Hymie needs to open a club is an idea and a loan of fifty dollars," Liebling wrote.[49] Billy Rose, as he did on Tin Pan Alley, fell into neither category but instead proved himself an adept. Dipping into his savings, which derived more from his songs than from his short-lived Broadway productions, Rose in 1924 invested $3,500 and joined entertainer Solly Violinsky, jokester and hoofer Joe Frisco, and veteran talent agent Jerry Hitchcock to create the Back Stage Club.[50] "'Sawdust'—At Last!" exclaimed *Variety*. "A class 'sawdust' place has opened in the Times square [*sic*] section. Everything else in the cabaret and night club line in the Broadway district is of the glitter and crass kind with high coveur [*sic*] charge among other higher charges." Rose's club at 110 West Fifty-Sixth Street took a different tack. "It's one flight up, nicely furnished but not gaudily, and permitting diners to see the original bricks on the side walls," an effect none but Rose was likely to have imagined. Other touches that suited the Back Stage theme included sandbags "hung around here and there to simulate the weights that pull up a curtain" and floodlights "stacked in one corner." Jokes between management and customers furthered the hip insider atmosphere and were chalked on the brick walls. One read, "Be kind to our hostess—she's working her way through Cartier's."[51]

A night of music and dancing included performances by Violinsky and Frisco and also a featured act that provided music for dancing, such as the orchestra of pianist and arranger Al Siegel, who later helped Ethel Merman create her distinctive singing style. No act, though, topped singer Helen Morgan, an iconic figure of New York's club scene. The "stunning brunette"[52] transmitted a "baffling emotional effect" alternately described as poignant, possessed of a "strange submissive quality," and "pensive, gently melancholy."[53] The *Times* attributed to Morgan "a somnolent, smoldering personality, with overtones of pathos."[54] One account of her performance at the Back Stage has columnist and short story writer Ring Lardner helping Morgan to the top of the piano to sing because she was too petite to be seen by patrons in the rear, initiating a cliché that has too much appeal to die.[55]

Crucially for Rose's future, the club and Morgan brought him to the attention of Fanny Brice. "The place was so crowded," Brice said. "Helen Morgan sang there. She always sat on the piano to sing because it was so crowded. She sang a song called 'In the Middle of the Night,' and I thought the lyrics were so wonderful." Two lines especially captivated her: "In the middle of a moment / You and I forgot what no meant." Brice wondered, "Who wrote that song, it's wonderful." A companion pointed out Rose. Brice could not believe it. "I said, 'Oh that little guy never wrote that song. He bought it from somebody.' That was the first time I saw him." Rose's account of the meeting captures the wised-up tone of their future relationship. In response to her disbelief he said, "I can understand your disappointment. You thought the guy who wrote it had eyes like the Albany night boat," suggesting Brice had fallen for the sentimental idea that the song's creator should beam brilliantly. That got a laugh out of comedienne Fanny Brice.[56]

In September 1925 the Back Stage closed. The first sign of trouble surfaced in May, when Hitchcock sold his share of the club to the singer Tommy Lyman.[57] His unwillingness to stay connected to the business likely stemmed from a prejudice against criminals. Al Capone was a club regular, Rose said, an unlikely story because by 1925 the Brooklyn-born gangster was well established in Chicago.[58] But other mobster customers included Arnold Rothstein, who came to own a piece of the joint. He arranged for the police to raid the club night after night and then had an underling offer Rose protection. "Broadway during Prohibition was as glamorous as a thumb in the eye," Rose said.[59]

HAREM TENDERS

News of his next club appeared in November, which meant he was working on the Fifth Avenue Club while the hull of the sinking Back Stage was still above water. That hardly counted as multitasking for Rose. He was also writing a play called *The Yes Man,* "a new comedy of American business life;"[60] forming or at least announcing a correspondence school to teach songwriting;[61] working on another stage production with writer Ballard MacDonald;[62] and also writing songs, including the 1925 hit "A Cup of Coffee, a Sandwich and You," an American update of poet Omar Khayyam's line "A jug of wine, a loaf of bread, and thou."[63] Rose wrote the lyrics with Al Dubin, who was the one who knew of Khayyam; Rose's education was minimal. In 1929, when he worked with Edward

Eliscu on a musical with biblical themes Eliscu suggested the line, "But sure as I know the Jordan will roll." Rose asked, "What's Jordan?"[64]

The Fifth Avenue Club was the polar opposite of the informal Back Stage. The new venue instituted a newsworthy five-dollar cover charge—the highest in the city—designed to appeal to elite society, and by not serving liquor the club was safe from the criminals Rose called "the broken fingernail set."[65] The cover charge was "in the nature of a gate fee as admission to the interior," which sported "a miniature theatre with a revue" written by the rising team of Rodgers and Hart. The club with a theater—its full name was the Fifth Avenue Club and Little Theatre—was Rose's first attempt to combine various entertainments into one attraction.[66] The formulation was a hallmark of his theatrical vision. His need for the strange and marvelous led him to meld "traditional popular forms into new and seemingly novel entertainments," and over the next several years Rose pursued this goal to its limit with clubs that overwhelmed the senses and defied categorization.[67]

"Various men and women of wealth have brought homes, shops and famous institutions to Fifth avenue, and Billy Rose, best known on Broadway for his song-writing proclivities, has given it a night club which upholds the traditions of the avenue in every way," *Billboard* announced in February 1926. The new spot operated from "quarters formerly occupied by the exclusive Criterion Club, directly opposite the University Club and within the very shadow of the Vanderbilt mansions. What's more, Samuel Untermyer lives right next door—so that's that."[68]

What seemed daunting to *Billboard* encouraged and even facilitated Rose's audacious move. Untermyer was a leading New York Jewish millionaire and by 1921 an outspoken Zionist;[69] the Criterion Club was one of the city's most prestigious Jewish men's clubs;[70] and the building at 683 Fifth Avenue that held the Criterion and then Rose's club was owned by Maurice Wertheim, investment banker and by 1914 a philanthropist for the Jews of Palestine.[71] Rose worked his musical and Jewish connections (there was often no difference) to clinch this deal. An important introduction was to the jazz saxophonist Roger Wolfe Kahn, son of the millionaire banker Otto Kahn, partner at Kuhn, Loeb & Co., patron of the arts, and a frequenter of nightclubs who relished "a wild good time" and who ended one nightclub excursion with his face covered in lipstick lavished there by a showgirl.[72] Rose's business partnership with the younger Kahn to jointly own and run the club lasted just long enough for Rose to secure the lease for the second-floor space vacated by the Criterion Club, which had moved around the corner.[73] Despite the end of their partnership, Rose kept Kahn happy by keeping him on as head of the Fifth Avenue Club Orchestra.[74] In these years, when Rose's relationship with Bernard Baruch was in abeyance, he found other Jewish men of fame, wealth, and faithfulness to their co-religionists to help and inspire him.

His Jewish affiliation also revealed itself in a penchant for Near Eastern motifs. As *Billboard* described it,

> No expense has been spared in any direction to make the club an artistic triumph as to mural and other decorations, surpassing anything ever seen here or abroad. Clara Tice has covered the walls with sketches expressing no less than 45 moods and longing for personal liberty, both from social restraint and clothes—all feminine, of course. As marvelous an array of nymphs as one would wish to see. There is a "perfumed garden" away from the dining and dance room which is presided over by a harem tender, who stands guard at the iron gate. The garden has a blue-sky effect, gold columns, flowers, and neither chairs nor tables, but a lounge built around the walls, plentifully supplied with luxurious cushions.[75]

It was the Turkish harem look again, as in Rose's first apartment. The perfumed garden even featured "three Assyrians playing weird Oriental tunes for the atmosphere," and the nude murals aided the effect he had in mind.[76] "Billy Rose commissioned me to do the murals . . . some forty-five nymphs in silver, rose and gold," Tice wrote.[77] The look was a nightclub version of the Moorish architectural style that in New York was associated with Jews. Fifth Avenue's Temple Emanu-El, built in 1868 at the corner of Fifth Avenue and Forty-Third Street and still standing in 1925, was "the first building in New York that was clearly identifiable as a Jewish house of worship" because, paradoxically, it displayed the domes, slender pillars, and cusped arches of the Islamic Near East. By 1870, "New York hosted more Moorish-style synagogues than any other city in the world. . . . The use of the Moorish style marks a wider Jewish engagement with modernity and with the surrounding religious and secular culture."[78] So both the club's location and its design were influenced by Rose's membership in the Jewish community. But his attraction to the harem theme had other sources, too, including a desire to collect and control women, and photographs of an unsmiling Rose coolly appraising half-naked women, deciding which he would hire for his shows and which he would dismiss, became a newspaper staple. This authority over women overturned the dynamic that prevailed between his parents. Though he admired his mother, he made sure no woman would do to him what she had done to his father. Rose relished his supremacy over females. His father could not cope with one woman; Rose made himself the master of hundreds.

In August 1926, Rose sold the money-losing Fifth Avenue.[79] "It was the beginning of my delusions of grandeur," Rose said. "I instituted an impractical policy of a $5 a person couvert charge. Outside of Saturday nights, the club played to no business." But as with his version of his mother's failure at home ownership, Rose invented a tale that made someone else the sucker. "My dear," Rose supposedly told highly valued nightclub hostess Cecil Cunningham, who worked at the Fifth Avenue before taking a better offer. "You could make the Fifth Avenue Club a sort of salon. Why, you could be mistress of conversation and go from table to table conversing with your customers."[80] Cunningham's criminal boyfriend bought her the club and it promptly failed, Rose said. This lie built up Rose's image as nobody's fool. He did take advantage of Cunningham, but not so spectacularly. Using the strategy Fields employed on *Melody Man,* Rose had Cunningham work for a piece of the profits. There were none, so she did not get paid.[81] He did the same to Rodgers and Hart. "The promised royalties for our revue score failed to arrive," Rodgers wrote. "As I recall it, we never collected a dime for our efforts, but Billy was the kind of promoter who somehow made you feel he had paid you double."[82] Rose's dazzling charm was as much a business asset as his appetite for confrontation.

FORD'S APOLOGY

The infamous antisemitism of Henry Ford made its public debut on May 22, 1920. That was when his weekly newspaper, *The Dearborn Independent,* featured on its front page an article headlined "The International Jew: The World's Problem." It was the first of ninety installments that reprinted excerpts of *The Protocols of the Elders of Zion,* the forgery that purports to be a Jewish plan for world domination. Ford had taken control of the suburban paper serving his small town of Dearborn, near Detroit, in 1918, and over the next eight years grew its circulation from the tiny 1,200 to an impressive 700,000. His wealth allowed him to distribute it free to schools, libraries, and colleges, and he ordered his auto dealerships to turn customers into subscribers. In this way, Ford for the first time gave American "antisemitism a national platform."[83]

Rose took notice. His songs were often a form of journalism: he spotted revealing trends, manners, pastimes, and products, and crafted lyrics that brought attention to the topics, often with humor. "Barney Google" was one such, but so was "Since Ma Is Playing Mah Jong," which comically asserts that in the early 1920s, when the Chinese board game became a sensation—especially among women—it threatened American family life.[84]

For Rose, Ford's continuing attacks on the Jews hit close to home. The car manufacturer slandered prominent men Rose admired, such as Otto Kahn and Bernard Baruch. In response, Rose went on the offensive. He took his first swipe at Ford with the 1926 song "Yiddishe Charleston." It seems Rose was waiting for Ford to make himself ridiculous so the songwriter could leverage the buffoonish moment to treat Ford as a joke, instead of objecting to him as a threat. Opportunity arrived in August, when dance instructors held a "'Henry Ford' Night" at New York's Waldorf Astoria to "discourage the Charleston and other eccentric dances." Ford preferred the "minuet waltz" and the "heel and toe polka."[85] The timing was perfect, because just a few months earlier the dancer Joe Frisco, Rose's former partner at the Back Stage Club, wowed audiences at the Palace with the "Jewish Charleston," a performance that "stopped the act cold."[86] Rose took advantage of both Ford's and Frisco's focus on the dance to create an absurd convergence of the twain. He nudged Ford's titanic antisemitism against the comic iceberg of the "Yiddishe Charleston" to make fun of the great American success:[87]

Oy that—oy that Yiddishe Charleston
Oy that—oy that Yiddishe Charleston
Henry Ford is learning how to Yiddishe Charleston now.

A year later, another news event gave Rose a second crack at Ford. One of the *Dearborn Independent*'s Jewish targets filed a lawsuit against Ford for libel, the case went to trial in early 1927, and it was settled out of court in July, after Ford decided a public court case was not worth "the controversies and ill feeling." Instead, he offered to present a public apology to a Jewish leader who could accept it on behalf of American Jewry. Louis Marshall, a founder of the American Jewish Committee, was that leader. He negotiated with Ford, and each got what he wanted. In return for the public apology, the car manufacturer was allowed to claim that his paper had printed the offensive articles without his knowledge. He also pledged to end the scurrilous articles. On July 8, 1927, the apology was front-page news and the country learned that Ford "was 'mortified' to discover that the *Independent* had become the 'medium of resurrecting exploded fictions'" about the Jews.[88]

Ford's claim of ignorance was a joke to many, and newspapers ran parodies. "John Hancock declared his shock at discovering that his signature appeared on a document titled 'The Declaration of Independence,'" was one example. Rose's Jewish response was "Since Henry Ford Apologized to Me," which a *Variety* columnist got an advance look at and called the "funniest song lyrics we have ever heard."[89] With false sincerity and Yiddish accents the Happiness Boys sang Rose's song.

> I was sad and I was blue
> But now I'm just as good as you
> Since Hen-ry Ford a-pol-o-gized to me
> I've thrown a-way my lit-tle Che-vro-let
> And bought my-self a Ford Cou-pe
> I told the Sup-'rin-ten-dent that
> the Dearborn In-de-pen-dent
> Does-n't have to hang up where it used to be
> I'm glad he changed his point of view
> And I even like Edsel too,
> Since Hen-ry Ford a-pol-o-gized to me
> My mother says she'll feed him if he calls
> "Ge-fil-te-fish and Mat-zah balls"
> And if he runs for President
> I would-n't charge a sin-gle cent
> I'll cast my bal-lot ab-so-lute-ly free
> Since Hen-ry Ford a-pol-o-gized to me.[90]

"Yiddishe Charleston" and "Henry Ford" marked Rose's first public allegiance to the Jews. He did not revisit a Jewish topic for ten years.

five

CRAZY QUILT

In 1910, Fanny Brice's debut in the Ziegfeld Follies was cheered as a revelation. "This strange and fantastic young woman of the willowy form and the classic face doesn't sing her songs at all—she just sort of kind of remembers them," the *San Francisco Chronicle* observed in its review. "Her gestures and facial play mark the climax insanity, but she is bubbling with natural fun and life."[1] Nearly twenty years later, Brice was still considered a treasure. "Fannie [*sic*] Brice represents Broadway less by being its product than a comment upon it," began a 1929 *New Yorker* profile. "Her talent, rare in that environment, is to make fakes look ridiculous."[2] The *Times* toasted the Brice of the "slightly crossed eyes, the broad grin and the comic awkwardness of a gawky east side young lady . . . [that] reveal Fannie [*sic*] Brice playing confidently on the home grounds. Most of us are content to see her at her best. At her best, she is unparalleled."[3] Her ability to wring pathos out of song was not bad either. Brice premiered her signature torch song, "My Man," at the 1921 Follies. Rose was there to witness the performance of his song "Ain't Nature Grand" and described her as "thunder in the mountains."[4]

But when Rose met Brice at the Back Stage Club in 1925, her husband Nicky Arnstein was in prison for his part in the 1920 theft of $5 million in bonds, and the intervening years had taken their toll. In 1923, Brice briefly lost faith in comedy, announced that she desired dramatic roles, and got her nose straightened. Florenz Ziegfeld was furious and Dorothy Parker delighted. "I want Fanny to make 'em laugh—that's what I pay her for," said Ziegfeld in a quote nobody remembers. Brice "cut off her nose to spite her race," said Parker in a pun that has never been forgotten. Disappointing shows followed. David Belasco's 1926 *Fanny* was a terrible show that starred Brice as a "Jewish girl out West among the

Cowboys," and in early 1927, she headlined *Hollywood Music Box Revue,* another flop. In September, Brice divorced Arnstein and sued for custody of their two children: Frances, eight, and William, six. The strain made her look "tired and worn."[5] Brice, at thirty-six, was on the ropes.

Rose, at twenty-eight, was full of bounce. *Variety* described a confab where Rose, "song writer extraordinary," was "surrounded by a flock of people and having a great time."[6] Everything was going his way. After his Fifth Avenue Club closed, he returned to songwriting and produced standards that elevated his reputation. "Tonight You Belong to Me" appeared in the summer of 1926, and he taunted the publishers that missed out on the evergreen hit. "Rose said he would like to see all the big publishers in line and have each one take a bow" for turning him away. Nobody bowed, but there was likely a gnashing of teeth among those who passed on it, because in March 1927 it sold well even during the Catholic holiday of Lent. The "axiom about the hit songs always selling applies at all times," explained *Variety.*[7]

Rose topped that song a few months later with "Me and My Shadow." Detractors have tried to deny him this standard recorded by Frank Sinatra, Judy Garland, and many others by relying on a biographer's allegation that Rose changed a single word and on that basis took credit for the song. Unfortunately for the biographer's posterity, he preserved his interview notes with "Shadow" composer Dave Dreyer. "Billy wrote the words [to] Me and My Shadow. . . . Me and My Shadow was not his title. But he wrote the words," Dreyer said. Rose bought the title for fifteen dollars from a "titler." Dreyer's music was originally written for another song for Al Jolson, but Dreyer felt his tune better matched Rose's lyric. So when Jolson demanded to hear the song he commissioned, Dreyer and Rose gave him "Shadow." "Jolson fell in love with the song," Dreyer said. Rose was the one who put it over. "I played the piano and Billy sang the song."[8] Its opening lines capture the solitary's exclusion from love with the evocative couplet, "Sweethearts out for fun / Pass me one by one."

In the summer and fall of 1927 Rose wrote sketch material with Ballard MacDonald, a sometime drunk who wrote for Brice. When MacDonald's sometime occurred in October, Rose stepped in and created the act Brice needed for her November 21 show at the Palace. His songs steered her back to the Jewish material rooted in the "gawky east side young lady" persona that had first made her a success. Rose was primed to write such material because of his recent "Since Henry Ford Apologized to Me." He also mined his Fifth Avenue Club's Turkish harem theme and Otto Kahn connection to whip up in two weeks what Brice called "the best act I ever had."[9]

In "Sascha, the Passion of the Pasha," Rose served up a comic Jewish version of the sensual East by imagining Brice as what the song calls one of those "harem dames." She complains that the sultan mainly "hangs around," though she does appreciate his amorous attentions. "Oh, how he appreciates a little kosher meat," Brice sang. And in "Is Something the Matter with Otto Kahn (Or Is Something the Matter with Me?)," Brice again played the unworldly young Jewish woman crashing a foreign land, this time that of the rich German Jews and their love of high culture. She wants Otto Kahn to hire her to sing opera, but what does she know from opera? Finally, in "Mrs. Cohen at the Beach," Rose wrote a brilliant comic monologue that became a pillar of Brice's act. Over the course of six minutes, Rose's Mrs. Cohen unwittingly reveals her loving but overbearing and husband-destroying personality. The influence of Rose's mother is obvious. Directing her children to play with their shovels and sand buckets Mrs. Cohen inevitably comes to the point. "'Go on, dig,' she commands, 'Dig a hole and bury your father.'"[10] The image also recalls Rose's childhood terror.

Brice's show was a winner and a turning point for her, Rose, and their relationship. *Variety* called her return to the Palace a "Bricean triumph" and the recently divorced woman took stock of Rose. "I think I'll marry this guy," she said. "He is clever. He might make life very easy for me."[11] When Brice was on tour in Los Angeles in January 1928 Rose made news by flying to see her. The trip took him through stormy weather, and he was "believed to be the first professional ever to make the trip from New York to Los Angeles by air." Brice met him when he landed.[12] Rose stayed in California for three weeks and returned again in July, when Brice was in Los Angeles filming her first movie, *My Man.* Here Rose again proved his value as he demonstrated that his talent for staring down song publishers was transferable to the new talking picture business. When he learned Brice was offered $25,000 for *My Man,* named for her famous torch song, he did some quick math: if the Warner Bros. film played in ten thousand theaters, that was just $2.50 a house.[13] Testing figures this way kept Rose from being unduly impressed or blasé about money. "In other words, suppose someone asked him for a $5 a week raise in salary. It sounds like very little. But to Rose it automatically became a $260 a year raise in salary, which is a figure to examine and study," said the press agent Wolfe Kaufman. More complex computations were also at his fingertips. "I never gamble," Kaufman recalled Rose saying. "When I bet I want the odds my way." Kaufman added, "And he gave a whole long and boring list of odds on every sort of gambling to prove that it was always impossible to win."[14] That many were bored by such statistics worked to Rose's advantage. He persuaded Warner Bros. to pay Brice $125,000 for *My Man*.[15]

Rose's marriage proposal to Brice could have been lifted from or used in a screwball romantic comedy. "One day he said, 'Why don't you and I get married? We're good for each other,'" Brice recalled. "I thought it over and said, 'Oh, not yet Billy. I'm not sure.' He turned around and kicked me because I said 'No.' I thought that was funny, so I said 'Yea, all right.' There was also a little revenge in my mind too. I thought 'What will this do to Nicky?'" There were other conditions that made the match less than romantic. "I didn't love him," Brice said. "I had great admiration for his talent. I liked him. Later on, Billy told me he felt the same thing." But there was one stipulation Rose would not abide. "I had a whole lot in common with Billy—everything, but nothing physical. I said to Billy, 'We're such good friends Billy, we shouldn't have any affairs.'"[16] Brice was surely too worldly to expect him to abide by this condition, and it seems her main concern was to avoid the public humiliation of playing second fiddle to a mistress. When Rose broke that rule their marriage ended.

Rose and Brice were married on February 8, 1929, at New York's City Hall. Mayor Jimmy Walker performed the civil service and also read the Jewish marriage vows in an English translation provided by Temple Emanu-El's rabbi, Nathan Krass. Rose forgot to buy a wedding ring, so the couple used the one Fanny had handy. "It was a gold carved ring, and inside of it was engraved 'To my darling Fanny—with love, Nickey [*sic*].'"[17]

Brice's mother attended the ceremony. Rose's mother did not. Six months earlier, on August 24, 1928, Rose had purchased a home for her on eighteen acres in Park Ridge, New Jersey, which Fannie Rosenberg imagined she could turn into a resort business.[18] It kept her busy, anyway, and out of Rose's life in New York. For him, one Fanny was enough.

MAMA'S BOY

Two months after their wedding Rose half-jokingly wrote an associate that he "bulled" Brice into the marriage.[19] Who came out on top was a question inherent to the match. For Brice, Rose was a source of great material and good company. Rose, as usual, insisted he got the better deal. "I wanted to marry her because she was like a medal I could wear," he said.[20] In their wedding photo he does look like a hunter posing with a prize catch. They were not in love, and her stated wish for a sexless marriage made the union a business merger, though the lack of interest in a physical relationship was apparently mutual. "There was no passion in our life," Brice said. "He never kissed me with any real passion."[21] The Oedipal aspect of the relationship defeated ardor. Brice bore Rose's mother's name, was his elder, and was more famous. Rose compounded the problem when he created for Brice that great comic portrait of the Jewish mother, "Mrs. Cohen at the Beach." "I am really Mrs. Cohen at the Beach in that number," Brice said. "I mean I am *with* that woman." Pygmalion created his dream lover; Rose created a substitute mother. Brice's psychological problem was complementary; she could only love shiftless charmers like Nicky Arnstein, who resembled her father. "If I go to a party," she said, "and there is one son-of-a-bitch in the room, a no-good bastard—I'd go for him right away." As a result, said Brice, "I never *liked* the men I loved—and I never *loved* the men I liked."[22] She liked Rose. He could not love her either. It was a match made in an analyst's nightmare.

Yet both shared attitudes toward their lives and work that drew on their Jewish identities and no-nonsense characters. Both pledged allegiance to the Jewish community and fought its critics. Rose lampooned Ford; Brice sent her children to Jewish religious school at New York's Temple Emanu-El, where daughter Frances stayed until her confirmation in 1934 and son William until a bout of poor health in 1933. She also battled Rose when the coarseness of his early "Ain't Nature Grand" style crept into his Jewish song material. "Billy said he had an idea and told me about a song called 'River Side Rose.' I told him why it was not good. I told him that I never did a Jewish song that would offend the race, because it depended on the race for the joke, so we got into an argument."[23] Brice won.

Each also knew the value of a dollar. "Tipping like a whore again, eh?" was how Brice chided Gypsy Rose Lee's extravagance. "They can talk all they want about scrapbooks, but it's the bankbooks that count."[24] Frugality funded charity, which Brice, like Rose, performed quietly. Rose arranged to get songwriter Chester Conn the copyright to "I Want to Be Loved," which Conn wanted to reintroduce. "It's the unwritten law among publishers never to give a copyright away," Conn said. "No one has ever heard of such a thing. Yet Billy said, I can get the copyright for you."[25] John Murray Anderson had a similar experience. When the director went broke in Hollywood he sent his brother to New York to ask Rose for $5,000. "I'll make out a check right away," Rose responded. "Shall I send it over or do you want to pick it up?"[26] For her part, Brice helped support Ziegfeld in his last days, "bought a layette for her doorman's granddaughter, and paid hospital expenses for a wardrobe woman."[27]

Perhaps most importantly, the two agreed that profound emotions were reserved for song and stage and the desire to employ deep talk in day-to-day life was the surest sign of a fool. "He had a bitter sarcastic sense of humor that appealed to me," Brice said.[28] A representative sample is Rose's cynical take on the purported connection between a songwriter's situation and his work. "At the time I was writing ["Me and My Shadow"]," he recalled, "there was a boisterous party of 35 eating, swilling and necking in my joint on 52nd Street. Alone? Why, I was never alone. I never had less than a dozen guys and gals in my place. Yes, I have heard this theory that a man can be lonely even if he has crowds of people around him, but I do not put any stock in it."[29] Brice was likewise wary of deep ideas. When the novelist Jerome Weidman, a candidate to write Brice's biography, said he thought she was "a lonesome woman," Brice quickly sized him up—"Oh, I said to myself, is this the slant?"—and then outlined her own earthy theory of unhappiness to her preferred biographer, the recording executive Goddard Lieberson, who sometimes referred to himself as "Der Schlemiel." He was the kind of guy Brice could open up to. "Of course, I'm like any other person," she said. "I've laid in my bed and cried at nights, why . . . because, perhaps, I wasn't pissing enough and every time this would happen to me I would get up and look in the mirror and say, 'you crazy Jew son of a bitch, go back to bed,' which I did, let out a big *futs,* and off to sleep I went, and this you call lonesome?"[30]

If there was a mismatch between Brice and Rose, it was that she derived greater satisfaction from Rose's ambition than he did from her fame. Rose was "the man hardly anyone knew when he became the husband of Fanny Brice," Gilbert Seldes wrote. "People said, 'Who?' You do not eclipse Miss Brice, no matter how good you are."[31] When asked what it was like to be married to Brice, Rose replied, "It was like being in the shadow of Gibraltar."[32] This drove him to work all the more feverishly to secure his reputation, but it also made him jumpy. Brice remembered that when Rose and she were married, he and Edward Eliscu were writing songs for the stage musical *Great Day!*

> When Billy would be working, he'd come in and say: "Come on in, Fanny—I want you to tell me what you think of this . . . " And he'd sing the song for me—and I'd

say: "I like it. I like everything but this one line ..." And invariably he'd say: "That's funny—that's the best line in the song." I'd say: "I'm very sorry—but I don't like that line." He'd say, "What the hell do *you* know about song-writing!" And I'd say, "What did you ask me for then? That line doesn't sound good to me." There'd be an argument, and he'd go back and work with the guy again—and he'd come out and say: "Listen to it now." And he'd do it *without* that line. And I would never say, "See?? I'm glad you took it out." I would never say that. I'd say, "Gee, I think it's fine now." Wouldn't mention anything about the line.[33]

The scene smacks of maternal selflessness, tact, and patience. As a Brice biographer wrote, her life was a contest between her roles as child and mother, and "it seems quite clear the 'mother' really won."[34] If Brice had to play at being Rose's mother, it was no burden, as long as Rose was hard at work. Her ex-husband Nicky Arnstein had frustrated her. "That man was just *talking* and never doing *anything*," Brice said. Rose was a welcome change. "You see, what I found thrilling with Billy—I was with a man who was creating all the time—doing something."[35]

TEACHER'S PET

The first thing that needed doing was to get Brice another movie deal. In February 1929, just a month after their wedding, Rose and Brice struck a two-picture deal with United Artists, she as the star and he as the writer of songs and story.[36] The contract was a testament to Brice's star power and Rose's writing talents and business savvy, because *My Man,* Brice's earlier movie, was panned by critics and did poor box office. Rose's contribution offered the film's only worthy moment. "Miss Brice's outstanding offering is 'Mrs. Cohen at the Beach,'" reported the *Times.*[37] Despite the film's weakness, Rose was able to win Brice another $125,000 paycheck for her next movie. For his writing contribution, Rose secured $25,000.[38] In June, Brice relocated from New York to Hollywood to begin work on *Be Yourself,* and Rose periodically traveled from New York to California to work on the film's song material, including "When a Woman Loves a Man," which "has, if anything, a better, more sophisticated lyric than 'My Man.'"[39] The song illustrates that Rose's hardboiled dismissal of tender sentiment was his way of avoiding the corrupting power of sentimentality. Even Brice was amazed by the dramatic contrast of her husband's tough and empathic sides. "When I'd hear these lovely words he wrote," she said, "I couldn't believe this cold-minded person had written them."[40] "When a Woman Loves a Man" begins,

> Mountains snap their fingers at time
> Since this old world began
> But they're molehills compared to the mountains she'll climb
> When a gal cares for a man.

At this point in his life, Rose had only received such devoted love from his mother.

Rose also landed writing contracts with MGM and Universal, which in a coup worthy of a rainmaking con man paid him $10,000 for a few hours' work writing three completely unnecessary new songs for its 1929 film version of Jerome Kern and Oscar Hammerstein II's landmark musical, *Show Boat*. Only one Rose song appeared in the forgotten film, and he cheerfully considered the job one of his sweetest swindles.[41] Universal, wisely or obliviously, held no grudge. It hired him again in the summer of 1929 and he wrote "It Happened in Monterey," a song rich in sexy alliteration ("Stars and steel guitars and luscious lips") that in 1956 became a hit for Frank Sinatra. Rose wrote it for *King of Jazz,* a 1930 film that celebrated Paul Whiteman, the then-famous bandleader who, among other things, debuted George Gershwin's *Rhapsody in Blue* at the 1924 concert "An Experiment in American Music." The three-hundred-pound Whiteman possessed a musical range and expertise that put him "in his own category," as did his personal volume. "He would intimidate you," recalled the musician Larry Neill. "He was big and tall, and he would stand right up next to you, six inches away—invade your space—and talk to you in a booming voice. And so you were automatically in a position of defense."[42] In 1935 when Rose produced *Jumbo,* he hired this talented giant.

In September 1929, Rose returned to New York to write lyrics for a Ziegfeld production called *Ming Toy.* He turned thirty that month, an age that then especially signified the end of youth. Nick Carraway turns thirty at the end of *The Great Gatsby* and on his birthday sees ahead of him "a thinning briefcase of enthusiasm."[43] Rose would never suffer an enthusiasm deficit, but the milestone age might have made him decide against trying to start a new career in the movies and stick instead to Broadway, where he had spent ten years making connections, writing songs, and learning the theatrical and nightclub businesses.

Unfortunately, it was not a good time for either new beginnings or practiced pursuits. He was in New York in October for the disastrous Broadway premiere of *Great Day!* Despite excellent songs by Rose and Eliscu, including the frequently reprised torch standard "More Than You Know," later recorded by female vocalists from Sarah Vaughan to Barbra Streisand, the show opened on Broadway with a "soggy and pointless book" that yielded a "thoroughly routine show."[44] One week later the 1929 stock market crash began with the October 24 meltdown known as Black Thursday. *Great Day!* closed in November after one month onstage. Ziegfeld's *Ming Toy* never opened.[45]

As the Depression took hold, New York came to look "visibly down at the heel," and the "comfortable middle class began to show faces pitted with worry."[46] Rose lived in luxury. Upon his marriage to Brice he settled with her and her two children and the children's French governess at 15 East Sixty-Ninth Street, an Upper East Side seventeen-story residential hotel just off the corner of Fifth Avenue that was brand new when Brice moved in after her divorce from Arnstein. To accommodate Rose, Brice added two rooms to the apartment, and this addition served as his private quarters.[47] The couple did not share a bedroom. There was more than enough space in Brice's next home to continue this arrangement. In the fall of 1930, the family moved to 1111 Park Avenue. The building was one of the few on the tony boulevard that welcomed affluent Jews, and Brice's fourteen-room apartment was both palatial residence and Rose's university.[48] It was where he was home-schooled. "He learned everything from Fanny. How to dress, how to eat," said Helen Schrank. "I always lived good," Brice said. "That's the only thing I spent my money on."[49] Starting in 1923, when she purchased and furnished a townhouse at 306 West Seventy-Sixth Street, Brice studied up on art, antiques, china, furniture, and design, and listened carefully to important dealers such as James P. Silo, whose auction house handled estate sales for the Vanderbilts and other wealthy clients. According to Maurice Zolotow, Brice developed "very good taste. Very fine taste in art, decorations, furniture. She played or seemed to be a low type Jewish comic. Actually she dressed superbly, very cultured. She had a magnificent collection of paintings in her home."[50] Rose was eager to gain this knowledge and Brice was proud of her clever pupil:

This is one of the things that made Billy Rose very interesting to me—When he was doing his first show he said to me "I'm doing a show and they are talking costumes to me, and when they say satin, taffeta, talk about qualities etc., I don't know. I don't like to talk about anything—business, prices—if I don't know what I am talking about." He asked me to go around to the stores and get him samples of every material and quality. I went around to the stores for three days until I got a big box of samples of every kind of material in every quality. I sat down with Billy for three or four hours and explained to him how you know satin, how you know taffeta, what makes this quality, etc. He stayed in bed all the next day with that box of material, studying it. When I came home he said, "Sit down here. Take the price tags off." Then he said, "This is taffeta. This is the cheaper one. This is the good one, etc." He knew every piece of material, what it should cost and everything.[51]

Rose also took classes from theatrical producer Jed Harris, who in December 1929 returned to New York after an eight-month stay in Europe. "Harris had sprung out of nowhere with the velocity of a meteor streaking across the sky," wrote playwright Moss Hart, and he was known as much for his Broadway hits as for his unnerving and intimidating antics, such as receiving visitors in the nude.[52] Born Jacob Horowitz and almost exactly Rose's age, Harris in 1926 scored a tremendous commercial and critical success with *Broadway,* a drama that scuttled the corny theater fare of the day with a production marked by "intricate detail, colloquial language, and modern social ideas" that introduced a new Broadway stage style: "clever, tense, urban, dynamic, and above all, contemporary."[53] It ran for 603 performances, earned $1.2 million at the box office, and in 1928 won Harris the cover of *Time* magazine. Rose was then still learning the ropes, so when he had the chance through Brice to meet the boy wonder, Rose paid attention. "He went to the public library, after being stimulated by Jed's discourses, and steeped himself in the classical plays, and he probably read a lot of books that Jed himself had never read, even though Jed talked of them in a very authoritative way," said Richard Maney, who was first Harris's and then Rose's publicity man. "Rose impressed me with his energy and seriousness."[54]

By May 1930, Harris and Rose became business partners in a musical revue Rose planned to produce starring Brice, but before that show opened, Rose and Harris made another deal that revealed Rose's grit. For nearly a year, Harris had planned to produce *The Vinegar Tree,* a comic play one newspaper called "'quadrangular.' It deals with an artist, a middle aged woman, her married sister and the married sister's daughter."[55] But when Harris lost interest in it Rose trusted his own judgment, optioned the play, and then sold the option to another producer for a 25 percent share of any future profits. The play proved popular and ran for a year. He netted $30,000. Rose had his own abilities, and he was also Harris's equal in the hard-as-nails department. In 1927, an actor in *Broadway* had to stand in front of Harris and demand his pay envelope. Harris handed it over. In 1932, when Harris and Rose's musical revue became a moneymaker, Harris had to sue to get his share.[56]

WHISTLING SOFT GODDAMS

"Billy was resourceful. He never gave up," Richard Maney said.[57]

It took three tries for Rose to generate a return on his and Harris's $25,000 investment in their musical revue—first called *Corned Beef and Roses,* then *Sweet and Low,* and finally *Crazy Quilt*—and along the way Rose transformed it into an excellent piece of brash American entertainment. "Haphazard, occasionally loutish, almost always strung together with chewing-gum and old kite-string, they not only appeased the vast public hunger for a good three-dollar thump at inhibitions, these revues, but they amassed for the minute Mr. Rose a comfortable and cozy sum of cash," cheered the *Literary Digest.* Gilbert Seldes celebrated him: "A good showman. Good? He is wonderful."[58]

Brice and renowned vaudevillian George Jessel starred in Harris and Rose's *Corned Beef and Roses* when it previewed in Philadelphia on October 14, 1930. It was supposed to open earlier and, despite the postponement, was not nearly ready when it premiered. A big problem was that Harris, "while he was highly skilled in the drama, didn't know anything about [a] musical."[59] Jessel, who had been onstage since he was ten years old, a star since 1915, and a hit in 1925 playing the lead in the stage production of *The Jazz Singer,* offered advice, but Rose and Harris brushed him off. "I was reminded that I was just a performer in this show," he later wrote.[60]

Corned Beef closed three days after *Variety* panned it. The paper's chief objection was a Jessel routine the reviewer deemed not "just off color; it was lower-class, stag-smoker stuff" that if performed in New York would be a "black eye both for Broadway and for the theater in general."[61] Jessel's Professor Labermacher sketch, later considered a classic and a favorite of the theater critic George Jean Nathan, who made efforts to see it as many as seven times, featured Jessel playing an old-world lecturer "so near-sighted that he mistakes the lantern slide of a voluptuous hussy for Niagara Falls" and unwittingly gives a comically indelicate talk about the female anatomy.[62] But the *Variety* review of the show was far from an outright rejection. It was thrilled with the revue's opening number, saying that "it looked like the smartest, most original, up-to-the-minute revue of the lot." David Freeman, Eddie Cantor's ghostwriter, wrote the script, but the description of it as ultracontemporary suggests Harris's touch.

The opening also included "plenty of smut, but generally funny," which reflected Rose's native roughness that when cowed and made to obey orders rendered up smart, funny, slyly suggestive, and even lovely works. The trick was for Rose to keep his smelly but fertile inner compost heap productive, not stinking. In "Poor Mr. Shufeld," he managed it. "It is a take-off on happenings in the office of a producer," played by Jessel. Shufeld was a laugh at the theater-owning Shubert brothers, and the sketch is an example of how theater people frequently found the theater business a great subject for theater. In a scene worthy of Mel Brooks's *The Producers,* chorus girls, according to *Variety,* invade Shufeld's office dressed in "decorous black gowns and then disrob[e] to demonstrate flashing pink undies, in which they do a wiggle dance in a big way." Also, Shufeld's back is killing him because "he has been up all night working on the play." The nature of this work is clarified by a sign over the couch: "Casting tonight."[63]

After the failed show closed, Harris left the scene. Rose reworked the revue as *Sweet and Low* and in less than a month opened it on Broadway. The losses at this point came to $36,000 and Rose would be $150,000 in the hole before he recouped almost all of it with a nearly six-month run.[64] *Sweet and Low* retained Jessel's Professor Labermacher sketch and Rose won a victory over *Variety*'s dire predictions when the *Times* enjoyed it as "a highly amusing, if considerably less than immaculate interlude."[65] True to its vaudeville roots the revue's entertainments ranged from smart songs that became popular hits, such as "Cheerful Little Earful," by Ira Gershwin, to Brice as "Babykins," a Rose inspiration that heralded her later "Baby Snooks" act, and Borrah Minevitch and His Harmonica Rascals, a high-energy act of "semi-midgets playing the harmonica" that was a top act in the twenties and one appreciated by *Sweet and Low*'s opening night crowd.[66]

Rose managed to keep the show open until April, despite the financial panic making the 1931 theater season "the worst in Broadway history." The achievement was considered heroic. "In this day and age a show that runs 22 weeks is regarded as something more than a success. Producers will be only too happy to tell you that it's something in the nature of a miracle," wrote the columnist Mark Hellinger.[67] Desperation was the mother of this miracle. If the show failed,

Rose knew he would go "back to being Fanny's husband again, and I was a mite tired of that."[68]

When *Sweet and Low* closed in mid-April, Rose in just three weeks again reworked and reopened the show under a new name. *Crazy Quilt* premiered in New York on May 19, 1931. The title first appeared as a phrase in January 1915, when George M. Cohan employed it to describe his musical revue, *Hello, Broadway*. Jessel borrowed it later that year for his act, "Two Patches from a Crazy Quilt." The coinage captures the vaudeville formula that allowed for "everything: from the puritanical to the licentious. . . . High art, low art, and no art stood cheek by jowl."[69] Rose's production followed that formula, and his persistent reinvention paid off. The revue was better than ever. "There is a piling zest to this show," reported the *New York American*'s Gilbert W. Gabriel, an early *New Yorker* writer. "It begins with a couple of bad steers and heavy stumbles—or, so it did last night—and then manages a safe walk, a comfortable jog-trot... until, all of a sudden, it is galloping in wild, giddy ways and taking all the hurdles like a champion winner."[70]

Rose's venture soon chalked up a fourth iteration when in September *Crazy Quilt* left Broadway for a tour of the provinces. "The road, you have heard, was dead," Seldes wrote. "Billy Rose didn't even know it was sick."[71] It was a great part of Rose's terrific confidence to challenge accepted wisdom, ignore experts, and trust his taste and what he saw with his own eyes. "Rose had had enough of the wise boys," Hellinger wrote.[72] They were the ones who told him to quit after the failure of *Corned Beef and Roses*, and the same thinking applied now. "Following a moderately successful New York engagement, *Crazy Quilt* should normally have sought refuge in a warehouse," wrote *Stage* magazine.[73] Instead, Rose hired the publicity agents Richard Maney and Ned Alvord, the former an expert with newspapermen and the latter an advertising rogue who considered purple prose too self-effacing. Alvord promoted *Crazy Quilt* as "Three Shows in One," "Theatrical Colossus," a chorus of "Notable Nymphs," "Statuesque Odalisques," "Dashing Demoiselles," and the following mouthful: "A saturnalia of wanton rhythm, fastest of all dancing shows, a maelstrom of lithesome sprites in divertissements of exotic and daring conception, culminating in the terpsichorean piece de resistance, El Bolero."[74]

Rose and Alvord "told the customers it was the hottest show they had ever seen; they came and found one of the funniest," Seldes said. Jessel left to do other work, but Brice stayed and toured Chattanooga, Sioux Falls, Omaha, Oil

City, Tulsa, Cleveland's Hippodrome, Buffalo, and other "cities where nothing but movies" had appeared in years, and where the locals were "hungry for first-hand sight and sound."[75] On the road, Brice continued to tutor Rose. "I taught Billy how to talk to the performers," she said. "He would jump on them and I explained to him, 'Even if they give a bad performance, you don't tell them—they know, and they don't need to hear it from you. They don't go out there to give a bad performance.' He didn't know people were that way. He wasn't sensitive to anybody."[76]

Others submitted contrary testimony. "I was his friend—and my honest belief [is] he was mine—until the day he died," Alvord said. "I couldn't have run my end with less supervision from the throne had I been 100% proprietor instead of hired hand. With most of his enterprises I had a cut of the profits which in most cases [was] substantial."[77] John Murray Anderson staged the *Crazy Quilt* road show and brought back stories of generosity. "Billy told me that he hadn't realized how much work the show would involve, that he was more than pleased with the result, and asked me to disregard the contract we made, because he wanted to double the amount of the weekly royalty . . . and each week thereafter Billy paid me exactly twice as much as my contract called for."[78] Maney "had great fun with him. He didn't care what I said about him." That made Rose a perfect client, because Maney's approach to publicity was to insult his show business clients through deployment of a "system of invective that sounded like swearing but was in fact as innocent as Mother Goose," a strategy that yielded up what the *New Yorker*'s Wolcott Gibbs, a Maney admirer, termed the "disinfected epithet." Maney explained, "It's much easier to write sardonically. I gloried in [Rose's] ignorance but he didn't care. I invented all these ideals for him . . . Basement Belasco . . . Penthouse Cagliostro. . . . He reveled in them."[79] All these Rose portraits—brutish, open-handed, considerate, comically broad-minded—are accurate, said Vicki Walton, daughter of Rose's third wife. "He was nice, he was loving, he was gentle, he was a cocksucker," she said. "He was all of that. He could be a son of a bitch if you were in business with him and you tried to cross him. . . . But by the same token he was loving and adorable and funny."[80]

Crazy Quilt toured for forty weeks, until June 1932, and along the way it tallied receipts that made "most Broadway grosses look paltry." *Stage* recognized Rose's importance as an innovator: "The most extraordinary barnstorming of the season has been the nationwide tour of Billy Rose's musical show *Crazy Quilt*. . . . The junket is significant not only because of its success but as an augury of what other theatrical attractions can accomplish by considering the country at large and not merely Broadway."[81] Weekly box office amounts regularly topped $40,000. Wrote Gilbert Seldes, "As *Variety* reported the gross receipts . . . in towns which Broadway had never heard of, local producers compared their own sheets and whistled soft goddams."[82]

THE SUGAR CRUSHER

Upon returning to New York in the summer of 1932 Rose immediately moved the offices of William Rose, Inc., where he was president and Brice vice president, from a fourth-floor office at Forty-Second and Seventh Avenue to the fifteenth-floor penthouse of the Wurlitzer Building. Located a little further east at Forty-Second and Sixth Avenue, the lavish ten-thousand-square-foot space was recently home to the Brunswick Radio Corporation, a division of Warner Bros. Pictures.[83] Rose could now afford to be on a par with big players. *Crazy Quilt* made him a bundle, and Brice was very pleased. "We went out on tour and just cleaned up," she said.[84] The profit was about $200,000 and the new penthouse office trumpeted his success.[85] "Centered under a forty-foot ceiling, Rose's desk was as big as a billiard table," wrote Maney. "An enormous black block in the Delft-blue carpet bore his initials."[86] According to a reporter, "Great walls were tapestried with a revue-producer's notion of something pretty 'fly' in the way of what the well-dressed wall will wear," and an adjacent terrace was "tiled with the glossy splendor of a Sultan's courtyard and pleasant fountains tinkled archly." The surroundings inspired Maney to greet Rose with a mocking, "A golden good morning to thee, Effendi."[87] To make sure their heads fit under the forty-foot ceiling, Rose and Brice commissioned comic portraits of themselves. There was "a replica of the Mona Lisa, with Fanny Brice's rolling eye and wicked leer taking the place of the famous head," Gilbert Seldes reported, and "an oil of Mr. Rose called The Sugar Crusher. It immortalizes the fury which comes over Rose at the laggard melting of sugar in these days of hard compressed tablets. Rose pounds the sugar in the cup with a spoon and chose to be painted in action."[88]

If these measures failed, Rose could always put the top down and fit into his 1932 Duesenberg Model J LeBaron Dual Cowl Phaeton J182. The convertible was chauffeur-driven because Rose almost never drove, and perhaps because New York mayor Jimmy Walker—forced to resign in 1932 but still beloved—also had a chauffeur-driven Duesy. Duesenberg's advertising campaign identified the vehicle's ideal owner as "a gentleman sportsman" at ease on his yacht. In reality, the luxury car was the choice, too, of the New York gangster Owney "the Killer" Madden, as well as those closer to the advertisement's target market, such as Clark Gable, Greta Garbo, the DuPonts, and the Vanderbilts. Rose's "Model J was the very embodiment of wealth, power, and success." Customers spent more than twenty times what they would for an ordinary car: Model J prices started at $13,500 and could reach $20,000 at a time when a Ford went for less than $600. Rose's purchase was especially noteworthy, because in 1932 the maker of America's most expensive car sold only ten vehicles.[89]

All the while Rose kept up his family obligations, and his sisters' career choices reveal that he exerted great influence and acted as substitute father. After his sister Miriam divorced her imported bridegroom and got married for the second time on April 21, 1931, to an optometrist named Frederick Stern, Rose was an official witness to the Jewish ceremony. Miriam was three days shy of thirty but listed her age as twenty-five. She also claimed the wedding was her first.[90] Her casual relationship with the truth and her occupation as a stenographer suggest an attempt to copy brother Billy's style and success, an achievement she could not fathom. Billy "was really smart and circumspect and shrewd. He really knew how to function," said Stephen Gottlieb, a stepson to Rose's sister Polly. For Miriam, however, Rose's success was just a matter of wishing it. "Miriam had once told my father that if she'd wanted to she could have been as successful as Billy," Gottlieb said. "That's what in all seriousness she said."[91] Miriam was like her father, said Helen Schrank. She inherited David Rosenberg's shallow character, unimaginative intelligence, and bitterness toward a world he did not have the gifts to exploit or even enjoy. Rose's enmity toward his father extended to Miriam. He never helped her financially.[92]

His sister Polly also did not possess Billy's business talents, but she exhibited their mother's energy. Polly was a "feminine version" of Billy, said a childhood friend. "She was quite a gal. Polly had spark and vitality. . . . She was very attractive."[93] Billy paid the tuition when Polly attended New York University in the mid-1920s, and in 1933 he probably helped her land a job dancing at a nightclub under the name Polly Porter. And when in her desire to become an actress she got her nose fixed, Rose paid the bill.[94] But for Rose, there was nobody like Fannie Rosenberg. "The mother, he adored her," said Schrank.[95]

A few months after Miriam's wedding, Rose reminded his business associates to watch their step. First he sued Joseph Schenk for reneging on his promise to produce two Fanny Brice movies, not just *Be Yourself*. The suit went on for nearly a year until March 18, 1932, when it was "discontinued without costs to either party."[96] Still, Rose had made his point. He was prepared to fight, despite the bother and expense of going to court. He also came to the aid of his fellow songwriters in their fight against music publishers. Since 1914, ASCAP had policed the public performance of songs, to demand payment on behalf of its publisher and songwriter members, but the advent of the talking movie business offered publishers a new way to shortchange writers. Film studios paid ASCAP a small public performance fee, while publishers got "large sums . . . for the right of synchronization, the right to use the music in pictures."[97] In addition, through the power of the Music Publishers' Protective Association, ASCAP reduced payments to songwriters from two-thirds of monies collected to half. During the Depression, publishers regularly paid next to nothing to buy a song outright, free of the need to pay the writer royalties. Songs were sometimes even sold for rent money or a meal.[98]

Rose's feisty response to the Music Publishers' Protective Association was the Songwriters' Protective Association (SPA), which he thought up in early September 1931, just before *Crazy Quilt* hit the road. To turn it into reality he descended upon Arthur Garfield Hays. "Now, when Billy Rose gets an idea, the fur begins to fly, for with him an idea means action, quick action, and plenty of it," said the prominent attorney. "He wants things done and he gets them done." Rose demanded that Hays draw up the incorporation papers for a Friday meeting of the SPA. "This is only Wednesday, so we have plenty of time," Rose assured him. This condition Hays could handle. A bigger problem was that songwriters "were accustomed to sleeping in the daytime, while we lawyers had formed the habit of sleeping at night." Meetings were held at "Dinty Moore's, Lindy's, and Sardi's," and a meeting "with two song writers would develop into a congregational discussion with twenty or thirty."[99]

Rose became the first president of the SPA (today's Songwriters Guild of America), senior officers included Ira Gershwin and Irving Berlin, and the songwriters secured their rights. When Rose died, the association—then called the American Guild of Authors and Composers—ran a front-page notice in its newsletter: "Thousands of songwriters and their families lead a better life today because of the efforts of Billy Rose."[100]

Such actions never dented Rose's reputation for toughness. There were good reasons. "Billy has a genius for not making friends," said Ben Hecht, who called him "as wistful as a meat ax" and "a kind of frustrated poet . . . a kind of slum poet and Jack the Ripper rolled into one."[101] And Rose was not satisfied with the biblical formula for justice, said Chester Conn. "It was two eyes for a tooth. If he could get the better of you." There was also the fact that "the characteristic of Billy's benevolence was he did it as a matter of course. He didn't go telling about it. He didn't sneak it under the table, either. He did it like a businessman," said the daughter of Rose's friend, the composer Deems Taylor.[102] Most of all, as his success with the many iterations of *Crazy Quilt* proved, his prime driver was to be, like his mother, an unstoppable, unappeasable force. As he told Mercedes McCambridge, "When you find yourself in a tunnel . . . don't turn back. Keep going until you see a steady gleam of light at the other end, and go for it with all your might, knocking down everything that stands in your way."[103]

"All my grandiose strains
stem right from my mother,"
said Billy Rose.

"He lives on shorthand," noted Rose's high school newspaper. Rose is at center.
Courtesy of Widener Library, Harvard University.

Rose is seated at left and Baruch stands at center at the end of World War I. Billy Rose Theatre Division, The New York Public Library for the Performing Arts.

Rose and Fanny Brice married by New York mayor Jimmy Walker on February 8, 1929. Billy Rose Theatre Division, The New York Public Library for the Performing Arts.

Billy Rose's *Jumbo* © The Al Hirschfeld Foundation. www.AlHirschfeldFoundation.org.

The forty-foot clown in Billy Rose's *Jumbo*. Photo by Vandamm Studio © Billy Rose Theatre Division, The New York Public Library for the Performing Arts.

Rose's sign in Dallas sells "Whoopee 45 minutes west" in Fort Worth. Courtesy W. D. Smith Commercial Photography Collection, Special Collections, The University of Texas at Arlington Libraries, Arlington, Texas.

Rose with Texas governor James V. Allred. Courtesy *Fort Worth Star-Telegram* Collection, Special Collections, The University of Texas at Arlington Libraries, Arlington, Texas.

Casa Mañana was "a unique combination of architecture and showmanship."
Courtesy *Fort Worth Star-Telegram* Collection, Special Collections,
The University of Texas at Arlington Libraries, Arlington, Texas.

Showgirls as cowgirls at Fort Worth's Casa Mañana. Courtesy *Fort Worth Star-Telegram* Collection, Special Collections, The University of Texas at Arlington Libraries, Arlington, Texas.

"It Can't Happen Here" finale at 1937 Fort Worth fair.
From the collections of the Dallas History and Archives Division, Dallas
Public Library.

Billy Rose is the 1936 "Man of the Year" in Texas. Elite Studio.

Grave of Rose's mother, Fannie Rosenberg. Courtesy of Matthew R. Ivler, Lebanon Cemetery Association of Queens, Inc., Mount Lebanon Cemetery.

Billy Rose's Diamond Horseshoe. Billy Rose Theatre Division, The New York Public Library for the Performing Arts, Astor, Lenox and Tilden Foundations.

In 1946, Diamond Horseshoe sold nostalgia with a look back at George White's Scandals of 1930. Billy Rose Theatre Division, The New York Public Library for the Performing Arts, Astor, Lenox and Tilden Foundations.

Staircase at Billy Rose's Diamond Horseshoe, 1947–49. The Herman and S. Helena Rosse Archive, Williams College. Photo by Bernard Pisarski.

six

A COSMIC SCALE

Despite his success and determination, Rose still depended upon his wife's steady and tasteful judgment. Brice was a check against his coarser show business instincts, and the first time the couple were apart that coarseness got the better of his judgment. In June 1932, Brice sailed for Europe with her two children and was away for three months. Her time back home was brief, because in October she left again for two months to perform on the road. While she was out of town, Rose made a producing mistake that cost him forty thousand dollars.[1]

Ben Hecht and Gene Fowler, both writers and newspapermen, approached Rose with a drama called *The Great Magoo,* which the authors cynically described as "a love-sick charade, drama full of passion and bird calls, something like Romeo and Juliet."[2] The play actually gets down in the gutter with the worst dives in show business, the demimonde, where grubbiness rules, despair hovers, and a producer with the I-dare-you-to-say-it name of Sam Kuntzmiller expects dancers "to sign on the dotted couch."[3] *Magoo* displays the kind of daring bad taste the *National Lampoon* ran with in the 1970s, and like it, *Magoo* was the creation of brilliant pranksters possessed of what Maney called "sheer arrogance."[4] "Recognition by these titans touched off gongs in [Rose's] skull," Maney said. He was not the only one whose thinking was short-circuited by the pair. "I confess that I was awed by Hecht and Fowler," said the play's director, George Abbott.[5]

Hecht, who had already won the first of his two Oscars for his Hollywood writing and screenplays, was a legend by 1924 when, at age thirty, he moved from Chicago to New York and left some in the Second City "calling for the flags to be flown at half mast." Hecht agreed to live by "conventional morality" but protested, "My manners don't reach into my mind."[6] In New York, he held much in contempt, including himself as a Jew. The literary critic Leslie Fiedler called Hecht's 1931 novel, *A Jew in Love,* "a work of inspired self-hatred: a portrait of the Jewish author as his own worst (Jewish) enemy."[7] Hecht reminds his audience that the gross characters in *Magoo* are also Jews. "I forgot—I ain't in a synagogue," says one, as he removes his hat.[8] It took the Nazis to liberate Hecht from his ambivalence, and in 1943 when he spearheaded the creation of the theatrical pageant *We Will Never Die,* to demand that the American government save European Jews from annihilation, his staunchest ally was Billy Rose.

"'The Great Magoo' is the low-down on low people," reported *Variety* after the December 2, 1932, opening. "Not diverting."[9] Maney, paid for his put-downs, said, "Knowing less about the drama than he knew about the migrations of the Arctic tern, Rose couldn't cope with *The Great Magoo* once it had been bludgeoned." Before it closed after eleven performances, Maney suggested filling the house by issuing subpoenas.[10] Rose recouped some of his losses by selling the film rights to Paramount, but the disaster's saving grace was the discovery of more future collaborators.[11] The scenic designer Herman Rosse's work for *Magoo* was featured in *Theatre Arts Monthly.*[12] He later designed Rose's Diamond Horseshoe nightclub. Hecht and Abbott became part of Rose's *Jumbo* team. In addition, together with the great lyricist E. Y. "Yip" Harburg, Rose wrote for *Magoo* "It's Only a Paper Moon," one of America's greatest popular songs. It deftly leavens cynicism with romance, as its worldly but lovelorn narrator admits that the cheap illusions of theater—"Just as phony as it can be"—can yield magic if graced with love. Hecht and Fowler's published version of *Magoo* attributes the lyric solely to Rose. That was not the case, but perhaps Harburg's willingness to credit Rose's contribution obscures the more sizable role he played. "Well, but I will say one thing about Billy Rose," Yarburg recalled. "I must give him due credit. He was a great editor. . . . Don't forget that I was writing poetry and free verse at the time and I had to make that terrible, terrifying transition from light verse to lyricism, to lyric writing, and he really helped me come down from Olympus to Broadway. So his editing did a lot of good for me. I was always grateful for it."[13]

A GOLD MINE

By the time *Magoo* folded at the end of 1932, it was clear that Prohibition was on its way out. In the November election, Franklin Delano Roosevelt and his fellow Democrats, nearly all in favor of Prohibition's repeal, had won the White House and Congress and states began voting to approve the Twenty-First

Amendment to the Constitution shortly after Congress passed a resolution to begin the process in February 1933. On December 5 of that year Utah became the thirty-sixth state to ratify the amendment and Prohibition was dead.[14] Ten days later on December 15 Rose opened the Casino de Paree, a theater-restaurant concept so new that "no exact name has yet been found" to describe it, reported Gilbert Seldes.[15] *Variety* agreed that its originality made it "truly the most unusual nite club in the world combining as it does the better features of the American theatre with the Continental supper club." The industry trade predicted it would be a "gold mine" and a peer of the world's greatest clubs. It was "a New York landmark comparable to the former Ziegfeld roof; Folies Bergere and Casino de Paris, Les Ambassadeurs or the Mouline [*sic*] Rouge of Paris; or the Kit-Cat and Cafe de Paris of London; or the Casanova, Haus Vaterland or Kempinski's of Berlin," wrote *Variety*. "For the New York spot is a combination of all."[16]

What Rose did was cobble together existing entertainments into novel juxtapositions and combinations to yield an attraction greater than the sum of its parts. Seldes spotted elements of "night clubs, restaurants, vaudeville shows, with several touches of the circus and the atmosphere of the cabaret and sideshow thrown in."[17] The physical space also represented a new hybrid. "Rose created the theater-restaurants, which put cabaret revues, entertainment, and dining service into converted theaters," explains the historian Lewis Erenberg.[18] Many theaters closed during the Depression and Rose invented a new use for them as venues for nightclub festivities on a scale that overwhelmed. His Casino de Paree accommodated well over a thousand customers, with 500 guests upstairs in the former balcony and 650 downstairs. Rose devised a seating innovation to permit such crowds. He tore out the seats in the New Yorker Theatre on West Fifty-Fourth Street near Eighth Avenue and replaced them with tables that dovetailed so that, as *Variety* marveled, "a party of four if becoming eight can so join the two tables that they mesh and yet have all the patrons" facing the stage.[19] This reconfiguration allowed six customers to fit in the space formerly occupied by just two theater chairs. Two bars served the two levels: the downstairs one, festooned with "caricatures of Broadway, stage, screen, journalistic and other notables," was "The Nudist," so called because of the image of a naked woman just six inches tall that waved from a fishbowl, while the upstairs bar was decorated by the whimsical illustrator and noted puppeteer Tony Sarg, who in 1928 had created for Macy's Thanksgiving Day Parade its signature animal balloons.[20]

Two orchestras spelled each other on the theater's stage to provide continuous and loud music. As Rose put it, "We play the 'St. Louis Blues' so you can hear it in Weehawken." The theater stage was a performance space larger than any typical nightclub could offer and was grand enough to also welcome customers who wanted to dance. "Patrons overflowed the stage and performed intricate patterns of the dance, coat tails flying, neckties streaming in the wind," a reporter observed. To up the sexual tension, Rose drafted chorus girls from the Ziegfeld Follies to open the revue-style show he also offered guests. These the reporter described as "a posse of nymphs attired in diaphanous garments of microscopic proportions."[21] However, Rose would not spring for Ziegfeld's extravagant costume budget, and some considered the showgirls' outfits drab. There was an inexpensive solution to that problem. "It was a relief to see the girls without clothes," wrote Gilbert Seldes, "a spectacle Mr. Rose did not fail to provide."[22]

For Seldes, a Rose fan, the excitement of the approach was how it "broke down all distinction between stage and audience" and allowed for an unparalleled atmosphere of "noise and excitement and well-being. . . . It may not be great theatre, but it is alive."[23] This vitality had Jewish roots. When the Casino de Paree opened, *Theatre Arts Monthly* praised New York's Yiddish theater of twenty years earlier in almost the same language for the same spirit: "The play began in the lobby or perhaps even on the sidewalk before the theatre. The audience was a part of the performance and the whole performance was alive."[24]

More than Rose's familiarity with the Yiddish theater—or the jolly chaos of his sister Miriam's wedding—determined his course. The model for the combination of entertainment and inexpensive dining for large audiences that Rose housed in a converted theater originated in Times Square in 1929 with the entrepreneur Nils Granlund's Hollywood Restaurant, and then in 1930 with his Paradise Restaurant.[25] But by the time Rose's Casino opened in late 1933, the dinner and entertainment model had also gone upscale. At clubs set within the Algonquin, Plaza, Waldorf, and St. Regis hotels, as well as at freestanding establishments such as El Morocco, "it used to be enough if they let you in," *Stage* remarked, "but now, even with dinner in most of the places . . . there is always something going on." The legal sale of alcohol revived the high end of the business, but with a new wrinkle: "Along with the emergence of glitter came the notion of entertaining the guests."[26] However, for Rose the trouble with following the lead of New York's so-called café society was its dependence upon a "socially exclusive appeal (with anti-Semitic overtones)."[27] His instincts toward large-scale entertainment, coupled with restrictive social realities, meant he had to stick to his native ground in the more Jewish Broadway district and go after an audience financially and ethnically excluded from the St. Regis with a modestly priced place that was loud and fun and unbuttoned. That suited Rose. "He is given to wildness, extravagance, a cheerful, inoffensive vulgarity, and everything slapdash, noisy, rough, and comic," Seldes wrote. These attributes delivered the key idea behind his Casino, which was to flip Granlund's Hollywood Restaurant formula on its head. As Rose explained, "A floor show is an effort to bring a little of the theatre into a restaurant. So when repeal came I said:—'Why not put a whole restaurant into a theatre?'"[28]

The result was fantastic. "All the knock-down, drag-out in my nature exudes rapture about the Casino de Paree," reported the *New Yorker*'s Lois Long under her pseudonym, Lipstick. "I knew it was the inside of a converted theatre, but I had no idea, really. Tiers and tiers of tables slope toward the huge stage; there is a colored hi-de-ho orchestra on one side, and a white-folks one on the other . . . it is all big and glorious, . . . you'll have the time of your life."[29] "The entire atmosphere of the place was one of a carnival" as it "combined the more delirious features of the Winter Garden, the Hall of Mirrors at Versailles, a Durbar at Delhi and the café of the Griswold Hotel at New London on boat race night. . . . The place was a sort of honky tonk on a cosmic scale," wrote the reporter Lucius "Luscious Lucius" Beebe, an outlandish character whose costume of evening cape and top hat was as florid as his prose.[30]

The Casino attracted the famous as well as the regular Joe. "On a Sunday night you see composers, vocalists, and celebrities marching up to the microphone to do their stuff," Seldes wrote.[31] To guarantee patronage by notables Rose hosted charity events that virtually commanded the presence of a Park Avenue set with names such as Countess Mercati and Mrs. William Randolph Hearst. Irving Berlin, George Gershwin, and George M. Cohan attended a benefit there for the Authors League Fund and Hollywood soon decided Rose's club would make a good setting for a movie.[32] Al Jolson starred in a film that during production was titled *Casino de Paree,* though released in 1935 as *Go into Your Dance.*[33]

The average customer's tab was just $3.00, but the club's weekly gross reached $40,000, thanks to up to three shows a night, starting with dinner hour, then eleven o'clock, and a final show at two in the morning if demand called for it. The weekly draw was "probably the all-time record high business which any cabaret-restaurant in New York, Paris, London or anywhere has done," according to *Variety.*[34]

The Casino opportunity presented itself while Rose was minding his business, doing only two things at once. In May 1933 he was preparing *Crazy Quilt* for a second tour and also thinking up a Ziegfeld Follies act for Brice when Rose's sometime songwriting partner, Fred Fisher, introduced him to one Yermie Stern, a dress manufacturer with underworld connections.[35] Stern "said he and some gentlemen who were interested had rented the [New Yorker] theatre and they wanted to turn it into a cabaret with the name of Casino de Paree," Rose recalled. They wanted Rose to run it for them. When Rose wondered who the backers were, Stern said, "Oh very fine gentlemen. The owners of King's [*sic*] Beer have an interest."[36] The Brooklyn brewery was one of thirteen in New York, New Jersey, and Pennsylvania owned by a Jewish mob run by Waxey Gordon and Abe Zwillman, along with partners from Italian mobs such as Charles "Lucky" Luciano.[37] Others may also have played a role. "Dutch [Schultz] told me he was the boss of Billy's [Casino]," said Charles Washburn, a Rose publicity man. "Billy owed me an overlooked $600 at the time of opening. Schultz paid me. 'Want a receipt?' I asked. 'I paid you, kid, didn't I?' he shrugged. Nobody asked him twice for dough."[38] Other investors were legitimate but ruthless businessmen. Sam "Subway Sam" Rosoff made millions in New York City subway construction and in the 1920s had many dealings with the gangster Arnold Rothstein. In the thirties, Rosoff, "an immigrant of incredible vitality . . . fat, swaggering—a dandy in dress," jointly owned twenty-six liquor stores with Morris "Little Ziggy" Zeig, a gunman who had graduated into less bloody underworld activities.[39] The subway builder was not out of his element in criminal company. In 1938 he was a suspect in the murder of a union organizer.

Rose hated the criminal type, but he knew them well. They had been his peers when he was a kid on the Lower East Side. The ones who bullied and beat him were now running New York nightlife, and Rose's familiarity and ease with criminals astounded many. "They respected him," Dave Dreyer said. "Dutch Schultz . . . thought highly of him, came to his office all the time. He talked just like them, too. Couldn't bulldoze him. He was only this high and he stood up to them toe to toe."[40] Maney was not impressed. "When he was running saloons I had an argument with him," he said. "I had an agreement I would never go into them. Backed by gangsters. Thugs. That was [all right] with him."[41] Such realism was not unique. Granlund also accepted the inevitability of gangster partners and described them as "'essentially . . . just a tough breed of businessmen.'"[42] Rose's equivalent toughness made him the target of the joke, "Who has the biggest prick in the world? Fanny Brice."[43] Another crack was that you could kidnap Rose, but who would pay to get him back? "I was known on Broadway as an intensely selfish fellow and a tough trader," he later admitted. "There was nothing especially endearing about the image I conjured up in those days."[44] Under the circumstances, though, his reputation brings to mind the gangster Mickey Cohen's quip: "I don't call a man a son of a bitch who's in a walk of life that calls for him to be a son of a bitch."[45]

SMALL TIME CAVALCADE

In the spring of 1934, still employed by Stern and the boys, Rose found greater visibility in a new venue. Billy Rose's Music Hall, Inc., leased the Manhattan Theatre on Broadway near Fifty-Third Street, around the corner from the Casino, and though the company's president was Stern, Rose got the publicity. The new club was called Billy Rose's Music Hall. Its name invoked comparison with the monumental Radio City Music Hall that had opened eighteen months before, attracted attention with an electric sign forty feet high, and began Rose's tradition of affixing his name to all his undertakings.[46] The space originally housed the Hammerstein Theatre, built in 1927 by Arthur Hammerstein to honor his producer father, Oscar Hammerstein I. Sitting empty in 1934, it offered the scale and grandeur Rose loved. The interior's domed ceiling and walls covered with mosaics evoked a Gothic cathedral.[47] A few weeks before the Music Hall opened on June 21, 1934, Rose had for once exhausted his capacity for promotional hype. He stole Beebe's line and predicted to A. J. Liebling that the club "will be a honky tonk on a cosmic scale. It will be the apotheosis of popular-priced amusement. It will be the nuts."[48]

And it was.

"There were undoubtedly flag raisings in honor of this and that among the Babylonians which embodied some of its cockeyed features. But as a monument of lunacy the Billy Rose Music Hall is in a class by itself," Beebe again reported.[49] Once more there were small dovetailing tables where the theater seating had been, room for one thousand, and "a madhouse of gayety . . . chaotic revelry in a strange combination of Mardi Gras–Beaux Arts Ball–Coney Island atmosphere."[50] All that, however, was to be expected, and Rose was not interested in duplication. Clearly experimenting, taunting the idea of limits, he turned up the volume and assaulted the senses from every imaginable angle. Now there were one hundred singing waiters who were "made up to look like old time tough guys, with red noses and all," and "gaudy nudes . . . daubed in hey-hey profusion over the red and gold walls" by Clark Robinson, who in 1933 was the art director at Radio City Music Hall.[51] In addition there was jazz music by Benny Goodman and his orchestra and a "multimedia extravaganza" provided by newsreels and a projection of the mob scenes from D .W. Griffith's *The Fall of Babylon*.[52] Open from 11 a.m. to 4 a.m., the Music Hall served lunch for fifty cents. Dinner and a show was priced at $1.00 and late-hour suppers topped out at $1.50, but Rose devised ways to generate additional income from liquor sales and the for-hire services of "100 hostesses for lonesome stags." This Lonely Hearts Club of young women "wore tight black satin dresses with red hearts over the left tit," Rose bluntly explained, "and you bought a lonely heart cocktail for $1 and you could dance with any girl."[53] The women approached customers and, according to one reviewer, came as close to illegal solicitation as the law allowed.[54]

But it was Rose's return to the nostalgia of his 1924 *Fatal Wedding* production that was the "socko highlight of it all." The "Small Time Cavalcade" will "become something in show biz history," wrote *Variety*. Lifted from Ben Hecht's unproduced play *Hearts and Flowers*, "Cavalcade" was the kind of emotionally moving production Brice could hardly believe Rose capable of. At first glance, it seemed a procession of show business grotesques. "It's truly a cavalcade of the varieties," *Variety* reported, "from the corniest of two-man song-and-dance teams, down through a succession of fire-eaters, magicians, musical clowns with bulbous noses and copiously weeping glims; strong women, bellringers, musical bottles and bones manipulators, comedy fiddlers, acrobats, gymnasts, casting acts, minstrel men, straight barytones, Irish tenors, clowns and the entire gamut of the lexicon of ring and rostrum entertainment." In front of a backdrop "painted like hundreds of faces looking down," some forty acts performed to "old-time melodies," until little by little they filled the stage and "a thin Irish tenor" sang Hecht and Rose's composition "Dreaming of Broadway," which Rose recited from memory thirty years later.[55]

Allow me friends to introduce
Professor, if you please,
The artists of the vaudeville stage that Broadway never sees
Masters of the laugh and tear
Clowns and jesters gay
Playing the tank towns year on year
And dreaming of Broadway
Give 'em that great big hand of yours
This is their one big shot
May I present the Small Time Cavalcade
The acts that Keith forgot.

Rose continued, "There was all the love and the torture and the tragedy and the hurrah of show business on these faces and they sang, 'We never made good on Broadway / We're playing the small-time still / We never made good on Broadway / But with a break, by God, we will.'"[56] The number drew three minutes of solid applause. Newspaper reviews called it "one of the most touching recitations we've heard in ever so long" and "really effective and not a little moving to those of us who knew vaudeville in the old days."[57] "William Morris, Sr. came in and cried like a baby and sent two cases of champagne to the company," Rose said and *Variety* reported.[58] Discussing the number near the end of his life Rose defended the show and its players with more sympathy and insight than his tough image would have predicted. These vaudevillians were not pathetic people, he said: "One of the things that motivates everybody, from Winston Churchill to Mahatma Gandhi, is the esteem, the affection, the admiration, the applause of his fellow man. Most people go through their lives without any applause."[59] The so-called small-timers received theirs.

A BEATIFIC GLOW

While all this was going on, Rose also was the creative force behind Brice's acclaimed 1933–34 Ziegfeld Follies performance as the humbled but still pompous Russian (Jewish) Countess Dubinsky. As Brice's character explains, before the revolution, "Nicolai and all his princes nibbled nightly on my blintzes." But gone now are the days of licentious interludes with aristocrats. In

New York she is an ordinary stripper. Referring to herself in the third person Brice's Dubinsky laments, "The Countess Dubinsky, right down to her skinsky, is working for Minsky now." *Stage* devoted a two-page spread to Brice's act and ran seven photographs of the Dubinsky number. "There are other points in the show," the magazine said of the Follies, "but when we recall Fannie [*sic*] Brice's Minsky number, we forget what they are."[60] The *New Yorker* agreed: "Boy, that Fannie [*sic*] Brice! She's marvelous!"[61] Her triumph was in good measure due to Rose. "The songs and sketches he helped create for her . . . 'fit' her perfectly and enabled her to impersonate a variety of memorable comic characters," writes the Brice biographer Barbara Wallace Grossman.[62] The custom fit was made from Jewish material. "Fanny was a Jewish comedian and the Follies was a very goyish show," Rose said.[63] But in 1933, the Jewish Shuberts licensed the Follies, for Ziegfeld had died in 1932 and his widow, the actress Billie Burke, had debts to pay. As Rose's Jewish Dubinsky, Brice soared to new heights. "She was better than she had ever been in previous appearances under the Ziegfeld banner," noted Grossman.[64]

With fascism on the rise in Europe and big government programs the hero at home, Rose's hardboiled cleverness, manic industriousness, and obvious pleasure in being Billy Rose stood for something. Just before she praised Rose's Casino, the *New Yorker*'s Lipstick announced, "America has come through. We sturdy pioneers can take it." Rose was one of the American individualists who H. L. Mencken in June 1934 recognized were unfashionable and under attack but nevertheless worthy, resilient, and necessary. In "Individualism Cheats the Coroner" Mencken took to task those on the left and right who demanded sacrifices for their favored abstractions, the people and the state. "To this unhappy faction belong all the tin-pot despots who now rage in the world, and the Brain Trusts which fill its air with blah. In Hitler, Mussolini and Stalin the fraternity has grand masters, and everywhere it has chapters." But such movements were doomed, Mencken wrote. "They all collapse when they are permitted to collide with the eternal nature of man. It is not in that nature for a man with what appears to be a likely idea for lining his pockets to yield up its execution to a gang of petty pedagogues and attorneys. . . . The progress of *Homo sapiens* in the United States, hereafter as in the past, will be carried on by men who follow their own ideas and serve their own interests."[65] That same month a *Vanity Fair* columnist also seemed to have had Rose in mind when he argued the importance of magnificence for the middle classes: "They crave color, splendor, pomp and ceremony. . . . They simply don't want these luxuries to be the other fellow's exclusive privilege." The columnist acknowledged that President Roosevelt's New Deal did crucial work in providing people with work and bread, but declared that "the people want a show, as well as a run, for their money."[66]

Rose agreed and as usual was thinking of his next and always bigger step. After the Music Hall opened, he applied for a passport, received it on July 27, and the next day settled into a first-class cabin to England aboard the *Majestic*, the world's largest ocean liner and the one that during the booming 1920s was considered by the elite as "the only way to cross" the Atlantic.[67] There was no shortage of reasons for Rose's journey. First, the Kings beer group was in financial trouble. After he set sail, news broke that Sam Rosoff called in his note of $700,000, and also voted a claim held by one Arthur Diamant worth $460,000 to force a reorganization of the business. Rose became aware of the impending problem no later than July 11, when Rosoff was appointed the brewery's "temporary trustee."[68] What this meant for Kings' investment in the Casino de Paree and Billy Rose's Music Hall was unclear, but Rose obviously decided not to wait and find out. Besides, Europe offered a number of enticements. *Variety* covered the doings there and in March ran a story about Paris's Bal Tabarin nightclub and its "formula for packing them in nightly."[69] Rose visited the Tabarin. Europe also was home to the writer Ferenc Molnar, a Rose favorite. The Jewish-Hungarian novelist and playwright was a Hungarian Ben Hecht, "a sentimentalist who shrewdly masks his sentimentality . . . [with an] extremely dexterous and most persuasive, derisory humor," wrote the theater critic George Jean Nathan.[70] In 1931, Rose wanted to produce Molnar's *The Play's the Thing* and news of the writer ran in the *Times* shortly before Rose's voyage, because Molnar's 1907 novel, *The Paul Street Boys,* had just been turned into the film *No Greater Glory.*[71] Rose traveled to Budapest and met Molnar.

The voyage also offered Rose the opportunity to reintroduce himself to his boyhood hero, Bernard Baruch. Among the many celebrities who enjoyed Billy Rose's Music Hall were Irving Berlin, Harpo Marx, Oscar Levant, and, on opening night, Baruch's friend Herbert Bayard Swope, together with Bernard's younger brother, Sailing Baruch.[72] Swope knew Rose from their WIB days, surely introduced him to Sailing, and Swope and Sailing must have secured Baruch's permission to share with Rose the news that Baruch was going to be in Czechoslovakia with fellow game hunters on the Count Karolyi estate, because that is where Rose visited Baruch in August. "They had breakfast at six A.M. and Baruch and 20 guests went out on horseback," Rose said. "Each guest had an attendant who carried his gun and loaded it.... Dogs and beaters flushed coveys of quail."[73]

But what most stoked Rose's interest was the chance to see *Star of the Circus*, a Budapest attraction *Variety* lauded as a "revue-musical-legit-vaude-circus entertainment . . . a real hit and something distinctly new." It told the story of a love affair between the daughter of a circus manager and an upper-class boy whose disapproving parents only agree to the match after their son "becomes an acrobat for her sake." What was new was that on this skeleton scaffolding, "scarcely more than an idea . . . brilliant acrobatics and dance productions [were] hung," love songs were crooned, clowns performed, and "trained bears" entertained.[74] The idea clearly caught Rose's imagination. He announced plans for such a circus musical even before he left New York. On July 26 the *Times* ran a short article with the long headline, "'Broadway Circus' Planned for Spring, Billy Rose Would Include 1,800 Dancers and Show Girls in Huge Human Spectacle." The Associated Press ran its story the day Rose sailed. "The circus has added nothing of consequence to its program since the days of Barnum. It has been static and the box office receipts have endured a steady attack," Rose said. But he had a remedy. "My experiences in the theater and night club field lead me to believe that mass entertainment, spectacularly presented, has great box office potential."[75]

In Budapest Rose met with Ladislaus Bus-Fekete, author of *Star of the Circus*, and reportedly "paid [a] $5,000 advance for [*Star of the Circus*] rights against a weekly percentage and gets 50% of the world film rights also."[76] Major press coverage was immediate. Before he returned to New York, a foreign correspondent for the *Times* interviewed Rose and reported on the showman's outrageous boasts, views, visions, pronouncements, and judgments. Rose became "swathed in a beatific and phosphorescent glow" as he imagined his forthcoming Broadway circus. "He tosses his mane wildly," the reporter observed, "and there is a fey glint in his eyes as he paints the possibilities of the half-million-dollar carnival." The traditional circus is through, Rose said. "The proprietors offer three rings because they're in league with the aspirin people. No human being can watch three rings at once." He argued that adults go to the circus at the demand of their children. "It's not a grown-up entertainment and, besides, it doesn't smell good. It's a badly lighted, constantly repeated bore displayed in a frowsy-looking tent. I want no part of it."[77]

Then Rose let fly with predictions that he and the *Times* were happy to treat as a virtuoso display of talk, performance art, a form of entertainment, and one not to be confused with information. "Statistics on Mr. Rose's circus are wooed from him easily," said the *Times*. "He states that he will have a ballet of 200, another 200 dancers schooled in the Tiller tradition, 100 show girls for pictorial purposes, a choral group of 250, still another hundred dancers of the Albertina Rasch kind, a Chautauqua of notables made up of slightly faded picture stars, politicians, authors, radio crooners and athletes, and two orchestras of 100 pieces each. A congress of stooges will be in the melee and a huge demonstration in magic will be a feature."[78] It was a vision apparently inspired by one of the vital tenets of Manhattanism divined by Koolhaas, which was a "hyper-density" of population, a celebration of congestion. It also expressed another of the great city's purposes that manifested itself in Rose: "to overstimulate the imagination and keep any recognizable earthly realities at a distance."[79]

NOBODY HOME

Rose's stand-up routine for the *Times* did contain one down-to-earth message: he was out of Kings' enterprises. This departure had nothing to do with poor management decisions made at the Casino and Music Hall clubs during his absence, as Rose later claimed. He and Yermie Stern made the split official a week before Rose returned to New York. It was probably all but over when Rose sailed to Europe accompanied by publicity for his planned circus. But it was not amicable. Rose said he was owed $16,000 in back pay for the weeks he was in Europe, that he "owned the scenery and costumes" at the Casino de Paree, and that Stern could not continue calling Billy Rose's Music Hall by that name. Stern disagreed on all points, and after Rose returned to New York on September 4, a meeting was arranged at the Casino de Paree. Rose brought along the powerful columnist Walter Winchell as a prominent witness whose presence would make violence impossible. Threats of violence were another story. When Rose insisted his contract supported his case, the gangster Spunky Weiss replied, "Why, Billy, while you was in Europe I took a look at that contract and I shot out all the clauses."[80]

It's a great yarn, and it keeps getting better. After the meeting, Winchell told Rose his life was in danger. Rose agreed and at five in the morning telephoned Bernard Baruch, who contacted Attorney General Homer Cummings, who called up J. Edgar Hoover, who dispatched three G-men to contact the criminals with the message that nothing had better happen to Billy Rose.[81] Unfortunately, the story is too good to be true. It is not credible that Rose asked such a favor of Baruch just weeks after reestablishing contact with him for the first time in fifteen years. In fact, nearly two years later Rose was still not certain of his friendship with Baruch and, addressing him in a letter as Mr. Baruch, apologized profusely after Fanny Brice's stockbroker contacted Baruch for financial advice. "I write this letter so that you will know that none of this was my doing," he said. "Despite the fact that I have spent hours in your company, I have never presumed on our friendship for guidance in the stock market."[82] In 1934, asking Baruch for protection from gangsters would have been an unimaginable presumption. Besides, Winchell could have helped Rose reach Hoover. Winchell received a personal note from the FBI director in April, and on September 6, at the time Winchell and Rose supposedly met with the gangsters, the columnist talked with Frank Fay, head of the bureau's New York office, who informed Hoover that Winchell "praised you highly for the attitude which you assume against gangsters and other so-called 'gorillas.'"[83] Finally, as Rosoff's lawsuit proved, by the mid-1930s even gangsters sought remedies in the courts. Rose filed three lawsuits against his former employers.[84] He was obviously not afraid for his life.

But he might have feared his life had not yet assumed the gigantic proportions he desired, a problem that could only partly be addressed with actual accomplishments. Invention was also required. Rose turned thirty-five in September 1934, and his résumé was a succession of sometimes very successful but brief engagements. His adventures with the Casino de Paree and the Music Hall lasted just over a year. Rose might also have been disheartened by the disruptions and loneliness of his life with Brice. In the summer of 1933, the Rose-Brice family moved from 1111 Park Avenue to a building at 32 East Sixty-Fourth Street.[85] When Rose went there after completing his 1934 trip to Europe, Fanny was not home. On the day he arrived, she opened the Follies in Chicago. It was the start of a nearly seven-month road show, and when Rose's month in Europe is tacked on, the separation of husband and wife lasted almost eight months, except for a week in December during the Christmas holiday, when Rose traveled with Brice's children to visit their mother in Kansas City. Frances and Bill called their mother's husband Mr. Rose, but he was warm toward them. "Rose had brought not just the children, but the presents, time, and spirit to make 1934 the greatest Christmas Fran and Bill had ever spent," writes the Brice biographer Herbert Goldman.[86]

Children brought out Rose's most charitable sentiments. Perhaps because of his own sufferings in childhood, or perhaps because children were unable to challenge or threaten him amorously or financially, he performed some of his kindest acts on their behalf. His decent behavior toward Brice's children hints that Rose's sister Polly may have been on to something when she insisted her brother was a wounded innocent. "He is the soul of kindness and goodness and generosity," she told a would-be biographer. "Billy is so soft and kind inside. . . . When Billy gets tough, he's protesting against himself. He's just trying to control himself, so his emotions won't run away with him."[87] It was a Jewish type that emerged from America's scrappy ghetto neighborhoods, and a fictional character appears in Saul Bellow's *Humboldt's Gift* with the affliction Polly attributed to Billy Rose. "He has fine feelings which frustrate him because they fiddle his heart, and he overreacts grossly," Bellow wrote of his character.[88] The Americanization of the Jews forced many to become emotional contortionists, twisting awkwardly to disguise traits that could hold them back.

seven

JUMBO

Back in New York but distant from his wife and separated from his theater-restaurants, Rose immediately began to produce what would become *Jumbo,* or Billy Rose's *Jumbo,* because he was not about to back off the titling innovation of Billy Rose's Music Hall. Initial plans called for the show based on *Star of the Circus* to open in the spring of 1935, and to move things along, after just one week Rose was already in search of a venue and in talks with Hecht and his writing partner Charles MacArthur to create the book. Such speed may have been spurred by fear that his former partners would submarine his new project. Kings Beer announced "optional acquisition of 'Circus Queen,' Hungarian play, for which Rose went abroad."[1] Kings could not have made the threat if Rose had truly purchased an option on the circus play as he announced, but he had not. He stole the story, and the author later sued him. While in Budapest, Rose "attended performances with a translator and took notes and sketched the scenery," charged attorneys for the author.[2] If the move by Kings was a dirty trick, it was made possible by Rose's own dirty trick. "He had the soul of a criminal or gangster," said Ben Hecht's wife.[3] But as club owner Granlund knew and Saul Bellow later observed, there is often not much difference in America between gangsters and other ambitious realists. As Bellow put it, although Jimmy Hoffa attracted the ire of Robert Kennedy, "the Hoffa school—in more than half its postulates, is virtually identical with the Kennedy school. If you didn't speak real, you spoke phony. If you weren't hard, you were soft."[4] Billy Rose had graduated from the same school.

When Rose contacted Hecht and MacArthur to write *Jumbo,* he was calling in a favor. He had recently helped the pair and film director Howard Hawks write a movie version of Hecht and MacArthur's hit play *Twentieth Century.* "We'd promised to help Billy Rose," Hawks said, because for five days Hecht and MacArthur "just talked the [*Twentieth Century*] dialogue, and Billy wrote it down [shorthand]."[5] The book for *Jumbo* took longer than five days. The job was enormous, but the eccentric schedule Rose had established during his years in the nightclub and theater businesses was well entrenched. He liked to "sleep 'till one o'clock in the afternoon like an actor, take his hot bath and get down to the office at two," recalled the writer and producer Will Morrissey. Still, his vibrancy always impressed. "For one so small Mr. Rose is charged with a super-electric vitality," wrote a reporter who watched him during *Jumbo* preparations.[6]

Rose's team was also essential. Years of contacts now paid off. Jed Harris's public relations man, Richard Maney, continued with Rose, and also through Harris came Jean Barkow, variously described as Rose's secretary and general manager, who knew "all about the business and where everything was." *The Great Magoo* fiasco brought George Abbott, who signed on to direct. John Murray Anderson would stage manage, as he did on *Crazy Quilt,* and Anderson brought on the scenic designer Albert Johnson. They had both worked on the Ziegfeld Follies that starred Brice as Rose's Countess Dubinsky. The twenty-three-year-old costume designer Raoul Pène du Bois had also worked that show and joined *Jumbo,* and Will Morrissey had known Rose since the showman had roomed at the Princeton Hotel.[7] His specialty was shoestringing, or putting on a show with virtually no money, and he was one of the small-time zanies Rose could not help loving. A typical conversation between the two started with Morrissey saying, "I need twenty-five hundred dollars," Rose replying, "I don't know you well enough to give you twenty-five hundred dollars," and Morrissey telling him, "I'll sit here until we get ACQUAINTED."[8] Morrissey brought an important asset to the table besides comic relief. He knew Allan K. Foster, the choreographer who had worked on the Shuberts' 1927 show *The Circus Princess,* which had featured circus stunts and performers.[9]

To write *Jumbo*'s songs, Rose first approached Jerome Kern and Oscar Hammerstein II, but the creators of *Show Boat* were working on a movie, so Rose turned to Rodgers and Hart, whom he had stiffed in 1925 at the Fifth Avenue Club. Hard feelings were, however, a luxury the songwriter team could not afford. They needed a job. For nineteen months the theater-owning Shubert brothers had kept the duo idle and in the dark about plans for their musical *On Your Toes*, so they jumped at Rose's offer to work and earn again. Rose later ignored the fact that he had first sought out Kern and Hammerstein to write *Jumbo*. Rodgers and Hart "were tops in their field," he said. "So I got 'em. I wouldn't have cared if they hadn't had a show in ten years."[10] Rose's bluster recalls that of an editor who reached out to every reporter in town before he found one available to do a job. The available reporter said the editor had "the knack of making you feel that nobody else can deliver the goods, which is the knack of lying your ass off."[11]

Rose and Morrissey brainstormed *Jumbo* in manic fashion. "Rose was a victim of CLAUTIFOBIA [*sic*]—MUST HAVE EVERYTHING BIG ... therefore he had big paper," the excitable Morrissey wrote in his slapdash memoir. "The paper looked like a big three sheet, then he'd write in big letters all the suggestions that either one of our 'brains' could dig up. . . . Ideas for pageants, plots, titles for songs. . . . We wrote 'Jumbo' words, music and book, three times that summer and winter. . . . All the songs that Rose and I had, we threw to Rogers [*sic*] and Hart. And all the ideas for the plot, we threw to Hecht and McArthur [*sic*]." Rose always believed in research, so the two went to the library to "look up data on all the 'old circuses come back,'" and maybe that is how Rose decided on the show's key comic element, a giant elephant named Jumbo. An article on Jumbo, the late P. T. Barnum's famous elephant, appeared in October 1934 in the *New-York Historical Society Quarterly Bulletin* and was filled with illustrations about the publicity the great animal attracted.[12] If Rose missed that item, there were other hints. *Stage* reviewed four new books about the circus and its lead was, "You have to have elephants." The showman Sam Gumpertz took charge of the Ringling Brothers and Barnum and Bailey Combined Shows during its 1933 New York run and planned to showcase forty-eight pachyderms. "You can't have a circus without elephants," commented *Stage*.[13] But the magazine agreed with Rose's attack on the big top's moribund condition: "The circus has no true novelty to offer this year." Other news also brought bad tidings. "Fairs Dropping Circus Acts as Customers Ask for Girly Revues," ran one headline. To counter this trend, circuses sought ever more spectacular acts. In 1934, a New York audience saw two men shot into the air by a single cannon blast. Rose's *Jumbo* booked a human cannonball act, but with a twist. Rose's cannon was loaded with a woman.[14]

By early 1935 *Jumbo* was far enough along to pitch to investors. Rose claimed that by then he had spent $40,000 on the show, but the true number was less than $17,000, mainly for advance royalties paid to the principal members of the team, including Rodgers and Hart, Hecht and MacArthur, and Murray Anderson.[15] Still, major expenses loomed, because Rose's vision for *Jumbo* included hundreds of acrobats, dancers, musicians, and clowns, as well as an animal menagerie that included everything from elephants and lions to horses and llamas. He had also not yet hired the cast, created sets, rented a theater, designed costumes, installed lighting, or built a stage. Morrissey wanted to go after backers who could invest $5,000, but Rose knew he needed to land a whale. "Nothing doing," he said. "This is a big promotion."[16]

John "Jock" Whitney was his man. Heir to a fortune of more than $100 million, Whitney was an expert polo player and fan of the theater, who in 1931 put $100,000 into *Here Goes the Bride,* a comedy about divorce by *New Yorker* cartoonist Peter Arno. It lasted seven performances. That did not scare off Whitney. As Rose worked on *Jumbo,* the multimillionaire and his wealthy sister, Joan Whitney Payson, put money into two more Broadway shows.[17] Rose reached out to Whitney's attorney and a pitch meeting was arranged for the first week in May at Rose's penthouse Wurlitzer office.[18]

At that meeting Rose further burnished his reputation as a fanatic for details, preparation, and professionalism. His passion to master every aspect of theater, which Brice had admired and nurtured, blossomed now. Rose delivered a sales pitch as carefully choreographed as a Broadway show. As the moneyed siblings entered Rose's office, their eyes were meant to be drawn to Pène du Bois's color drawings of *Jumbo*'s characters in costume that Rose had framed and mounted on the walls. Albert Johnson presented "elaborate models" of the planned theater sets, and Murray Anderson reviewed the staging of complex production numbers, such as the opening scene, "Over and Over Again," which would present circus performers rehearsing stunts that called for endless repetition and practice. That opening act included a woman shot from a cannon, who would be caught by her partner seated in the front row of the audience, followed by an acrobat in the balcony clenching a rip line in her teeth and sailing one hundred yards over the heads of the spectators to land on the stage. Stunts like that made the fantastic nature of the show clear from the outset. Hecht and MacArthur read their book for the Whitneys, and Rodgers and Hart played and sang the score.[19] When the presentation was done, Rose pivoted from master showman to grandmaster of chutzpah. According to Morrissey, he "*slapped* the desk (a 'big' slap) sat up and said: 'Jock, unless I get a half a million dollars, I'm not interested.'" Morrissey was mortified. "At that moment," he recalled, "I could have SHOT HIM." But Rose knew what he was doing. Just as he had in his negotiations with song publishers, Rose talked to Whitney not as a supplicant but as an equal and was respected as such. "Well, I'll talk to my lawyer in the morning and let you know," Whitney replied. By the end of August, Whitney and his sister committed to an investment of $150,000.[20] Rose had triumphed.

"It was my first experience of an audition for 'angels,'" recalled Murray Anderson, referring to *Jumbo*'s financial backers. "Today auditions are the rule . . . and I have given and attended many of them. But never have I seen one so expertly, thoroughly, and successfully given as this first one, planned and presented by Billy Rose for *Jumbo*."[21]

SWEET-TALKER

What the Whitneys heard at the audition was a *Jumbo* storyline similar to the original *Star of the Circus,* except that now the young lovers were heirs to feuding circus families. A more significant difference was the creation of a character from Rose's past: the incompetent father who ruins the family finances. In *Jumbo*'s first act, the circus owner John Considine is a drunk who causes the Considine Wonder Show to go bankrupt. To satisfy unpaid taxes, a US marshal sells the show's assets at auction, giving Considine's rival circus owner, Matt Mulligan, the opportunity to buy his competitor's best items and hire his best acts. This threatens to undermine the love between Considine's daughter and Mulligan's son. It also means the loss of Considine's beloved attraction and occasional drinking buddy, the elephant Jumbo. To avert the loss of Jumbo, Considine's press agent, Claudius B. (Brainy) Bowers, attempts to spirit the animal away from the auction site. The marshal stops him, and the confrontation sets up the show's great one-liner. Asked where he is going with that elephant Bowers replies, "What elephant?"

In the second act, Bowers, who has an unusual tic—he tosses around lit matches—accidentally sets fire to the Considine home, and the insurance money allows the irresponsible circus owner to buy back his show and Jumbo. Here the story retrieves an element from *Star of the Circus*. With the Considine daughter still miffed at the Mulligan son, he becomes an acrobat to be near her. Meanwhile, before Considine can reclaim Jumbo, the animal escapes Mulligan's circus and rampages through town. Considine agrees to use his special relationship with the elephant to calm him down if his arrest for arson—he is accused of burning down his home for the insurance money—is rescinded. The rival circus owners reconcile, and the musical ends with the wedding of their children.[22]

With the financing in place Rose moved forward in earnest. Since February he had been in talks with Jimmy Durante to play the part of the comic press agent Claudius B. Bowers, and he had also announced that the venue he required was the enormous Hippodrome on Sixth Avenue between Forty-Third and Forty-Fourth streets. In May he got both.[23] In June, Rose booked Paul Whiteman and his orchestra to perform the music,[24] and by the end of July he won another crucial battle. The Actors' Equity Association ruled that *Jumbo* was a circus and so did not fall under its jurisdiction.[25] As Jock Whitney's lawyer, John F. Wharton, had recognized and warned, Rose's $150,000 production budget ignored the possibility that *Jumbo* might be considered an Equity show. "If the production is held to come under the rulings of legitimate shows," he wrote, "this would amount to a rather large sum." Only after the favorable ruling did Whitney deposit checks into the account of Billy Rose's Jumbo, Inc.[26]

The usual time allotted for the rehearsal of a musical was about five weeks. Liberated from Equity rules, Rose worked his cast nearly four months to coordinate the movement of actors and animals and acrobats and clowns and showgirls with the music and songs and dance numbers. "There were dozens of horses, [and] numbers that were done with music with the horses," Rodgers said. "All that had to be synchronized with Paul Whiteman's band, up on a platform over the ring. It took a tremendous amount of doing."[27] Another matter was the Hippodrome, which was a construction site as Rose and Murray Anderson reconfigured, redecorated, and rebuilt every aspect from the lobby to the seating, including a new revolving stage and a catwalk "to hold lights, rigging and the occasional performer." A subterranean level was even turned into a zoo with "a papier-mache mountain swarming with monkeys, each of which wore a tag inscribed with the name of a Broadway celebrity."[28] With all the construction, acts were forced to rehearse in a variety of locations in Brooklyn and Manhattan.

It soon became a New York pastime to read and talk about the comically unwieldy rehearsals. A typical stage direction was, "The bandwagon will follow the calliope, then the llamas and the donkeys and white horse on the right. The black bear is wheeled off first. And will the lady with the dromedary move a few steps forward. All right, is everybody standing by?"[29] Morrissey was overheard on the telephone pleading, "Could you put up an elephant for me over the weekend? . . . Please? The poor thing is coughing his lungs out over at the building where they're sand-blasting."[30] Rose "plastered the side of a building" with the sign, "SH-H-H-H! JUMBO IS IN REHEARSAL!" Rehearsals continued virtually around the clock and "slumming parties from Harlem and Greenwich Village" finished their nights out with a visit to the Hippodrome to watch rehearsals. The *New Yorker* featured a depiction of the show on the cover of its April 27, 1935, issue, which included a profile of Rose, and Maney crafted lines for his boss that the press loved. The best included, "*Jumbo* will make me or break Whitney" and, to display Rose's sangfroid, a paraphrase of Caesar's fateful words before invading Rome: "I stand on the Rubicon rattling the dice."[31]

It was all very amusing to everyone except the exhausted cast. As non-Equity performers, they were not paid during their months of rehearsals. Instead, Rose was only obligated to feed them during working hours. "Six days a week until Thanksgiving and never paid them a quarter," Maney said. "It was a scandal."[32] At some point there was a revolt, and the moment tested and proved Rose's almost hypnotic ability to persuade people to believe and do what he wanted. It was a talent first noticed by his peers in high school. In debate class Rose argued that the *World* newspaper owed its great circulation to its sports page. "But the way he put it. He was a very convincing person," said a classmate.[33] He employed this gift when the cast of *Jumbo* quit working. "There was kind of an insurrection," Rodgers said. "And I remember Billy standing in the middle of the arena talking to the entire company, and he sweet talked them into behaving themselves. And he walked away and they were still in rehearsal, still carrying on. They were all going to quit."[34] Jimmy Durante also came under Rose's spell when the producer decided he needed Durante to lie on the ground while Jumbo walked over him. "You know what's wrong with that Billy Rose?" Durante said. "He can talk anybody into anything!"[35]

GREAT AND GLAMOROUS

Jumbo opened on November 16, 1935, to a stampede of New Yorkers eager to see the endlessly promoted spectacle, which got an important last-minute publicity boost. During the three weeks before *Jumbo* opened, the Texaco oil company sponsored weekly radio broadcasts of rehearsals featuring Durante as Bowers. The publicity worked. The opening-night crowd was enormous. "Sixth Avenue was jammed up to Fiftieth Street," according to *Variety,* and Fifth Avenue was also deadlocked. Ticketholders got out of taxis and cars and walked but could not reach the doors. "Pavements were blocked by rubberneckers, and the cops didn't seem able to handle the mob," *Variety* also noted. Once inside the lobby, customers had to maneuver around a cluster "of klieg lights for the newsreels."[36] Celebrity attendees attracted the cameras. There was the boxing champ Jack Dempsey, the department store magnate Bernard Gimbel, Irving Berlin, the stripper Gypsy Rose Lee, the heiress and socialite Gloria Vanderbilt, the automobile giant Walter Chrysler, the radio stars George Burns and Gracie Allen, and Rose's wife, Fanny Brice, who wore a diamond necklace that a *Daily News* society columnist called "big enough to stop a Cartier clock."[37] The show also drew every drama critic in town. For nearly three hours they witnessed "comic clowns with wonder-working costumes . . . bareback riders and tumblers and skilled performers on steel hoops high in the air." There were "people shot from cannons, beautiful girls, song birds, brass bands" and "a giant clown," nearly fifty feet tall, "sequined and silvery," which "epitomizes the magnificence of the extravaganza."[38] There was even an act that a contemporary theater historian notes anticipated "the helicopter scene in *Miss Saigon* by more than fifty years." The Kimris were "aerialists who perform[ed] stunts while hanging out of a miniature but nonetheless flying airplane."[39]

"It's great, it's glamorous, it's gargantuan!" cheered the *New York World-Telegram,* while the *Daily News* wrote, "There have been big shows in the Hippodrome before, but none so beautiful as this, I am sure. And never before have I seen a show which 'caught' the audience within thirty seconds of the parting of the curtains." The *New York American's* Gilbert Gabriel explained, "We've none of us ever seen quite the like of it before. It is chockful of so many sorts of thrills, musical, scenic, gymnastic and humanitarian, it deserves endowment as an institution." The applause was unanimous, and each critic had his favorite scene. For the *New York Sun* it was when the musical's love object, Considine's daughter, "dreams a circus. The circus she dreams is flamboyantly miraculous. There is a rhinestone clown which reaches to the roof and a blaze of dancing light which almost blinds the eyes. The ring is filled with crystal horses; overhead crystal girls hang by their teeth and whirl." The *New York Journal* wrote, "The day before yesterday, November the 16, achieved history. 'Jumbo' opened. It is huge and it is magnificent." What the paper loved best was the talented clown, A. Robins, "a fellow of quaint madness who is afflicted with the peculiar problem of having bananas grow in his left coat pocket." Brooks Atkinson at the *Times* also loved Robins and wanted more of him. "Otherwise," he wrote, "'Jumbo' is perfect as Mr. Rose has staged it—a gargantuan antic, a fool's paradise of bizarre and plain enjoyment." The *Herald Tribune*'s Percy Hammond assured Rose that "his new 'lunacy,' as he calls it, is a sane and exciting compound of opera, animal show, folk-drama, harlequinade, carnival, circus, extravaganza, and spectacle. If I have omitted anything from the catalog, he has my permission to put it in."[40]

Almost overlooked were the songs by Rodgers and Hart, which "did not stop the action, they were an intrinsic part of the action. The romantic ballads were crafted to suit specific characters in particular situations." These include "The Most Beautiful Girl in the World," "Little Girl Blue," and "My Romance," which "features some of the most elegantly wistful lyrics ever put on paper" and is "quite simply, one of the best songs Rodgers and Hart ever wrote."[41]

Over the next six months the show ran for 223 performances, and when it closed on April 18, 1936, it was reputed to have attracted more than one million people.[42] The actual number was half as much, just 597,033, and the tremendous production lost about $100,000, despite the Texaco-sponsored radio broadcasts that had brought in an unanticipated $12,000 a week for twelve weeks, or $144,000.[43] Poor turnout was not the only culprit. Whitney's attorneys estimated the show would cost $32,000 a week to produce without factoring in Rose's salary, which is not found in any records of the production, though when the show closed, he claimed to have pocketed $20,000 in the final week.[44] If that was typical, weekly production costs were far north of Whitney's estimate.[45] Anticipated costs also exceeded projections. The budget allocated $2,000 a week to rent the Hippodrome, but Rose's announcements that no other theater could contain his enormous project gave the landlord the upper hand, and the rent reached $6,000 during top box office weeks.[46] Rose also pulled a fast one at the box office. "Each week he wiped out his box-office staff in order to get an equitable distribution of 'the ice,'" said Maney, referring to the money that scalpers paid for tickets.[47] The practice was common in the twenties and was obviously a tradition Rose felt ought to survive at least until the end of *Jumbo*. He apparently decided, in the manner of the Clever Isaac characters in his high school newspaper, that Whitney's inherited fortune did not need his protection.

And he was never one to tremble at committing such larcenies. "I knew him when he started," said the songwriter Abner Silver. "He was very aggressive and he didn't have a dime in his pocket. All he had was nerve."[48]

THE SHOWMAN

But many forgave Rose nearly everything because he was scintillating, eccentric, original, charming, and unexpectedly fair and even generous. Women found both his formidable and decent qualities magnetic. "Rose radiated energy and power, which made him attractive," wrote Betsy Blair, who met her husband Gene Kelly while dancing at a Rose nightclub.[49] The Broadway actress Mercedes McCambridge testified that "when Billy wanted to be charming, you might just as well give in without a struggle." He could affect an almost kingly manner. One winter night he ordered McCambridge to remove her "ugly coat." When she did, he threw it into the street and then handed her "the softest, most beautiful natural Canadian wild lynx coat, and it had my name in it."[50] Singer Jane Morgan remembered him as "charming, witty, entertaining."[51] "His worst enemy would tell you he was a brilliant man," Helen Schrank said.[52]

One such was Rose's resentful publicity man Charles Samuels, a talented writer who worked with the blues singer Ethel Waters on her autobiography. "I don't give a goddamn how many times other people say he imitated," Samuels said. "He had a great eye for talent. He knew how to put on a show."[53] Rose's friend Abe Burrows remembered,

> Whenever we were talking, Billy would start off by saying, "Abe, you couldn't be more wrong." Whether we were talking about the theatre, the stock market, or life itself, he always told me how it was or how it should be, and I listened. . . . The simple fact [is] this was a very remarkable man. . . . Billy was good at everything. I admired him, I was dazzled by the things he did. But most of all I had a deep, deep affection for him. We'd differ, quarrel, grow angry with each other. But somehow or other I always found myself having dinner with him, spending a weekend with him, as though nothing had happened.[54]

The widow of a Rose employee said, "Likable, shmikable, he was a very gifted man. . . . He was a barracuda. One of the roughest [but] in his own business dealings was extremely fair."[55] Others were awed by his conversation and his ability to tell stories for hours and "never . . . repeat a story. Never."[56] Rose even made listening a memorable event. "He was a great audience," said the songwriter Burton Lane. "At parties he would pull a chair over from across the room and sit on top of me. He was most appreciative of things of quality."[57] Meredith Willson played Rose tunes from his show *The Music Man,* and was charmed by his attentions: "Billy is a very warm audience when he's reached—reacts like a European—patted me enthusiastically on the head as he stood behind me there at the piano." Brice was enthralled by his nimble mind. "He's clever, clever, clever. He's a smart little goose," she told an interviewer.[58] Gloria Safier, who in the 1950s became a powerhouse talent agent, worked for Rose in the thirties. "I adored him," she said. "Everything about him. . . . I thought he was brilliant. He was a fabulous man. The people that knock him . . . they never did anything . . . all men that get to that position are tough."[59] Richard Rodgers called Rose "very enthusiastic, terribly bright, very helpful, very shrewd." Hecht considered him a kind of wonder worker. "He had a marvelous capacity for throwing himself at a million projects and no theater was big enough," Hecht said. "He would have been good producing the landing of the Pilgrims or the battle of Gettysburg. That would have been ideal for Billy." Hecht considered him a great showman, for Hecht a "magical phrase" that described the rare individual who "casts a spell over himself in his youth and when he grows up he's able to move this spell over the world."[60]

That is what Rose accomplished with *Jumbo.* It brought him fame, adoration, acclaim—the public recognition of his talents. "There was nothing in the world but Billy Rose and he was going to get his," is how he described himself during these years.[61] He got his from the theater critic John Mason Brown, who wrote, "Billy Rose has proved to a long-waiting world that he is the successor to two great showmen at one and the same time. On his head he has put the hat of the late Florenz Ziegfeld and around his shoulders he has wrapped the voluminous cape of the great P.T. Barnum."[62]

"I was delighted to believe every one of the glittering syllables," Rose said.[63]

eight

IT CAN'T HAPPEN HERE

By the time *Jumbo* closed in April 1936, ten years had passed since Rose had mocked the antisemitism of Henry Ford, and during that time the ancient prejudice had become a chief characteristic of life in Europe and the United States. When Adolf Hitler first took power in Germany in January 1933, news of Nazi persecution of the Jews "touched a raw-nerve among the American people and not simply its Jewish citizens."[1] Governors from South Dakota, Arizona, California, and Montana sent words of support to the American Jewish Congress before its March 27 anti-Nazi rally, held at New York's Madison Square Garden. That evening twenty-three thousand people inside the arena and another thirty-five thousand on the street who listened to the proceedings over loudspeakers were joined by more than eighty similar rallies across the country. But this Jewish and gentile, New York and national environment of concern for Jewish welfare did not last. In September 1935, Germany's Nuremberg Laws revoked its Jews' citizenship rights, and Jews there issued a plea for refuge in "an appeal addressed to all nations."[2] The American response was muted. Domestic antisemitism was now widespread. By 1936, *Fortune* magazine reported that "leading members of the Jewish community in the United States—men who had previously looked to the future with confidence—have been shocked into fear. The apprehensiveness of American Jews has become one of the important influences in the social life of our time."[3] The security of American Jews continued to decline. "Before 1933 there were no official anti-Semitic organizations in this country," the historian Leonard Dinnerstein notes, but "by 1939 over one hundred existed."[4]

Rose addressed his Jewish identity at a business pitch in Texas in early 1936, when the subject could hardly be avoided, and he submissively assumed the burden of the widespread hatred. "Boys, thank you for your confidence in me," he said. "I feel I ought to say this. I'm a stranger here, and what's more I'm a

Jewish stranger and you'll have to take your chances on me giving you a square shake." Such humility was uncharacteristic, but in 1936 being a Jew required tact, rather than Rose's standard confrontation. His trepidation turned out to be unwarranted; Rose met with no antisemitism in Texas. Still, that did not blind him to the problem. He granted only that Texas was an exception as "the only part of the country" free of Jew hatred. It was a place "where a man was taken for what he was and admired or disliked on the basis of his personality and character rather than the shape of his nose or the sound of his last name."[5] For the time being he could put the world Jewish crisis aside and attend to business, though the problem gnawed at him, and within a year he made his first theatrical stand against the threat.

THE RETURN OF NOSTALGIA

Jumbo was still playing in New York in March 1936 when Amon Carter, Fort Worth newspaper publisher and the city's passionate ambassador, used his impressive network of contacts to present Rose with an opportunity. The centennial anniversary of Texas's independence from Mexico was to be celebrated that summer in Dallas, a prospect civic leaders in nearby Fort Worth could not abide. The smaller city resented its larger rival's money and power and the insolence the combination bred, and wanted its own summer celebration to deflate Dallas's ego and generate local jobs. But time was running short. Dallas planned to open an expo in June. Carter first reached out to Hollywood's Rufus Le Maire, a former Fort Worth resident who was director of casting at MGM. Le Maire declined to produce the event but suggested Rose. News of *Jumbo*'s success had reached California, and he was becoming a national sensation. "'Jumbo,' as finally revealed by Billy Rose, the little man who pulls battleships out of hats, is an awesome spectacle," reported the *Los Angeles Times,* and the *Hollywood Reporter* called *Jumbo* a "stupendous, colossal, gigantic success."[6] Le Maire did Carter's legwork and telephoned New York, but it turned out Rose was in Hollywood for a fruitless meeting with film studio RKO, which wanted to use bits of *Jumbo* as live entertainment in its movie theaters.

Le Maire met with Rose and pitched him on Texas but got nowhere. Rose's wallet was apparently so fattened by *Jumbo* that he could afford to be choosy about his next undertaking, and he did not understand why Texas desired festivities. "It is the hundredth anniversary of the battle of the Alamo but it seems the

Americans lost that battle. Why have a celebration?" Rose asked Le Maire.[7] Carter decided to try a different tack and telegrammed Jock Whitney. That did the trick. With Whitney facing losses on *Jumbo,* Rose was not in a position to refuse the millionaire's request to, as Carter put it, "drop over here to Forth Worth and give this project the once over." What's more, if someone in Fort Worth could reach Whitney, that someone was likely rich, and Carter in fact was a wealthy man and "fable-izer" of "Texanic" energy, a "phantasmagorical character" who occasionally "stood on banquet tables and fired his six-shooters."[8] He was Rose's match in showmanship and shrewd dealing. Carter's bested competitors spoke of having been "Amon Cartered," and he knew how to appeal to Rose's wallet and ego. "It will be an opportunity [for Rose] to make a substantial amount of money, well worth his time," Carter wrote Whitney. "With his genius and the financial backing we have there is no question of success."[9]

Rose flew to Fort Worth and learned what the city was up against. Dallas planned to spend $25 million on its state-sanctioned centennial celebration. Fort Worth budgeted half a million for its upstart challenge. This problem brought the chest-beating Rose to the fore, and in contrast to the soothing tone he employed when he spoke about being a Jew he tackled this business proposition with the nerve, straight talk, and confidence bordering on arrogance he had perfected in his dealings with music publishers and Whitney. To even the playing field Fort Worth needed beautiful women. "The only thing that could stand off $25,000,000 worth of machinery was girls—pelvic machinery vs. Diesel engines, and they would make the engines look sick," Rose said. More money was also a must. Two million might be required. "What I'm going to lay out for you boys is pretty big," he told the Texans.

"Nothing is too big for the state of Texas!" answered Carter.

"That's all I want to know," replied Rose. But there was one more thing Fort Worth needed to know. "And let's get this straight. This fair is not going to make any money. You can't build what amounts to a small town and expect to amortize it in 90 days. If you look at this venture as an experiment in civic exploitations you will not be disappointed. Some of your shows will show a profit on their operating costs, but the fair as a whole will lose about one million dollars." Rose said the Texans liked his style and reassured each other that "at least this guy isn't pulling our legs."[10] So on March 7, 1936, they named him director general of the Fort Worth Frontier Centennial. The officious title came with clout. By April he was in touch with Texas governor James V. Allred, who made requests Rose sometimes refused. "I have heard heaps about you and look forward to meeting you," Rose wrote the governor, as if Allred were a key staffer.[11] Rose had reason to assume a superior rank. His fee was $100,000, computed at $1,000 per day for one hundred days' work. President Roosevelt put in a full year for $75,000.[12]

Texas was the ideal setting for Rose's nostalgia-laced entertainments, which turned out to be far more prominent than female flesh at the Frontier Centennial. Just as his advertisements for *Crazy Quilt* had promised a dirty show and delivered a funny one, a reviewer of Rose's Texas attractions noted, "There isn't a naked woman on any of Billy Rose's stages. Only the peep shows house the nudity."[13] (The reporter apparently did not consider stripper Sally Rand's stylized nude act on Rose's main stage licentious enough to count as naked. Her "Nude Ranch," on the other hand, was surely the peep show he had in mind.) "Men like to see pretty girls, and so do women. But they want to see something besides nudity," Rose said.[14] Female nudity was widespread in the thirties. "Strippers performed in burlesque theaters, nightclubs, vaudeville houses, carnivals, and fairs," notes one historian. But it was because of innovations such as Rose's "Countess Dubinsky" number, which added laughs to striptease, that "women continued to watch it alongside of men."[15] Aware of these fault lines and what crossing them could mean for the bottom line, Rose featured showgirls but was careful not to let sexuality overwhelm what was essentially the same product he delivered at his Music Hall's Barbary Coast bar: "a rootin', tootin', shootin' old-time saloon." A public ground down by the seemingly endless Depression found relief in this kind of nostalgia, "a renewed interest in nineteenth-century pioneer life."[16] Rose brought down to Texas his production team from *Jumbo*, as well as the show itself and also the Paul Whiteman orchestra, and promised Fort Worth a "Living, Breathing, Highly Exciting Version of The Last Frontier." In addition, it would be gigantic, though with a Billy Rose production that was probably understood.[17]

Designed to operate only at night to escape the brutal daytime heat and distinguish it from Dallas's focus on instruction—"Dallas for Education, Fort Worth for Entertainment" was the Rose catchphrase that defined the distinction—Rose built Fort Worth a variety of Old West attractions. These ranged from staged gunfights and bank robberies to a "Last Frontier" show with warring Indian tribes and a buffalo stampede that had to be carefully timed, because "once it began, there was no stopping it."[18] But the Centennial's main attraction was the enormous and elegant Casa Mañana, an outdoor theater-restaurant that in some promotional materials was dubbed Billy Rose's Casa Mañana. It was an enormous two-story amphitheater of Moorish arches that welcomed guests with pedestrian lanes lined with trees and fountains. Inside up to 3,600 guests ordered dinner from white-jacketed waiters, while another 3,000 filled balcony seats.

Here nostalgic entertainment depended on a paradox: Casa Mañana delivered a vision of the past that owed its enchantment to the magical power of modern construction and 450-horsepower engines. The latter turned the world's largest revolving stage, measuring 130 feet in diameter, and also simultaneously moved it forward and backward, toward and away from the audience, as it seemed to float on a specially constructed lagoon of water 130 feet wide and 175 feet long. As this "floating" stage revolved, the nearly seven thousand customers watched the past slowly become the present. On the great stage Whiteman's orchestra and that of the popular Joe Venuti played as two hundred dancers enacted the twentieth century's world fairs. First came the 1904 St. Louis fair, and when that act ended the performers dashed to nearby changing rooms to don costumes for the next scene, before the stage churned its way toward a full revolution in one minute and forty-five seconds. They reappeared to enact the 1925 Paris fair and kept on changing to depict the Chicago fair of 1933 and the current expo, which again took spectators back to earlier days as the show recapitulated the history of Texas, from the days of the Comanche to the present, closing with a lagoon scene of cruising gondolas filled with showgirls. For the "grand finale, sixty-four jets of water lit by dozens of rainbow-colored lights suddenly erupted from the lagoon," and both orchestras "broke into 'The Eyes of Texas,' bringing the audience to its feet singing, whistling, and cheering."[19]

THE CASUAL GENIUS

The show's popularity with local audiences was essential to its success, but just as important to Rose was its reception in New York. The production was his first out-of-town audition for the city's recently announced 1939 World's Fair. He succeeded with this first step toward his goal. The Frontier Centennial opened on July 18, 1936, to reviews marked by awe. "A superb show . . . one of the gayest and most genuinely enchanting spectacles imaginable," was a typical response from the bowled-over New York critics.[20] Rose "presents a spectacle . . . that has no parallel in our curdled world," reported another.[21] Casa Mañana is "a night club that is beyond a Broadway Dream," exclaimed a third.[22] Damon

Runyon went to have a look at what Rose created and called it "probably the biggest and most original show ever seen in these United States."[23] Another reporter agreed with all of the above and surrendered in the face of it. The show, he wrote, is "so gargantuan, so fantastic, so incredible . . . that your correspondent is unable to figure out just what Fort Worth is going to do with it."[24]

Surrounded by raves, Rose adopted "the role he affected best . . . that of the casual and absolutely natural genius."[25] That is how a New York reporter found him after the reviews had poured in. "His feet were planted upon his broad flat top desk," the reporter observed, "just as they are when he's receiving at the Wurlitzer Building. He smiled mystically and blew smoke in neat spirals."[26] The act took in no one but was nevertheless appreciated for its theatricality. Rose "glanced casually at a letter from [New York] Mayor LaGuardia [sic]" and sent regards to his friends back home at the Lotos Club, where members included Rose's confederates in the show, newspaper, and public relations businesses: Lee Shubert, Herbert Bayard Swope, and Richard Maney, respectively.[27] And when Rose and the reporter discussed the future New York fair, Rose took the cavalier attitude to absurd heights: "That ought to be a great fair. . . . 1939 . . . that's a long way off. . . . I might be up in the Canadian wilds . . . or tiger hunting with Ben Hecht in Tibet."

In truth, he was scheming frantically. The *New York Sun* and the *Times* had speculated that Casa Mañana would do well in Central Park, so Rose wrote the city's park commissioner and planning czar, Robert Moses, to suggest the idea. The important letter to the powerful figure was polite and respectful and free of fawning or false flattery. It was smart and engaging, and displayed a flair for turning a phrase. Rose started on a note of irrefutable camaraderie executed with rhetorical grace: "As a New Yorker, I am familiar with your contributions to the gaiety of the City. As a New Yorker, perhaps you are familiar with mine, though they are not nearly so extensive, or important." Moses's response was friendly but unambiguous: "Of course I had heard of you before and you need no introduction, but I am sorry to say that the Casa Mañana will not fit into Central Park. It just can't be done."[28]

Still, the August 8 letter offered Rose two favors. Moses copied the fair's general manager, W. Earle Andrews, on the correspondence and in this way introduced Rose to the influential figure. In addition, he offered Rose a valuable suggestion: "By this time, you will probably have seen the representatives of the New York World's Fair who left for Texas a few days ago. They are the people to whom you should sell the Casa Mañana." Richmond H. Shreve of the New York architectural firm Shreve, Lamb & Harmon had designed the Empire State Building and was on the fair's architectural committee. He considered Casa Mañana "a unique combination of architecture and showmanship. The amazing thing, architecturally speaking, is that it is so large and yet retains the intimacy of a small cafe. I've traveled all over the world and I've never seen a show to compare in size or quality."[29]

Shreve and Rose discussed the upcoming New York fair for an hour, and on August 14, to harness this momentum, Rose telegrammed a pitch to W. Earle Andrews. But now all the winning elements of Rose's letter to Moses were absent. It was always a strain for Rose to behave properly, and his rough instincts frequently escaped captivity to undermine relationships with potential allies. Rose's note to Andrews began, "Would appreciate confidential expression from you as to how interested you are in having me participate in production of New York Fair." That was quite a how-do-you-do. It assumed not just Andrews's familiarity with Rose but a virtual preoccupation with the showman. Rose then applied the pressure of urgency. New opportunities were popping up and pulling him in several directions that might tie him up for years, he informed Andrews. After that came a declaration guaranteed to raise eyebrows: "Please believe me that this is no shenanigan to make you declare yourself." The undiplomatic insistence on innocence could only invite suspicion, and the error betrayed Rose's anxiety and desperation. He could not hide his eagerness. When he really needed it, the casual tone eluded him. Rose closed with a forced bit of levity: "Naturally the size and possibilities of your project appeals a little more to an imagination troubled with claustrafobia [sic]."[30]

Andrews responded the same day. He ignored Rose's failed attempt at chummy humor and also that Rose had misspelled his name as Earl instead of Earle. "It is premature to make any definite plans for the development of theatre and other features of Fair in which you are interested."[31] Andrews displayed the cool Rose lacked, and for the time being, that was that.

REST, MAMA

What Rose wrote Andrews was on the level. Other jobs beckoned. The Centennial did not close until November 1936, but from August onward he was flying to Hollywood, San Francisco, and Cleveland to investigate new projects.

RKO still wanted acts from *Jumbo* as live stage entertainment for its theaters. San Francisco was planning its 1939 Golden Gate Exposition, and Cleveland needed to improve the 1937 season of its 1936 Great Lakes Exposition.[32] Rose also visited New York to see his wife. Conflicting work schedules had forced long separations. During the summer and fall of 1935, when Rose was in New York preparing *Jumbo,* Brice was in Hollywood filming *The Great Ziegfeld.*[33] When Rose left for Texas in March 1936, Brice was starring in the Shuberts' 1936 Ziegfeld Follies, which kept her in New York from January to early May. Differences in their health added a new dimension to their estrangement. In the spring of 1936, Brice fell ill. Her teeth decayed, and that summer she had them all taken out and replaced with dentures.[34] When she visited Billy in July for the Centennial's opening, her condition must have made for an unflattering contrast with his relative youth, not to mention the beauty of the many young showgirls.

But the true beginning of the end of their marriage was the December 9, 1936, death of Rose's mother. Fannie Rosenberg was sixty-two and had been ill with heart disease for more than two years. She survived as long as she did because Rose retained the renowned cardiologist Franz Groedel, a German Jewish refugee, to extend her life. "I heard you were a great doctor. Use all your skill and talent to keep her alive," Rose told him.[35] In her last weeks she was much on Rose's mind. In November the Fort Worth Club held a luncheon in Rose's honor and presented him with a large silver loving cup inscribed, "In appreciation of a big job done well." Rose told his audience "of the pride his mother always had in trophies he won in early life for shorthand reporting," and referring to the new trophy said, "Why mother will get a bigger kick out of this than I did out of the entire Centennial."[36] At New York's Lenox Hill Hospital she slept with such a trophy in her arms and told her son, "When I die, dress me pretty, Willie."

Upon her death, he publicized her funeral with his usual ballyhoo and disdain for facts. Rose said he "cried steadily for 10 days" and that her funeral at Manhattan's Riverside Memorial Chapel attracted one thousand mourners. Many were the immigrants she helped come over from Russia. He claimed it was "a spontaneous outpouring of people from the East Side. People threw themselves on the grave," and that the Yiddish *Forverts* newspaper "wrote an editorial about her."[37] Riverside has no records of the funeral, but a search of the *Forverts* turns up only a brief December 10 obituary notice for Fannie Rosenberg, "the ritual slaughterer's wife's daughter." The *Times* noted her death the same day but did not follow up with news of the remarkable service. *Time* magazine likewise missed news of the crowds when it ran a notice of Fannie's death.[38]

Other Rose stories ring true. He wanted to get his mother a "bronze or a silver coffin, the finest in the world," but the rabbi reminded him, "Your mother, Mr. Rose, was a Jew—not a gangster." She was buried, according to tradition, in a plain pine box. A final Rose tale that sounds like a fable is factual. He had her gravestone inscribed with the words, "Rest, Mama." In her life of whirlwind activity, he said, that is the one thing she never did. The untraditional stone includes no Hebrew and omits her role as wife to her surviving husband, David.[39] Rose erased him from the family history. He never forgave him his failure as a provider or his concomitant failure to be a father who could act as a male counterweight to Fannie's female power. He "was never the head of the house," Rose said.[40]

Rose's version of his mother's death, like his pretense of indifference toward the World's Fair, surely camouflaged a frenzy of emotions. The evidence is overwhelming that he loved and even revered her, but it is likely that at age thirty-seven he was relieved to be free of her domineering personality and eager to end their quasi-marital relationship. A clue to the truth of this is how his mother's death affected his marriage to Fanny Brice, who was a maternal figure and a proxy for Rose's relationship with his mother. But now the time for mothers had passed. His freedom from one Fannie meant freedom from the other. He fled the chastity of his marriage to Brice and sought a passionate love life. He found one fast.

HAPPY WHEN RECKLESS

"Art, get an eyeful of that gal in there," said Rose. His attorney, Arthur Hays, later recalled in agreement, "She was decidedly worth looking at."[41]

In February 1937 Rose found, signed, and instantly fell for Olympic gold medalist Eleanor Holm, the swimming star of his upcoming Great Lakes Exposition Aquacade. Rose met her when he was, as usual, juggling several major projects at once, including planning the Cleveland Aquacade, producing a second season of the Texas fair, and keeping his name in front of the powers at the New York World's Fair. He soon added to the mix an affair with Holm and a public feud with Brice. Rose outfitted his life with romantic entanglements, high-wire acts, and special guests, until it resembled one of his spectacular productions.

A return date at Fort Worth in 1937 for the Frontier Fiesta (the new name because the centennial year had passed) was in the cards for Rose even before the 1936 season closed. The city was more than pleased with him. Instead of the fair's losing $1 million the shortfall was less than $100,000.[42] The Cleveland job came his way after he visited the fairgrounds there in October 1936, when press reports of Rose's victory in Fort Worth were fresh and alluring to Lincoln G. Dickey, Cleveland's fair manager and, as former head of New York City's Convention and Visitors Bureau, a man attuned to the New York papers. In Cleveland Rose saw an act praised in *Variety*, one that "combines precision swimming and fancy diving with a fashion parade. Seats are packed and it's free. It's perhaps the best show on the grounds."[43] With only twenty-four female swimmers, no admission, and no name, the performance was ripe for a Rose makeover into his first Aquacade. The popularity of women's synchronized swimming was already proven. Swimmer Katherine Curtis pioneered so-called ballet or rhythmic swimming set to music in the 1920s, and by 1933 Busby Berkeley's *Footlight Parade* featured "the first known water ballet sequence on film." The same year, Chicago's Century of Progress fair hired Curtis to create "Modern Mermaids." Ten thousand people showed up three times a day to watch thirty-five women swimmers perform to live music. Sam Snyder's International Water Follies expanded this kind of show to include "swimmers, divers, comedy divers and water ballet swimmers."[44] Snyder also made news by luring Olympic swimmers away from amateur competition to appear in his shows as professionals. In 1936, he was interested in Eleanor Holm.[45] So was Rose. In 1936, everyone was interested in Eleanor Holm.[46]

The twenty-two-year-old Brooklyn native had been a vivacious and charming swimming sensation since 1927, when at age thirteen she nearly beat the national champion, Adelaide Lambert, who went on to win a gold medal at the 1928 Olympics. The press found Holm irresistible: "scrappy," a "mermaid," and delightful in her youthful "impetuousness."[47] At fourteen she defeated Lambert, set a new world record in the women's three-hundred-yard medley, and was the subject of a feature story in the *Brooklyn Daily Eagle* that quoted her father unwittingly predicting his daughter's future achievements and stumbles. The fire department captain was "so rotten scared" when at age eleven Eleanor took her first ocean swim. "But that kid hasn't a nerve in her body," he said. The youngest of seven children "was always getting knocked around. . . . But she takes it like a prizefighter, game as a pebble." As the reporter gathered, she "[is] never happy unless she's reckless."[48]

Holm qualified for the 1928 Olympic team and competed again at the 1932

Olympics in Los Angeles, where she won a gold medal in the hundred-meter backstroke and, according to the *Eagle,* "set these Olympics on its ears by her looks as well as her prowess in the water."[49] At eighteen, Holm was a beauty with a pinup figure, dark hair, and eyes and a smile that bristled with an exciting, even alarming radiance. Warner Bros. signed her to a film contract and moved her to Hollywood for six months of training.[50] Despite the job, she contended that because her contract did not specify swimming performances, she could still compete in the Olympics as an amateur, and that is what she did after her film career quickly fizzled. Holm trained and qualified for the 1936 Berlin games. By then, she was married to a musician named Arthur Jarrett, toured with him as he played nightclub and theater gigs, and gained a reputation "as a blase [*sic*] young lady who trained on champagne and late parties and thought the trip to Berlin should be a 'joy ride.'" Holm denied it. "There's nothing at all to those stories," she said, "and whoever started them must be insane. . . . I've trained harder than anyone knows for these try-outs."[51] Two weeks later the American Olympic Committee ejected Holm from the team for attending late-night parties and drinking.

The judgment was issued while the Olympic Committee, Holm, and 333 other Olympic athletes were aboard the SS *Manhattan,* which on July 15, 1936, set sail from New York to Hamburg. Trouble started immediately. On the first night at sea chaperone Ada Sackett found Holm "on a deck chair surrounded by a group of young men." It was past ten, the curfew hour, and Holm refused to go to bed "until I get ready." The minor incident was followed by more serious missteps. On July 17, she spent the afternoon "'shooting crap' with a group of men" and seemed "to be under the influence of alcohol." That night she went to a party, and her cabin mates did not see her again until six the next morning, when two men helped her to her room. She was drunk. Holm missed breakfast and lunch that day and by noon was no longer in her room. Her cabin mates did not see her again until the afternoon, when Holm was newly intoxicated. She continued to drink and remained drunk until eleven that night. "The next day (19th) Mrs. Jarrett complained of being ill and remained in bed," reported fellow Olympic swimmer Mary Lou Petty. After she recovered, she began drinking again. On the night of July 23, as the ship cruised Germany's Elbe River, Sackett spotted Holm "walking on the forward deck with her arm interlocked with the arm of a young man whom I did not know. They came past me. I observed immediately that Mrs. Jarrett was intoxicated. She staggered as she walked. She was bleary-eyed. I went after her. The young man disappeared." Sackett helped Holm to her room. Once inside, Holm "went to the porthole from time to time and shouted to persons on the shore using vile language." When the ship's doctor arrived to examine her, Holm was "in bed in a deep slumber which approached a state of coma." The physician found her "pulse slow and of poor volume, pupils of eyes contracted and somewhat uneven." His diagnosis was "Acute Alcoholism."[52] That night an onboard American Olympic Committee of twenty met and unanimously voted to drop her from the team. She would not swim in the upcoming contest.

The Holm story ran in papers across the country. "Never did a bit of ocean-going wassail receive such publicity," Hecht wrote. "The entire civilized world was set agog. Had the S.S. *Manhattan* hit an iceberg and gone down, she would have received no more newspaper space."[53] But the Olympic Committee was admirably close-mouthed regarding the details of Holm's drunkenness and likely adultery. It did not want to slander her, and that allowed Holm and the newspapers to soft-pedal the story and generate sympathy. Her punishment seemed too harsh for ignoring curfew and drinking champagne at a party attended by Charles MacArthur, Ben Hecht's writing partner on Billy Rose's *Jumbo*. Holm's husband said "he saw nothing wrong in his wife's drinking champagne if she wanted," and Holm picked up on the theme. "I like a good time, particularly champagne," she said.[54] She was lucky to have as her foe Avery Brundage, president of the American Olympic Committee, who was infamous for slandering those who wanted the United States to boycott the Nazi Olympics as "un-American" spreaders of "malicious propaganda."[55] A Brooklyn newspaper columnist saw the Holm incident as another aspect of Brundage's fascist sympathies and alleged that he "implanted in the other members of the [Olympic] committee a pretty forceful impatience with the haphazard way in which Americans go about doing, frequently, what they please without asking any fuehrer's permission."[56] Holm pleaded for readmission to the team but could not keep a note of umbrage out of her apology: "I know I have been drinking too much and I'm all wrong. . . . I've been night-clubbing and having a good time for the last three years, always doing as I pleased, going where I liked, drinking what I wanted and when I wanted."[57] Holm stayed in Germany to watch the Olympics from the sidelines and returned home on August 20, claiming, "'I'll never be happy again.'"[58] But she displayed no indolence or other sign of depression. Instead, she and her husband fashioned a nightclub act that leveraged her notoriety, but by October poor reviews and the example of other amateur swimmers had her looking to go pro and join Snyder's swimming shows. Rose intervened and made sure he got her.[59] He called up her agent, "Blinky" Lou Irwin, met with her at his New York office and again in Cleveland, where she and Jarrett performed in January, and sold her on his vision for the Aquacade.[60] "There had been water shows before," he said, "but they were poorly routined and poorly rehearsed, and were raggedly disciplined. . . . The shows consisted mainly of stunts and diving exhibitions. This was not to be an exhibition. This was to be a show, an elaborate and lovely musical revue but with songs and dances in the water."[61] A history of the sport acknowledges that Rose was "the showman who correctly read the signs of change. He recognized that if a swimming show was reasonably priced and [according to Rose] had 'the sheen, the fun, the zest and romance of a Ziegfeld musical . . . millions, not thousands, would throng to see it.'"[62]

KNOCKING OVER PYRAMIDS

Rose's show business vision and money brought Holm onboard, but it was a close call. Sam Snyder's swimming outfit claimed that in October 1936 Holm made a verbal agreement to join its act for $1,250 a week. In December a judge ruled that this was not a contract and that she was free to do as she liked. In February 1937 she signed a written contract with Rose for a weekly salary of $2,000.[63] Their romance began in the spring, when Aquacade rehearsals put them side by side.

Eleanor Holm was quite a change from Fanny Brice. At age twenty-three, the swimmer was fourteen years younger than Rose instead of eight years older, and at five feet, two inches, was roughly the same height as Rose, rather than several inches taller. That Holm was a Catholic and her popular appeal based on her sleek sexual allure and not on a comedy of awkwardness made the young athlete as far from a maternal figure as Rose could hope to find. Other differences were less agreeable. Brice was intelligent and insightful. She told an interviewer, "Comics are the philosophers of the stage, because they can't accept a thing on the surface, they have to look behind it."[64] Such awareness made her interest in art a natural outgrowth of her taste and discernment, which Rose studied. There was not much he could learn from Holm. A reporter characterized her taste in furniture and art as "Flatbush triumphant," and when she was drunk, her antisemitism surfaced and she called Rose a "dirty Jew."[65] Given that tendency, the timing of their match could not have been worse. The two crossed paths just as Rose began to put his thumb on the Jewish side of the scale to balance the energy he spent on his businesses and his people. When New York's Mayor La Guardia suggested in March 1937 that the coming World's Fair include a "chamber of horrors" to document Germany's antisemitic outrages, Rose volunteered to produce it. He "deposited $5,000 as earnest money" to create a five-acre exhibit on Nazi "concentration camps, the blood purge, book burnings, etc."[66] The fair rejected the proposal, but as the world Jewish situation became more dire Rose's devotion to Jewish causes grew, and in 1949 when he became interested in doing promotional work for the new state of Israel, Holm resolved to derail the project.[67]

But in 1937 Rose was smitten with her, and the photographic record of their courtship confirms that she felt the same. Holm was the image of exuberance and pride as she gazed on Rose with wonder. Though not Brice's intellectual equal, she was clever enough to admire Rose's smarts. "He has one of the most amazing minds I've ever seen," she said.[68] He also had money, and that mattered greatly. Unlike Brice, Holm did not have her own fortune or a career that might prove lucrative. Nevertheless, she had a "love of cash," and after they married, Rose satisfied that love. He had his secretary prepare for Holm "a large straw basket, doll it up with ribbons and pretty paper, then stuff it full of crinkled ten dollar bills."[69] Riches were an important element of their relationship from the start. Rose wooed her with "images of their future life together—moonlight on the Ganges, staying at the Shepherd Hotel in Cairo, living in a penthouse with the blue sky around them. Luxury, voluptuousness, foreign lands, eternal variety, continual excitement, jewelry, furs."[70] To Rose, a proposal was a proposal, and making a pitch for a marriage was not much different than making one for business. "Billy was a salesman right from the start," said a friend. "All the way. A certain type. Talk talk talk. Talk you out of your eye teeth."[71] Except this was no act. Rose was crazy about Holm. One minute he was a formidable player and the next he was a bowl of mush.

Rose was riding high. He had a contract in his pocket to produce a second fair in Texas for $50,000 and another for an Aquacade in Cleveland that promised him $100,000.[72] Those paydays, combined with the $100,000 he had earned in Texas the previous summer, amounted to very big money in 1937, and it was during this first flush time that the confident, powerful, brutal, and charming Billy Rose fully emerged, the one who had great faith in people ("If you thought you could do it, Billy did. This is a marvelous thing"[73]); was merciless to underlings ("If he thought you were broke that would kill you"[74]); flaunted eccentric habits such as always cadging but never buying cigarettes ("He said, 'You know I never buy cigarettes.' At the time it seemed logical"[75]); and greeted people at home wearing pajamas, a silk robe, and slippers embroidered with his initials, a getup he even wore when he went "next-door [to the] Chinese restaurant for a snack. One could often find him there, conversing with friends in evening dress, Billy in his comfortable silk dressing gown, his little feet sockless in Moroccan slippers."[76]

Sometimes there was nothing under that dressing gown. "He wore a robe at his desk. I never saw my husband as naked as I saw him," Schrank said. "When he turned to answer the phone the robe would open."[77] And he deployed multiple desk phones until he was "strangled in cords in the manner of Laocoön and the serpents."[78] This was the Rose who "when he walked he bounced." "Billy walked like a guy swimming. With his arms swinging. His chest up," and "despite the $140 suits and the $45 shoes he wore, he looked like an undersized motion-picture gangster."[79] On this all agreed. "He looked tough, he looked formidable."[80] He was a "manly man, although he was small. One was impressed with his guts."[81] "I was a little afraid of him," said another.[82] All these traits are apparent in a news photograph from the time Rose met Holm. He stares ahead steadily, calmly, and unsmilingly, wearing a look somewhere between a quiet challenge and an implied threat. His thick head of dark hair is slicked back and what his sister Polly's friend called his "good looking dark eyes" seem, like their owner, to be able to do two things at once.[83] The right stares straight at the viewer; the left appears focused on a distant opportunity. He looked the part the news story announced: that in the field of show business Rose was Texas's "Man of the Year."[84] This mastery went out the window when it came to Eleanor Holm.

"Sugar plum candy mouth and things they hang on Christmas trees if you think you're contented you ought to see me." That was the opening rhyme of one of his telegrams to Holm. It was June 8, 1937, and Rose was in Fort Worth. He had to commute between that city and Cleveland to oversee his two summer productions, and when he was away he wrote Holm and longed for her. On June 11 it was, "I adore you," and on June 18, "Don't be scared about anything my love . . . as long as we love each other we can knock over pyramids." He sent similar telegrams on June 19 and June 20, when he summed up his condition: "Remember a lonesome guy on a prairie is nuts about you."[85]

In Cleveland, Holm starred in what an enormous sign announced as Billy Rose's Aquacade. She was "Aquabelle Number One," and her male lead, Johnny

Weissmuller, was "Aquadonis Number One."[86] In 1924 and 1928, Weissmuller won Olympic gold medals for swimming and since 1932 had starred in several popular Tarzan movies, including *Tarzan and His Mate,* which exhibits Weissmuller in a loincloth and a body double for Maureen O'Sullivan in nothing as they frolic underwater. The Aquacade borrowed titillating elements from that film and also stagecraft from Rose's Casa Mañana. Like the latter, the Aquacade's newly constructed amphitheater had a stage that moved forward and back on the water, except this time it truly floated, because the stage was not constructed on an artificial lagoon but on Lake Erie. The floating stage faced a theater on the mainland that accommodated seven thousand guests. When it was time for the customers to dance, engines propelled the stage toward the theater to create a dance floor, and when the Aquacade show began the stage retreated into the lake to create a natural pool. The set included sixty-five-foot-tall diving towers that divers and an "Aquaclown" employed "to run, bounce, and fall off five different diving boards."

The theme of the show was America's beaches, past and present. Scenes were set in Coney Island circa 1905, Miami, and elsewhere, and the opening number included eight lifeguards singing about the women they protect. As the men ogled "a swimsuited chorus of Aquadolls," they chanted, "We haven't yet been wet, although we follow the She / Eight handsome sons, sons of a beach resort are we!" Then Holm made her entrance fully covered in a mink coat. Overdressing was a strategy that soon paid off. She let the fur fall off her body and stood comparatively naked in her "shimmering silver swimsuit."[87] Then came a moment of palpable sexuality. "Eleanor put on her bathing cap. She put it on like a woman alone in front of a mirror," Rose said. This inattention to the audience created a voyeuristic atmosphere. The audience was an unobserved observer. "Then I sensed a tenseness in the audience," Rose continued. "It seemed more fascinated by this natural and intimate bit of business than all my manufactured hoopla."[88] Rose attributed the suspense to Holm's absentminded innocence. She forgot he asked her to dispense with the adjustment of the cap and just get on with the show. But the expert on female sex appeal was being coy. "When it comes to judging beauty, the wolf whistle is much more important than the tape measure," Rose wrote. "The experts tell you that a girl should have a 24 waist, 34 hips, and 34 you-know-whats. Arkus-malarkus! If she gives you goose bumps, hire her."[89] And Holm, constantly surrounded by men on the cruise to Europe, was also aware of the spell she cast. Beauty, vitality, youth, perfect fitness, and a taste for flirtation and rule breaking made her an unsettling force.

All this was standard Billy Rose fare, but in the summer of 1937 his Cleveland and Texas shows featured something new that revealed a politically aware Billy Rose. In both cities he produced finales based on *It Can't Happen Here,* a drama that on October 27, 1936, had debuted simultaneously in eighteen cities across the country as part of the Works Progress Administration's Federal Theatre Project. The show was adapted from the 1935 novel of the same title. The Sinclair Lewis book responded to the rise of fascist governments in Europe, and its ironic title warned that in fact it could happen here, in the United States. The government-sponsored 1936 stage version presented "democracy as a key feature of the American national community" and was "propaganda for democracy," with condemnations of book burnings and other aspects of fascist societies that then filled the newspapers.[90] However, the production was a straight play, without music, and it was wedded to a strict realism, with sets that offered a faithful rendering of daily life in ordinary homes. These mundane aspects, combined with a modest cast of only twenty-three in the English-language New York show (it was also performed in Yiddish), failed to deliver an emotional wallop or even "the ordinary excitement of good theatre," complained the *New York Times.* The play and its theme "ought to scare the daylights" out of its audience, the *Times* critic said.[91]

Rose understood the need to transport an audience, and he knew how to do it, but he decided not to frighten his audience with the prospect of fascism but instead elate it with a victory over fascism. His truncated version of *It Can't Happen Here* "blatantly mixed spectacle with politics," and he crowded the stage with "huge banners symbolizing fascism, nazism, and communism, [and] armies wearing black shirts, brown shirts and red shirts [that] clashed in mock battles." Cleveland's lake and Texas's lagoon swarmed with model battleships firing cannons, and patriotic, almost jingoistic lyrics stirred fervor.[92] "Let cannon thunder over the sea, / Let men be slaves who used to be free; / Let Hell appear, but never fear— / IT CAN'T HAPPEN HERE!" went one of the show's songs.[93] The magnificently theatrical culmination that saw American power vanquish evil, and good triumph over darkness, employed sets, costumes, and lighting to imbue the moment with a mood of redemption reminiscent of the religious. As a reporter described the scene, a woman dressed as a "Symbol of Peace" and dozens of the two hundred cast members ascended "countless chromium steps to the sky. As if this edifice were not tall enough, elevators shoot boys and girls still higher and higher. This is without a doubt, the most complete overpowering of the senses that a revue producer has ever devised."[94]

Rose explained his *It Can't Happen Here* productions as being "completely in the spirit of the times."[95] He was not more specific, but given the times and his recent interest in using the World's Fair to publicize Nazi atrocities, the comment was doubtless a reference to antisemitism at home and abroad. Though Rose's production did not explicitly address Jewish concerns, it matched the efforts of several Jewish playwrights in the thirties who created secular antifascist dramas as a way to voice concerns about Nazism without making it a Jewish issue, which they feared would exacerbate antisemitism. According to the theater historian Garrett Eisler, S. N. Behrman's 1934 *Rain from Heaven,* Harold Jacob Rome's 1937 *Pins and Needles,* and in 1939 Kaufman and Hart's *The American Way* and Hecht's *Let Freedom Ring* all "provided Jewish-American artists a significant opportunity to finally represent 'The Jewish Question'" without making explicit reference to Jews.[96] Rose's production adopted this model and incorporated other influences, too. In January 1937, the Jewish historical pageant *The Eternal Road* opened in New York at the Manhattan Opera House and achieved "a particular fusion of theatre and ritual that caused many a critic to talk about the performance as 'a religious experience.'"[97] This religious feeling was crucial to the emotional uplift Rose's work delivered, and the sacred atmosphere was appropriate to the underlying theme of saving millions of lives from the ravages of Nazism.

It Can't Happen Here was Rose's first participation in the Jewish effort to persuade America that Nazi Germany needed to be fought and defeated. He would work on several more antifascist productions that avoided explicitly Jewish themes, until news of the mass murder of the Jews made such timidity absurd.

nine

LET'S PLAY FAIR

Rose's triumphs in Fort Worth and Cleveland boosted his fame and his national celebrity. MGM sent a crew to Fort Worth to make a film short about him, and on July 19, 1937, the mass-circulation *Life* magazine introduced Rose to America, devoting two double-page spreads to the producer. The first showcased his Fort Worth and Cleveland productions and the second, titled "William Rosenberg, Shorthand Champion, Becomes Billy Rose, Mass Entertainer," illustrated his life with twelve photographs depicting him from infancy to the present.[1] He was a star.

There were, however, complications with both productions. Not everything went smoothly in Texas. The show included a staged adaptation of the 1936 novel *Gone with the Wind,* featuring a Southern plantation–style mansion with columns twenty-six feet tall that was one of the largest buildings ever created for live theater.[2] The act's only flaw was a legal one: in a replay of his *Jumbo* production, Rose never got permission from the author. Margaret Mitchell sued, Rose closed the Casa Mañana Revue on September 25 instead of October 16, and the loss of three weeks' revenue badly damaged expected profits. In Cleveland, the complications were personal. There were rumors of a Rose and Holm romance, but instead of hurting business, it delivered a boost. People wanted to see the young beauty who had caused Rose to jilt Brice, especially after Holm announced in July that she was divorcing her husband. Rose and Brice continued to deny he was involved with the swimmer, but their divorce record suggests that by July they had decided to split. The couple formally separated on June 10.[3]

Yet this does not clear up the female complications Rose indulged in after his mother's death. Brice may have left Rose in June not because of Holm but because he was having an affair with a Texas showgirl. His overlapping relationships with Brice, Holm, and the showgirl mirrored his taste for simultaneous productions in

Cleveland and Fort Worth. Rose's need for excitement, for stimulation—sexual, emotional, theatrical, and financial—suggests a Manhattanist hunger for a degree of action that approached combustion. Multitasking also may have distracted Rose from the loneliness many saw in him. "He was desperately lonely," said the talent agent Gloria Safier.[4] "A marvelous person, a brilliant and terribly lonely man," said Mercedes McCambridge.[5] The writer Doris Julian said that Rose was, according to his close friend the screenwriter Paul Osborn, "always very lonely," and that he hungered for the kind of closeness that "would take 25 years of marriage [to] . . . achieve. How can you get that when you marry a woman for a while."[6] Near the end of his life Rose said he knew why he had "been a failure as a husband," but he did not elaborate. It is doubtful he did know, because he quickly added that a woman "should be the sweet part of a man's life," without realizing the ideal was at odds with his lifelong infatuation with his powerful and anything-but-sweet mother. And he had an unusual way of calculating the price he paid for his failure to sustain a relationship. "One of the tough things about being on your own," he said, "is if you make a great score, if you suddenly make a great deal of money, you're in a heck of a spot if you've got no one to brag to." When he had such a day in the 1950s, he said, "I looked around the big empty house in which I was rattling around and there was no one to tell about it . . . there was no wife to tell it to."[7]

Revealingly, Rose felt the pains of loneliness most acutely when he could not boast about money. Its accumulation was paramount. It proved he was an American success and nothing like his father, and if he could not win the love of a woman that matched what he received from his mother, he could always lie and pretend he did. He could not do that when it came to money. A poor man cannot credibly assert he is rich. But the existence of love is harder to prove or disprove, and that allowed Rose to say that Brice bore him no ill feelings when he left her for Holm. "If you love her, there's nothing to discuss. Good luck, kid!" he reported her as having told him. "That's a lot of baloney!" Brice told a columnist. "All I told him straightaway was, 'Just pay me what you owe me—and SCRAM!!!'"[8]

TOO BROADWAYESQUE

After the Cleveland and Fort Worth shows closed in September 1937, Rose returned to New York to try and secure some sort of role in the 1939 World's

Fair. In 1936 he had received encouragement toward that end from Robert Moses and then discouragement from Earle Andrews. In August 1937 the wheel had turned again. John Krimsky, the fair's acting director of entertainment, liked Rose's Casa Mañana. "This attraction . . . was not only the main feature of the Fort Worth Exposition, but represented the only drawing power at the gate," Krimsky wrote his superiors.[9] To sustain such interest, Rose brought a version of the attraction to New York. In January 1938, he opened Billy Rose's Casa Mañana on the site of the defunct French Casino, one of the most spectacular of the theater-restaurants inspired by Rose's pioneering Casino de Paree, and from Casa's premises on Seventh Avenue at Fiftieth Street he launched a campaign to become a major player at the World's Fair.[10]

The path to that position was not clear. Despite Krimsky's backing, by the end of 1937 Rose had made little progress in cracking the fair. An October list of suggested names for a fair committee is notable for his absence. It included Rose's production team member John Murray Anderson, appreciators John Mason Brown and Damon Runyon, the *Jumbo* songwriters Rodgers and Hart, and its director George Abbott. An updated list on November 18 included Ben Hecht.[11] "Rose felt he was the only showman qualified to preside over the Fair's amusement section. He was also certain that those who financed this folly would rather put it to the torch than permit him to operate a shooting gallery in it," Maney wrote.[12] This was not quite accurate. The financiers were the public bondholders, and everyday citizens admired Rose's rise from poverty, enjoyed his wisecracks, and were impressed by his guts. An example of this appreciation is found in Philip Roth's novel *Portnoy's Complaint*, when Portnoy suffers through Rose stories as his Depression-era father begs him to follow in the footsteps of this sharp dealer. "My father plagued me throughout high school to enroll in the shorthand course," the narrator says. "'Alex, where would Billy Rose be today without his shorthand? Nowhere! So why do you *fight* me?'"[13]

But Portnoy's father and the millions like him were not running things, and the powers at the fair thought Rose "too inelegantly Broadwayesque for a great cultural rodeo. They didn't realize that they were snooting the cleverest of modern showmen," wrote a reporter whose adoration is more evidence of Rose's popularity.[14] However, as the reporter understood, what appealed to the public offended the fair's bigwigs. The problem was not just Rose's unrefined street-kid image, which had first proved to be an obstacle when as a teenager in Washington, DC, he talked too loud and wore the wrong clothes. The problem was that Rose's image correctly identified him as a booster of popular tastes, while the fair president, Grover Whalen, was part of what Koolhaas calls the "patronizing puritanism of the Urbanism of Good Intentions," personified in 1938 by Robert Moses, whose antiurban bias revealed itself in his "dreams of lawn-flanked parkways and trim tennis courts." Whalen and Moses were proponents of "the reformist urbanism of healthy activities" preferred by the elite, and enemies of "the hedonistic urbanism of pleasure" desired by the masses.[15] The latter was Rose's specialty.[16]

But fair officials wanted their stupendous project to offer attendees an idealistic, educational, and uplifting experience. Set on 1,200 acres in the borough of Queens, the fair prepared for its expected fifty million visitors two hundred pavilions built by sixty nations and dozens of corporate giants such as AT&T and General Motors. It promised a look at a better World of Tomorrow, the fair's theme. That optimism was hard to sustain, as fascism engulfed Europe and the world edged toward war. The determinedly cheerful theme smacked of a childish embrace of wholesomeness that could not accommodate adult realities. Evidence of this willful avoidance surfaced in two statements from the fair's president. "Forget 1938 with its bewildering succession of disturbing world events," said Whalen. "The year 1939 will be a GOOD Year!"[17] That masterpiece of naiveté made predictable his announcement that the fair "would contain no indecent exposure and that the amusement area . . . would be kept scrupulously 'clean.'"[18]

No show business professional could hear this without smirking, and even *Life* considered the proscription laughably "high-toned." Rose saw the fair as a typical if gargantuan show business production whose success required the display of scantily clad women. A history confirms he was right: the fair, a historian of striptease argues, "needed a midway full of naked women to make it run."[19] To make his case, Rose decided to produce a stage show at his new Casa Mañana nightclub titled *Let's Play Fair,* which he gambled would amuse and flatter Whalen and also excite the interest of New York's newspapers and the general public, as well as the city's more worldly sophisticates. His behind-the-scenes campaign had failed. It was time to apply public pressure. Rose outlined his realistic view of the fair in an invitation to *Let's Play Fair* that he telegrammed to Whalen. "My forthcoming production . . . will be [*Let's Play Fair*] and will in genial fashion satirize the preliminaries to our World's Fair. . . ." he wrote. "As a character in the sketchy story you are played by Oscar Shaw and if the show is as successful as I hope it to be I suspect it will be an excellent ad for the Fair. . . . Should you care to see the manuscript or drop in at rehearsal please let me know. . . . The theme of Let's Play Fair is that feminine beauty is the one sure crowd magnet."[20] Whalen was not amused. "I am overwhelmed with work as you can readily understand," he wrote Rose. "Best wishes for success."[21]

This was not enough to dissuade Rose. He was determined to produce an attraction at the fair and was certain his approach was the right one. When a reporter asked if he had confidence in *Let's Play Fair,* he replied, "Confidence? Why, I have a hundred grand of my own dough in it." Desperation played an equal role. After almost two years in Texas and Cleveland "he longed for New York," Maney wrote. "Only there could his thirst for recognition be slaked."[22] The fair was going to be the greatest exposition in American history and an unmatched opportunity for a showman to make a fortune. To miss it, to be relegated to the sidelines, to lose this chance as he approached forty might mean the end of the fame and affluence Rose had attained in the hinterlands and the beginning of a slide back into anonymity, irrelevance, and failure.

As he renovated the Casa Mañana to include a stage that not only revolved and thrust forward and back but also elevated, Rose launched a public relations blitz to spark advance coverage of *Let's Play Fair.* Newspaper headlines included, "Billy Rose to Spoof Coming World's Fair," and the *Herald Tribune* ran a large cartoon entitled, "In Advance of Billy Rose's 'Let's Play Fair,' at Casa Mañana," which depicted scenes from the upcoming show, including one in which the Whalen character is delighted by a comic sketch highlighting the attractions of female beauty. Rose also dispatched a winningly low-key and self-deprecating telegram to desired guests: "If you enjoyed my shenanigans in the past and want to be part of an exciting opening night may I suggest premiere of Casa Mañana formerly French Casino Tuesday January 18. Lavish girl show will genially satirize New York World's Fair."[23]

It all worked. Rose outmaneuvered Whalen. On January 18, 1938, despite his initial rebuff, the fair's president attended the opening night of *Let's Play Fair* at Billy Rose's Casa Mañana. He could hardly refuse, as his absence would have been more newsworthy than his attendance. Rose's press antics and personal invitations cajoled a crowd of celebrities to the show's premiere performance. An extra attraction for the moneyed set was a guarantee that they would not be pestered by hoi polloi. The opening-night ticket price of ten dollars assured the bigwigs that they would be in exclusive company. Edward G. Robinson was there, and so was former mayor Jimmy Walker, the theater power J. J. Shubert, the celebrated boxing champ Barney Ross, the humorist Robert Benchley, and *Jumbo*'s lyricist Lorenz Hart. Amon Carter traveled from Texas to see the show. The society columnist and hostess Elsa Maxwell was among the "good-sized slice of Park Avenue" that arrived, including "Mrs. William Randolph Hearst, protected against the cold with a very fine chinchilla cape."[24]

The two-act "revusical" rested on the slim story of a talent scout "roaming the world in search of novelties" for the World's Fair and then presenting his discoveries from "Paris, Ethiopia, Salzburg, Shangri-La," and other locales to Whalen, played by Oscar Shaw, an actor then popular in musical comedies. With a nod to George Jessel's Professor Labermacher sketch, Rose's show also featured an actor playing the role of "a professor of anatomy hot to convince the Grover Whalen character that displaying women's bodies would bring in big bucks." The professor touts the drawing power of featured stripper Sally Rand by noting that she made the Chicago fair a success: "'Without her hips . . . it would have been a bust.' Double entendres were not in short supply. When a nearly naked Rand danced with a globe the professor observed, "Here we have a bit of astronomy . . . showing that when a globe passes before a heavenly body, we have an eclipse of the moon."[25]

Such comedy had the advantage of being honest about sexual attraction and pleasure, and it followed the formula prominent writers had recently outlined in defense of sexual entertainment. "Personally, I like a show with a certain amount of good, clean dirt in it, just as I like a racy story if it is not too smutty, and is funny, too. But I don't like a show which is all rough stuff and nothing else," wrote a *Stage* magazine contributor in May 1935.[26] In March 1936, the poet E. E. Cummings dared *Stage* readers to say they did not enjoy such entertainment as much as he did. "And, lo! here, in its full flower, was strip-teasing," he wrote of a burlesque show recommended by the novelist John Dos Passos. "The essence of the Irving Place burlesque was, is, and I hope will continue to be, *Das Ewig-weibliche* [the eternal feminine]—alias Miss June St. Clare . . . and if you think I exaggerate, one of two things is a fact. Either you haven't seen her, or you didn't deserve to."[27] In addition to the nude enticements, Rose produced his show per his "fabulous reputation by staging [a] lavish, opulent, eye-aweing, glittering and expensive looking entertainment." And crucially for Rose's goal, the main point was not lost in the fanfare. As a newspaper headline the next day explained, "Billy Rose Opens Night Club, Showing Whalen How to Spend Millions on Fair."[28]

Let's Play Fair was a turning point but not a victory. Two weeks later on February 4 Rose telegrammed Whalen again: "I've recently been approached by members of your organization relative to taking space in the amusement section of the fair. I have given such a project careful consideration and have evolved a plan of entertainment of such major proportions and involving so great an investment that I do not propose to discuss it with anyone of less importance than yourself."[29] The fast-talking promoter was back. Modulating his tone to suit nonboisterous occasions was always a struggle, and one of the greatest payoffs of Rose's future wealth was relief from the need to try. When Rose became rich he could use rough language in fine company and the fine company had to sit and take it. But now such a telegram was a liability. It was also nonsense. Rose had no plan.

Whalen did not meet with him, but George McCaffrey, the fair's technical adviser, did, and he learned that Rose considered a plan a kind of reward. As McCaffrey wrote Whalen, "The nature of the attractions has not yet taken form and cannot be developed until Billy Rose receives from the Corporation some indication that the Fair Corporation wants his attractions sufficiently to offer special terms and conditions and financial help not granted to other concessionaires. . . . Obviously the Fair Corporation could not offer such inducements without definite knowledge of the attractions so the question goes around a circle." In addition, McCaffrey reviewed the financial statements for Rose's *Jumbo*, Casa Mañana, and Cleveland Aquacade and found that although they had "fair drawing power" they did not make money for their backers. Fortunately for Rose, McCaffrey realized that the fair's New York State Amphitheatre was the perfect venue for one of Rose's popular but money-gobbling productions. It would not cost the fair or Rose anything to build; the state footed the $1.6 million construction bill. And because of its great size the Amphitheatre would probably not house a profitable operation of any kind, so the fair would not be sacrificing a lucrative space to lure Rose. Finally, McCaffrey said, "under the proposed agreement with the State, half of any net profits realized [by the fair] from the amphitheatre operation would have to be paid over to the State in any event."[30] In other words, the fair had little to lose by giving it to Rose.

Rose could not take yes for an answer. The pugnacious slum kid did not know when to put down his dukes. He was in the tricky position of being a success but not, as it were, a made man. It was a delicate situation that called for equal parts nerve and tact. Instead, Rose made the young punk's mistake of annoying his admiring but formidable superiors. When fair officials met with him again on April 1 he surprised everyone by threatening to open "Billy Rose's World's Fair on Broadway" to compete with the fair. In May, he insisted that any agreement "had to be arranged so that he would have a chance to make 'a killing.'"[31] At this point, Earle Andrews started talks with Lee Shubert. Was Shubert interested in the fair's State Amphitheatre? Shubert was, and on May 14 he submitted a two-page offer to produce "a musical production of the spectacle type" there. Two weeks later the Shubert organization was so eager to close the deal that it offered to withdraw one of its conditions if that would accelerate the process. This seems to have brought Rose to his senses. On June 7, 1938, Andrews composed a brief memo to John Krimsky. "The Corporation," he said, "has decided to go ahead with the contract of Billy Rose."[32]

UNHOLY ZEST

After Rose nailed down the fair, he devoted little thought to what he might produce there. That detail could wait. His contract gave him until December 1 to submit a proposal and until January 15, 1939, to deposit $100,000 in escrow to guarantee the funding of an attraction.[33] This gave Rose a lot of latitude, which the fair came to regret. As one of Rose's business partners explained, "Most people haggle in the beginning. But Billy was not that way. He haggles afterwards! . . . And once you're hooked, there's no way out."[34] Rose did haggle before he signed the fair contract, but the experience seems to have taught him that the best approach was to sign the contract and then drive his partners up a wall. That is what he did after signing with the fair. Whalen announced the Rose agreement on July 1 and told the press Rose planned "a musical extravaganza with a cast of 1,000" for a show with "a modern American theme . . . [that] will picture contemporary life or foreshadow the future."[35] This idea did not represent an investment of Rose's thought and imagination. It represented trouble. As with *Jumbo* and the *Gone with the Wind* productions, the notion belonged to someone else. "When I talked with Mr. Rose he used, in describing his spectacle, word for word what I had submitted to the Fair Corporation as our idea of the American Cavalcade," reported Messmore Kendall, president general of the National Society of the Sons of the American Revolution.[36] Kendall complained to Whalen but received no response.

If Whalen was looking into it, he may have been delayed by an inability to reach Rose, who was busy. In July, his Casa Mañana nightclub demanded his attention and benefited from it with a hit show starring Jimmy Durante, who, "dynamic as ever," according to *Variety*, "hurls telephones and epithets at Vincent Lopez and his musicians, scatters sheet music right and left, mauls a piano and bullyrags the grinning waiters and captains."[37] It was not much of a leap from that to surrealism, and on July 14 when the fair ran into a problem with Salvador Dalí's representatives regarding how to split the receipts of Dalí's "Dream of Venus" attraction, it turned out the problem was Rose. "It has developed that [the architect I. Woodner Silverman and the art gallery owner Julien Levy] have been talking to Billy Rose," a memo explained. "And it seems that he has suggested that 20% [of the gross receipts paid by the Dalí attraction to the fair] is too high, and that if they can't get this reduced that [Rose] can 'go to the top and get it.'"[38] Other unpleasant surprises were forthcoming. Word got around that Rose planned to place a Casa Mañana–type attraction in the fair's Amusement Area, where the "class" as opposed to "mass" attraction "would be fatal" to the draw required to fill adjacent shows. Ironically, it was now the fair that wanted shows with mass appeal. There was no need to worry, Rose wrote Whalen. He planned a cowboy-themed Pioneer Village that would attract crowds that would also patronize neighboring shows.[39]

This plan lasted a month. By September, Rose had changed his mind. Now he proposed new ideas for three Amusement Area sites. On one he wanted to build a "Barbary Coast" show that would feature "the San Francisco earthquake and fire every fifteen minutes." On another would be "Killers of the Deep," featuring a man fighting a shark, and the third site "would consist of a combination of girl show and aquacade, the girl show being emphasized at night, and the [swimming] tank activities being emphasized during the afternoon hours, such stars as Eleanor Holm and Johnny Weissmuller taking part in the aquacade show."[40] By now the fair's staff understood that in Rose it faced an unpredictable partner, and regarding Rose's aquacade proposal noted that "it is highly speculative as to whether or not this show will develop into the negotiation stage with the Fair Corporation."[41]

This was Rose's first mention of an aquacade for the fair, and if it was held in the Amusement Area, it was not clear what he would do with the Amphitheatre. But even his seven-track mind could not make room for that problem, because in October he dreamed up two new projects. In the space of a week, he announced he was going to open a second nightclub, a temple of nostalgia called

Billy Rose's Diamond Horseshoe, and, at the opposite end of the political and artistic spectrum, produce *No for an Answer* by Marc Blitzstein, composer and librettist of the 1937 left-wing theatrical sensation *The Cradle Will Rock*.[42] His Casa Mañana nightclub, meanwhile, was still in operation, and in October Rose opened a new show there called "Streamlined Varieties" that, the *Times* cheered, proved Rose "continues to be Broadway's most astonishing phenomenon. For Mr. R. is not only a little man with a fat purse (which accounts for some of the magic) but he is also an impresario bursting with big ideas and he knows a good act when he sees it."[43] Before the month was out, Rose's lawyers notified Brice that he would not contest her suit for a divorce, which meant he did not have to appear in Los Angeles Superior Court on October 27. Given his schedule, he could hardly have squeezed it in.[44]

All this was more evidence of the incessant industriousness that left Rose no time for introspection or reflection, which might have been its chief benefit. Though he was proud of the fact that he drank no alcohol, he nevertheless resembled someone addicted to stimulants. Project juggling thrilled him. It excited his energies and delivered him a manic high. As he excitedly wrote Hecht about another jammed schedule, "This feels like the old Texas days—working around the clock," a situation he comically asserted was not his doing. "Don't ask me how this all happened—my answer would be that I got sucked into it and that answer would be a God damned lie."[45] He met overwhelming challenges "with unholy zest," wrote the *Times*. "Unholy zest? Even avidity!"[46]

Still, even Rose had his limits, and the multiple projects combined with delayed plans for the Amphitheatre could not go on much longer. Rose hired Lincoln Dickey of the Cleveland Great Lakes Exposition to run his World's Fair operation so he could meet the December 1 deadline for a synopsis of his plan and also have time to build out the Diamond Horseshoe. To delegate required a decision, and on November 14 Whalen received the welcome news that Rose was "beginning to see [the] light."[47] Two days later he and the fair agreed to a contract. The fair received Rose's check for $60,000 to fund construction of an Amphitheatre swimming pool—partial payment of the required $100,000. Rose agreed "not to produce an historical pageant" there. In return, Whalen conceded to Rose's demand that the aquacade face no competition, so the fair barred from the Amusement Area "any other Musical Comedy, Review [*sic*] or Girl Extravaganza" seating more than 1,500 spectators. To give Rose flexibility, the contract did not mention the word "aquacade," but it was clear to fair officials that Rose would produce "an Aquacade similar to the Cleveland show."[48] Press coverage ended the speculation. A November 17 headline announced, "Eleanor Holm to Swim at Fair in $60,000 Billy Rose Aquacade."[49]

GOYIM NACHES

By this time, Rose had introduced Murray Anderson to the future home of Billy Rose's Diamond Horseshoe, where the director saw a "dreary cellar room in the Hotel Paramount on West 46th Street. . . . The room at first glance looked like a place where the Count of Monte Cristo might have been glad to dig himself out of, but Billy was right."[50] When it came to mass entertainment, Rose was nearly always right. History's verdict is that Rose was the operator "who perhaps understood popular entertainment better than anyone else in his time."[51] Rose's contemporaries agreed. "It is likely that no more dynamic combination of artist, psychologist, businessman and salesman has ever struck Broadway," said one.[52] In 1934, his theater-restaurants Casino de Paree and Billy Rose's Music Hall had immersed patrons in a whirling, chaotic atmosphere that amplified the quick pulse of New York and combined, in those first months after Prohibition's repeal, the modest prices required by the Depression with the atmosphere of "old Broadway [that] was carefree, what the hell."[53] In 1938, the watchword was still value, but the appetite for a wild atmosphere had leveled off. Perhaps, like *Gatsby*'s Nick Carraway, the public had tired of "riotous excursions."[54] They desired limits and the assurance that they would not be exploited.

This guarantee was especially important to the lucrative tourist and convention market that "Rose was probably the most aggressive in pursuing." At Casa Mañana he "displayed cards on every table promising honest value for the money . . . [and] claimed the Casa was dedicated to the interests of 'Mr. Forgotten Man (the guy who pays the check).'" Such assurances allegedly dampened spontaneity. Rose "commercialized the Broadway nightclub into an institution more palatable to larger audiences" and made it "the forerunner of the Las Vegas show with the patrons more an audience than participants," one historian observes. Another demerit was that Rose's new tourist-oriented nightclubs "depicted but did not provide the intense excitement of the big city." Yet if this new model represented a loss of the authenticity enjoyed by the elite in "intimate urban" hideaways, it was a boon to a middle class hungry for diversion and fun. Short of money and time, Rose's audience wanted a sure thing on its night out, and the informality of the Diamond Horseshoe allowed this crowd to enjoy itself without restraint, offering an acceptable substitute for the "action and excitement" available to a more select group of nightclubbers.[55] "Some of us got up on our chairs and yelled and cheered" at a Diamond Horseshoe show featuring silent film stars, recalled the columnist Louis Sobol.[56] Rose was "the key figure of the new Broadway," as *Literary Digest* put it in 1934.[57] He "refined the 'volume' concept to an art form," and in early 1939 his Casa Mañana and Diamond Horseshoe clubs "were the two most successful theatre-restaurants on Broadway."[58]

The new Diamond Horseshoe competed with Rose's Casa Mañana, and the latter closed in May 1939. The former stayed in business for twelve years and became a legend. It was derided as a "bedlam, basement bordello," mocked as an "overblown nightclub [where] the women guests dressed up like sequined handbags," and given its due as what "may have been the greatest, gaudiest nightclub in the world."[59] It was also the object of the most withering Jewish insult. The Diamond Horseshoe "is exactly what we used to call 'Gojim-Naches,'" émigré composer Kurt Weill wrote his wife, Lotte Lenya, using a Yiddish term "to mean that this kind of fun was so stupid that only a 'goy' might enjoy it."[60] American Jewish culture had experienced a sea change that made it unintelligible to European Jewish intellectuals and artists, and Rose was an agent and emblem of that change. As Saul Bellow joked about another European Jew who never understood the "American-Jewish contingent," Weill "had the misfortune to be educated in Germany."[61]

Rose's schooling was different, and his Diamond Horseshoe proved he was an adept pupil, because his club "hint[ed] at one of the inescapable conditions of American Jewish culture: its bias toward mass entertainment."[62] This made Rose the mirror image of Weill, and it may have seemed to Weill that Rose, as Bellow wrote of one fictional character in *Humboldt's Gift,* had given his "Russian Jewish brains away out of patriotism" and become "a self-made ignoramus and a true American."[63] This was untrue, but Rose was still insecurely and haltingly feeling his way toward an identity that could pledge allegiance both to his brash and powerful native land and to his despised but doughty Jewish brethren. Without knowing it, he had already laid important groundwork. Because in America "vulgarity is not as destructive to an artist as snobbery," the more elevated achievements of postwar Jewish literature and culture derived their sensibility from Rose's earthy and informal world, "the vaudeville theaters, music halls, and burlesque houses."[64]

Descendants seeking inspiration from such an illustrious ancestor can start with Rose's take on schnitzel, the Austrian breaded and fried veal cutlet. For Rose, a schnitzel was entertainment served up right, plain and popular. "It's an obvious schnitzel—all black and white—no subtlety," was his seal of approval. The Diamond Horseshoe had schnitzel all over the place, such as the loud musical commotion known as a fanfare. "Fanfares are a specialty of the Horseshoe," Rose said. "A fanfare says lay down your knife and fork, here comes the Indians." Another schnitzel was the garishly decorated Horseshoe interior done up, he said, like "most of the great cafes of the world . . . painted a bright red, like the cafes in Roumania and Hungary. That rich Roumanian red."[65] Rose knew what he was doing. "You have to keep in mind that 600 people are wrestling with a five course dinner. . . . I got to figure out how to give them the illusion of a good time. A big wacky enterprise like this I got carefully figured out like a chess gambit. My success is no accident. It is the result of very careful preparation."[66]

To ensure a successful opening night, Rose advertised the club in the New York papers with a nearly three-hundred-word letter to the public that positioned him as a regular Joe with bad grammar at odds with the "Broadway smart boys (anyone with a camel-hair coat and a buck and a quarter)." They had told him that with the Casa Mañana, "I'd lose my shirt," and they were wrong, Rose boasted. (There is no evidence anyone said this.) Now they were at it again. "The same smart guys with the same camel-hair coats (a little less hair on them now) tell me that times are bad—the location is on the wrong side of Broadway—and that I'm wacky if I think I can make any money selling a good dinner (or supper)—a lavish John Murray Anderson production—'name' dance orchestras—plus the most glamorous room in town—ALL for a ONE DOLLAR MINIMUM. So the boys say—but fortunately I don't hear so good." Other ads sought to beguile admirers and detractors with a pledge "to take care of all who come to my opening nights (those who come to see me 'hit,' and those who want to see me 'miss')."[67]

In a move that signaled that Jews were likely to be overrepresented at the Diamond Horseshoe, Rose opened the club on Christmas night, December 25, 1938, and any in the crowd who showed up to witness him strike out were disappointed.[68] The *Times* called the club "the most zestful, gorgeous and lovable pleasure palace in town," and *Variety* and *Billboard* vouched that Rose "has a winner."[69] "The Diamond Horseshoe was luxurious," said Betsy Blair, who danced there in early 1940. "Near the entrance across the whole width of the room was a Gay Nineties-type bar, brass railed and mirrored. The walls were red velvet.

There were crystal chandeliers. At the far end was the proscenium stage, with a horseshoe-shaped runway coming out of it. The inside of the horseshoe lowered between shows to become a dance floor."[70] The club's name was borrowed from the choice inner ring of seats at the Metropolitan Opera House, and the design tipped a hat to its namesake, "with boxes flanking" the stage. Other influences were also obvious. "A huge bar fronts the room, and above the bar is the stage. It's a replica of Rose's Frontier" show from Fort Worth, *Variety* correctly noted.[71]

For Rose, originality was overrated. His new club was the perfection of the nostalgia formula he first attempted with *The Fatal Wedding,* reworked with "Small Time Cavalcade," and expanded into magnificence at Fort Worth's Casa Mañana. The Horseshoe's opening stage show was "The Turn of the Century," and it celebrated the great acts and personalities of New York's Gay Nineties, such as the early Ziegfeld star Anna Held, whose reputation owed much to Ziegfeld's racy and invented story that she bathed in milk. The revue also presented scenes set in that earlier day's glittering restaurants, Rector's and Delmonico's. Festivities started on the way down the two-flight staircase that led to the below-street-level club with walls enlivened by "Police Gazettes and other late 19th century literature," and inside the club, chandeliers, the western-style Silver Dollar bar, and the nude attraction of a beauty preparing to take a milk bath evoked the world of New York's grandest turn-of-the-century pop figure: "Diamond Jim Brady, that Paul Bunyan of playboys," wrote the *Times.* "How he would have loved the Diamond Horseshoe!"[72]

In addition to being Rose's most polished example of nostalgia, the Horseshoe was also his most successful attempt to make a profit in the nightclub business. He was no longer a hired manager or producer on a salary provided by gangster or millionaire or civic backers, and so he had to figure out the business side of show business. "It took me two years on the midways at fairs," he said, "to analyze why my production of 'Jumbo' failed ... and why Ziegfeld died owing $2,000,000 after he had produced 100 hits.... [He] didn't know how to count. And neither did I. I was weak on economics."[73] He figured it out. "After a lot of costly experience Billy learned how to be a businessman," reported *Fortune,* which in July 1939 published a study of his Diamond Horseshoe operation because it was a notable exception; as the magazine observed, "The night-club business ... has been making money for very few people but Rose."[74] He took what he had been doing right on the show side, with a theatrical staff comprising professional costume designers, lighting experts, scenic designers, and more, ruled by Murray

Anderson, and applied it to the business side, with the experienced specialist Ernest G. Borden, who had formerly managed the Hotel Ambassador, to run the kitchen, a key profit center. Keeping an eye on both Anderson and Borden was "a small, tight-lipped young CPA by the name of Charles Orenstein," who as manager of the Paramount Hotel introduced Rose to the Horseshoe space and probably the Horwath accounting system used to detect revenue diverted into employee pockets.

Despite attention to every penny, Rose did not skimp on quality. The Horseshoe "was the only club I was ever in where you got the best food obtainable at a reasonable price. No gyping [sic]," said one associate.[75] Rose's ferocious attention to detail was key. "He used to go up to his office and send someone downstairs to take food out and eat it and see how the food was. Not only the customers' food but what the help used to eat," said Sal Imbimbo, the dining captain. "He was hard but he was also a good boss." When a customer called the club to ask if anyone had found a wristwatch worth $1,500, "a broom boy, a Greek fellow, he said he's the one who found the watch," Imbimbo said. The watch's owner rewarded the boy with $5. "Billy Rose happened to be there and said, 'I had one honest man in this place and now you've made a thief out of him.' The man gave the boy $25."[76] On other fronts, Rose's promotion team targeted convention business, concessionaires paid handsomely for rights to the club's coat check and cigarette-girl franchises, bartenders poured drinks in "big-looking glasses" that held "not a drop more than an ounce and a quarter, instead of the usual one and a half or two ounces," and Rose hunted down and knocked off every unnecessary expense. One act wanted confetti but could not have it. Rose axed it after he discovered its true cost by factoring in the time required to sweep it up.

Brutality was also part of the mix. When Betsy Blair auditioned for the chorus, Murray Anderson was ready to toss the sixteen-year-old from the lineup. "She's got no tits—she looks twelve years old."

"Don't mention ages," responded Rose. "Yeah, no tits, but she has got the long stems." And those legs were perfect for a chorus line "advertised as 'Billy Rose's Long Stemmed American Beauties.'" (Rose loved to make wordplay out of his shortened last name.) Blair had another run-in with Anderson during rehearsals, when she made an error and he demanded, "Kneel down in front of me and apologize." To avert humiliation, she made "a sweeping gesture like a medieval courtier" and said, "I'm sorry, Sire."[77]

Public shaming was common. When a woman auditioned as a dancer, Imbimbo remembered, Rose said, "'Stand over there. Pull your dress up.' She pulls it up a bit. 'Come, come, show me what you got there.' She had bad legs. There's a lot of girls around. He said, 'You go home and get yourself a man and have six children. Show business isn't for you.'"[78] A young Gene Kelly choreographed a football-themed dance number. Rose nixed it, saying, "They don't come to the Diamond Horseshoe to see a fucking ballet." And when Blair wanted to leave the club for a part in a Broadway show Rose threatened her with the classic, "You'll never work on Broadway. I can stop you." She did, and he could not.

But Rose was mercurial. One minute he was a terror, the next beneficent. After a young dancer tripped and fell in the middle of a show, she was fired. "But Rose had me come in once a week and I had a complete meal and it was practically saving my life, frankly, because I didn't have anything to eat," said Dorothy Rice Chase. "So I didn't starve to death. I could order anything I wanted. It was a wonderful gesture to do. He understood my situation. In his way he did look after me. I admired him. He was very decent in his way."[79]

The Diamond Horseshoe was a success on all counts. It generated torrents of publicity, including a profile of Rose in the *New York Times* Sunday magazine section, and it was a hit with critics, popular with the public, and "the most profitable pre–Las Vegas nightclub in American history."[80]

Conveniently, the club closed at around two in the morning, allowing Rose to then sit in front of a "titanic sandwich" at Lindy's and shoot the breeze with "producers, columnists, booking agents, [and] actors" such as Jed Harris, Jake Shubert, Lou Holtz, and Irving Berlin.[81] "Here you find Rose at his best. He is amusing and gay. He cracks wise with the very best of them," reported *Fortune*.[82] "He became rich and famous producing spectacles. But for his own entertainment he demanded small talk," said the sportswriter Jimmy Cannon.[83]

If he got to sleep by four and woke before noon, he still had a good part of the day to oversee the Aquacade.

PERSONALITY POWER

"Many thanks for your note calling attention to the enthusiastic press notices of Billy Rose's show. With this sendoff he should continue to do a very fine business. More power to him and to the Fair!"[84]

The May 8 note from George McCaffrey to Whalen was part of an exhale of relief that many in fair management felt after Billy Rose's Aquacade officially debuted on May 4, 1939, a few days after the fair's April 30 opening, and immediately won over the press and the public. Employing the Cleveland Aquacade's beaches-of-yesteryear theme and its stars, Holm and Weissmuller, the cast of more than two hundred swimmers and stage-based dancers, live band and the Fred Waring glee club, solo crooners, and a slapstick comedy team delivered a sixty-five-minute show that fulfilled Rose's vision of popular entertainment. "It's a gigantic show that the diminutive Rose has devised. And it's a vision of loveliness, color and lights," read a typically enthusiastic review.[85]

As was the case with many of Rose's triumphs, from Casino de Paree to *Jumbo* to the Casa Mañana in Texas, the Aquacade combined elements from so many genres that it required some explanation. The *New York Journal American* did its best: "Last night in the huge Marine Amphitheatre at the World's Fair, [Rose] gave New York its first sight of a seagoing musical comedy, and New York found it a brilliant show, beautifully clothed and unclothed, part revue, part sports carnival, part floating ballet, and altogether spectacular."[86] Brooks Atkinson at the *Times* agreed that "as usual, Aquabeau Rose has thought of everything, including the moon supplied by courtesy of celestial providence, and the 'Aquacade' ought to be good Summer entertainment in any man's town with or without a World's Fair to serve as bazaar and background."[87] In May, the *New Yorker* also recommended it. "There is a sort of cock eyed majesty in every project undertaken by Billy Rose, and the Aquacade is no exception. As far as I can see, it has everything—beauty, skill, size, humor, music, and, these chilly nights, a strong undertone of muted suffering. Of all the exhibits at the Fair, it is the one you are most likely to report to your grandson."[88] A month later, another writer for the weekly let herself go and confessed that the Aquacade "seems to get better every time I see it. This is probably why more and more people are practically living in the New York State Amphitheatre."[89] The business-minded *Variety* appreciated other aspects. Tickets priced at $0.25 for children and from $0.40 to $1.10 for adults made it "a super-bargain" facilitated by the promise of volume sales at the ten-thousand-seat venue. The entertainment trade deployed the shorthand argot of Broadway to rapidly tally Rose's likely take. "The show needs $30,000 weekly to break; can hit a phenomenal $150,000 weekly gross if sold out three shows a day, which Rose thinks will happen more than once during July and August," *Variety* said.[90]

The early signs were good. On its first weekend, the Aquacade attracted fifty thousand people, or more than 10 percent of the fair's attendees. In addition to a good show at low prices, Rose benefited from being denied permission to act on his worst instincts. On February 20, apparently stimulated by the previous day's news headline "Fair Decides to Go Girlie in Fun Zone," which celebrated the reversal of the previously prudish policy, Rose asked Whalen to "seriously consider the advisability of my engaging Sally Rand for the Aquacade. I think that this gesture will once and for all eliminate the impression that we are going to have a sissy midway."[91] Rose either interpreted the news coverage as bad publicity or wanted to convince Whalen it was not as good as it seemed, in order to win his point. In any event, the stripper found no place at the Aquacade, and Rose later took credit for this as an example of his shrewd showmanship. "You remember when the entertainment committee urged me to hire Sally Rand for the Aquacade," he said. "I felt she'd maybe attract a few hundred thousand—and keep out a few million. I felt I didn't want to flaunt Topic A. A hundred girls in wet bathing suits was sufficient sex. The Catholics put Jumbo on their white list, right on top and it taught me an important lesson. It's very important to get on the lists of these Catholic papers. It means thousands of mothers and their children will come to your show."[92]

Rose's insistence on always being right and his compulsion to fabricate falsehoods to create a biography without blemish—except in stories of roguish exploits that made him more colorful, stories that were also often invented—reveal him to be a publicity event in his own right. This need for notoriety was a common affliction. As Liebling wrote about the third-string show business operators of the day, they liked "to be thought of as characters. 'He is a real character,' they say with respect, of any fascinatingly repulsive acquaintance."[93] But the desire to be interesting, an object of attention and fascination, was not limited to these comic types. In the early twentieth century shifts in the culture favored the cultivation of personality as a way for the average citizen to rise above the crowd and be somebody. According to the historian Warren Susman, the goal became the development of a personality that was "*fascinating, stunning, attractive, magnetic, glowing, masterful, creative, dominant, forceful.*" Rose succeeded in having his name associated with all these traits. "The social role demanded of all in the new culture of personality was that of performer," Susman writes.[94] Rose was better at it than almost anyone, and his personality was as much a production as his theatricals were. Yet he never fell victim to the illusion he created. Rose remained a canny operator quick to take advantage of every new opportunity. This required knowing the difference between reality and fiction. His victories over the fair's management prove he was always alert to that distinction.

Two examples prove the point. On January 15, 1939, the deadline for Rose to deposit $100,000 in escrow came and went and on January 17, lacking the full amount, the frustrated fair management gave the Shuberts another shot at the Amphitheatre.[95] The two sides speedily agreed on terms. Still, the fair gave Rose one more week to set things right. He held out until the last minute and signed a new contract with the fair on January 23.[96] Incredibly, Rose won a better deal. The fair agreed to reimburse him the additional $160,000 he needed to spend fixing up the Amphitheatre by allowing him to collect this sum from ticket sales without the fair taking its 10 percent cut. Participation in revenues would begin only after Rose was recompensed the full amount. When the director of concessions, Maurice Mermey, learned of the new contract he wanted at least to reverse the fair's ban on other entertainments serving more than 1,500 viewers. He felt the condition handed Rose an unnecessary competitive advantage at the fair's expense and that the new contract was an opportunity to claw it back. But Rose was too quick for him. A handwritten reply to Mermey's memo admitted defeat: "Nothing can be done." The contract was signed.[97]

That victory seems to have encouraged Rose to haggle again at an even later date, when the fair had no way out. On April 18, Rose and the fair signed another contract, and this appears to be when the fair virtually waived its 10 percent participation in the Aquacade's gross revenue.[98] McCaffrey's note reminded Whalen that from the start Rose had wanted to deny the fair a slice of the gross. In the spring of 1939, he achieved his goal. According to the fair's financial director, by early September 1939, after four months in operation, the Aquacade's gross revenue was $1,761,611. The fair collected just $4,280, which it split with New York State, leaving only "$2,140.30 . . . net revenue of the Fair from the sale of admission tickets up to and including September 5, 1939."[99] The amount was so tiny because Rose managed to persuade the fair to forego participation in the first $1.6 million of Aquacade revenues.[100]

But though Rose shortchanged the fair, he delivered full value to his audience. He produced a wonderful and beautiful show. Agnes de Mille, the ballet dancer and choreographer of *Oklahoma!* and *Carousel* and no fan of Rose's, deemed the Aquacade swimmers "a gorgeous sight to behold."[101] More than five hundred people earned a salary from the Aquacade, and five million people, or about 20 percent of the fair's patrons, enjoyed it. "All God's chillun got forty cents,"

Rose joked about the reason for his show's success, but in fact the Aquacade's affordable entry price helped make the fair what Rose believed it should be: "a poor man's paradise!"[102]

BIGGEST MEDAL

Given his contract, Rose was set. The Aquacade grossed, on average, more than $100,000 a week. On good weeks during the summer months, when the Aquacade held four shows a day, the numbers would have been large enough to support the "crazy lurid figures [Rose told Eleanor about] in the car as they rode home together after the late show. '$96,500 this week for the bank.... I'm banking $103,000.49.... I'm putting away $99,000 this week."[103] Rose also collected "approximately $174,116" from the concessions and advertisements bought by the Pabst Brewing Company, Chesterfield Cigarettes, Gruen Watches, and Pepsi.[104]

"When the Aquacade opened, I knew I would soon be fantastically wealthy," Rose told an interviewer.[105] That confidence, if genuine, did not distract him from minding every expense. "When he built the Aquacade [*sic*] ... he whittled down $1.76 from a bill for 186,000," said one associate.[106] This obsessive focus on saving even tiny amounts suggests that Rose suffered a fear of poverty that no amount of money could assuage. Late in his life, when his wealth was in the tens of millions, Rose reviewed a bill from his personal chef and found he was charged twenty-five cents more than he should have been. "Billy sent me a full page typewritten letter to the effect that if he had managed his business like I did, where would he be? A pauper for sure," said Dione Lucas.[107] The fair was not nearly so careful with its expenditures. It was a financial bust. Instead of the expected fifty million visitors, it drew half that number and by summer flirted with bankruptcy. Desperate to increase admissions, the fair in September offered free entertainment away from the Amusement Area, which undercut concessionaires there. Double-crossed by the fair, they threatened "direct action" against management.[108] Rose's endless bargaining ensured he was protected against such betrayals. He knew fairs to be an economic swindle. "The fundamental fraud in connection with all fairs and expositions," he said, "is to sell bonds as if it were a genuine investment. They make you think you can get your money back. It is impossible to amortize the cost ... in the running time of the average fair."[109] Sure enough, the fair's bondholders were taken to the cleaners. The unions, businesses, and ordinary citizens that bought nearly $28 million in Fair Corporation bonds lost 60 percent of their money.[110] Nearly every amusement attraction also faced bankruptcy. Rose was a ruthless negotiator, and he did not play fair, but it was the high-minded fair managers who hurt the average citizen.

"Let's don't talk about how much money I made at the fair," Rose told columnist Earl Wilson. "It's bum taste this season."[111] Fascination with his wealth, however, could not be quelled. His 1939 income was astonishing. "Probably a new show business record is the more-than-$1,000,000 net profit cleared by Billy Rose on his Aquacade in 24 weeks at the N.Y. World's Fair, now that the final figures have been audited," *Variety* reported.[112] The exact figure was closer to $1.4 million, the equivalent of about $24 million today. This put him in very select company. A newspaper reported that in 1937, the most recent year of data then available, only forty-nine Americans made a million dollars. "If none of them [slipped] this year," Rose was number fifty. In addition, he "netted some $150,000 from his night club, the Diamond Horseshoe, so far this season."[113]

As befits a master showman, his riches arrived at a turning point in his life. In September 1939, Rose turned forty. On November 3, he received a judgment of divorce from Fanny Brice, and on the fourteenth he married Eleanor Holm in a New York judge's chambers in the presence of "forty newspaper photographers and reporters," allowing Rose to turn the ceremony into a publicity event. "You stage it and I'll restage it," Rose joked with the judge. Rose's sister Polly was there, identified as Polly Rose, having adopted her brother's last name, though she was married to a Charles Silverman. Rose's influence was clearly determinative, and following his mother's example he edged out his father, who did not attend the wedding.[114]

The Aquacade ran again at the World's Fair's second season in 1940 and also that year at San Francisco's Golden Gate Exposition, which was on the verge of licensing a rival show, until Rose sent Lincoln Dickey to San Francisco to deliver "all sorts of legal threats."[115] Rose called the Aquacade his "liquid slot machine" and he was not going to let anyone steal it.[116] In 1940, it again earned him more than $1 million in New York and $600,000 more in San Francisco, while the Diamond Horseshoe surely surpassed its first-year profits, as it made its way toward a 1943 performance that netted him $1.25 million. All told, Rose probably grossed $2 million in 1940, boosting his net worth to about $4 million.[117] By the time the New York and San Francisco fairs closed in the fall of 1940, the three productions of the Aquacade over two years on both coasts had been seen by "more than fifteen million people and had become the most popular world's fair entertainment of all time."[118]

For Rose, the acquisition of riches was the realization of a lifelong dream. It meant everything. When he later argued with Murray Anderson about a production at the Diamond Horseshoe he yelled, "I have been in this business for 30 years and I have five million dollars to show for it. What have you got?" Anderson replied, "One friend."[119] Rose was not chastened. He told Alan Jay Lerner, the gifted cocreator of *My Fair Lady* and *Camelot,* "Never argue with someone who has more money than you."[120] Wealth was the ultimate standard. "Money . . . is the diploma that says you won," Rose said. "It's the biggest gold medal of them all."[121]

Ten

SAVING KURT SCHWARZ

Rose's Aquacade and Diamond Horseshoe triumphs overlapped with the German invasion of Poland on September 1, 1939, which marked the start of World War II in Europe and the growing desperation of Europe's Jews. The latter was a crisis that had been on Rose's mind for some time. As early as January 20, 1938, he made it clear that he wanted to add to his nightclub and producer credentials the role of Jewish hero. "Disraeli," he replied, when asked to name his favorite historical character. "Disraeli was a gentleman, who got many chuckles out of life, and a great deal of satisfaction out of being a Hebrew who commanded the respect of the whole world."[1] Money was not the only gold medal that denoted victory. The chance to become a Jewish leader was also compelling and offered something money could not promise: the allure of historic immortality and, equally important to Rose, the chance to exceed his mother's achievements in the realm of Jewish service.

Rose's regard for Disraeli as an inspiring example almost certainly stemmed from a January 17, 1938, radio drama presentation of the well-known play *Disraeli*, first produced on Broadway in 1911 and made into a silent film in 1921 and a financially and critically successful talking picture in 1929. The radio play allowed Rose to see himself as a Disraeli, a Jew born at the bottom but "climbing, climbing on hands and knees with his eyes fixed on the summit," and one who seeks help from a wealthy Jewish banker, a parallel with Rose's cultivation of Bernard Baruch.[2] Rose and Baruch's reacquaintance in Europe in 1934 had by late 1936 begun to bear fruit. On October 23 of that year, Rose wrote Baruch about his success in Texas at the Frontier Centennial and greeted him as "Dear Bernie." Baruch's reply began, "My dear Billy."[3]

Rose's new conception of himself as someone ready to take on the role of Jewish historical figure represented an emulation of his mother's early twentieth-century adventures helping Jewish refugees flee Europe, and her recent death made it easier for him to advance into the Jewish territory she had formerly held. He had boasted that she had achieved a Jewish fame that was recognized at the time of her death by the crowds at her funeral and, crucially, newspaper coverage—the invented editorial about her in the *Forverts*. Now the Jews faced an even more terrible persecution than the Russian pogroms that had energized his mother, and so the fame and gratitude to be reaped from Jewish activism might be exponentially greater. His mother would certainly have been pleased by his ambition. Rose's ability to rack up gaudy show business successes while he volunteered to fund a World's Fair depiction of Nazi horrors and vanquished Nazis in his *It Can't Happen Here* productions satisfied her twin desires, which she shared with her immigrant generation. "It was the unspoken hope of the immigrants," wrote Irving Howe, "that their visions and ambitions, the collective dream of Jewish fulfillment and the personal wish to improve the lot of sons and daughters, could be satisfied at the same time."[4] Rose became the embodiment of that hope.

SOMETHING QUIET

His mother's example, however, was necessary but not sufficient. Rose's ten years of silence on Jewish issues after his satires of Henry Ford's antisemitism speak to a weakening of his attachment to the Jewish community. New York, because its more than two million Jews formed more than one-quarter of the population of America's largest city, was unique among American Jewish communities in its ability to offer Jews both cosmopolitanism and Jewish culture.[5] The city and the Jewish community were large enough to afford both. Rose, however, was more interested in cosmopolitanism. In 1937 when he left Fanny Brice for Eleanor Holm, a move impossible to imagine during his mother's lifetime, Rose was heading toward intermarriage at a time when the rate of such unions was vanishingly small. Even at the start of the 1960s, Jewish intermarriage rates in America were under 10 percent.[6] But Rose was in show business, and as with other Jewish songwriters and playwrights and producers, his job was to tap into Jewish energy and verve to create American, not Jewish, entertainment.[7]

It seems clear that only world events revived Rose's Jewish identity, as it did that of his peers, whose example also seems to have been a powerful goad to his growing involvement in Jewish causes. In February 1933, the columnist Walter

Winchell used his "On Broadway" column to rail against Hitler.[8] Winchell continued to use his column to defend the Jews, and this seems to have made a deep impression on Rose. In 1944, he confessed to Winchell his admiration for the columnist's work, which he intimated contained something meaningful. "I think I have done pretty well with my own career," he said, "but by comparison with what you have done with yours, it seems pretty empty."[9] Another influence was Rose's hero, Bernard Baruch. In Europe during the summer of 1934, Rose listened to Baruch discuss Hitler's sports and flying clubs. "Baruch knew Hitler was arming," Rose said.[10] And in 1935, while Hecht and Rose worked on *Jumbo,* the screenwriter appeared as a guest columnist for Winchell and used the powerful bullhorn to decry Nazi antisemitism and explore the meaning of the shock it held for America's assimilated Jews. Hecht understood their pain as part of a necessary awakening from their slumbering Jewish identities. "It is not without a certain thrill—this spectacle of financiers, society leaders, literary talents emerging as Jews under attack," he wrote. "Painful though it is, I have a feeling that this Jew consciousness is rather good for the seemingly assimilated Jew."[11]

Part of Rose's attraction to these men was undoubtedly their alert Jewish consciousness. If he had wanted to avoid reminders of Jewish solidarity, he could have aligned himself with show business Jews who were hardly so engaged. In April 1934, columnist Louis Sobol recognized that "something unusual happened" when New York's Jewish Theatrical Guild honored the non-Jewish George M. Cohan and "Harry Hershfield told half a dozen stories which were quite funny, too, but not a single one in which a Jewish gentleman was mentioned."[12] That crowd exhibited the assimilationist traits Hecht condemned. It was not Rose's crowd.

His identification with Disraeli as a Jewish hero came five months after he staged *It Can't Happen Here* and just three months after an October 3 rally at New York's Madison Square Garden drew twenty thousand people to a German Day celebration that included more than one thousand uniformed Nazis.[13] The cause-and-effect relationship between anti-Jewish acts and Rose's Jewish activism became most plain after *Kristallnacht,* the "Night of Broken Glass." The organized violence against Germany's Jews on November 9 and 10, 1938, destroyed one thousand synagogues, left ninety-one dead, and saw thirty thousand Jewish men arrested. News of the outrages appeared on the front page of the *New York Times.*[14] "Nazis Smash, Loot and Burn Jewish Shops and Temples until Goebbels Calls Halt" was the headline on November 11. The next day the front page alerted readers, "Arrests Run to Thousands." Less than a week later, in a news story of November 17, 1938, Rose hinted he was interested in doing something out of character, something "that will be quiet, altruistic. More than that he would not say."[15]

In fact, he would never say, but he did act. On December 6, 1938, Rose offered to help an Austrian Jewish refugee trapped in fascist Italy. "If you come to New York will definitely give you employment in one of my enterprises," he wrote.[16] Over the next three months this modest offer grew in scope until Rose took full responsibility for rescuing the young man from Europe, a project that included paying his travel and living and visa expenses for immigration to Cuba.

Rose's rescue of Kurt Schwarz from Italy in the winter of 1938–39 reveals unpublicized aspects of his character. One was his determination to do something about the threat facing Europe's Jews that went beyond expressions of concern and protest. Another was his ability to remain anonymous. The latter is the more shocking of the two. After twenty years seeking attention, Rose seemed the last person likely to avoid publicity, but when it came to good deeds he preferred anonymity. In 1942, owing to a mistake made by New York's draft board, the public discovered that Rose supported his father, three of his uncles, and his sister Polly.[17] As Polly later explained, her brother "has a person[al] WPA, and keeps dozens of relatives on his payroll."[18] This he kept to himself, and he likewise never told anyone he saved Kurt Schwarz—not Brice, not Holm, not his sister Polly, nobody.

LIFE AND DEATH

Schwarz was born in Vienna on May 19, 1917, the only child of Helene and Ludwig Schwarz, Jews secular enough that in one letter from his mother she noted the date as Easter Sunday.[19] He pursued a business education at a commercial academy in 1935–36, and in 1937, at age twenty, started his career in the hotel industry as a clerk at Vienna's grand Hotel Bristol, an 1892 monument to sophistication and culture that attracted guests such as Enrico Caruso, Gustav Mahler, and Sergei Rachmaninoff.[20] But on February 8, 1938, Schwarz quit his job, said goodbye to his divorced mother, and left for Rome.[21] It was a smart move. One month later the Nazis invaded and absorbed Austria, and soon afterward, in response to the arrival of many refugees, Italy made it illegal for Austrian Jews to enter the country. Schwarz found work in Rome at two of the city's most luxurious hotels, the Flora and the Majestic, where he was assistant manager, but his Italian refuge was brief. In May 1938, Adolf Hitler made a state visit to Italy and many German and Austrian Jewish refugees, apparently including Schwarz, were arrested in advance of the visit. Then on September 7, under German pressure, Italy ordered all recently arrived foreign Jews to leave the country by March 12, 1939. To ensure compliance, the Ministry of the Interior compiled a secret list of the country's approximately ten thousand foreign Jews. Schwarz was on it.[22]

The Italian government faced a problem carrying out the Jewish expulsion: there was no place for the Jews to go. No country would accept them. For the Italian authorities this was a bureaucratic headache, as they could not expel the Jews according to the official timetable. For Jewish refugees such as Schwarz it was a crisis, and he investigated many means of escape to avoid being repatriated to Austria, a prospect that also terrified the German Jews in Italy, and these two groups, "in particular, made desperate efforts to find alternative places of refuge," notes the historian Susan Zuccotti.[23] A stamp in his passport from the Chinese consulate confirms that Schwarz considered going there. He also sought and received help from an unidentified Marquis Nikolas and also Carlo Alberto Viterbo, an important leader of the Italian Jewish community who "worked tirelessly to help Jewish refugees."[24] Viterbo served as the Italian government's official in charge of the Jewish community of Ethiopia and in the fall of 1938 there were reports and rumors, official and apocryphal, that Italy might consider its newly acquired colony as a place for Jewish settlement. Schwarz seems to have investigated that, too.[25]

Rose's December 6, 1938, telegram dangled the tantalizing prospect of immigrating to America, the most desirable choice, and Rose's offer of employment is obviously a response to an earlier and lost Schwarz inquiry. How and why Schwarz reached out to Rose is unfortunately an unsolved mystery. According to a Schwarz friend named Herb Hillman—the man who shared Schwarz's story with Saul Bellow, who transformed it into the novella *The Bellarosa Connection*—Schwarz had a girlfriend in Rome who learned that Rose was running an underground rescue operation on behalf of Italy's stranded Jewish refugees.[26] This is unlikely, though Rose could hardly have avoided learning of Italy's Jewish expulsion order and its implications. On September 2, 1938, the *New York Times* ran the story of the upcoming order on its front page.[27] But if Rose had masterminded a secret operation of any great extent, it would have almost certainly come to light by now.

A more plausible explanation is that Schwarz probably wrote letters seeking help to several prominent Jewish Americans, and Rose was the one who responded. In late 1938 it was not unusual for American Jews of some renown to receive letters from European Jews pleading for the help that might save their lives. In November of that year, the playwright S. N. Behrman received a letter from a correspondent whom he had merely chatted with during an earlier visit to Vienna. "I regret to trouble you with my sorrows, but I beg you to understand that these sorrows have become literally questions of life and death for me," the man wrote. Behrman brought him and his wife to America.[28] In 1939 the famed *New York Times* cartoonist Al Hirschfeld received a letter from a Jewish widow in Budapest born with the Hirschfeld name. She used this slim connection to "beg you have the kindness in informing me, whether would you have the goodness to facilitate the immigration one of my sons into the United States of America."[29] Hirschfeld's response is unknown.

Rose sent Schwarz a second telegram on January 29, 1939. Much had happened to both men during the intervening seven weeks. For Rose, the refugee crisis had grown into a serious concern, which did not mean he was committed to earnestness or self-abnegation. On January 13, he was master of ceremonies on the radio station WHN's "refugee program," a good place to promote his upcoming January 24 Casa Mañana show starring European refugees.[30] The "Refugee Revue" featured "actors and musicians driven from Germany and Austria by the Nazis," and Rose's touch was evident in a comic send-up of Nazi intolerance. Whenever the performance included music composed by Jews, such as Oscar Straus's "Chocolate Soldier" or Mendelssohn's "Wedding March," the Austrian actor Max Willenz "held up his hand and said: 'Verboten!'"[31] The *Times* commended the show and Rose for "putting these people to work where their talents may be seen," and in February, Rose donated his Casa Mañana to a benefit for refugee children.[32] Refugees were on his mind.

For Schwarz, life had become grimmer, as he surely informed Rose. The September 1938 legislation that called for the expulsion of Italy's foreign Jews also instituted "anti-Jewish laws [that] affected Italy as a whole, not just its political, social, economic, or cultural life. . . . Mussolini had decided that Fascism and Italy as a whole were to be Aryan and anti-Semitic."[33] A normal existence was essentially outlawed, and the foreign Jews who needed to leave the country faced doing so without their assets, as Italy restricted the amount of Italian lira they could take out of the country to the equivalent of little more than one hundred dollars.[34] This created a demand for the illegal acquisition of hard currency before emigration, and in January 1939 Schwarz was arrested for helping Jews buy British pounds. His position at the Majestic gave him access to foreign visitors willing to trade currency on the black market. He did this in concert with a Jewish refugee named Karl Marx (not a descendant of the author of *Das Kapital*), who became one of postwar Germany's more important Jewish journalists, and on January 26 the Italian police arrested Marx and Schwarz for illegal currency trading.[35] They were still in jail on February 9 when the Italian political police suggested to the Foreign Ministry that both men be expelled from Italy. The report added that Schwarz was "unemployed and without means."[36]

Schwarz's January 26 arrest surely accounts for the urgent tone of Rose's January 29 telegram and his comprehensive plan for Schwarz's exodus: "Will pay transportation third class Rome Havre thence French Line Havanna [*sic*] through American Express. Contact American Express immediately. Arrange passage visa. Will deposit money Cuban government soon visa issued. Rose."[37] Three weeks later on February 22 Rose sent Schwarz a third telegram: "Arranged everything. Contact American Express." Using the money Rose sent, Schwarz visited the Cuban consulate in Milan on March 6 and paid $200 for a visa to enter that country. The next day he went to the American consulate in Rome and secured a transit visa to permit him to stop in New York on his way to Cuba. This means Schwarz had his ship ticket by March 7. Rose paid for that too. Schwarz's passenger log for the journey from Naples to Havana—a simpler scenario than Rose's original travel plan—notes an "Am Express passage order" number.[38]

Schwarz wrote his mother in Vienna about his forthcoming escape from Europe before he finalized all these arrangements. Rose's February 22 telegram was assurance enough. Helene Schwarz received her son's letter on March 4, 1939, one week before Italy's expulsion deadline. By this time most of her family had fled Austria for India, Australia, and the United States, but she still had the company of her sister Gisela and niece Gerta, and she opened the letter from her son in their company. It was not something to face alone. There was no telling what news the envelope contained. Schwarz's mother scanned the letter in silence, leaving her relatives in an agony of anticipation. "Read," insisted Gerta, who grabbed the letter and read it aloud. "He's going to Cuba," she announced. "He's leaving, thank God."[39]

On March 16, 1939, Schwarz sailed from Naples to Havana via New York.

On the day her son left the dangers of Europe, Helene Schwarz sent a letter to Billy Rose.

"Dearest Mr. Rose," she wrote. "If ever in your life you have a special inner wish that calls for fulfillment, think of the mother who prayed for her beloved son every day and included in this prayer the one who saved her child."[40]

THE ENIGMA

Schwarz arrived at New York's Ellis Island on March 23 and soon played an unwitting part in an absurd juxtaposition. The young Jewish refugee hoped to enter the United States. He planned to use his transit visa's permission to stop in New York on the way to Cuba as an opportunity to make his case for immediate immigration. To accomplish this, Schwarz highlighted his relationship with Billy Rose. Despite his visa to Cuba, Schwarz told the United States immigration inspector that his destination was "7th Ave. 50str. New York Casa Mañana," Rose's nightclub, and for evidence he carried with him the three telegrams he had received from Rose, so he was held in detention until a hearing could decide his case. Rose telegrammed Schwarz on Ellis Island to say, "Pardon my not coming to see you but it was impossible because of several shows in rehearsal."[41] That excuse was flimsy enough. The truth was ridiculous. On March 27, Schwarz had his hearing, testified before an Inspector Smith, and lost his immigration appeal.[42] That same day Billy Rose sat in the display window of the Ansonia Bootery on Broadway at Forty-Seventh Street and judged a beautiful legs contest.

It is an unflattering contrast, to say the least. What's more, this was not a last-minute plan. Rose clearly prepared the stunt to coincide with Schwarz's hearing date, which Schwarz likely provided him. To ensure a crowd, Rose was joined in the window by Eleanor Holm, George Jessel, and a radio announcer from WMCA who offered a live broadcast of the proceedings. Rose produced it like a pro, and it all worked. The police had to be called because the leg contest generated disruptive crowds in the street outside, and Rose got what he apparently wanted. No reporter learned that a European refugee in New York Harbor had a terrific story about one of the most famous men in New York.[43]

Schwarz was deported to Cuba on March 29, but that did not end his contact with Rose. In a letter dated May 7, Schwarz's mother tried to cheer her son with the reminder, "Rose invested a lot of money in you" and so was unlikely to abandon him, though on May 14 she wondered why Rose had not answered her letter, and on May 17 she confessed, "Rose is a puzzle to me."[44] Then on June 21 the enigma sent Schwarz in Cuba one last telegram: "Have American Express cable their office here immediately procedure necessary bring you America." Nothing came of this. In December 1939 Schwarz married an American Jewish tourist during her visit to Cuba and joined her in New York in August 1940.[45]

LOVE AND MONEY

Rose's lifelong silence about his rescue of Schwarz can be chalked up to a becoming modesty about matters that were truly profound. He dismissed the idea that he was lonely when he penned "Me and My Shadow," one of the great popular evocations of loneliness, because it showed no class to seek applause for sensitivity or moral attributes. The journalist H. L. Mencken, Rose's contemporary, approved of this approach. "There is always something embarrassing about unqualified praise," he wrote. "A man knows, down in his own heart, that he doesn't deserve it."[46] This was almost certainly the same reason that Rose kept mum about Schwarz.

But his failure to visit Schwarz on Ellis Island, and the leg contest publicity stunt, require a less flattering explanation. His actions suggest that Rose considered any association with the refugee too risky. The association threatened him on all sides: psychological, political, commercial, and sexual. He could have had someone translate the German letter from Schwarz's mother and compose a response, but given Rose's history with his mother-wife Fannie Rosenberg and his wife-mother Fanny Brice, he likely wanted to avoid entanglement with another Jewish mother. In addition, he needed to ward off controversial political questions that might sink his Diamond Horseshoe and Aquacade. Everything he did was newsworthy. If he went to Ellis Island, the visit would have wound up in the papers, and then the inflammatory political issue of Jewish persecution, refugees, and antisemitism would have been his issue. That would have damaged his prospects at the upcoming World's Fair on two scores: it would tarnish the hopeful "World of Tomorrow" theme and make him the fair's highest-profile Jew during a period of rising antisemitism.

As Rose realized, much of his Aquacade's success was due to the green light given by the Catholic authorities that it was decent entertainment. That support might not have been issued if Rose had appeared to favor American involvement in the European war. In 1936–37, Catholic newspapers in Brooklyn, Boston,

Connecticut, and Ohio railed against Jews for their anti-Franco stand in the Spanish Civil War, a position seen as anti-Catholic and pro-Communist, and also because the Jews were "too prosperous, too successfully grasping."[47] This American Catholic anger increased even after the horrors of *Kristallnacht,* when, ten days after the violence, the notorious demagogue Father Charles Coughlin used his radio address heard by 3.5 million people to blame the Jews for their victimization.[48]

Finally, Rose had to consider how the Schwarz project would affect his antisemitic-when-drunk future wife, Eleanor Holm. The beautiful young woman apparently broke a pathetic pattern in Rose's life: despite his charisma, intelligence, and wealth, many women did not want to sleep with him. His tiny stature and not-very-attractive visage apparently repelled them. Brice was not interested in a physical relationship with him, and other women he squired, including Gypsy Rose Lee, the singer Jane Morgan, and a former Miss Israel named Miriam Hadar, felt the same.[49] "Sooner or later he'd expect it to become physical and I couldn't bear that," Lee said about why she would not consider marrying him.[50] Rose appeared to try and make light of such rejections by saying, "Sex has never been the most important thing in my life."[51] But this did not mean it was unimportant. Like his role model Baruch, Rose still had a powerful sexual appetite in his sixties, when he crudely and forcefully tried to seduce the actress Lee Grant, twenty-eight years his junior.[52] When he rescued Schwarz, Rose was not yet forty and had just been released from a sexless marriage with an older woman. He could not afford to alienate his young lover. Holm provided an invaluable service. Schwarz had to go to Cuba.

Rose almost certainly saved Schwarz's life by bringing him out of Europe, but he kept the project quiet. He was vulnerable in a myriad of ways. Rose's big public Jewish move had to wait.

eleven

WE WILL NEVER DIE

After he rescued Schwarz, Rose continued to live a double life that saw him become one of the country's richest and most famous purveyors of light diversions for the masses and also an important part of American Jewry's campaign to win support for American intervention in World War II—a campaign Jews described in terms that were purely American, such as the defense of liberty, and deliberately did not frame as something of special importance to Jews.[1] Rose's double life and the careful Jewish campaign were part of the common Jewish American condition. Many believed that Jews were not wholly American and that Jewish concerns were by definition not American concerns. American isolationists, led by the aviation hero Charles Lindbergh, attacked Jews for advocating war "for reasons which are not American."[2] A Jewish American identity that allowed Jews to embrace both sides of the identity's equation, and allowed non-Jews to accept it, was still to be achieved.

In their effort to win American action in Europe, Jews found a home in the political movement known as the Popular Front, a loose conglomeration of socialists, Communists, labor organizations, intellectuals, and refugees from Nazi Europe. It arose in the mid-1930s in response to the Depression and the apparent collapse of capitalism, and to the growth of fascism in Europe. It was hardly a fringe group; by 1942 a poll found that 60 percent of Americans favored or were open to the leftward social movement that was antifascist, anti-imperialist, and in favor of greater civil liberties for African Americans.[3] However, as the Nazi persecution and mass murder of the Jews emerged as a singular focus of that regime, Jews in the Popular Front became impatient with camouflaging specifically Jewish concerns behind more general American themes. In response to the increasingly desperate conditions, Jews created three works for the theater that more forcefully than anything that came before put explicitly Jewish concerns at the center of the action. This change marked a fundamental break with the reigning model of Jewish identity in America. According to the historian Garrett Eisler, the public assertion of Jewish issues "anticipated and influenced a postwar shift to a more openly professed Jewish-American identity."[4] The three theatrical productions that pointed the way forward were *Fun to be Free, We Will Never Die,* and *A Flag Is Born.*

Rose played a role in all of them.

NO HAY

Rose's first involvement with a Popular Front drama was his December 1939 financial backing of the Theatre Guild's production of Ernest Hemingway's *The Fifth Column,* a drama that over the previous two years had been discussed, considered, and rejected by several Broadway producers. The play is based on Hemingway's experiences in the Spanish Civil War of 1936–37, and tells the story of an American fighting with the Loyalists against Franco's fascists. The American reluctantly accepts the inglorious and distasteful but necessary assignment to ferret out fascist spies—the fifth column—in the Loyalist ranks.[5] It was a timely subject. Nazi propaganda stoked fears that Europe and the United States were laced with enemy saboteurs, and in January 1940 the *Times* worried that "popular fear of the Fifth Column threatens to run into panic."[6]

Rose's support was far from trivial. In an article that appeared a few days after the play opened on March 6, 1940, the *Times* diagnosed one of the ailments afflicting that season's Broadway as runaway costs. "A producer cannot give an author a public hearing without a preliminary expenditure of ten thousand dollars, more likely twenty or twenty-five thousand and perhaps thirty-five thousand dollars," Brooks Atkinson wrote. "The Ernest Hemingway 'The Fifth Column' represented a preliminary investment of about fifty-five thousand dollars when it opened at the Alvin Wednesday evening. As the Broadway vernacular has it, that ain't hay!"[7]

The *Times* applauded the Hemingway play. "During the last few years Ernest Hemingway's 'The Fifth Column' has passed through so many hands that most of us have despaired of it. Obviously, we despaired too early," said Atkinson. The play "is a profoundly convincing and moving drama of death in the night, murder by day."[8] The paper promoted the work again ten days later, when it devoted another article to a detailed dissection of its plot, the acting by stars

Franchot Tone and Lee J. Cobb, and the direction by the Group Theatre's Lee Strasberg, and called it "a stirring play" that "pierces closer to the chaotic agony of the contemporary world than anything we have had this season." Its lack of ideological dogmatism earned Hemingway the enmity of some in the Popular Front because his complex play "emerges as a portrait of torture by warfare. That is the main thing. The impact of the Spanish civil war . . . reminds us that warfare is no heroic subject, but degradation of the spirit. Among those it destroys are the idealists."[9] Additional acclaim came from *Life,* which called it "good entertainment," and the *New Yorker,* which praised it as "astonishingly good" and "emphatically worth seeing."[10] Despite such press, *The Fifth Column* enjoyed "a merely respectable" run of eighty-seven performances. It closed in June.[11]

Rose contained multitudes, and his appreciation of quality works such as *The Fifth Column,* combined with his determination to score popular successes through baldly executed public relations and showmanship efforts, could yield comic complaints. A good example is the telegram he sent to the Theatre Guild about the early closing of the play. "The lack of imagination in selling The Fifth Column to the public makes me slightly ill. . . . Despite the fact that the phrase 'Fifth Column' is front page news today because of what is happening in Europe, we make no use of it. I would say as a fairly expert showman that the difference between what we are doing and what we are not doing is costing a minimum of five thousand dollars a week at the box office. . . . I adore all of you at the Guild but sincerely I think I am getting a bum run for my money."[12]

HE'S INTERESTING

Rose could afford it, and he went from one public-service, no-fee, and money-losing production to the next. All shared the Popular Front's theme of antifascism, and before long a Jewish argument for America's war against Hitler. In early 1941, Rose helped the War Department's Committee on Entertainment arrange for movie and radio stars to perform for servicemen in army and navy training camps.[13] One of his innovations was so-called "mobile entertainment units" consisting of trucks designed with sides that dropped to form stages.[14] Productions at Fort Dix were launched within ten minutes of the trucks' arrival, allowing Rose to stage three performances there in one night. Milton Berle and the African American tap dancer Bill Robinson entertained twelve thousand troops, and the *Times* crowned Rose the "head-man of mass entertainment."[15]

He was joined in this work by the playwright George Kaufman, who in the twenties wrote scripts for the Marx Brothers and during the thirties wrote hit Broadway shows with partner Moss Hart, including *You Can't Take It with You* and *The Man Who Came to Dinner*.[16] When Rose came to dinner he "horrified" Kaufman's wife "by describing the way he treated his father when the elder Rose came to ask for money. 'I never see him personally,' said Rose. . . . 'I keep him waiting for an hour or more, and then I send a servant out with a few dollars. And I tell the servant to *throw* the money at him.'" After Rose left, Mrs. Kaufman assaulted her husband. "'The man's an utter bastard. . . . How can you possibly stand him?'

"'I think he's interesting,' Kaufman said mildly."[17]

Rose was certainly that, and part of the interest was due to his raw and un-refined Jewish personality, one marked by a peculiarly Jewish style that the literary critic Mark Shechner called "ghetto cosmopolitanism." In Jews such as Rose, "vulgarity and sensibility go hand in hand; his coarseness of manner is not inconsistent with high orders of intellectual and aesthetic discrimination." In other words, he might simultaneously produce a "girlie" swimming show and a Hemingway drama—and complain that the latter was underpromoted. Shechner wrote that this personality "is a puzzle to non-Jews, for whom education implies refinement, decorum, *breeding*."[18] It seems also to have been an intriguing puzzle for Rose's more assimilated Jewish peers. Kaufman and his wife Beatrice were born to assimilated German Jews.[19] Richard Rodgers and Lorenz Hart also stemmed from the "German Jewish upper crust."[20]

Ben Hecht's family left the Lower East Side when he was a child, and he attended high school in Racine, Wisconsin. But with the rise of Hitler they all were now compelled to consider their Jewish identity, which for Rose had always been a given. When in early 1941 Hecht began writing his "1001 Afternoons in New York" column for PM, a New York newspaper staffed by Popular Front members, he largely ignored editor Ralph Ingersoll's advice to "get out the old files of THE WORLD around 1900 or 1910, say, and see what's happened to some of the big news subjects of that day."[21] Instead, he wrote much about the Nazi threat and about the kind of Jew who "in nearly all his dealings, dreams, and expressions [is] no more a Jew than his uncircumcised neighbor."[22] Hecht's attack on such Jews in "My Tribe Is Called Israel" insisted that Jews understand the world conflict as not just a fight between freedom and slavery but also as a direct attack on them. This idea could have served as the credo of the Jewish voice within the Popular Front. It is also a testament to the value of a Jewish identity such as Rose's, which was the mirror image of the one Hecht derides: "I write of Jews today, I who never knew himself as one before, because that part of me which is Jewish is under a violent and ape-like attack. My way of defending myself is to answer as a Jew, whether my answer is unhistorical or unethnologic, or whether it is even in some way troublesome to those Jews who think they can remove themselves as targets by turning their foolish backs to the battle."[23]

Rose's Jewish childhood in New York's Jewish neighborhoods ensured he was awake to the part of himself that was Jewish even during the years he paid it little mind. He shared the condition that the historian Michael A. Meyer summarized so well: "For the Jew in the modern world Jewishness forms only a portion of his total identity. . . . And yet external pressures and internal attachments combine to make him often more aware of this identification than of any other."[24] So it is not surprising that when Rose and Hecht played important roles in *Fun to Be Free* they contributed the show's most Jewish material.

The October 5, 1941, performance at Madison Square Garden, broadcast live over radio station WEVD, was a political rally with entertainment, a patriotic assembly featuring New York's Mayor La Guardia and the 1940 Republican presidential candidate Wendell Willkie urging America to join the fight against fascism in Europe, and also a stage show written by Hecht and MacArthur that starred George Jessel, Jack Benny, Ethel Merman, Betty Grable, and other show business names who celebrated American freedom of speech and, in stark contrast to the Nazi vision of society, the freedom for religious and ethnic and racial minorities to live in peace. Willkie enunciated this theme when he denounced those who would "divide the United States on the basis of race and religion."[25] The night's entertainment also drove this message home, and the page-one article in the next day's *Times* emphasized the theme in its lead: "Bill Robinson, no Aryan, tap-danced on Adolf Hitler's coffin last night."[26] Robinson's act was part of *Fun to Be Free*'s variety show. Billy Rose produced that segment and included in it the "Verboten Overture" he had created two years earlier for his Refugee Revue.[27] It made the case for the freedom of America's Jews to live and think as Jews, in contrast to the violent silencing they suffered under the Nazis.[28] Hecht's part of the show also pressed for Jews to be fully recognized and accepted in America, and he made his case by adding to the roster of American patriots the "Paul Revere of the Jews—Haym Salomon," who fought in the American Revolution. Hecht depicted a mythical scene of Salomon interrupting the holy service of Yom Kippur to collect money to fight against the British and for American freedom. *Fun to Be Free* argued that America faced the same choice now, and that once again American Jews rightly argued for war in the cause of freedom. Such performances made the production "effectively a protest against Jewish persecution at home as well as [for] intervention abroad."[29]

THE BERGSON BOYS

Two months later on December 7, 1941, the Japanese attack on Pearl Harbor ended America's isolationist stance toward the wars in Europe and the Pacific. The work of the Popular Front was now obsolete. The United States was at war. The work of the so-called Jewish cultural front, however, was not over. Its most important battles to draw attention to the unfolding Jewish catastrophe were yet to come. Rose engaged in those battles alongside the Bergson Group, also known as the Bergson Boys, a group of five core members. Nearly all of them were from the Jewish settlement in British Mandate Palestine and in the late 1930s were members of the militant, right-wing Irgun Zvai Leumi, or National Military Organization, a rival Jewish army to David Ben-Gurion's Haganah, the defense organization loyal to the left-wing Labor Zionists. The Bergson Group, led by Peter H. Bergson, a.k.a. Hillel Kook, came to New York in the summer of 1940 to raise money for a Jewish army to be based in Palestine that would join the fight against Hitler.[30]

But Bergson and his comrades were spurned by mainstream groups such as the Jewish Agency and United Jewish Appeal and made little progress until August 1941, when Bergson discovered Ben Hecht.[31] Bergson read Hecht's "These Were Once Conquerors," a short essay in PM that reflected on a photograph of a Polish Jew being forcibly shaved by Nazi soldiers. Hecht saw in the Jew's strikingly composed expression a man "full of great will-power, as well as learning. . . . He stands looking directly into the averted eyes of his tormentor. And if this young Jew were standing on a rostrum in Jerusalem many years ago, receiving the acclaim of his people, his eyes could hold no prouder look."[32] Bergson telegrammed Hecht, "Thanks for giving . . . expression to the pride and spiritual heroism which for centuries accumulated in the soul of the genuine and conscious Jew. By the creation of a Jewish army we intend to transform this heroic spirit into heroic deeds."[33] Hecht said he "bumped into history" when he met Bergson, who worked closely with Sam Merlin and Yitshaq "Mike" Ben-Ami. Hecht had never

First successful song by the newly minted Billy Rose.

Variety called Rose's first nightclub the most unusual
in the world.

Billy Rose's Aquacade. William A. Dobak / Museum of the City
of New York. X2012.66.121.

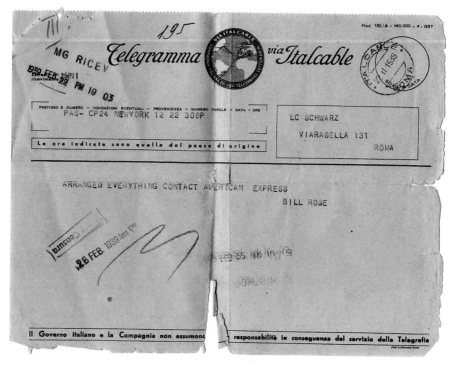

Rose's third telegram to Kurt Schwarz in Rome. Kurt Schwarz papers,
United States Holocaust Memorial Museum Collection, Gift of Idy Sherer.

Ben Hecht and Rose worked on this Popular Front production.
Courtesy of the Weill-Lenya Research Center, Kurt Weill
Foundation for Music, New York.

Cover of *We Will Never Die* program. United States
Holocaust Memorial Museum, courtesy of Gregg
and Michelle Philipson.

Rose was the silent backer of *A Flag Is Born*.

Rose and his last wife, Doris Vidor Rose, in 1965. L. Arnold Weissberger (1907–1981) / Museum of the City of New York. 67.32.1.

met Jews like them. "They were contained, smiling and wary," he said. "Their eyes glinted with the mood of adventure. They were unmarked by memories of suffering."[34] This assessment confirmed the success of the culture the Zionists had created in Palestine over the previous twenty years, when the ideal of "toughness was central: It was promoted and lauded," writes historian Nina S. Spiegel. "There were no tensions surrounding this objective: All strands of Zionism agreed on the need for strength and toughness."[35] The Bergson Boys convinced Hecht to join the Committee for a Jewish Army of Stateless and Palestinian Jews, which announced its existence on January 5, 1942, in a full-page advertisement in the *New York Times* entitled, "Jews Fight for the Right to Fight."[36] Hecht wrote it.

Rose met Bergson and his group through Hecht and found them easy to like. They gave Rose his first contact with the Zionist Jewish culture that would deeply influence the future state of Israel he came to love. It was a culture that celebrated the physical strength and bravery the Zionists believed the Diaspora Jew lacked, and Rose's embrace of the soldierly Bergson Boys put him at odds with much of the American Jewish community. Most American Jews preferred to imagine the future Israel as a "'model state' [that] represented American liberal intellectuals' fondest and most romantic visions of a better world. . . . Zionism conjured up a grand vision of ardent young men and women earnestly engaged in the selfless task of creating a new and better humanity."[37] But as the Bergson Group member Yitshaq Ben-Ami explained, their embrace of militarism was a rejection of such ideals and what they saw as the "historical fatalism and passivity in Jewish life."[38] Rose was with Ben-Ami and Bergson. He was not a liberal intellectual but a slum kid who never forgot the harsh lessons he learned on the Lower East Side. Passivity was not his style. When his secretary feared that a fired employee might return to attack her, Rose said, "Let me know if he comes up. . . . I'll break his hand with your typewriter." "He was dead serious," she said. "He admired only toughness."[39]

It was a preference that among American Jews was associated with those outside polite company, such as the gangster Mickey Cohen, who also learned about Bergson from Hecht and was thrilled to find that the group shared his outlook. "These guys actually fight like racket guys would, they didn't ask for a quarter and they didn't give no quarter," he said.[40] Unfortunately for what it says about human nature, Cohen and Bergson's approach suited the moment far better than that of Rabbi Stephen Wise, the great luminary of American Jewish life, head of the American Jewish Congress and Jewish Institute of Religion, and a Bergson foe. Wise's "liberal humanistic worldview was based on the assumption that there existed a civilizing spirit in the world which could be mobilized when minorities like the Jews were threatened," writes historian Henry L. Feingold. The Holocaust proved, however, "that such a spirit did not play a part in the world."[41] Rose's worldview was made of sterner stuff and the tough proto-Israelis of the Bergson Group thrilled him. "These boys are only wonderful," he wrote Hecht.[42]

In late 1942, reports of the Holocaust appeared in American newspapers and Bergson shelved his goal of a Jewish army. Scattered news of the crime had surfaced since late 1941, including a "sensational and remarkably accurate report" filed by the Jewish Telegraphic Agency about the "merciless, systematic extermination" of "52,000 men, women and children" in Babi Yar, Russia. By June 30, 1942, headlines in London announced, "1,000,000 Jews Die."[43] Three weeks later, on July 21, American Jews organized at New York's Madison Square Garden what President Roosevelt called a "mass demonstration against Hitler atrocities" that drew messages of support from British prime minister Winston Churchill, who "revealed that more than 10,000 Palestinian Jews were serving" with British forces, a statement seen as a "reply to the continuing agitation" for a Jewish army by Hecht and the Bergson Boys.[44] Their full-page advertisement, formation of a board that included prominent non-Jews such as Samuel Church, president of the Carnegie Institute, and strenuous congressional lobbying were having an effect. But on November 25, 1942, when newspapers reported and the US State Department confirmed that "about half of the estimated 4,000,000 Jews in Nazi-occupied Europe had been slain in an 'extermination campaign,'" Bergson changed course and formed the Emergency Committee to Save the Jewish People of Europe.[45]

TEARS OF RAGE

In February 1943, Hecht published "The Extermination of the Jews" in the *American Mercury*. The article also appeared that month in condensed form in the mass-circulation *Reader's Digest*. The article imagines a postwar convocation of nations gathered to seek justice from the defeated Germans. Every people is represented but the Jews, because the Jews have no nation, and because the Jews of Europe have vanished, "reduced from a minority to a phantom." In his article Hecht gave voice to the dead Jews who "will remain outside the hall of judgment, to be heard only when the window is opened and the sad, faint cry drifts in—'*Remember us!*'"[46] This refrain became part of the most moving section of Hecht's Holocaust pageant, *We Will Never Die: A Mass Memorial to the Two Million Jewish Dead of Europe.*

It was not easy for Hecht to enlist the Jewish theatrical help he needed to stage this event. At Kaufman's home in early February 1943, he addressed "thirty famous writers (and one composer). . . . All had written hit plays or successful novels. . . . What would happen if these brilliant Jews cried out with passion against the German butchers? . . . How loudly they could present the nightmare to the world." Hecht beseeched them to do as he had done and contribute their writing skills and star power to publicizing the Jewish crisis, in order to move the American government to take action that might save lives. But his fervent appeal compelled very few to work on the *We Will Never Die* project. Beatrice Kaufman tried to soothe Hecht's disappointment. "You asked them to throw away the most valuable thing they own—the fact that they are Americans," she told him.

Hecht disagreed. They behaved "like scared Jews," he said.[47]

The historian Garrett Eisler's view splits the difference between these two judgments. "Ultimately," he argues, "what Hecht was up against . . . was the still unresolved nature of Jewish-American identity."[48] Few Jews knew how to manage both aspects of their lives and to simplify things they sacrificed their Jewish identity to their American one. Of the thirty writers at the Kaufmans' home, only Moss Hart and Kurt Weill volunteered to help. Weill's personal experience of Nazi Jew hatred in his native Germany made him a predictable ally, but Hart, whose assimilationist tendencies "pushed Americanization to its outer boundaries," was unexpected.[49] However, he apparently never shed the influence of his poor Jewish childhood with its allergy to pretension and its emphasis on *tachlis,* down-to-earth reality. When friends of his non-Jewish wife Kitty Carlisle talked about hunting pheasants and "great houses and shoots and beaters," Hart interjected, "When I lived in the Bronx we used to have the same kind of sport. It was called a relative shoot, and we used to beat the relatives out of the tenements."[50]

Rose was not at the gathering where Hecht sought help, but he soon joined Hecht, Hart, and Weill to launch *We Will Never Die.* "He needed no briefing," Hecht said of Rose. "He came under his own steam, which was considerable."[51] Rose produced the spectacle, and he and Hecht served as the national co-chairmen of the *We Will Never Die* committee. The Committee for a Jewish Army sponsored the production and solicited donations to support it, because

Bergson did not form his Emergency Committee to Save the Jewish People of Europe until July. Hecht, Weill, Hart, and Rose agreed to secure the committee against any financial loss and cover the $25,000 cost in New York if ticket sales were not enough to meet expenses.[52]

The *We Will Never Die* theatrical that Hecht wrote, Moss Hart directed, Kurt Weill composed for, and Billy Rose produced harnessed the emotional power of theater to elicit an almost traumatic reaction in the audience, who would then hopefully be moved to public action. These spectacles were elaborated into pageantry through a mixture "of art and propaganda . . . to affect public opinion and to stimulate communal cohesion," writes Stephen Whitfield, adding that "such aesthetic events are really political gestures."[53] For Rose it was familiar terrain. His *It Can't Happen Here* trod the same ground. But *We Will Never Die* was not meant to stir action through a single performance. The plan from the start called for a national tour of all the major centers of Jewish and national life, so that its effect would build over weeks and months and its name become known as a call to action.[54] It also departed from the tone most natural to Stephen Wise and other mainstream American Jewish leaders, which sought to win sympathy for the Jewish plight. Their emphasis was on "defending the victim." For Rose, Hecht, and the Bergson Boys, the "guiding principle [was] directly attacking the criminal."[55]

The four theater talents went to work and incorporated elements from earlier Jewish pageants into *We Will Never Die*. Starting in 1932, Meyer Weisgal of the Zionist Organization of America produced three Jewish pageants that pioneered many of the dramatic strategies used in the Holocaust pageant. *Israel Reborn* employed "traditional music known from the synagogue," and Weill did the same for *We Will Never Die*, with a "medley alternating between the Zionist anthem 'Hatikvah' and the ancient Aramaic litany *Kol Nidre*," recited by Jews on Yom Kippur, the day of atonement. *The Romance of a People* positioned onstage "a giant Torah scroll which was placed, unrolled, on an illuminated altar," and for its opening in New York the city's mayor, John O'Brien, declared September 24, 1933, to be "Jewish Day." For *We Will Never Die* Rose surpassed this on both counts. He outdid the giant Torah with "two 40-foot high tablets on which were written the ten commandments in Hebrew."[56] Over the tablets floated an enormous "illuminated Star of David. The aesthetic principle of the spectacle was this: more is more," writes Whitfield, accurately capturing Rose's approach.[57] And Rose topped Weisgal's mayoral proclamation with one from New York's governor, Thomas E. Dewey, ordering that the day of the show "be set aside by the citizens of our State to offer prayer to Almighty God for the Jews who have been brutally massacred."[58] (Rose tried to get recognition from the White House, but President Roosevelt's staff would not cooperate.[59])

Finally, Weisgal's 1937 *The Eternal Road,* directed by the German Jewish exile Max Reinhardt, "electrified the spectators" through "the energy of the masses occupying the space—245 actors, singers and dancers." Rose's production tripled that number with more than seven hundred people, including one hundred rabbis, a chorus of two hundred, and about four hundred actors. He gathered this vast team through visits to New York's Yeshiva University, where he invited young men to serve as cast members, and also the Israel Orphan Asylum.[60] Dozens of children from that institution appeared onstage.[61] In a measure of the enthusiasm the show generated, people of all stripes volunteered to play roles in the production, including the non-Jewish lesbian nightclub owner Spivy.[62] Finally, Reinhardt's staging of *The Eternal Road's* large cast may have influenced Moss Hart's approach to the masses Rose assembled. "I did the Memorial Pageant 'We Will Never Die' at Madison Square Garden with Ben Hecht, Billy Rose and Moss. It was a very effective show," Weill wrote Ira Gershwin. "Moss did a wonderful job of staging. I called him Moss Rein-Hart when I watched him directing the masses through a microphon [*sic*]—and did he like it!"[63]

In addition to the hundreds of anonymous cast members, Jewish stars of Broadway and Hollywood such as Paul Muni and Edward G. Robinson narrated portions of Hecht's script and were crucial to capturing publicity. Hecht "used his connections to recruit an array of prominent actors for the pageant's cast," and so did Rose, who managed to nab Muni.[64] Once a star of the Yiddish stage, Muni was on Broadway in the winter of 1943 in a show produced by John Golden. "Mr. Golden talked with Muni over the long distance wire today," the company's manager, Max Siegel, wrote Rose. "Muni said he would do it if Mr. Golden was satisfied, and Mr. Golden has decided to give his consent to Muni's appearance at Madison Square Garden." However, Golden and Siegel insisted on certain businesslike conditions, ones that a producer such as Rose surely had no trouble understanding. "I want your Committee to see to it that this action on the part of Mr. Muni and Mr. Golden will insure some special announcements mentioning Mr. Golden's and Mr. Muni's contribution, and the fact that Muni is starring in Mr. Golden's production of 'Counsellor-At-Law,'" Siegel told Rose.[65] The demand that Rose plug a Broadway show at a memorial for Jewish victims of mass murder proved that Rose made his living in a tough business. It was not the only time that some in the theater made Rose seem like a sweetheart by comparison.

Advertisements for the March 9, 1943, show at Madison Square Garden were headlined, "Action—Not Pity," which became the pageant's motto, and featured the illustration "Tears of Rage" by the artist Arthur Szyk, depicting a helmeted Jewish soldier holding aloft a rifle in one hand and with the other supporting an old bearded Jew in chains and additional Jewish victims. The same illustration appeared on the front of the pageant's souvenir program. The title phrase, "We Will Never Die," paraphrased the Hebrew prophet Habakkuk's assurance regarding the permanence of the Jewish people, "They shall never die." It also was a reminder of the 1934 play *They Shall Not Die,* which told the story of another injustice, that of the "Scottsboro Nine," African American men falsely accused of rape. The pageant sold out its twenty thousand seats a week before the March 9 show, so an encore performance was scheduled for later that same night.[66] Publicity, almost certainly arranged by Rose, generated demand. On March 7, New York's WMCA broadcast a preview of the show featuring cast members Stella and Luther Adler.[67] Rose had employed the same approach with *Jumbo.* The night's second show also sold out, and thousands who could not get tickets to either performance stood outside and listened to the proceedings over loudspeakers.[68] The evening's audience exceeded forty thousand.

The action began with a prayer to "Almighty God . . . for the two million who have been killed in Europe because they bear the name of your first children—the Jews."[69] An address to the audience was more direct and disturbing: "The corpse of a people lies on the steps of civilization. Behold it. Here it is! And no voice is heard to cry halt to the slaughter, no government speaks to bid the murder of human millions end."[70] Then followed an honor roll of the names of Jews who throughout history contributed to civilization, "from Moses to Einstein." Next came a tribute to the American Jews fighting in the war, and then arrived the final act, "Remember Us," which was the "episode that proved most affecting":[71]

[It] comprised a series of short scenes where groups of dead Jews from across Europe confront their German murderers at the peace table. Each tragic vignette ended with the charge to the assembled governments—and to the audience the "dead" were facing—to remember the annihilated millions who had no voice to accuse their tormentors or negotiate with them. . . . "Remember us in Wloclowek. The Germans came when we were at prayer. They tore the prayer shawls from our heads. Under whips and bayonets they made us use our prayer shawls as mops to clean out German latrines. We were all dead when the sun set—a hundred of us. Remember us."[72]

Another actor delivered the testimony of a dead woman from Poland: "We hung from the windows and burned in basements. . . . We fill the waters of the Dnieper today with our bodies. . . . Remember us."[73]

GREAT PRIDE

After New York, *We Will Never Die* appeared on April 12, 1943, in the nation's capital, where a smaller venue required that the Ten Commandments tablets be "reduced to 20 feet from 40 feet."[74] Still, as Rose's letter to a friend reveals, the show was still overwhelming and the project still excited him. "This coming Monday at Constitution Hall, in Washington, we are presenting the memorial pageant that we recently staged at Madison Square Garden. There are several hundred people in the cast—we are doing a new set for Washington. It involves rounding up and transporting a great many performers and cantors— and so, with one thing and another I have been kept jumping," he said.[75] For the Washington performance Hecht added a special appeal to the audience, which included "seven Supreme Court justices, two cabinet members, thirty-eight Senators and hundreds of Congressmen, and the representatives of forty nations." Among the latter were nine "representatives of the European countries occupied by Germany" whom the event's invitation credited as the production's patrons. More prestigious than all these was the presence in the audience of the first lady, Eleanor Roosevelt.[76] Hecht's appeal began, "We, the actors who have performed for you tonight are nearly done. But there is another cast of actors involved in this tale whose performance is Not done. This cast is our audience. Our audience tonight is a notable cast playing vital roles on the stage of history. It is to this audience more than to any group of human beings in the world that the dead and dying innocents of Europe raise their cry, 'Remember Us.'"[77]

As in New York, the Washington production had the desired effect of stirring the sympathy and attention that Bergson and Hecht were determined to transform into American government action that could save Jewish lives. On April 14, Mrs. Roosevelt devoted part of her nationally syndicated "My Day" newspaper column to "the mass memorial . . . dedicated to the two million Jewish dead of Europe . . . one of the most impressive and moving pageants I have ever seen. No one who heard each group come forward and give the story of what had happened to it at the hands of a ruthless German military, will ever forget those haunting words: 'Remember us.'"[78]

Additional performances were sponsored and produced by local committees in Philadelphia, Chicago, Boston, and on July 21 Los Angeles. There, a publicity flier trumpeted the first lady's words and advance stories in the city's newspapers drew eighteen thousand to the Hollywood Bowl show, which was broadcast live over KFWB, a radio station owned by the Warner brothers, who devoted this resource to the Jewish pageant.[79] It was a valedictory end to the show's tour. The Los Angeles production was the pageant's last performance. More were planned, but opposition from the American Jewish Congress scuttled plans for showings in Buffalo, Baltimore, Pittsburgh, and other cities. A battle over the power to represent American Jewry was in play. But Rose was gratified by the work he did on behalf of the Jews.

"I can't think of any show in my life that I remember with greater pride," he said.[80]

Twelve

ABRACADABRA

Meanwhile, Rose reveled in a New York version of the Paris of the twenties, when artists, entertainers, and writers apparently lived in a colony that limited interactions to only one another. His watering holes included his Diamond Horseshoe, where he introduced the film mogul Samuel Goldwyn to the showgirl and future movie star Virginia Mayo; the exclusive Stork Club's "sanctum sanctorum"—the Cub Room, a.k.a. the "snub room," whose entrants were limited to the elite, from the famous and brilliant (Orson Welles) to the simply rich (playboy Tommy Manville); and also "21," where Rose cheered the stripper Gypsy Rose Lee after Simon and Schuster would not host a launch party for her 1941 book, *The G-String Murders.* "Fuck 'em," Rose told her, according to the author Michael Korda, "if the lousy cheapskates weren't going to give her a party, he would take her out to dinner to celebrate instead."[1]

At that point, Rose was in the middle of his own dealings with a publisher. Harper & Brothers wanted to bring out his autobiography, to be ghostwritten by the New York journalist Stanley Walker, author of *The Night Club Era.* Rose was officially famous. He had even been the butt of a James Thurber *New Yorker* cartoon, the ultimate certificate of celebrity, especially if the celebrity could stand the inevitable Thurber sting. In Rose's case, it was to be put in the company of the assassinated Austrian fascist Engelbert Dollfuss. In the cartoon a tiny man explains to a large woman, "Lots of little men have got somewhere—Napoleon, Dollfuss, Billy Rose." That would not have bothered Rose. He was happy to lampoon himself. He stayed in touch with the painter Thomas Hart Benton after buying the artist's 1939 *Weighing Cotton,* so that in 1941, when Benton claimed he was tired of the effeminate art world and wanted to see his paintings displayed in "whorehouses and saloons," Rose took him up on it and hung Benton's *Persephone* in the Diamond Horseshoe. The enormous painting of a nude young woman spied upon by an old man addressed "themes of sexual conquest and frustration" that Rose knew well, both personally and as a merchant of the same.[2]

But mostly Rose's social world revolved around Lindy's, the delicatessen that was New York's version of the Paris café, and late at night he could be found there with Irving Berlin, Harold Clurman, or Stella Adler, the celebrated actress, cofounder of the Group Theatre, and daughter of Yiddish theater royalty Jacob and Sara Adler.[3] This group also rotated through Rose's home on Beekman Place, one of Manhattan's smallest, quietest, and most desirable streets. It extends just two blocks along the East River from Forty-Ninth to Fifty-First Streets, and its residents then included John D. Rockefeller's daughter and Archibald Roosevelt, son of President Theodore Roosevelt, as well as at least one wealthy Jew. William Paley, the founder of the Columbia Broadcasting System, lived in a townhouse at 29 Beekman Place. Rose became his neighbor on December 26, 1939, when the showman purchased the five-story home at 33 Beekman, where he and Holm lived with the help of a cook and chambermaid. During the day there was also a butler. "Billy liked high living. He was the first one I knew that lived in a brownstone in . . . midtown New York when everybody was living in apartments," said his songwriting partner Dave Dreyer.[4] Paley's proximity may have made the house especially attractive. Like Rose, Paley was the son of Russian Jewish immigrants who was certain he "was born with a sense of what was important to the American public."[5]

In May 1940 *Life* published a profile of Rose to showcase his beautiful new house, furniture, art, and bride. The furnishings by the interior decorator William Pahlmann included eccentric inventions, including coffee tables fashioned from "bandmaster drums" and a working fireplace framed to give the illusion that it hung from the wall like a painting.[6] Holm was delighted with her conventionally luxurious bedroom, which sported "ice-cream-colored trimmings."[7] But Rose distanced himself from the showy furnishings of his home's public rooms. He had a small bedroom where he slept on a minimally adorned, twin-sized mahogany bed. Husband and wife had different tastes. Rose recognized quality and, surprisingly, appreciated the restrained. For a man whose life and fortune derived from his taste, these differences spoke to a profound marital mismatch. "During decoration of the house, the biggest domestic feud was when Billy, an ardent art collector, bought the Modigliani [portrait of Jean Cocteau]. Eleanor wept, wouldn't live with it," *Life* reported. Rose removed it from public view and hung it in his fourth-floor bedroom. The painting is considered one of Modigliani's finest works.

Holm, meanwhile, was excited about her heated bathroom towel racks, "so that you can always have a hot towel. 'Colossal!'"[8] Married less than six months, Holm was ready to seal off Rose's life from her own. Her husband conducted business from the phones in his bedroom and "often . . . carries on four different business appointments in his house at the same time," one reporter observed. "Continually calling at odd hours are his numerous theatrical pals." Holm showed a reporter the home's elevator. "This . . . is so Billy's cronies can come in and go straight up to his room without bothering anyone else," she said. "I'm going to have the doors locked to all other parts of the house."[9]

Prominent guests enjoyed an open-door policy. When the playwright Ferenc Molnar arrived in the United States in 1940, he was the guest of honor at a Rose dinner party that included George Kaufman, Moss Hart, Ben Hecht, the symphony conductor Leopold Stokowski, the writer Edna Ferber (whose novel *Show Boat* was the basis for the great musical), George Jessel, and Edward G. Robinson. When everyone was seated, there was still an empty chair next to Rose. "It is probably for God," Kaufman jibed.[10] He was close. It was for Bernard Baruch. Molnar wrote that he "took a great liking to Billy Rose, who is vital and always full of great plans." He also appreciated Rose's gift for flattery. Molnar said the "kindest joke" that anyone ever told him came after he said to Rose, "If I'm ever broke, I'm going to ask you for the butler's job." Rose replied that he would not be able to help Molnar in that way, because "unless I'm broke, you can't be broke. And if I'm broke, I shan't be able to afford a butler."[11]

A new painting also brought people over, because Rose could not resist showing off his art and sharing his disbelief in his ownership of it. In August 1940, Clurman and Elia Kazan went to see his new El Greco, and the next night Rose invited over the playwright Clifford Odets, who had been riding high since the 1935 success of his landmark plays *Awake and Sing!* and *Waiting for Lefty* had made him "king of Broadway."[12] Odets was suitably knocked out. "It is a Saint Francis, the hands pierced, the whole design whirled around and tapered up to a lighted vent of sky," he wrote. "A real El Greco in every inch. There it was in his bedroom—I can't get over it! No, I can't!" As the two men descended in the home's elevator, Rose soothed Odets's awe with a wisecrack. Odets had gotten carried away and "suggested a bedroom in which were hung five nudes, one by

Renoir, by Manet, Goya, and two others. Said Billy, 'I will take one nude Paulette Goddard in the bed instead.' That has its points too," noted Odets.[13]

For the Jewish Odets, Rose was fascinating, both repulsive and attractive. He wrote in his diary, "Last night . . . ate at Lindy's, there meeting and talking for an hour with that sordid little clown, Billy Rose, who pretends aloud that he cannot understand, lying, as he said, in Eleanor's room, what he did to deserve all of this, the money and the luxury and the lady's breasts, I suppose. By which he means to say that he has done pretty well for a little Jew boy from nowhere. . . . He sees himself as some little Napoleon, and not so little at that."[14] Rose had an obvious affinity with Odets's father, whose "business morality" often made Odets feel contempt for his own idealism and "its ineffectuality in the 'real' world."[15] Rose's "morality is that of the master," Odets wrote. "Billy always manages to let you know what enormous income taxes he is paying, how gifted he is, how altogether attractive he is. He is not bad, merely ambitious. I don't dislike him."[16] That would change. In December 1941, Rose produced Odets's *Clash by Night* and pressed for tough terms. As Clurman remembered, "I received a wire from Odets saying that Billy Rose was going to back his play, but that he wanted so large a percentage of the profits in return for his investment that there would be none left for the Group Theatre as such. What did I say? I said: 'Go ahead.' Another wire followed shortly after, informing me that Billy Rose did not wish to use the Group Theatre's name in billing the play. What did I say? I said: 'Very well.'"[17]

As usual, after winning the business negotiation, Rose worked hard to deliver the best possible show. "Mr. Rose has given a very fine production to one of Mr. Odets' worst plays," wrote the theater critic John Anderson. The "unrelievedly sordid" story of a love triangle in which the husband kills his wife's lover seems to bear the scars of Odets's relationship with Rose. The character of the lover offers an insight into Rose's boasting when he says, "I don't enjoy my life. I enjoy only the dream of it." Odets also appears to have made use of Rose's marriage by noting the obvious—that Rose was a tiny man and his wife Eleanor a powerful, beautiful athlete. So the wife in *Clash* longs for "big, comfortable men" and complains of those who are "little and nervous."[18] As for Rose, his production of this bleak play about unlikable characters recalls *The Great Magoo,* and taken together they speak to his deep cynicism. Prepared for the worst, he always carried a revolver. "I never go anywhere without my gun," he told the public relations man Wolfe Kaufman, who saw the pistol on a table next to Rose's bed.[19] The upside of his hardboiled character was a sometimes cheerful and witty acceptance of rough treatment. It confirmed his outlook. After the drama critic John Mason Brown savaged Odets's play, Rose wrote him,

> I enjoyed your piece in last Saturday's paper. I doubt very much whether Odets did, but anyone who aspires to be an apostle must expect to be hit over the head with a tablet now and then. . . . A gimlet eyed assistant has instructions to close "Clash By Night" the first week it loses over eight dollars. . . . If the intake and outgo refuse to keep company, it will fold—and the hell with it. I just don't know how to get "artsy"-"craftsy" about show business. I like it when it roars. A peep show with a high hat (flop legit) is not my cup of tea.[20]

Clash closed in February 1942 after forty-nine performances.

IF GOD HAD MONEY

Odets's drama lost Rose $30,000, but he was so rich that the then-quite-sizable debit did not even slow his spending on art and real estate.[21] Still, he liked to flaunt his reputation for thrift. "Not with my dough. . . . Sunshine is for apricots," is how Rose facetiously insisted he had no interest in buying a country home when Eleanor informed him that that was what they were going to do.[22] In May he paid $60,000 for a fifty-eight-acre estate in Westchester County's Mount Kisco. Only forty miles from Manhattan, it was a popular spot for moneyed weekenders. Gertrude Berg, the Molly Goldberg of her hit radio show, *The Rise of the Goldbergs,* was nearby, and Benny Goodman soon joined them.[23] Writing partners George Kaufman and Moss Hart chose Bucks County, Pennsylvania, for the site of their country estates, but they were all part of a phenomenon that the Jewish songwriter Arthur Caesar termed "Poland to polo in two generations."[24] These children of immigrants were dizzied by their rapid rise from poverty and fulfilled their American dreams with dream homes. "What are you doing here?" Rose wondered to himself about the estate he and Eleanor named Roseholm. "Don't you know this setup was intended for people with long, thin faces and stylish ancestors?"

Feeling like a trespasser, however, only added to the thrill of wandering his lawns and gardens and filling his twenty-six-room mansion with rambunctious friends. "The kick I get out of tramping around my own land," he said, "is something only another kid who was raised in the dust and thunder of an East Side slum can understand. . . . Many a night Eleanor and I have sat out on the porch and heard our guests laughing in the game room—laughing the way you're not supposed to laugh in Georgian houses with white columns."[25] And using language on the tennis court not heard at Wimbledon. Rose "was a rabid tennis player," said the songwriter Chester Conn. "One afternoon he was in the midst of a heated tennis match between me and his wife and somebody else . . . [and] right in the midst of this excitement the phone bell rang and pretty soon the valet came to the tennis court. He said, Mr. Beaverbrook is on the phone. Billy was just about to receive a tough service. He said, Oh fuck Mr. Beaverbrook," who was in fact Churchill's cabinet minister and the newspaper magnate Lord Beaverbrook. The incongruity was just too much. "We all collapsed. Fell down."[26] As Rose confessed, he and his friends were just "a generation or two removed from another kind of world."[27]

Regular guests included friends Ben Hecht, the composer Deems Taylor, and Rose's sister Polly and her husband, and occasional visitors ranged from Orson Welles to Jimmy Durante, Benny Goodman to George Jessel, and Laurence Olivier to Nicky Blair, Rose's manager at the Diamond Horseshoe. Blair delivered the thrill of secondhand contact with gangsters, because he "certainly 'knew all the boys,'" said Wolfe Kaufman, who called Blair "a delightful character and definitely a toughie with 'connections.'"[28] At the other end of the spectrum were great personages. In 1946, "Bernard Baruch brought Winston Churchill to Mount Kisco," Holm said. "Holy father!"[29]

Rose did everything he could to make his home and grounds grand enough to impress anyone, indulging an approach Wolcott Gibbs formulated when Moss Hart told him, "I've moved this oak so that it shades my library," and Gibbs replied, "It just goes to show you what God could do if He only had money."[30] Rose turned part of his estate's stables into a private movie theater, and when he wanted to screen a film he asked and got Goldwyn to provide it.[31] A manmade paradise strewn with art greeted the playwrights Ruth and Augustus Goetz when they visited Roseholm in the years after the success of their 1947 Broadway play, *The Heiress,* based on Henry James's *Washington Square:*

> The approach to Billy's house was through a gateway, then a mile long drive planted with pink dogwoods on either side, and a distant view of low-lying turn-of-the-century barns and stables, well out of the view of the manse which lay across the top of a gentle ridge. The house was Georgian, in the usual Boarding School for Young Ladies style of grandeur, except that here a Bourdel [*sic*] nude and Rodin's

bust of Balzac flanked the front drive, which the average boarding school doesn't bother with. . . . He had bought Rodins and Manzus and Bourdels [*sic*] and Daumiers and Lipschutzs [*sic*] and Nadelmans and Renoirs and Remingtons and Noguchi and Hepworths and perhaps fifty more of lesser and greater sculptors and his woods were alive with their silent people. He had read every book on the art that had appeared since Vasari, and he knew how good or bad his examples were and how he meant to improve or add to it in the coming years. His bedroom slippers were always muddy at Mt Kisco, because he would take a walk through his woods a few times a day when he was there, and he would be plotting and campaigning for the next acquisition, and where he would place it and how he would plant around it.[32]

As Rose joked about his Beekman Place address, the only thing out of place at Mount Kisco was himself. When he greeted Goetz and her husband, Rose "was wearing old black evening trousers with a silk stripe down the sides, a soiled grey sweat shirt which gaped at his neck because it had been stretched over his head so many times, his hair was long and greasy and fell in ribbons behind his ears, and his fingers were stained yellow from the million cigarettes that had preceded the one he was smoking now."[33]

Roseholm was a showcase and theater for the display and performance of American success, and the energy and time and money Rose lavished on it were a measure of how much its primary benefit meant to him. In 1943, at virtually the same time he produced *We Will Never Die,* he produced a patriotic war bonds rally at Mount Kisco's St. Francis Auditorium, featuring his wife Eleanor as a star of the entertainment.[34] And though he insisted he liked delicatessen, in Westchester he ate at the local and fine French restaurant, La Crémaillère, and ordered frog's legs.[35] "He was a *feinshmecker,*" said his friend Karl Katz. "Had good taste in everything."[36] As Rose made clear to Lee Strasberg in 1955, the country home was a refuge from his Jewish self and concerns. "Over the past fifteen years," he said, "come Hell, high water or Hitler, I have spend [*sic*] all my holidays in Mount Kisco."[37]

ADMIRED AND HATED

Given a choice, the press preferred to ignore Rose's Jewish work and write instead about his mansions and other glitzy achievements, and there was always a choice, because he juggled both simultaneously. In July 1943, just a month after the last production of *We Will Never Die, Life* magazine ran its fourth feature on Rose's Diamond Horseshoe for no discernible reason except, perhaps, to dispel from readers' minds anything they might have heard about his Jewish activism, which the magazine never covered.[38] Another press opportunity to shift the focus toward the lighthearted surfaced in December 1943 with Rose's production of Oscar Hammerstein II's *Carmen Jones.* Rose began work on the African American adaptation of Bizet's opera in late 1942, and so was involved with it at the same time that he produced *We Will Never Die.* But his hard-nosed approach to *Carmen Jones* signaled that it was a business venture and not eligible for the generosity he bestowed on his Jewish projects.

"Billy Rose, whom I admired tremendously and hated even more," said Dick Campbell in a reminiscence of the man he fought with over the salary of Muriel Rahn, who played *Carmen*'s title role. Campbell demanded that Rahn, who was his wife as well as his client, get a star's salary and not the paltry $150 a week Rose offered, but Campbell could not get anywhere while Rose had what he thought was a suitable replacement for Rahn. "He kept holding Muriel Smith over my head," Campbell said. "I worked up a scheme." Knowing that Smith's voice would not weather eight shows a week, Campbell allowed Rose to replace Rahn with the less experienced singer, whose voice soon faltered. "And that's when I got Billy Rose," Campbell said. Rose had to pay Rahn $500 a week or close the show. Campbell regretted the gambit that undermined Smith, but a battle against Rose was no holds barred. "I was dealing with a fellow who was rough," he said.[39] Rose was so rough that it almost seems he needed to counteract the good work he did on *We Will Never Die* in order to restore his equilibrium. He told the press agent Charles Samuels, "I know what [my employees] are saying, 'Look at this little boss. Let's get some shit out of the toilet and dump it on him.' I don't care what they say."[40] Samuels believed him.

Carmen Jones was a smash. "Billy Rose is a little man with gigantic ideas, which at suitable intervals explode over the city like a burst of fireworks," was how the *Times* welcomed its premiere. "The display last evening was one of the grandest of them all." Yet another profile of the hometown hero was in order, and the *New York Post* delivered one in December 1943 that featured photographs and quotes and a by-now-familiar retelling of Rose's triumphs, including his rise from shorthand wiz to songwriter to producer of *Jumbo,* the Fort Worth Centennial, and the Aquacade, all of which led to his current winner, *Carmen Jones.*[41] The Holocaust pageant from earlier in the year was ignored. The omission was significant, because for New York Jews the *Post* was, as one Jewish woman put it, "our paper." Owned and run by Dorothy "Dolly" Schiff, who was Jewish, it offered Jews "a message of what it was possible to aspire to" and was "very much identified with glamour for Jews," in the words of its readers. As a "primer on how to become an American," the *Post* spoke to the Jewish American identity struggle that required constant recalibration.[42] Its profile may have hinted to Rose that his Jewish identity needed to be toned down.

ABRACADABRA

"It is true that I did stage the pageant, 'We Will Never Die,' both in New York and at Constitution Hall in Washington for Ben Hecht, who wrote it," Rose told the *Washington Post* in October 1944. "I did it because it was a good show. That was my only connection to the pageant."[43]

Rose's disavowal came when his enthusiasm and even love for the Bergson Boys was at its height, when his work to publicize Hecht's 1944 *A Guide for the Bedevilled,* a furious denunciation of Germany, excited his energies, and when a heated dispute between the Bergsonites and the American Jewish Congress (AJC), the main umbrella group of American Jewry, had metastasized into hatred and even sabotage. The timing of this feud seems to have caused Rose to suffer a relapse of the Jewish wariness that in 1939 made him create a diversionary publicity event to obscure his rescue of Kurt Schwarz. The risk of losing money might have also played a role. As with Schwarz, Rose's 1944 erasure of the Jewishness of *We Will Never Die* overlapped with a producing project. In December 1943 he had (somehow) pulled strings to guarantee that his offer of $630,000 would win the sealed-bid auction for the Ziegfeld Theatre. Built in 1927 by Flo Ziegfeld with money provided by the newspaper magnate William Randolph Hearst, and designed inside and out by the Vienna-born artist Joseph Urban, whose credo that "form followed fantasy"[44] made him a Manhattanist brother to Rose, the Ziegfeld was considered one of the greatest theaters in the country, and on September 1, 1944, Rose celebrated his ownership of it with a party there, after which he shelled out another $260,000 to restore "its old lush loveliness" and banish the slovenliness that had accumulated during its eleven years as a movie house.[45] By October, he was masterminding the Ziegfeld's premiere production, *Seven Lively Arts,* a revue scheduled to open on December 7, the anniversary of Pearl Harbor, as a kind of thumbing-of-the-nose at America's enemies.[46] One of the aims of *Fun to Be Free* and *We Will Never Die* was to defeat the idea promoted by bigots such as Lindbergh that American Jews needed to choose between such patriotism and allegiance to the Jewish people, but despite his participation in both productions, Rose apparently did not trust the public to embrace this broad-minded idea. The grand opening of his Ziegfeld Theatre meant big money was on the line, and to protect his investment Rose hedged his bets by denying that Jewish projects were important to him.

Rose adored Bergson's aggressive approach to the Jewish cause, but over the course of 1944 it put him in a spotlight that revealed his Jewish stage fright. The wrenching melodrama of *We Will Never Die* and the newspaper advertisements that cried out, "Action—Not Pity, Can Save Millions Now!" demonstrated that Bergson's group "had a better understanding of the needs of the hour and the sentiments of the Jewish masses" than the AJC.[47] Even the Labor Zionists, natural foes of the right-wing Bergsonites, recognized that the latter "succeeded in catching the legitimate Jewish organizations off guard and in demonstrating the inadequacy of Jewish leadership." In addition to the publicity front, Bergson relentlessly lobbied Congress far more actively than more pedigreed Jewish organizations did, and his group succeeded in its efforts when the legislature supported the creation of an agency to aid refugees. This victory came despite Rabbi Wise's testimony before the House Foreign Affairs Committee that Bergson's was "an irresponsible group." Bergson's group won its greatest victory on January 22, 1944, when President Roosevelt established the War Refugee Board, which succeeded in rescuing some two hundred thousand European Jews. Bergson's efforts to save millions failed, but historians give his group most of the credit for the birth of the WRB.[48] In April, Rose wrote Hecht, "These direct action boys delight my heart."[49]

Rose kept tabs on the War Refugee Board's creation through conversations with Baruch, who Rose was excited to tell Hecht called him "from Washington at the crack of dawn a couple of days before the announcement appeared about the boss's appointment of a Refugee Commission. . . . He is definitely of the belief that something will happen and happen quickly." The boss, in Rose's lingo, was President Roosevelt. Not surprisingly, Rose was eager to claim some credit for the creation of the WRB. "I am not under-rating the great contribution made by [Bergson's] organization. I think it helped plenty but I wouldn't be a bit surprised that our friendship with the old boy [Baruch] helped bring this to a head."[50] Baruch played a very minor role, but Rose's wishful thinking attests to his continuing desire to be a Disraeli, a figure influencing Jewish history. Though there is no correspondence between Rose and Baruch during the early 1940s, Baruch was a guest at Rose's Beekman Place home in 1940, and per Rose's letter to Hecht the two were in contact in 1943–44. That Baruch trusted Rose with confidential government information strongly suggests that a relationship based on mutual respect had been formed.

Rose was especially pleased to tell Hecht about press reports quoting government sources that "specifically stated that [the WRB] was to save Jews. It's the first thing stripped of abracadabra." This turned out to be false. The magician's trick of diverting attention away from the crucial action was still in use. The executive order that created the WRB did not mention Jews but referred instead to "victims of enemy oppression who are in imminent danger of death."[51] As it had been since the mid-1930s, the government was "sensitive to the charge . . . of American subservience to Jewish concerns."[52] That even the government believed the American public in 1944 harbored suspicions of the Jews suggests that Rose was not paranoid or foolish to protect himself by denying a Jewish interest in *We Will Never Die*. Baruch also followed the government's lead and avoided public affiliation with Jewish causes. He told Rose he was "very insistent that his name never be mentioned in connection with any work he may have done for this cause."[53] Rose, as always, followed in Baruch's footsteps.

In early 1944, Rose devoted himself to a new Jewish project: publicizing and distributing Hecht's *A Guide for the Bedevilled*, a fiery attack on German antisemitism and German character itself. The promotion effort brought Rose and Bergson into the closest working relationship they ever had. Both men practically swooned over the book and its roaring anger. "Only genius can combine so much love and so much hatred. . . . This book must become not only a best seller but also a starting point for an unprecedented crusade," Bergson wrote Hecht, and Rose wrote Winchell, "Ben has dipped his pen in blood and punched as only he can punch when he's mad. . . . I am afraid, and I know that you are too, that the world will soon forget and what is worse, forgive the bestial enemy we are fighting. Those who read Ben's book will never forget and unless they are made of mush, will never forgive." Rose had sent Winchell a chapter called "A Talent for Murder." "It took the top of my head off," Rose said.[54] At Scribner's publishing house, the editor Maxwell Perkins, who had worked with Thomas Wolfe, Hemingway, and F. Scott Fitzgerald, felt the same way. He wrote Hecht, "I wanted to publish the 'Guide' the moment I saw it, just on principle, and then very much more after I read it for its fire and power as literature."[55]

The book appeared in March 1944 and Rose and Bergson worked separately and together to get *Bedevilled* its greatest possible audience. The two met that month and "were in perfect agreement as to the necessity and advisability of a large scale campaign.... [Rose] is very enthusiastic about the whole thing and is pounding away with his usual zest," Bergson wrote. Rose promised Hecht "that a very excited friend of yours is ready to start swin[g]ing with two capable hands and a well filled purse to ensure its being read by a great number of people." But in a harbinger of his future statement to the *Washington Post,* Rose said he wished to do this work "quietly."[56]

Still, he fought for the book on every front. He overcame Scribner's hoarding of its ad allocation to win *Bedevilled* eight additional ads in the *Times* and the *Herald Tribune,* and when he heard the publishing house would not print enough books to meet demand, he went down to Scribner's to look into it and fix it.[57] He got the playwright Sam Behrman to write the book's ad copy, and when he was not happy with Behrman's work, had him go back and rewrite it.[58] He made a deal with the *New York Post* to run *Bedevilled* as a serial "in daily instalments," he told Hecht. "This as you know gets a good deal of hurrah and advertising and its three or four hundred thousand circulation is not to be sneezed at."[59] He even came through with money, as proved when he complained to Hecht that Scribner's would not devote more of its newspaper ad quota to *Bedevilled,* "even though we pay for the ads."[60] Rose may have spent as much as $13,000 to publicize the book, as Bergson projected that the publicity campaign would cost $15,000 and his group contributed only $2,000.[61] This did not diminish his estimation of the Bergson Boys. When the group's newsletter, *The Answer,* advertised the book, Rose was "filled with admiration for this hard hitting little outfit."[62] Rose also encouraged Hecht to serialize the book in the *Chicago Tribune* with the great hardboiled line, "WE WOULD DRINK THE ENEMYS [*sic*] BLOOD WHY NOT HIS WINE" (the paper's publisher, Robert McCormick, was a staunch isolationist).[63]

The result was that *Bedevilled* hit number seven on the nonfiction bestseller list, causing Rose to quip, "I don't know exactly what this means in terms of books—but as the lady said to the sailor—'It's nice.'"[64] Two weeks later, with decency and without the Broadway attitude, Rose declined to take credit for the book's success. "Please believe me when I tell you I don't think my efforts have contributed very much to the showing the book has made," he wrote Hecht. "I think they may have helped a bit, but I think the book is doing its own job."[65]

His childhood memory of his mother pleading for the Jews of Kishinev was the model for all of Rose's Jewish projects, and in another note to Hecht he described their relationship as a familial one, with Rose in the superior position. He signed himself, "your loving father."[66] And in May, in the midst of publicizing Hecht's book, Rose was even inspired "to take a spite at an anti-Semite in my own way. I bought Donald Ogden Stewart's play, tentatively entitled 'Emily Brady.' This is an impassioned attack on Mr. Ford."[67]

It was at this moment, when Rose was basking in feelings of Jewish family love, enjoying the sales figures for Hecht's book, and admiring the Bergson Boys, that the fight between the Bergsonites and Wise's AJC hit a new low and put Rose on the spot. In May 1944, Bergson founded the Hebrew Committee of National Liberation and opened an "embassy" in Washington to represent the Hebrew nation, as opposed to adherents of the Jewish faith. The move anticipated Israeli identity, but at the time few had the patience or interest to decipher Bergson's innovation, and Wise, who in December had even warned Secretary of the Interior Harold Ickes that "the time will come and come soon when you will find it necessary to withdraw from this irresponsible [Bergson] group," now stepped up his attacks.[68] Nahum Goldmann, an ally of Rabbi Wise, urged the State Department to either draft or deport Bergson and reported that Wise "regarded Bergson as equally as great an enemy of the Jews as Hitler, for the reason that his activities could only lead to increased anti-Semitism."[69] On July 6 and August 31, the Zionist Emergency Council, a group aligned with the AJC, targeted Bergson allies with mail campaigns that denounced Bergson's groups.[70] Bergson returned the venom and castigated the "inferiority, cowardliness ... [and] degeneration of our so-called 'Jewish Leaders.'"[71] The AJC called the Bergson group fascists and Bergson an "irresponsible adventurer ... without credentials."[72] Bergson was, in fact, a hard man to pin down. Even an admirer agreed that he struck some "as a confidence man" and that it was never clear whether Bergson was a "prophet or promoter."[73] The similarity to Rose is striking and may explain why, when Bergson was under attack, he called on Rose for help.

On October 3, 1944, the *Washington Post* ran the first of what became a series of four front-page investigative articles that questioned Peter Bergson's character and background, raised suspicions about the source of his funds, and quoted his foes at the AJC saying that his Hebrew Committee was a "fraud, a buffoonery, and a comic opera drollery, if it were not so tragic." Bergson was certain the articles stemmed from the "pathological trickery" of his foes. On October 4, the second

Post article appeared, and in response to a reporter's question about his funding Bergson said that part of it "was provided for by Billy Rose." The *Post* contacted Rose, and he refuted his beloved direct-action boy. "Let him show one single check I ever signed," challenged Rose, who then went beyond what was required by saying he only worked on *We Will Never Die* "because it was a good show."[74]

Given Rose's crocodile skin, he may not have felt humiliated by his embarrassing behavior. He never referred to the incident. Bergson and Hecht seem to have taken it in stride, and before long both were again working with him. For men like Bergson and Rose, lying to outsiders was a forgivable offense, and the wording of Rose's denial may have even been a maneuver that allowed him to make a getaway, while sending a knowing wink to his friends. He likely spoke the literal truth: Rose probably never did send Bergson a check. There is evidence, though, that he gave cash. In the margin of a letter from Rose to Hecht, the latter, or his wife, wrote, "We didn't *take* money from the Irgun fellows. Sometimes—not often though—we gave cash in $1000 lots."[75]

BLACK BOOK

Further evidence that Bergson spoke the truth about Rose's financial support is that at virtually the same moment Rose also gave money to President Roosevelt's reelection campaign. This was also a form of Jewish philanthropy. In addition to the president's popularity among Jews, in New York Rose visited the offices of the Liberal Party, run by David Dubinsky, head of the powerful garment workers union, and while there saw David Niles, a Jewish White House staffer and Roosevelt adviser. "I gave Dubinsky a check for $1000 and I shall contribute at least $2000 more to the local [campaign] efforts here in New York," Rose wrote in a letter afterward. On top of that, Rose was in touch with Harry Hopkins, one of Roosevelt's most trusted advisers and a man who had three children by his Jewish first wife. Rose sent Hopkins "a couple of thousand dollars for the Roosevelt Fund" and shared all this news with Morris Ernst, cofounder of the American Civil Liberties Union, whom Rose addressed as "my darling."[76]

Rose's success had carried him to one of the loftier heights of American society, a climb made possible by the equivalent success of his Jewish peers, who were his only contacts at this altitude. Niles, Dubinsky, and Ernst expanded Rose's circle of powerful Jewish friends, associates, and contacts whom he had valued since he met Baruch at the War Industries Board, and his affection for Ernst suggests that these relationships were informed by Jewish family feeling. They spoke the same unsentimental energetic language. Dubinsky, born in Russia, spoke with a Yiddish accent, and his style was pure ghetto cosmopolitan. It ratcheted back and forth from "that of global statesman to that of a dead-end kid," according to his *Times* obituary. Ernst fit the same mold. He was an "unlawyerlike" lawyer who was always "bouncing back with a bright idea, an angle, a plan of action. And, inevitably, advertising his intimacy with the great."[77]

Within a year Rose was at work on a Jewish project that called for action on a scale suited to such company, but as a kind of appetizer he first took on a relatively modest piece of work. In the spring of 1945, victory in Europe was just weeks from being concluded when Gen. Maurice Rose, the highest-ranking Jew in the American military, was killed in action in Germany. The circumstances were not clear, but American Jews had no trouble believing the highly respected tank commander and son of a rabbi was unjustly killed, and in his hometown of Denver the Jewish community decided to dedicate its plans for a new hospital to the general. Toward that end, it sent a representative to New York to get help for its fundraising effort. Rose volunteered to be the chairman of the nationwide campaign, and his first move was to send telegrams to a variety of show business stars and urge them to attend Denver's $1,000-a-plate fundraising dinner scheduled for May.[78] Telegrams to Orson Welles, James Cagney, Spencer Tracy, and Humphrey Bogart were likely identical to the passionate one Rose sent Irving Berlin:

> Dear Irving, you undoubtedly were as shocked as I was to read news accounts of the brutal murder of Major General Maurice B. Rose of our Third Army on being captured by the Nazis. The citizens of Denver, the General's home town are preparing to perpetuate his memory by the erection of a million dollar non-sectarian hospital. This is a cause very dear to me. On Sunday May twentieth a citizens committee with the assistance of the Denver Post is giving a thousand dollar a plate dinner as the kickoff in the fund raising drive. I know that you are very busy but I wonder whether you can possibly appear at that function. Your presence would be a great stimulus. . . . If you can make it, I will arrange plane transportation and all accommodation.[79]

Rose's offer to pay Berlin's travel and hotel costs is more evidence of his open-wallet policy when it came to Jewish causes, and his characterization of the general's killing as a "brutal murder" links it to the Holocaust. By this time, Rose had read the grim *Black Book of Polish Jewry*, published in December 1943 by the American Federation of Polish Jews. Hecht brought it to his attention, and the edited collection "emphasized the small-scale—of the fate of individuals and small groups—in an effort to personalize the horror." The volume also included photographs "of mass graves stacked with the naked corpses of Jewish victims."[80] Rose clearly viewed the German killing of General Rose as part of that nation's crime against the Jewish people.

None of the entertainers Rose contacted were able to lend a hand, but Rose did get Paul Whiteman to dedicate his May 20, 1945, *Philco Hall of Fame Hour* radio show to General Rose, drawing national attention to the cause. Rose served as chairman of the General Rose Memorial Hospital Campaign until the end of August.[81] Three years later, on August 31, 1948, Gen. Dwight Eisenhower, General Rose's former commander, laid the cornerstone for the hospital, which opened on May 1, 1949.[82]

ROSE'S MISSION

In the fall, another report on the Jews stirred Rose. With the war at an end, the need to resettle millions of European refugees prompted President Truman to send Earl G. Harrison, who had recently served President Roosevelt as commissioner of immigration and naturalization, to investigate conditions of "displaced persons," in particular "the problems, needs and views of the Jewish refugees . . . especially in Germany and Austria." Harrison's report, *The Plight of the Displaced Jews in Europe,* was presented to Truman in August, released by the White House on September 29, and revealed to readers of the *Times* the following day. The findings and assessments were Harrison's and, free of bureaucratic language, they hit hard. One of the most shocking statements appeared on the newspaper's front page: "As matters now stand, we appear to be treating the Jews as the Nazis treated them except that we do not exterminate them. They are in concentration camps in large numbers under our own military guard instead of SS troops. One is led to wonder whether the German people, seeing this, are not supposing that we are following or at least condoning Nazi policy." On the other hand, Harrison's most insightful observation received almost no attention: "The first and plainest need of these people is a recognition of their actual status and by this I mean their status as Jews. . . . The general practice thus far has been to follow only nationality lines. . . . [But] Jews as Jews . . . have been more severely victimized than the non-Jewish members of the same or other nationalities. . . . Refusal to recognize the Jews as such has the effect, in this situation, of closing one's eyes to their former and more barbaric persecution."[83]

This refusal to recognize the Jews as Jews confounded not just American officials but also American Jews, as Hecht had argued in the PM articles that exposed the conflicted American Jewish identity he dredged from his own experience. Rose had no such problem, and a month after Harrison's report became public, he contacted Baruch. Rose had to investigate the DP situation himself. "Dear Bernie . . . Would dearly love to get into Germany especially Nuremberg. Understand this only possible by invitation of member of military government. If not out of line wonder if you could get General Patton or General Bedell Smith to issue invitation. If any reason needed could come in as entertainment consultant."[84]

On November 3 Rose flew to London, where he investigated some entertainment business opportunities, and by the end of the month was in Germany. He did not visit Nuremberg to witness the war crime trials that began there on November 20, but otherwise Baruch apparently delivered, because Rose met with Gen. Bedell Smith, who had been General Eisenhower's chief of staff, and conducted a tour of Germany and Austria with the assistance of a military escort behind the wheel of a Plymouth. One of his first visits was to the Dachau concentration camp near Munich. "I thought I was prepared, but I wasn't," he said later. "I walked out of there plenty angry, an angry Jew, if I may say so. I hated their gory guts."[85]

Then he toured DP camps to inspect conditions among Jewish inmates. On December 2, the Jews at the Zeilsheim camp near Frankfurt unveiled a monument to the millions of murdered Jews and Rose was there to witness the ceremony. Zeilsheim was a model settlement of three thousand where Jews lived in normal homes that were requisitioned for them from local Germans. General Eisenhower's special adviser on Jewish issues and a *Boston Herald* reporter had also just visited. The United Nations Relief and Rehabilitation Administration (UNRRA) officials who operated the facility took Rose's visit seriously, and the team director introduced him to DPs, most of whom were survivors of Buchenwald, Bergen-Belsen, and Dachau. Rose knew enough Yiddish to communicate with them. UNRRA was so cordial because it wanted good publicity. This was a game Rose knew well, and he issued, via telegram, a quote that UNRRA distributed: "What I've seen so far indicates great consideration, amazing sensitivity on part UNRRA and US army officials. There are undoubtedly many problems to be solved, but startling essential fact that only bigoted person can deny is both UNRRA and US Army approaching situation with heart and compassion."[86]

A week later Rose visited the New Palestine camp near Salzburg, Austria, and his appearance left behind an indication of his fame and renown among American Jews. The chaplain there, an Eli Heimberg, noted in a December 8 letter to his wife that paperwork had kept him from the camp that day, "and therefore I missed meeting Billy Rose, the showking [sic] and the big cheese of the musical extravaganza field." Nobody seemed to know what Rose's mission was, but Heimberg was certain it was more than the rumored preparation for an entertainment. "I think his real mission is being kept secret and it is as an inspecting authority on the Jewish problem," he wrote. "Most people forget that Billy Rose is not only a great producer of musicals, but a very intelligent and brilliant man."[87] That same day Rose met with the US general Mark Clark, a key commander in the 1943 invasion of Italy, to discuss entertainment for servicemen and the conditions facing Jewish DPs. He then lunched with the general and several of his staff.[88]

When he returned to New York on December 16, 1945, Rose immediately contacted the *Times* with the story of his visit, which the paper printed the next day. What Rose had to say was news. He did not focus on the DP camps but instead talked about the conditions facing Jews in Poland. According to the *Times,* "Mr. Rose said that his knowledge of Yiddish had enabled him to obtain a vivid picture of the plight of the Jewish people in Poland by questioning Jews in camps in Germany and Vienna. He declared that the treatment of returning Polish Jews 'is as ferocious as by the Nazis.'" This information reflected the anti-Jewish violence that had occurred in Poland over the summer months and that would break out again in 1946. About the UNRRA camps in Germany he was largely complimentary, citing as a problem only the overcrowding, which the story implied was driven by the arrival of Jews fleeing Poland.[89]

But at the end of December, in a private letter to General Clark, Rose was more critical of the job done by the army and UNRRA. He wrote that his "visit to ROTHSCHILD Hospital SIEGASSE Number 9 and other JEWISH Displaced Persons Installations distressed me very much. On coldest day of the year these buildings were without heat and old people who had somehow lived through 3 years of concentration camp in CZECHOSLAVAKIA were huddled up in filthy beds because rooms were too bitter cold to get up. Evidence of over crowding unbalanced diet inadequate medical supplies apparent everywhere. I am sure a personal inspection of your part would be productive of real act of mercy." He closed his note with a request that Clark confirm the "improvement of conditions for this remnant of a race." He received no reply.[90]

Thirteen

A FLAG IS BORN

Rose raised one more issue with the *Times,* and that was Jewish immigration to Palestine. During his visits to DP camps he saw firsthand what Earl Harrison had noted some months before: that the desire of the Jewish DPs to immigrate to Palestine was widespread and profound and the only moral path forward. "The civilized world owes it to this handful of survivors to provide them with a home where they can again settle down and begin to live as human beings," Harrison wrote. Just before Rose visited Germany and Austria, an UNRRA official reported that "a general strike which occurred simultaneously in all Jewish camps . . . [was] a demonstration against the British deal of preventing their immigration into Palestine. More trouble of this sort was expected." During Rose's visit to Zeilsheim he would have observed that the Jews embraced Zionism as a "Jewish national approach to their problems." They resented UNRRA authorities who tried to "force their educational and cultural program into a pattern that is Polish or German, or English, and not Jewish."[1] As for the New Palestine camp, its name made its inhabitants' hopes plain. So Rose raised the issue with the *Times* but, as usual, hedged (or fudged) his position. "I'm not a Zionist, I do not know enough about it," he said, "but I would like to see Palestine made quickly available as a place of refuge and rescue."[2]

This was not on the level. After more than two years working closely with Hecht and Bergson, Rose knew a good deal about Zionism, and his continuing connection with Bergson and his new organizations, the Hebrew Committee of National Liberation and the American League for a Free Palestine (ALFP), make it clear that Rose was a Zionist. In the fall of 1946 he told a friend that he helped unnamed groups working for the Zionist cause, and later he was more explicit when he told Lee Strasberg, "I helped buy a fairish amount of guns for the Irgun."[3]

Because America's closest ally, Great Britain, opposed Jewish immigration, in order to placate Arab objections, Zionism was controversial, but it was also very popular among Jews. The former New York governor Herbert Lehman urged the opening of Jewish immigration to Palestine, and in 1946 the famed liberal journalist I. F. Stone published *Underground to Palestine,* an account of his experience running the British blockade against Jewish immigration. He wrote it not "merely in search of a good story, but as a kinsman, fulfilling a moral obligation to my brothers."[4] The symphony conductor Leonard Bernstein "sympathized with both the Irgun and the Haganah," and in 1947 he conducted the Palestine Philharmonic Orchestra while the British and Jewish militias fought each other in violent battles.

The Jewish American public also supported the Zionist movement. In 1945, membership in America's Zionist organizations reached one million, a dramatic rise from the sixty-five thousand in 1933. Such general agreement made the moment a historic one. "At the war's end, American Jews confronted the enormity of the destruction of European Jewry and the . . . struggle for Jewish sovereignty in Palestine," notes the historian Arthur Goren. "Linking the solution of the problem of the survivors with the attainment of statehood created a unity of purpose on a scale unprecedented in the modern history of the Jews."[5]

THE BIG BOYS

Rose played a part in this extraordinary moment. In March 1946, two of the wealthiest and most important players in American Jewish life—Edward M. M. Warburg, heir to the great Warburg banking and investment fortune, and William Rosenwald, a former director at retail giant Sears, Roebuck—reached out to him for help with the United Jewish Appeal's "Campaign for Survival" to raise $100 million. The campaign helped the Jewish causes Rose cared most about, as half the amount raised funded the American Jewish Joint Distribution Committee's work with DPs and another 40 percent funded Jewish settlement in Palestine.[6]

Rose was an almost inevitable choice. His fame and riches were now greater than ever. *Carmen Jones* remained a hit throughout 1944 and netted Rose $40,000 a week as it played until February 1945 for a run of thirteen months. *Seven Lively Arts* at his Ziegfeld Theatre ran for five months, until May 1945, and though it was not a critical success the revue's parade of top talent, with sketches by Kaufman and Hart, songs by Cole Porter, music by Igor Stravinsky, dance by the ballerina Alicia Markova, and the return from England of the great comedienne Bea Lillie, won him terrific publicity, including another multipage spread in *Life* and yet another newspaper profile, this one in the *Times,* which stayed true to the established format by mentioning virtually his every endeavor except his Jewish-themed productions.[7]

His Diamond Horseshoe was still so popular that on April 12, 1945, the night of President Roosevelt's death, every club "in town was waiting to see if the Diamond Horseshoe would stay open" or go dark in mourning, said Kitty Carlisle Hart, who then sang at the Club Versailles. "They were all waiting on Billy. And he decided to stay open, and we all went to work."[8] And when one Billy Rose production folded, another opened, to provide uninterrupted publicity. Just before *Seven Lively Arts* closed, 20th Century-Fox released *Billy Rose's Diamond Horseshoe,* a musical film the *Times* called "probably the most expensive advertisement that a night club ever had." Not only did Rose not pay for the ad; he got paid for it. "It didn't cost me a moment's effort and it brought in thousands. I had to do something for Eleanor," Rose told an associate struck by "the topaz in Eleanor's bracelet," which, she said, "was the size and shape of an old-fashioned reading glass. The stone was easily as big as the palm of my hand."[9]

In October, Rose was again in the news, this time for spending $75,000 on a Rembrandt, the highest price paid for a work of art that year. "I'd have paid a million for it," Rose told his Jewish mentors Bernard Baruch and Samuel Untermeyer about *A Pilgrim at Prayer.* "I'm in love with it." At that moment a Diamond Horseshoe manager interrupted the meeting to say, "I finally got that guy who has the bird act to stay in the show for seventy-five dollars."

Rose shouted, "Seventy-five dollars! How do ya like that! Seventy-five dollars! Well all right. But we don't feed the birds!"[10] Such tales, this one in Winchell's column, got a chuckle out of millions and surely helped persuade Paramount Pictures in February 1946 to buy the rights to a film about Rose's life (the *Diamond Horseshoe* movie did not feature an actor playing the boss). The studio paid him $200,000.[11]

Given this résumé and Rose's work on behalf of *We Will Never Die* and Jewish DPs, Warburg and Rosenwald wanted Rose for the UJA campaign and asked him to chair the theatrical division and raise money from Jews and sympathetic non-Jews in that industry.[12] Rose joined up, and his first volley of telegrams to people in the business displayed the showman's characteristic style. It also exposed the chip on his shoulder toward the sector of the population that had once tormented him. Referring to the money-raising job he had taken on he said, "The big boys of our business promised me every help and cooperation. Let's see if it will be forthcoming." This pitch was sent to a select group invited to a luncheon at the Hotel Astor, where fifty "big boys" such as Warburg and Barney Balaban, president of Paramount Pictures, would brainstorm "arranging a big dinner party in honor of Mrs. Eleanor Roosevelt." At the Astor luncheon, Rose set a goal of raising $1 million and established an organization to get it, naming Ed Sullivan, then a *Daily News* columnist, to head the "nitery division" and others assigned to squeeze songwriters, costume pros, designers, orchestra leaders, and ticket brokers. "A million dollars may seem a lot," Rose said. "But it means the difference between life and death to people overseas. I think we should all do our share not only in giving but in going out and getting."[13]

Rose did both. To get he wrote emotional pleas that pressed potential supporters to donate. "It will help us so much in our work of bringing life and hope to the Jews overseas if you will join Mrs. Roosevelt, Bob Sherwood, and leaders of Amusement Industry at our UJA dinner at Sherry's on Tuesday, April 30," read an April 22 telegram to Theresa Helburn of the Theatre Guild, and on April 25 he made an "impressive address" to the Independent Theatre Owners Association that raised $80,000.[14] His passion for the cause was also decisive at the dinner for Eleanor Roosevelt. Rose "presided and spoke with deep feeling of his experience visiting displaced persons' camps in Germany," reported Mrs. Roosevelt in her newspaper column "My Day."[15] His words complemented the first lady's, which were also about her visit to DP camps, and the evening raised $501,900 from the 150 guests, nailing down half of Rose's fundraising goal at the one event.

The biggest donors included the three Warner brothers, who together gave $100,000, and the Balaban family, which donated $70,000. Rose donated $20,000, twice the minimum donation of $10,000 that qualified one as a major donor, and for months afterward he continued to pay close personal attention to the fundraising effort.[16] Irving Berlin had promised to donate 10 percent of his royalties that quarter to the UJA, an amount that would have been about $3,200. However, "in view of the present emergency," he said, "I have decided to increase my donation. I am enclosing my check for $5,000." A personal thank you from Rose was in order. "Dear Irving," he wrote. "On behalf of the United Jewish Appeal, accept my sincere thanks for your check. Spelled out in medicine and things to eat, it will buy a great deal."[17]

Rose's group eventually raised $850,000, short of the $1 million goal but still six times more than the amusement division had ever raised before. This reflected the general success of the fundraising effort. Though the UJA's $100 million goal was three times the amount raised in 1945, the organization managed to exceed that amount. It raised $131 million, a figure four times the previous record.[18] But New York's Federation of Jewish Philanthropies was not interested in putting Rose's fundraising success in context. Instead, the organization took accurate measure of his achievement, wealth, and fame and decided it could raise money for the 116 hospitals it helped support by holding a fundraising drive in his honor. On December 12, 1946, a dinner was held at the swanky Hotel Pierre, and Herbert Bayard Swope, from Rose's WIB days, served as emcee. Bernard Baruch presented Rose with an award for his "distinguished achievements as a showman, journalist and humanitarian."[19] That last description undoubtedly elicited an ironic laugh from many, but his public and secret Jewish philanthropy justified it.

A FLAG IS BORN

This alignment with mainstream Jewish groups was a departure for Rose, who since 1941 had worked closely with the Jewish renegades Hecht and then Bergson to bring attention to and initiate action on behalf of Europe's Jews, and despite his October 1944 repudiation of them, he continued to help the two men while he labored for the UJA. In May 1946, Bergson of the Hebrew Committee asked Rose to pressure UNRRA to aid the Jews of the Balkans. Rose brought the issue to Warburg.[20] Bergson of the ALFP funded the Irgun's "repatriation effort" that smuggled Jews into Palestine on boats that tried to evade the British blockade. Ben-Gurion's Haganah made the most progress here with a campaign that succeeded even when it failed. Ships filled with stateless Jews turned away by the British, especially in the case of the SS *Exodus*, "focused embarrassing attention on London's harsh policy."[21] The ALFP had less success with its own repatriation program, but Rose contributed one hundred dollars to the cause.[22] However, the heart of Rose's work with Hecht and Bergson had been producing theatricals designed to energize the public on behalf of Jewish causes boldly stated, and in 1946 he partnered with them one last time as the prime financial backer of the ALFP's production of Ben Hecht's play *A Flag Is Born*.[23]

"You, out front, are not in a theater tonight, you are on a battlefield." That was the direct call for donations issued from the stage after every performance of the play that was both the first Holocaust drama and the first Zionist drama, appearing as it did two years before the Jewish state became a reality.[24] Its two themes were intertwined to make three emotional pleas: to view the Jewish survivors as Jews with Jewish national needs; to foment American anger at the 1939 British restriction against Jewish immigration to Palestine that before the war trapped Jews in Nazi Europe and after the war prevented them from attaining a national homeland; and to raise money for ships that would defy the British blockade by bringing Jewish DPs to Palestine and fund the Jewish fight to establish the State of Israel.[25] *Flag* was the culmination of the theatrical efforts that saw the Jews claim their right, as Americans, to argue Jewish interests. "It was their Jewish identity that spurred them to civic action in the American public sphere," writes Garrett Eisler.[26]

However, this transformation into full-fledged Jewish Americans able "to embrace both sides of that equation equally," as Eisler puts it,[27] did not happen overnight, and the habit of prudent care that enabled Rose to escape a childhood clouded by failure and poverty now reasserted itself. In contrast to his work on *Fun to Be Free* and *We Will Never Die,* and his statement to the *Times* that the DPs should be allowed to reach Palestine, Rose wanted no public connection to *A Flag Is Born.* Bergson and Hecht's actions were going too far for the Jewish showman. On July 22, 1946, six weeks before *Flag* opened in New York, the Irgun bombed Jerusalem's King David Hotel, headquarters of the British government in Palestine. Every American Jewish group but Bergson's ALFP condemned the attack that killed nearly one hundred. Hecht acted as the exceptional group's spokesman when he told the *Times* two days after the bombing, "The hand which writes British policy in Palestine is directly responsible for detonating the bomb at the King David Hotel."[28]

Rose at that moment was fundraising for the hardly radical UJA, and such statements surely dissuaded him from any further public affiliation with Hecht or Bergson. But there is little doubt about his willingness to finance Hecht's play. "Rose was my chief ally," Hecht said. "His pocketbook was one of the chief arsenals for Jewish liberation, no less than his talent as a producer."[29] And two years before *Flag,* Rose had made it clear he would even finance Hecht works he disliked. That was when Rose in July 1944 pleaded with Hecht to ditch a play he was working on because the anti-Nazi theme "already feels like a period piece." Rose wrote, "I will produce it or if you want to produce it I will finance it but as a dear friend of yours who never wants to see you strike out I would like to see you sell it to the movies or scrap it. I don't think it is fresh enough or distinguished enough and I have a fierce and possessive pride about anything that you write. Please don't get mad at me because I love you."[30]

A Flag Is Born was not a period piece but, as stated above, something new, and it seems likely that Rose's 1944 letter helped Hecht turn away from a reiteration of Nazi horrors and toward a play about the Jewish future. *Flag* did this through the story of three Holocaust survivors trying to make their way across Europe to the Land of Israel. Two are an old married couple, Tevya and Zelda, who are remnants of the *shtetl* world of Sholem Aleichem, and the third is David, a despairing young Jew who "has lost faith in God and in his fellow man." The theater stars Paul Muni and Celia Adler played the old couple, who die during the journey. David, played by Marlon Brando, takes up with "fighters of the Hebrew resistance in Palestine." At the play's close, David carries the future Israeli flag and with his new comrades sings "Hatikvah," the Zionist anthem that became Israel's national anthem.[31]

Flag was a popular and critical success and its four-month run raised $275,000 through ticket sales and additional donations. This paid for a ship renamed the SS *Ben Hecht* that in March 1948 attempted to bring six hundred DPs to Palestine. The British intercepted it, took the DPs to Cyprus, and arrested the American crew.[32] No records regarding *A Flag Is Born* mention Billy Rose. Like his rescue of Kurt Schwarz, the production proved Rose's ability to keep a secret.

FRUSTRATED FATHER

Rose undertook yet another secret operation while helping the UJA and the ALFP, and that was an American version of Hecht and Bergson's effort to bring refugees to Palestine. In August 1946, while *Flag* was in rehearsals, Rose paid $70,000 for a thirty-room house on 131 acres.[33] He did not publicize this purchase or tell anyone what he intended to do with this second Mount Kisco estate, adjacent to his first, until March 1947, when he revealed that he wanted to house twenty-five war orphans there. They would be his and his wife's children. The couple was going to adopt them from European DP camps. Rose and Eleanor's adoption trip to Europe was in the works.

The adoption plan was Rose's attempt to implement what the US government had announced as its policy but had largely failed to enact. In December

1945, President Truman ordered that DPs be given preference to immigrate to the United States as "an example to the other countries of the world [and] . . . it is hoped that the majority will be orphaned children."[34] But Truman's order had little effect on overall refugee immigration numbers and minimal impact on Jewish arrivals. By December 1946, a year after the president announced his plan, only 6,213 refugees had entered the country, and of these a mere 177 were orphans. In addition, though American Jewish lobbying was part of what led Truman to issue the immigration order, American Jews did not dare request special treatment for Europe's dispossessed Jews, so they were admitted per their share of the refugee population, which was about 20 percent. This meant that over the course of a year, the United States admitted about thirty-five Jewish orphans.[35] In this context, Rose's plan was enormous.

The needs of the Jewish refugees, the vileness of the Nazis, and the quirks of Rose's character joined together to yield his ambitious and bizarre adoption plan. In November 1946 he published an article in PM about the Germans he saw during his 1945 DP tour. He wrote that while in Munich he visited "the big Red Cross Club which played to something like 7000 GI's a day" and was astounded to learn that the band was composed of former SS soldiers from Dachau. Rose asked a staffer, "Do you think it's a good idea . . . to allow the Death Head Brigade to ingratiate themselves with these kids by playing dance music for them?" The answer infuriated him: "What's the difference? . . . The war's over." After the band ended its set, Rose sized up the departing Germans:

> They were laughing as the truck pulled away in the direction of Dachau. I won-
> dered what they were laughing at, and what the joke was. And then I felt a little
> drop of ice water trickle down my spine. I knew what the joke was and who the
> joke was on. It was on the Red Cross, on the soldiers in the club, on you and me,
> and on the hundreds of thousands who had preceded the SS men at Dachau. . . . I
> wasn't much surprised at anything I saw in Germany after that. I wasn't surprised
> when we investigated Nazis in public office with a whitewash brush in our hand.
> And I wasn't surprised when the Nurenberg [sic] Court looked at atrocity pictures
> for a year and then decided to hang only eleven of the twenty-one defendants.[36]

This contempt for what he saw as the naiveté, stupidity, and indifference to-ward Nazi crimes was part of the general derision for accepted opinion that had always driven Rose to go his own way. His adoption program was in alignment with this aspect of his character and also another trait that had previously only been hinted at—his view of himself as the essential father. Having replaced his own father when he was a teenager, Rose assumed the role toward nearly everyone. His mother encouraged and his sisters accepted his assumption of that position within the family and he extended its reach to more distant relations, as his draft board revealed when it announced that he supported three uncles. He also "adopted" friends, as when he called himself Hecht's "loving father," despite Hecht's being five years older. Another show business colleague received the same treatment. "Don't get excited, boy," he chided Will Morrissey, who reflected, "Him calling me boy, he was a kid and I was an *old man then.*" This conception of himself as a paterfamilias was surely strengthened by his financial success and the acclaim he received from the entertainment and Jewish communities. Another factor also may have played a role. It appears his affair with a Texas showgirl in 1937 resulted in an out-of-wedlock child he never acknowledged, and to avoid similar mishaps in the future, he underwent what turned out to be an irreversible vasectomy. His sister Polly said the procedure was the reason he never had children with any of his wives. His childless life apparently frustrated his paternal impulse, which expressed itself in this grandiose gesture.[37]

Word of his plan to adopt twenty-five orphans appeared in the *Times* on March 21, 1947, along with a protestation that he did not want publicity. Circumstances behind the scenes, however, suggest that he engineered the press attention to overcome objections to his adoption goal. Through an intermediary, he had communicated his proposal to the United Service for New Americans (USNA), "a strictly Jewish agency" that deliberately took a nondenominational title to evade antisemitic opposition.

On March 19, two days before the *Times* article appeared, the USNA rejected Rose's plan. The idea was impossible for a host of reasons, from the legal structures that governed adoptions to the needs of the orphans, said the USNA's Joseph Beck. The process required, first, that an umbrella organization, the US Committee for the Care of European Children, sign the required immigration affidavits guaranteeing economic support of all immigrant children. The committee then entrusted Jewish children to the USNA, which placed them in foster homes through a subsidiary, the European Jewish Children's Aid. In addition, the children needed individual attention and not "group care, for this is merely a repetition of camp life that they had in Europe," Beck said. "They want to get away from that, which calls for the type of care they can get only in a home."

There were additional issues that Beck was reluctant to discuss, "since it would be harmful to our whole immigration procedure if information of this kind got out." Some of the children had tuberculosis. What's more, "they are a suspicious, tense, difficult lot of adolescents. . . . The mark of the concentration camps is a mark on the spirit, soul and the personality of these people." Privately, Beck worried that "moving these teen aged youngsters into [Rose's] . . . 'posh' naborhood [*sic*] could be detrimental to the program. An attempted rape, or a drunken 'ball' with its potential publicity could be fatal to admission of refugees."[38]

Rose was surely made aware of Beck's concerns, but he did not accept Beck's answer, and the *Times* article was clearly his counterattack. Reactions to the unveiled idea varied. To a colleague at the UJA, it was proof that Rose was "the amazing Billy."[39] To officials at UNRRA, it was evidence of madness and a reason to marshal troops.

"Would it not be possible to cable appropriate agencies in the U.S.A., possibly State Department and U.S. Committee [for the Care of European Children] to stop this wild scheme," wrote an UNRRA child search officer, Cornelia D. Heise, to UNRRA headquarters in Paris. "We shall be glad to alert our military authorities if in your opinion there is imminent danger of [Rose] arriving in the U.S. Zone for the alleged purpose of adopting children." Heise then had a moment of doubt about her passionate reaction and asked a superior, "OK to send this out? Enough trouble with agencies—to say nothing of the Roses." There was no problem. The organization was with her. "Heartily concur," came the reply. "Approved for sending."[40]

Still, Rose had reason to think he could get his way. Others within the adoption bureaucracy "were inclined to accept [his] offer." And Rose was in no mood to give up the fight. He "was furious: there is no person more insulted than the generous donor whose gift has been refused by a philanthropic agency," Beck wrote. "He said that he would cut off all his charitable contributions and in particular his large gift each year to United Jewish Appeal (which was the source of our funds). Ed. Warburg became involved." In May, UNRRA offices in Washington sent UNRRA's Displaced Persons chief in Paris the latest message from the US Committee for the Care of European Children: "The only additional information I can give you about Billy Rose at the moment is that we are discussing our program with him with the hope that we might somehow work together toward helping displaced children in whom he is interested."[41]

That discussion went nowhere, and over the course of the summer Rose came to accept the fact that he would not be able to carry out his outlandish scheme to adopt twenty-five children. In addition to official objections, it can be taken for granted that his wife would never have agreed to be a mother to Yiddish-speaking orphans. He and Holm did not journey to Europe to find children to adopt. Those whom he might have cared for remained under the jurisdiction of the authorities who sought conventional homes for them in America, and that is where Rose redirected his passion for the project.

On June 13, he wrote an open letter to Secretary of State Gen. George Marshall on behalf of all Americans who wanted to adopt European orphans. The letter appeared in his new syndicated newspaper column, "Pitching Horseshoes." He started the column in April 1946 as a series of (relatively) subtle and diverting paid advertisements for his Diamond Horseshoe that featured Rose's editorials on "Life, Art, Reforestation and Sex among the Aborigines" of New York. He ranged widely, sometimes endorsing quality cultural products, such as Roberto Rossellini's film *Open City*. These musings caught the attention of John Wheeler, president of the Bell Syndicate, who told Rose, "You shouldn't give that column away or pay to have it published. I can sell it."[42] By the summer of 1947, it appeared in more than seventy papers across the country, and Rose joked, "I'm now a real newspaperman. I carry a press card and talk tough to cops."[43] With a showman's gift for the appeal of sentiment, *schmaltz,* what he once called "the real corn," he wrote to General Marshall about the children who needed homes,

I got a close-up of these small fry a year ago last November when I was in Europe. I particularly remember some I saw at Landsberg, Germany. A full-scale blizzard was doing its stuff as I trudged past the shacks in which 6,500 DP's were waiting for a confused world to make up its mind what to do with them. Off in a corner of the camp, I heard laughter coming from one of the shanties. I walked in and found myself in a makeshift laundry. I ducked under some wet clothes hanging over a dirt floor. Near the washtub, there was a group of kids playing with a doll they had made out of knotted rags. And they were laughing. Laughing like kids anywhere laugh. I'm afraid I wept a little when I saw them, because I couldn't think of any set of kids anywhere in the world who had less to laugh about.[44]

This depiction had little to do with the harsher reality of the typical orphan. Beck had advised that the "children are largely a teen age group. There are very few young children alive in Europe," and that the concentration camp experience had made them very unlike "kids anywhere." In his private notes Beck elaborated that they "sought safety in the woods, in abandoned buildings, in the slums. In small gangs they begged, foraged for food, stole, to maintain life. These were a hardened group of youngsters by the time we got to know them. They would lie without provocation or reason. It had become habitual. Sometimes they would change their names from one interview to the next as if continuing to hide identity." Rose surely got a taste of this at the DP camps he visited. At Zeilsheim, a report noted that the Jews "have developed a certain hardness and toughness of personality; it is that of course which was largely responsible for their survival." At Landsberg, officials noted that black-market activities were rife: "They have had to trade and bargain to exist in the past. They don't consider it wrong to continue." This was not information anyone in favor of helping the survivors wished to publicize, and Rose's fairy tale put the USNA in a bind. It helped the adoption cause but also made Rose a saintly figure the organization could not afford to criticize. As a result, Rose's adoption wish was still being discussed as a possibility as late as August 1947, when a memo to Warburg revealed the scale of Rose's desired impact: "Incidentally, part of Billy Rose's idea is that if Mt. Kisco could be used for children, it would not only be of value for the children, but as a possible visual demonstration in connection with the whole emigration situation."[45] This was the last reference to Rose's plan.

Proof that his desire to care for children was not a mere infatuation or publicity stunt is the quiet work he performed the following year on behalf of another group of Holocaust orphans. In 1948, Rabbi Michael Weissmandel, a survivor of the Nazi carnage, established in America a yeshiva to succeed the "Nitra Yeshiva, one of the jewels in the crown of prewar Hungarian orthodoxy."[46] The rabbi found a site in Mount Kisco, where his Yeshiva Farm Settlement, with a student body of Jewish orphans, purchased a 250-acre estate for $100,000, which money, Weissmandel said, "we got from somewhere."[47] Rose was likely one of the donors. In 1948, he was invited to a meeting of influential Jews who agreed to back the yeshiva against Mount Kisco opponents who wished to deny it a permit. That was not the end of the story. In 1950, Rose donated some of the $12,000 the yeshiva needed to pay for a new well and water system. The following year he made an additional gift.[48]

The extraordinary Jewish events of late 1947 drew Rose's attention toward a new project. In November the United Nations approved a plan to partition Palestine into Arab and Jewish states. The prospect of a Jewish state immediately inspired Rose's deal-making imagination. Two weeks after the UN vote, on December 15, Rose used his newspaper column to send an open letter to Chaim Weizmann, soon to be Israel's first president, to suggest the Jewish state raise the money it needed to develop its economy and build an army by issuing bonds. The column's syndication included Jerusalem's *Palestine Post,* and the following month Israel undertook a study of the plan's feasibility because "there was a growing recognition that there was a limit to funds available from charitable contributions." Rose's back-of-the-envelope figuring and assessment of the bond market's attitude toward lending the new state half a billion dollars at 3 percent interest covered some of the ground a team of researchers delivered to Ben-Gurion. According to the historian Ilan Troen, "It is difficult to fix a date and an author to the idea of Israel Bonds," but Rose's column puts him in the running for the credit. "Who'll buy these bonds?" wrote Rose. "Well, to begin with, the people who contributed over $200,000,000 in the past couple of years to United Jewish Appeal. It figures that if they dropped that kind of money into a tin cup, they'll do even better when you offer them paper which is a first claim on the present and future assets of New Judea. . . . And I think a lot of investors will believe you when you tell them that folks who weren't frightened by concentration camps, immigration quotas and Arab tribesmen aren't going to be frightened by 3 per cent."[49]

This last bit of romanticism echoed the thoughts of many Jews amazed and inspired by the prospect and then the advent of Israel in May 1948. I. F. Stone's *This Is Israel,* with photographs by Robert Capa, the famed war photographer and ladies' man whose assimilated Jewish identity was apparently quickened by the attractive female soldiers he depicted, presented Israel's story as heroic, and Arthur Koestler's 1949 *Promise and Fulfilment,* "one of the liveliest and freshest accounts of Israel's war for independence ever written," lionized the Bergson Boys—who were castigated by official American Jewry—with a "passionate defense of [their] role . . . in the creation of Israel." In this spirited climate, when it seemed giants walked the earth and all was possible, it is not surprising that

Israel's government became interested in "a rather fabulous character . . . by the name of Billy Rose."[50]

Rose's Israel matchmaker was Alfred Strelsin, who introduced the showman to the Jewish state's top people. Strelsin was a successful New York advertising man who had been a friend of Rose's since at least 1943, when both worked with Bergson. But Strelsin's affluence and interest in Jewish projects were not the only bases of their relationship. The two also shared the eccentricities and passions that, more than similar ideals, often make for the fondest bonds. Like Rose, Strelsin embellished his accomplishments "tenfold in the telling . . . [and] was always surrounded by a bevy of beauties." In September 1948, he discussed with Rose the idea of helping Israel, and then during a visit to the country in October Strelsin proposed it to Israel's government officials, including Prime Minister David Ben-Gurion.[51] When Strelsin returned home in December he arranged for Rose to lunch with Arthur Lourie, Israel's new consul-general in New York; Eliahu Elath, Israel's ambassador to the United States; and Isaiah Kenen, spokesman for Israel's delegation to the United Nations. Lourie wrote to Israel's Ministry for Foreign Affairs about the Rose meeting:

> I must admit that a little to my surprise—and also to that of Eliahu, we were gen-
> uinely and favorably impressed with him. He is decidedly a person, and we were
> both convinced that he is sincere in his desire to be of service and that more than
> that, he is really capable of rendering an important contribution. He has excep-
> tional contacts not only in the literary and artistic world, but also (as *vide* his close
> and continuing friendship with Baruch) in other spheres. He has imagination and
> organizing ability and it should be added that he is today a man of independent
> means. . . . I am not going into the details of our discussion at the luncheon. You
> will have the opportunity yourself when he comes to Tel Aviv of talking things
> over with him. But I do want to emphasize that we here . . . regard this as a matter
> of genuine importance which we think should be given favorable consideration
> and energetically followed through.[52]

Rose's upcoming visit to Tel Aviv was just one stop in a round-the-world tour he had once joked about taking in a letter to Winchell. Now he was about to set off on such a trip with Eleanor. Their journey began on January 7, 1949, and saw them travel through South America and Mexico, then Hawaii, Japan, China, and India, followed by Turkey, Greece, and Israel, with final stops in

Rome, Paris, and London, before returning to New York in late April. But the only destination that required advance planning was Israel, because it was the only place where Rose intended to be more than a sightseer. In late December 1948, Lourie rushed Israeli officials to prepare for Rose letters of introduction to Weizmann and Ben-Gurion. Rose had asked for them, and Lourie felt "it [was] appropriate that he should receive such letters." They were delivered in one day. Both were signed by Eliahu Elath and were identically worded. The letter to Ben-Gurion read, "My dear Mr. Prime Minister: I wish to introduce you to Mr. Billy Rose of New York. I am sure that the name of Mr. Rose is familiar to you, for not only is he a well-known figure in many fields of activity in the United States and one of the most popular figures in journalism, but he is also a good Jew and a friend of ours."[53]

What Israel hoped to derive from all this efficient preparation was the realization of Strelsin's assurance that Rose wanted to help Israel win positive reception in the world press. Strelsin said that Rose was "excitedly interested in heading what he terms 'The Israeli Information Bureau,' with offices possibly in New York, Paris, London, and maybe Rio de Janeiro or Buenos Aires." This was a singular opportunity because, Strelsin explained, "Rose, the columnist . . . has obtained more free [press] space than possibly any other man in America," and his "publicity know-how . . . would make [him] the ideal man to head such a venture. Under his management, I am sure Israel would find itself in the top magazines and newspapers of the world, disseminating subtle propaganda on the highest level, and with the material so slanted that it would attune America particularly to a recognition and full acceptance of Israel as a sound investment field and a future industrial center linking the Near and Far East."[54]

WINE, WOMEN, AND WORDS

Strelsin's buildup was backed up by Rose's most recent triumphs. First, Bennett Cerf at Random House took over the Rose biography project from Harper's after that firm failed to deliver, and Cerf got Rose to cooperate on the book with the writer Maurice Zolotow. On February 15, 1947, *Collier's* magazine began running a series of excerpts from Zolotow's forthcoming biography, which was entitled *Billy Rose of Broadway*. A month later the Lerner and Loewe musical *Brigadoon* opened on Broadway at Rose's Ziegfeld and ran for 518 performances. Rose had wanted to produce the show, but under onerous conditions. "The contract Billy Rose wanted us to sign negated Abraham Lincoln's Emancipation Proclamation that freed the slaves," Lerner said. Instead, it played at Rose's theater, and he boasted, "I made more money out of the show this way . . . and without taking any risks."[55]

On June 2, 1947, *Time* magazine put Rose on its cover and the accompanying article sold the public on his already well-established image as a success who lived life as promoters of the American Dream promised it could be lived—in luxury and at ease, with money in the bank and a beauty by his side. The magazine avoided any hint of his interest in Jewish causes and ignored not only Rose's work on *We Will Never Die* but also his 1945 visit to Jewish DP camps and his then-still-ongoing effort to adopt refugee orphans. Thirty years after the *Gregg Writer* congratulated Rose for his American virtues, it was still easier, safer, and more acceptable to describe Rose without reference to anything Jewish.

Meanwhile, Rose signaled he was having second thoughts about his forthcoming biography, because he struck a deal for Simon and Schuster to publish his autobiography. Max Schuster had been interested in a Rose book since December 1943, when he watched Rose follow Oscar Hammerstein's remarks on *Carmen Jones* at New York's Dutch Treat Club with a talk that "knocked the boys cold." Rose's "Pitching Horseshoes" column reawakened the publisher's interest. "Pardon my ignorance," began an internal S&S memo, "but has anyone ever published or thought of securing an autobiographical book by Billy Rose? His stuff in PM makes the best reading in the paper, and he must have a swell story to tell." The answer was that Schuster was on it, and a deal was struck for Rose to produce a memoir in the form of a humorous collection of stories, including some new material and the rest reworked or simply reprinted from his column. The only question was which book should appear first: Random House's Zolotow biography or the autobiography? Cerf argued that his firm's biography should take precedence. It "can only *help* the book of columns later. . . . If the Horseshoe book [the autobiography] comes first, on the other hand, the biog will be just one big anticlimax," he said.[56] Max Schuster agreed, but Rose had other ideas, and in 1947 he decided to issue his autobiography ahead of Zolotow's biography. Cerf then withdrew his approval for the biography, which was never published. Lawyers forced Rose to compensate Zolotow for his trouble, and in October 1948 Simon and Schuster published and promoted Rose's *Wine, Women and Words*, featuring original illustrations by Salvador Dali.[57]

Zolotow's biography included the tale of Rose nearly being buried alive, and the showman may have decided it was not a story he wanted known. Besides, Rose had managed his image successfully for thirty years and likely had no interest in delegating the job. The book also may not have been Jewish enough for Rose. Its opening line shared *Time* magazine's outlook that his story was that of "a poor but honest American lad."[58] In contrast, Rose's autobiography made room for a piece called "Somebody Hold My Coat," which objected to all prejudice and racism and to antisemitism in particular. In high school, a fellow student "tried to pin a murder rap on me," Rose wrote. "I told him I had an airtight alibi: I wasn't anywhere in the neighborhood when *He* was killed, and I had witnesses to prove it." And in "Me and My Pea-Shooter" he made a playful but not flippant case that he may have motivated Hitler to commit suicide. As Rose recounted the tale, in June 1941 the British arrested the high-ranking Nazi Rudolf Hess, and Rose wrote Lord Halifax, British ambassador to the United States, to suggest that he be allowed to put Hess on exhibit in a cage. "The coast-to-coast tour of Mr. Hess would take at least two years, and by that time, Mr. Hitler himself might be available as a follow-up attraction."

Lord Halifax got into the spirit of the thing and in his reply assured Rose, "We are currently doing our utmost to secure Mr. Hitler for you."[59] Rose released the correspondence to American newspapers in July, and the publicity brought it to the attention of the Nazi newspaper *Völkischer Beobachter,* which attacked Rose, as he proudly put it, for being a "loud-mouthed American showman, of a certain frowned-upon ancestry, who had the audacity to talk about putting *Der Fuehrer* on exhibition like an ordinary monkey." When Hitler killed himself, part of his stated reason, quoted in Hugh Trevor-Roper's *The Last Days of Hitler,* was, "I will not fall into the hands of an enemy who requires a new spectacle, exhibited by the Jews, to divert his hysterical masses."[60] Was Hitler thinking of Rose and his plan to put the Nazi leader on display? "I don't know, but I certainly hope so," Rose wrote.[61]

The publicity drumroll for *Wine* began on July 6, 1948, when *Look* magazine published the first in what was to be a series of eight installments of the book to herald its publication. "Move over, De Maupassant," was the headline of a self-deprecating full-page ad in the *Times* book review section that sold the author as a lovable roughneck. "Guess who's written a book!" was the attention grabber atop another ad, and anytime Rose liked he could attract publicity with a provocative open-letter "Horseshoes" column, such as the August 27, 1948, letter to George Sloan, chairman of New York's Metropolitan Opera, suggesting that

Rose take over its management. That set off fireworks. "Pitching Horseshoes" had also sprouted a new branch, with Rose sounding off Monday through Friday in five-minute radio broadcasts heard on 392 stations. The column appeared in about 245 newspapers. Rose's thoughts blanketed the nation and brought him unsolicited applause from powerhouses such as Walter Annenberg, publisher of the *Philadelphia Inquirer.* "I frankly admit to you a mistake in editorial judgment was made . . . in having failed to contract for your column Pitching Horseshoes," he wrote Rose. "You are doing a magnificent job and I salute you cordially."[62]

Several ghostwriters, such as Jerry Tallmer, later of the *Village Voice,* and the author Bernard Wolfe, helped Rose sustain the pace demanded by a daily column, but all agreed Rose made it his own. Wolfe Kaufman also wrote many columns, "though," he said, "I repeat, I could not have made them half as effective if [Rose] did not re-write and edit them . . . [and] there is the fact that he loved 'the magic of words.' He really and truly did, and he was mighty good at toying with words." Charles Samuels, author of a bestselling biography of the singer and actress Ethel Waters, remembered how Rose tested the columns: "He would sing them, hum them, whistle them . . . to see if they were rhythmic." And the widow of the writer and Rose ghost Lee Rogow said, "Lee could have written that column and it could have been dead. It was Billy who made that column. When Lee said it was Billy's column he was not only fulfilling his obligation. . . . Billy made that column. . . . Billy was a relentless editor."[63]

Rose struck a bold deal with Simon and Schuster. He put up all the money to publish *Wine, Women and Words* and in return split the profits with the publisher fifty-fifty. He dedicated the book to "B. M. B," Bernard Mannes Baruch. Its first chapter is titled, "Look, Ma, I'm Writing." The book was a bestseller.[64]

DISCREET HOSTILITY

Despite this résumé and Strelsin's puffery, the Israelis were wary. Arthur Lourie made additional inquiries about Rose and spoke with Meyer Weisgal, producer of the epic Jewish theatrical *The Eternal Road.* Weisgal agreed that "Billy Rose has excellent contacts and is capable of being extremely helpful," but there was also the warning that, as Lourie delicately put it, "Billy Rose being what he is, we should be ready to avail ourselves of his help quietly."[65] The irony was perfect. After years when Rose was careful to preserve his American credentials by segregating his Jewish work from his business career and even publicly rebuking Jewish allies such as Bergson, Israel now wished to keep its new Jewish image respectable by hushing its relationship with the loud Broadway operator. Rose's dealings with Israel, Lourie said, should be carried out "more or less in an unofficial way, and [we must] make it clear to him that we are anxious to have his cooperation, but it would be very inappropriate for him to appear as a spokesman or a representative of the Government." This was not what Rose wanted. He believed he was now ready to be a public Jew and official ally of Israel. "He is definitely opposed to being an arm of the Zionist Organization, Jewish Agency, or any organization that is not the government, per se," Strelsin advised Ben-Gurion.

Rose requested, and Israel made, all the necessary arrangements to ease his arrival. Because his travel itinerary included a flight from New Delhi to Istanbul that made a refueling stop in Syria, his travel agents advised he delay getting his Israeli visa until after that leg of the trip. So at Rose's request Lourie contacted the Israeli Consul in Athens with instructions to issue Rose a visa when he landed there on March 8. When the time came the visa was ready, and on March 9 Rose and Eleanor boarded a Czech Airways flight from Athens to Haifa, where, as Rose had requested, they were met by a government representative.[66]

"From the beginning of his trip, it was clear that the sight-seeing was of little importance to him compared with the contacts and discussions which he hoped to have in connection with the schemes he had in mind," wrote Rose's handler, Monica Dehn. Nevertheless, he managed to see almost the entire small country and visited "Jerusalem, Jaffa, Nazareth, Tiberias, Safed, Haifa, Acre, the immigrant childrens' reception centre at Onim and the Misrachi children's village at Ra'anana. He also had an evening at the Habimah and Mograbi theatres." Like many future American visitors to Israel, Rose "was disappointed when he considered something done here less efficiently than, say, in the United States . . . [but] he considered [the War of Independence] 'heroic' and said it 'made every Jew proud.'" Israel's military elan was likely reinforced by Rose's dinner with Lt. Col. Mordecai Maklef, who had been a senior officer during the war.[67] The spirit of the young country also touched him when he saw the celebrations for the raucous holiday of Purim that celebrates the Jews' deliverance from genocide in ancient Persia. "The streets of Tel Aviv were alive with young and old Israelites singing and dancing. It was as though an entire nation was having a block party," Rose told Polly. One of Rose's Israeli contacts remembered that he observed the scene less with jubilation than with profound emotion. In an understated way that hinted at deep feeling, Rose said, "Let these people have a good time."[68]

Dehn learned to disregard Rose's practiced air of casual indifference and perceived that "despite an apparent apathy, the general impression gained was that he was strangely excited by what he saw." Perhaps the most fascinating opportunity was the chance this small Jewish nation offered to increase his stature and historic role. His reception by the government's top echelon surpassed anything he ever achieved in America. He never met Roosevelt or Truman and could not even get his White House contact, David Niles, to fix his Syrian transit visa problem. But on his first visit to Israel he met with and received orders from Ben-Gurion. In a diary entry of their March 16 meeting Ben-Gurion recalled,

> Billy Rose came to me from New York. He thinks that the appeal this year will not be very successful. Jewish businesses in particular have suffered. . . . And we need money, money, and money. But there are many rich Jews that have vast amounts of wealth. We need to get them to invest in the country by means of appropriate advertising. He is prepared to open such an office in New York. . . . He gave me a list of rich people such as Harry Warner, Harold Lasker, Danny Orenstein, and others. I told him—he should *act!*[69]

A plan was set in place. Rose and Israel would partner to fund an annual $250,000 public relations program in the United States to promote business investment in Israel. Israel would provide $75,000 of the budget, to be paid in three installments of $25,000, and Rose was expected to donate personally and find additional backers to come up with the remaining $175,000. To avoid the complications of getting Israel's Treasury Department to approve the expenditure, the prime minister's office requested the money and directed it to what became "popularly known as the B.R. Fund."[70] The thrill of the Israel publicity plan was in the way it permitted the little showman to punch far above his traditional weight. Broadway was nothing compared to his new ability to sway and excite a government. Another thrill was Israel itself. When he returned to the United States, Rose got a call from Bernard Baruch, who wanted to know if Rose thought Israel would survive. "I had come away from Israel with the general impression that its people were (a) intelligent, (b) tough as nails, and (c) prepared to work like all get-out to make a go of their new lives," Rose later recalled replying. Baruch responded, "A business or a nation with those qualities usually gives a good account of itself."[71]

Israel was eager to implement Rose's publicity plan. Less than a week after

Rose returned to New York on April 17, 1949, the government wired $25,000 to the Israeli consulate, made payable to Billy Rose. Lourie thought this unwise and had the draft canceled and replaced with one made payable to the consulate.[72] Lourie also made it clear that Rose would not have free rein to do publicity work as he wished. Instead, Rose would be "an associate member" of Israel's Joint Public Relations Board. "Within the framework," Lourie wrote Rose, "your own advice and cooperation would be of the greatest value and would be warmly welcome." However, Lourie knew Rose would not like this. Rose was not an organization man, and Lourie telegrammed his government colleague Esther Herlitz, "DOUBT HIS READINESS ACCEPT CONDITIONS."[73] Plus, Israel insisted that Rose remain a silent partner, a stance confirmed in a memo to the powerful Zeev Sherf, who served both as Israel's first government cabinet secretary and as director of the prime minister's office. Sherf's press officer assured him that Rose "would of course function in an honorary capacity and without any official position. His connection with this operation would also be kept private."[74] All of these conditions helped doom the enterprise, and Eliahu Elath wrote Lourie, "I doubt . . . that Billy Rose will return to [the United States] very much encouraged by Tel Aviv's reception of his proposal." Sure enough, by the summer, communication between Rose and Lourie came to a near halt. When they met on July 27 at Rose's home, the two had not spoken in many weeks, and their discussion made it clear that Rose was drifting away. Dressed for the meeting in "silk pajamas" he gave Lourie "the impression that Mr. Rose's enthusiasm for the project has diminished considerably and that it is unlikely that anything will come of it."[75]

Nothing did, and a contributing factor was the influence of Rose's wife. Though Rose claimed Holm had joyously joined Tel Aviv's Purim dancers, this appears to have been another example of his need to depict the women in his life as founts of love and support, such as when he falsely claimed Brice bore him no malice when he asked for a divorce. Eleanor did not embrace Israel. On the contrary, she communicated a "discreet hostility" toward the country, Monica Dehn wrote, and "was clearly anxious to prevent [Rose] from becoming personally involved in Israel's affairs."[76]

UNCAGED TIGER

"Eleanor and I have a great deal to be thankful for this year, and so we've decided to spread ourselves and throw a whoop-de-doo of a New Year's party for the people we like," Rose wrote Baruch in December 1949. "I'm transforming the rehearsal hall on the 8th floor of the Ziegfeld into an intimate cabaret, and the hundred people that will attend will represent darn near the cream of the theatre."[1]

The decision to celebrate was well timed, because 1949 turned out to be the last year for several that Rose was untroubled by bad health, domestic strife, a conflagration, death, an attempted suicide, and divorce. In December he still had many reasons to relish his enviable position. A highlight of his round-the-world trip was a visit to Florence and the great art historian Bernard Berenson. The connoisseur of Christian art thought often about his Jewish origins, and the subject "seemed to rise to the surface each time he made the acquaintance of a fellow Jew."[2] Rose brought Berenson's Jewish ambivalence to the surface. "At first glance as repulsive as a rat," Berenson wrote of Rose, "but turned out to be the quintessence of sheer cleverness. According to his own account (which I dragged out of him) he was one of the clowns in chief to the sovereign city of New York, and enjoyed his job, to which he recently has added that of columnist." For Rose, Berenson briefly became another revered Jewish elder, and upon returning to New York, Rose wrote him, "If there's anything I can do here for you—dig up a book, get the straightaway on a painting which may interest you, or what have you—feel free to command me." Rose and Berenson must have made an odd couple at the latter's villa, but they shared at least one interest. Berenson, Rose said, "took me by the elbow, led us out into the garden, and said to me: 'Now, Mr. Rose, tell me about those amazing long-legged American chorus girls.'"[3]

Rose also treasured his increasingly close relationship with Baruch. In November 1948 Baruch invited Rose to an event at his home and afterward sent him a heartfelt letter of praise. "You turned [the party] into a love feast," Baruch wrote. "You know how proud I am of you. Your conduct last night was so dignified and gracious, you made me still prouder."[4] Rose returned the feeling on May 22, 1949, when he served as toastmaster at a Waldorf Astoria dinner in honor of Baruch's generosity to the Williamsburg Settlement and Brooklyn Philanthropic League, and again in August, when he wrote about the statesman for a South Carolina paper celebrating its fiftieth anniversary. "There's an old saying that a man is never a hero to his valet," Rose said, "but like a lot of old sayings it's only partly true. For instance, I know of a certain native of South Carolina who, after thirty-two years, is still a hero to his old stenographer. And to stop beating around the blarney, the Carolinian is Bernard M. Baruch and the stenog is me."[5] That fall, Baruch invited Rose to Hobcaw, his sixteen-thousand-acre South Carolina hunting retreat. "If you and Eleanor can get away for a few days," he wrote to Rose, "nothing would give me greater pleasure than to see you."[6] Rose adored him, and in his New Year's invitation he informed Baruch of a "remarkable photograph of yourself in the Charleston News and Courier." Like a starstruck teen, Rose was unembarrassed to tell Baruch that he had ordered several prints, "because I think it's one of the best photographs of you I've seen in a long time."[7]

Added to all this was Rose's continued success, which in 1949 got a last-minute boost when *Gentlemen Prefer Blondes* opened at his Ziegfeld on December 8. "The attraction can gross $49,000 a week, and my 'take' should be a happy-making thing," he told Baruch. Rose had also invested in the show and expected to reap profits after seventeen weeks.[8] The show's 740 performances kept it open for twenty-two months and confirmed Rose's prediction to Paramount's Adolph Zukor that *Blondes* "looks like it will keep everybody eating for a long time to come."[9] With all that positive momentum behind him Rose's New Year's party was a smash. He turned the Ziegfeld "into a nightclub for the occasion and labeled it 'Chez Eleanor,'" and the guest list included the star performers Ray Bolger, Mary Martin, Oscar Levant, Milton Berle, Carol Channing, and Henry Fonda, the songwriters Frank Loesser and Arthur Schwartz, the theater critic George Jean Nathan, and the writers Abe Burrows, Irwin Shaw, and Clifford Odets.[10]

Rose was still rolling merrily along in early 1950, when he invested in the Theatre Guild productions *As You Like It* and *Come Back, Little Sheba* without expectation of a return. As he once explained to Hecht, when the money flowed in it gave him the freedom to have some costly high-class fun. "I will now be able to start work on the stylish shows that will probably wind up in a red ink bath," he said.[11] He took this attitude when a play that Rodgers and Hammerstein produced, *The Heart of the Matter,* closed and he lost $6,000. "I didn't want to see these two old friends of mine, for the sake of any group of investors, bring a show to New York which might chalk up a red mark against their outstanding achievements," he said.[12] None of this good cheer and benevolence indicated a fundamental shift in the man. In August, William Pahlmann, the decorator of Rose's Beekman Place home, invited Rose to appear beside him in an advertisement for Lord Calvert whisky. Rose's answer was wonderful. "As for being photographed in connection with a Man of Distinction ad," he said, "I'm afraid the answer must be a firm No. The lads and lassies I chum and bum around with would kid the pantaloons off me if I got mixed up with any such shenanigan. I'm not saying it isn't O.K. for you to do. It's good publicity, and you have the face and figure to swing it. But for an old hepster like me—well, I'd rather be hit with a baseball bat."[13]

Besides, at that moment Rose and Baruch were engaged in a secret Jewish project. On July 6, Abba Eban, Israel's ambassador to the United States, contacted Baruch on a "matter of very grave concern to the State of Israel."[14] America's Tripartite Declaration of May 1950 limited arms sales to Israel and its Arab neighbors, so that "only a small trickle of weapons" reached the Middle East.[15] To circumvent this policy, Israel wanted to buy arms from private dealers. On July 2 Ben-Gurion wrote to his diplomat Arthur Lourie, "There are a number of vital and urgent transactions involving eleven million dollars [but] amount required immediately is 5,5 million." A Harold Goldenberg was to raise this money in America; Eban mentioned him in his letter to Baruch. But the fundraising did not go well. On July 14, Goldenberg informed Ben-Gurion that potential donors believed Israel's "security can come only at the governmental level between Israel and the United States. This point of view was particularly emphasized by Mr. Baruch," who refused to contribute.[16] But Baruch stayed connected to the project and in August brought in Rose. The two met with another agent of the Israeli government, who on September 5 delivered to Rose Israel's shopping list of weapons, which ranged from Sherman tanks and antiaircraft artillery to twenty-five thousand ground-to-ground rockets and twenty-five tons of explosives. Whether Rose donated money is unknown, but he enjoyed the skullduggery. He sent Baruch the weapons lists by messenger and in a note referred to their

Israeli contact only as "the gent we lunched with," perhaps in case the letter fell into enemy hands.[17]

Then, as with the death of his mother, the prospect of mortality changed everything.

IDIOT LIFE

"If you're ever invited to purgatory—don't go, they don't treat you very nicely there. Which is my roundabout way of referring to the recent operation I underwent," Rose wrote Odets on November 27, 1950. "To hear the medicos tell it, it was 'a minor one.' That can be as it may—all I know is that it involved a fantastic amount of sustained pain."[18]

Rose's specific malady is unknown, but according to his statements it was clearly a heart ailment, and it alarmed him sufficiently that he scaled back his operations. First he ended "Pitching Horseshoes" with a last column on December 4. "For the past year," he wrote, "my doctor has been waving blood counts and cardiograms at me, and hinting that all work and no play makes Jack a dead boy. . . . Up to now I haven't paid him much mind, but my current bout with the miseries has finally brought me around to his way of thinking." A month later in January 1951 he closed the Diamond Horseshoe, which over the previous twelve years had hosted about five million guests and grossed $20 million. These two moves allowed him later to claim that his surgery caused him to embrace a more reasonable way of life. "I was balancing six balls on one nose. . . . I came to a cold decision—I decided that I was leading an idiot life," he said.[19] Actually, that life was only just beginning.

When death paid another visit six months later Rose's response was an about-face; instead of scaling back, he ramped up. Rose's father died in Miami Beach on April 19, 1951. Rose consigned David Rosenberg to oblivion in Florida instead of next to Fannie in New York, but the event nevertheless hit home. As with his mother's death, his father's apparently set in motion the dissolution of Rose's marriage. Rumors that Rose was having an affair with a showgirl named Joyce Mathews while still married to Holm date from this time, and the relationship seems a desperate rebuff of death, a way to prove he was still in the prime of life. "There are certain people that are not realistic or don't want to face reality—that everyone must die. He was one of those," said the songwriter Chester Conn.

"Every time the thought came to him he threw it away. He didn't want to think about it." Conn spoke from experience, because after he recovered from a heart attack, he approached Rose about a venture and Rose told him, "I don't want to go into business with anybody who has one foot in the grave." Conn later told an interviewer, "That shook me. That startled me so. I said, Billy, no one has a lease on life. You may get a heart attack too."[20] However, Rose's aversion to death was apparently accompanied by a morbid fascination, because his relationship with Mathews was also touched by death.

On July 15, 1951, Rose and Mathews were in his private apartment at the Ziegfeld Theatre when, Rose later told police, she "locked herself in the bathroom, screaming hysterically that she was going to slash her wrists." She was not bluffing. She did it. It was not the first time Mathews attempted suicide; she had done it twice before, using sleeping pills. She was good at faking suicide, including wrist slashing—"That was not a real suicide attempt at all"—to get what she wanted, said her daughter, Vicki Walton.[21] The lurid story amazed the Broadway crowd that thought it knew Billy Rose. According to a report in the *American Weekly*,

> there wasn't an expert from Lindy's to Shubert Alley . . . who wouldn't have de-
> scribed Billy Rose as a slick, sharp, canny, cagey cookie to whom nothing embar-
> rassing would ever happen. The way they figured him, he was a lad who thought
> twice before he said hello and called his lawyers before he bought a sandwich. . . .
> Other men might lose their heads over a girl . . . but not Billy Rose. . . . But on
> that historic Sunday afternoon, as ambulance bells rang up Sixth Avenue and an
> anguished voice crying "Hurry! Save her! She tried to kill herself!" echoed in the
> halls of the Ziegfeld Theatre Building, Joyce Mathews proved that even a little Na-
> poleon may have an Achilles heel. . . . And she had found it.[22]

She had indeed found Rose's weak spot, which was his inability to love a suitable woman. Fanny Brice had been a maternal figure. Eleanor Holm was, in the words of Tom Wolfe, the kind of "young and frisky animal" with whom older wealthy men reward themselves for their success, but she objected to Rose's Jewish interests. Mathews was a needy and unbalanced woman of thirty-one who had already been married three times, including twice to Milton Berle, with whom she had adopted a baby girl, Vicki, who was six when her mother cut her wrists in Rose's office. The basis of Rose's relationship with Mathews was as unstable as his previous unions. "She had a father complex," Walton said. Rose liked to don the role of father and reciprocated. "Joyce Mathews was like his daughter and he treated her like a daughter," said the writer Doris Julian. And the fact that Mathews had a daughter allowed Rose to be a real father, a role he fulfilled admirably. "Can you tell I adored him?" Walton said. "He was so good to me."[23] But his kindness to his stepdaughter did not preclude nastiness in other realms.

Rose's divorce from Eleanor began in November 1951 and was a gift to New York's tabloids, which ran headlines for months in a font too grandiose for a declaration of war. "RAINED RICHES ON WIFE: ROSE," shouted the front page of the *Daily News* on August 9, 1952. The so-called "War of the Roses" went national with coverage in *Life,* and crowds lined up outside the Manhattan courthouse to get a seat and view the proceedings. Not covered was Rose's complaint to friends that when drunk, Holm called him "a little Jew bastard, [and] was thoroughly anti-semitic and nasty." That treatment—and his determination not to lose a substantial part of his fortune to her—apparently drove Rose to bring the divorce fight into the gutter. He tried to show that their marriage was invalid because Holm never obtained a proper divorce from her first husband, and when that failed, he accused Holm of carrying on a lesbian affair with the wife of a friend.[24] It was tawdry and ugly, and according to Helen Schrank, "Of all the evil things [he did,] that was the most evil."[25] It was also self-defeating. Rose was forced to recant the false charge and ended up paying Holm a $200,000 settlement and alimony of $30,000 a month, as well as $1 million to lawyers.[26] Holm also got a painting by Renoir that she later discovered was a fake. Rose had reason to believe it was not genuine when he surrendered it, because he had by then established a friendship with the great art collector Albert Barnes, who on a visit to Rose's Beekman Place home told him, "Now Billy, take this off the wall, it doesn't belong in your collection." But Barnes softened the blow when he wrote Rose "about your Rembrandt, which I think is tops."[27] Rose kept the Rembrandt.

Amid the chaos, on April 30, 1952, Rose produced an Israel Independence celebration and Israel Bond rally at Brooklyn's Ebbets Field. Eleanor Roosevelt addressed the crowd, and thirty-two thousand attendees heard a recorded message from Ben-Gurion on Israel's fourth birthday. The program included a concert by the New York Philharmonic conducted by Izler Solomon and featuring the violin soloist Mischa Elman. Rose "bought the first bond at the celebration and also directed the sale of bonds to the audience."[28] All else in his life was in flux, but his Jewish identity was solid ground.

Rose and Holm were finally divorced on February 27, 1954, and the settlement payment and end of a chapter led him to sell the Mount Kisco estate once intended for orphans, as well as his Beekman Place home, the Rembrandt, and paintings by Frans Hals and J. M. W. Turner. However, he immediately set about replacing what he had lost and purchased Rodin's sculpture *Honoré de Balzac* and a new Rolls-Royce Silver Wraith.[29] (Rose rarely drove but had firm ideas about how it should be done and directed his chauffeur from the passenger compartment via a telephone that allowed communication with the driver. "He drives the way I tell him to drive. It's stupid to drive on the left. That's where all the accidents happen because it's closer to the oncoming traffic," Rose told Gypsy Rose Lee.[30]) The December 1953 opening of *Kismet* at his Ziegfeld also helped heal wounds as the hit show grossed $58,000 a week, refilling Rose's wallet.[31]

Rose also worked on his friendship with Baruch. In March 1952, Holm's famous divorce lawyer, Louis Nizer, spread the word that the ugliness of the divorce displeased the old gentleman. "Mr. Baruch now has profound contempt for Billy Rose," Nizer said.[32] Baruch's letters to Rose gave little sign of such disapproval, but it seems to have worried Rose, whose letters to Baruch tried to elicit a confirmation of continued friendship. On March 25, 1953, Rose wrote to anoint himself Baruch's "illegitimate son." Then a December telegram wishing Baruch a good new year read, "Next to the love of my parents you are the one fine thing in my life which has endured. All my love."[33] That got Rose the reply he needed. "Your nice telegram gave me a great deal of pleasure," Baruch told him. "It is heartening, indeed, to know that the people you have known over the years retain respect and affection for you. I know of no one who could detect a 'phony' quicker than you. May good fortune and peace attend you. As ever yours." But he also added, "Eleanor sent me a very gracious charming note." A year after Rose's divorce, Baruch still tempered his praise for Rose with reminders of his gaffe. On January 20, 1955, Baruch wrote, "You are one of the few people I know that have imagination and vision, but keep your feet on the ground." However, Baruch closed the letter with the reassurance, "My house and my heart and my mind are always open to you."[34]

As Rose rebuilt his fortune and friendship with Baruch, disaster struck. On April 2, 1956, his Mount Kisco home burned to the ground. As one wag put it, Billy Rose had to have a big fire, a big loss, since "it couldn't have been a small one."[35] Much of his art collection was destroyed. "I fear it is too much to hope that any of the paintings could have been spared," the art dealer Germain Seligman wrote Rose. It was, but the sculptures that decorated the grounds survived, including Rodin's *Adam* and *Balzac* and also a work called *Young Woman,* by the contemporary expressionist sculptor Doris Caesar.[36]

The fire put the tally of Rose's losses in the almost six years following his 1949 New Year's Eve party at his father, his health, one wife, three homes, and many paintings. He resided in his one remaining lodging, the apartment in the Ziegfeld Theatre equipped with a sliding panel that offered a view of the stage, and he set about replacing everything he had lost, starting with a wife. On June 2, 1956, he married the would-be suicide Joyce Mathews. As Rose's friend Ruth Goetz observed when she visited Mount Kisco, Joyce "was not to be shaken. She wanted him, she loved him, she needed him."[37] When Rose discussed the match with Ruth's daughter, the young woman said to him, "You are not going to marry this woman—what are you thinking of?"

"Well, I'm rattling around the house," Rose replied.

"Hire some jugglers," Judy Goetz Sanger advised.

"Well, she wants to," Rose said.[38]

Perhaps the woman who as a teenager in 1947 got Rose to be her prom date understood the marriage best. Ethel Ferezy and her girlfriends in Brooklyn tried to get famous men as prom dates, and she wrote Rose, who agreed to it. When the time came his mood had changed, but he still went. "He sort of got stuck into it," Ferezy said. "I'm sure he was where he didn't really want to be. But he had no choice. . . . He backed himself into that corner."[39] Sanger saw the same forces at work. "I think half the time Billy ended up in bed with someone because he didn't want to be a cad," she observed.[40] There was also the unresolved battle between Rose's need to dominate and collect women, as he did for his various entertainments, and a certain timidity toward them. Forceful women frightened him. He would rather go to a restaurant than ask his personal chef, Dione Lucas, who had once starred on her own television cooking show, to fix him one of her famous omelets. "She's very tricky," Rose explained to Sanger. "Kind of a pain in the ass. Why don't you just meet me at Sardi's. It's easier."[41] The spell of his mother's female power never abated, and he seemed to take his defeat by women for granted. "If they want me, they got me," was his philosophy, he told his sister Polly. The self-deprecating line was also an admission that he was trouble.[42]

The women were not unarmed either. Mathews and her friend Jacqueline Susann, the future author of the bestselling *Valley of the Dolls,* together with about five other women, "called themselves the Jockey Club and they had lunch together all the time at '21,'" Sanger said. "These babes would have lunch together and get all dressed up in the clothes and the hats . . . and gossip. . . . I know that my mother felt that they were really tarts. The phrase was 'married tarts.' They were on the lookout for the next husband. And they passed information back and forth like the witches in Greek mythology. . . . And I guess in that world in that time, somebody like Billy would have been helpless, in a sense, if a Marilyn Monroe–Joyce Mathews blonde decided that he was her next victim."[43] Rose may have also felt he did not have time to find someone else. When a friend consoled Rose on the loss of Roseholm his reply revealed thoughts of death: "Thanks for your feeling and knowing letter. Yes, another God damn setup will rise out of the ashes. But it's the September Song for fellows like you and myself, and I begrudge the new setup the couple of years it will take."[44]

It took just one year. Despite his dour thoughts, Rose's energy and willfulness were still intact. "He looked as beaten as an uncaged tiger," wrote the Fanny Brice biographer Norman Katkov of Rose during the worst of the divorce publicity.[45] Two weeks after the fire Rose and Joyce dined with the Goetzes, and they told him of a Manhattan mansion for sale. "When the dinner was ended," Ruth later wrote,

> Billy said, "Let's go see the place." I said, "It's eleven fifteen, Billy. You can't look at a house now!" "Why not," he said. "Tell the driver where it is." I did, and just before midnight all five of us, chauffeur included, stood in a dark side street in NY pounding on the great oak doors which had been carved in France, and ringing all the doorbells we could find. . . . We walked through this most ravishing of all New York houses. . . . The next morning at eight through a haze of sleep I heard, "I bought it."[46]

In fact, Rose had not bought it, but he developed a scheme to buy it, because he had to have the twenty-three-thousand-square-foot, fifty-five-room mansion at 56 East Ninety-Third Street. Built in 1932 for the stockbroker William Goadby Loew, the home was one of the last great houses constructed in New York. And though situated on a city block and not on expansive grounds, "it nevertheless succeed[ed] in evoking the grandeur of the vastly more extravagant turn-of-the-century millionaires' mansions."[47] With a sense that his time was running out, Rose needed to find a residence that would confirm his rise from the bottom to the top, and this was it. The house was promised to the government of Czechoslovakia for its delegation to the United Nations, but as Rose later told a reporter, he "managed to get rid of them."[48] He bought at auction the furniture and other contents of the property and publicized these purchases as evidence that the owner had promised to sell him the mansion. Then he informed the Czechs that if the nation tried to buy the place, it would find itself involved in the lawsuit Rose brought on May 4. The Czechs backed out, and the owner vowed he would never sell the mansion to Rose. There was a way around that, too. Rose's wealthy friend John Wohlstetter bought it on September 18, 1956, and Rose bought it from him the same day. But just as he had in his Beekman Place home, Rose spurned luxury and bunked in an "ascetic chamber for a monk, with a single narrow bed, like a cot."[49] The house was for show.

With a new wife, a city mansion, and the beginnings of an expanded sculpture collection, the only piece of his former life Rose still needed to replace was his country estate at Mount Kisco. That he did in September 1957 when he bought Tavern Island, a retreat in Long Island Sound a half mile off the shore of Norwalk, Connecticut, accessible only by boat. The island's properties included a thirteen-room Elizabethan house, a five-room cottage, and on the mainland a seven-room house and garage. For Gypsy Rose Lee and her son,

> It was extraordinary: four acres of fairy-tale serenity; the place where Prince Charming and his bride live happily ever after. The moment the boat's engine was turned off, tranquility descended over everything like an eiderdown. It wasn't quiet, but all the sounds were comforting: the ocean washing over the rocky shore, the raucous caw of sea gulls mixed with the gentle music of songbirds, and the wind rushing through the leaves of trees and bushes. And standing on the gravel path to the house, next to a magnificent bronze by Malderelli [sic] entitled *Seated Woman,* a miniature deer kept a watchful eye on us as it nibbled the grass.[50]

When Rose was in residence, he took a flag that sported the image of a rose and hoisted it up the flagpole.[51] Prominent guests included the New York senator Jacob Javits and, after the death of Ernest Hemingway, his widow, Mary Hemingway. Permanent residents included peacocks, a Chinese rooster, African crowned cranes, and an ostrich Rose imported to create another fantasy world for him to enjoy and inhabit.[52] The floors of the main house were strewn with animal hides. "He filled the entrance with the heads of big game," said Rose's friend Tex McCrary. "He used to say, I like to see those big teeth spread out on the floor. . . . Made him think that this is what happened to big game. Some bum shot him." The same trophy impulse, but with a Jewish twist, inspired the display of paintings "of the tallest most pink-cheeked typical English people" on the walls of his new mansion, McCrary recalled. "He enjoyed seeing them there saying, 'No relation of mine,' with a smile. To move among these ancestors, to be able to buy them and hang them on his wall, put a twinkle in his eye. He had a sense of humor about it. . . . These were big-toothed people, they were not lying on the floor but they were hanging on his walls."[53]

His reemergence was a victory he relished, and he would not allow detractors to satisfy, at his expense, a belief in comforting clichés about the unhappy rich. The columnist Louis Sobol admitted he was being trite when he remarked to Rose

> that so many people who had everything—money, fame, etc., seemed unhappy. At this point we came toward the Ziegfeld Theatre. Billy said: "Look at that beautiful building. Think of all the great stars who performed there. And I own it—every brick and tile and proscenium light—free and clear. No mortgages. I could rip off that name, Ziegfeld, and put up my own, if I wanted to. I wouldn't do that. What I'm getting at is I've got money now, I've got property, that mansion of mine, my place in the country, and I think I have fame, too. Louis, I'll tell you something confidentially—I'm not unhappy at all."[54]

The following year Rose put in place one final element to ensure that his wealth and name would continue after his death. On October 6, 1958, he established the Billy Rose Foundation, Inc.[55] His American legacy was secure. His Jewish legacy needed work.

ISRAEL MUSEUM

"I've got time on my hands and would like to start a new project. Maybe something will come floating in."[1]

It was October 22, 1959. Rose had recently turned sixty and was being coy with the press, just as in 1936, when he feigned indifference toward the World's Fair. Something was up. It was true he had time on his hands. He was single again. Joyce Mathews had divorced him in July after three years of marriage, on the standard grounds of incompatibility.[2] Other business was also completed. The New York decorator Melanie Kahane had finished furnishing his palatial new home, and in August 1960 eight photographs of the great rooms done in Louis XVI and Jacobean styles—and graced with sculptures by Hugo Robus, Elie Nadelman, and Jacob Epstein; tables, chairs, and a mirror (the last a gift from Baruch) by Chippendale; antique Aubusson rugs; fabric-covered walls and tapestries by Fortuny of Venice; and more—would appear in *Interiors* magazine.[3] Also behind him was the purchase and renovation of another New York theater. Rose had bought the National in June 1958 for $1 million and immediately hired London's Oliver Messel, "a major presence in the history of British theatre design," to redecorate it. After a further expenditure of $500,000 it reopened on October 18, 1959, as the Billy Rose Theatre.[4]

Its owner was richer than ever. Rose started purchasing AT&T stock in 1954, and in 1958 bought more in anticipation of the three-for-one stock split of April 1959, which left him with eighty thousand shares. This holding alone gave him the then-mighty income of $264,000 a year in dividends, the equivalent of $2.2 million today, and his Ziegfeld had also become a reliable producer.[5] In 1956, NBC signed a seven-year lease for the theater and produced television shows there. "It's like having a seven-year hit in a house," Rose said of the regular cash flow. He flaunted his new prominence and defied bad news. Word of his 1959 divorce hit the papers on Thursday, July 23, and Rose made sure his columnist friend Leonard Lyons had a story to run that day about the fabulous time he had the previous Monday kidding around and shooting pool at his mansion with the screen stars Eva Marie Saint and Sidney Poitier, the playwrights Paddy Chayefsky and William Inge, and the famed African American diplomat Ralph Bunche, who in 1950 had won the Nobel Peace Prize for negotiating a 1949 ceasefire between Israel and Arab states.[6] Reporters still loved him. "We just happen to like cocky guys with ability, who can transform dreams into reality," wrote a columnist. "Rose, beyond most men we have known, can do just that." And as Rose hinted, a new project had floated in, one that became the greatest of his life and that "in size and emotion makes my Jumbos and Aquacades look like peep shows."[7]

FREE THE HERZLS

Israel had a job for him. In 1958, after a three-year wait, the Jewish state won United States approval to use $822,000 in American funds to kick-start the creation of a new museum in Jerusalem, and by 1959 the planning was in its infancy but under way.[8]

Rose's connection with it began with a March 19, 1959, letter from Nahum Goldmann, whose titles included president of the Jewish Agency for Israel, the World Zionist Congress, and the World Jewish Congress, and who some years before had been an enemy of Rose's friend Peter Bergson. Goldmann wanted to enlist Rose on a special mission. "It concerns members of the family of Dr. Theodor Herzl, the great founder of the Zionist movement," Goldmann wrote. The Herzl relations were two sisters, Magda and Elisabeth Herzl, imprisoned in Romania. "Maybe you could approach the Rumanian [sic] Ambassador whom you know and ask him to intervene so that they should be allowed to leave Rumania and join their families in Israel."[9] Rose first met Ambassador Silviu Brucan in 1956 when they planned a tour of Iron Curtain countries Rose took that fall, and Rose's friendly dealings with him may have owed something to the Romanian's Jewish origins; in 1916, he was born Saul Bruckner. It is not known whether Rose was willing or able to help the sisters, who were soon allowed to immigrate to Israel, but as a result of his letter Goldmann learned about the sculpture collection Rose had built since the Mount Kisco fire had destroyed many of his paintings, and he asked the childless bachelor about its ultimate destiny. This question quickly made the rounds among those interested in the new museum. Goldmann contacted Gershon Agron, who had been the publisher of the *Palestine Post* when Rose's "Pitching Horseshoes" column appeared in it, and who in 1959 was mayor of Jerusalem, and Agron spoke to Walter Eytan, chairman of Israel's Bezalel Art Museum, the institution the new museum would replace.[10] In the summer of 1959 Eytan wrote Rose to expect a visit from a young American art historian, Karl Katz, the Bezalel's director, and Rose perked up at the prospect of this new Jewish action.[11] "Israel—and I know it like the palm of my hand—has excited me," he wrote Lee Strasberg on September 25.[12]

Israel intrigued him in a new way that year when he spotted Miriam Hadar, Miss Israel of 1958, at the "21" restaurant and walked up to her table to say hello. The twenty-four-year-old beauty had a boyfriend and was not attracted to the sixty-year-old showman, but she did find him fascinating company. "I'm five-eight and six feet with heels. He felt so little next to me," said today's Miriam H. Weingarten. "But when you speak with him and get to know him better he's eight feet tall." Rose attended the talks the Jerusalem native gave in New York for the American Friends of Hebrew University, and they knew people in common, including Agron.[13] Then on October 21 Katz wrote Rose, "I plan to be in the States this winter and would be grateful if you could spare some time for me to see you."[14] A meeting was arranged for early December.[15] "We were grasping at every straw to try to find money," Katz said.[16] The museum got more than money. It got Billy Rose.

"CUT THE BULL____"

"He was living in that *incredible* house ... it was *unbelievably* palatial ... over the top plush," Katz recalled.[17] The showman's instincts still hit bull's-eyes. Rose knew the power of staging, and the house, with a "living room that may have been slightly smaller than Madison Square Garden," was one of the ways he defended himself and conquered others.[18] When he and Moss Hart argued over an unattractive character in Hart's 1949 *Light Up the Sky* that resembled Rose, the house eventually made the peace between them. "Moss wanted so badly to see his house," Kitty Carlisle Hart said, that he patched things up in order to visit.[19] When the butler admitted him, Katz also was awed. Then "this little guy walks in, I'll never forget," Katz said, "in bedroom slippers, with a red shirt on with a rose in blue on the pocket of the shirt, and said, 'OK, kid, what's that?' He pointed to a piece of sculpture. And I said, 'I think that's a Daumier.' He said, 'Right. What's that?' 'I don't know—I think it's a little study by Rodin?' 'Right. What's that?' 'Oh, I think that's a Zadkin [*sic*].' 'Right. OK, come on in.' I said, 'What if I didn't pass the test, Mr. Rose?' He said, 'I wouldn't have let you in.'" (To make sure his interviewer understood the nature of this meeting with Rose, Katz yelled out Rose's lines.)[20]

The two men then went to an office, where Rose sat in a barber's chair and looked over the plans for a museum on a hill in Jerusalem. Rose already knew what he wanted. "I think you should have a sculpture garden," he said.[21] Katz thought it was a terrific idea, since "there weren't many sculpture gardens in the world at the time: there were three or four."[22] Things now moved quickly. The next day Katz "was so excited" that he ran to talk with Ralph Goldman, an American who had left his position in Israel at Ben-Gurion's office to head museum fundraising at New York's America-Israel Cultural Foundation (AICF). "I remember we had lunch together at the La Terrain Hotel on 45th Street," Goldman said. "We spent two good hours getting all excited" about Rose. But Goldman, as "the practical person, was trying to think how can we get Billy Rose to commit himself to give this particular gift."[23]

There was an opportunity to accomplish this on an upcoming Friday, either December 11 or 18. That evening a kind of museum-awareness event was scheduled at the Manhattan home of Siegfried and Lola Kramarsky, important art collectors. Goldman thought it an ideal place for Rose to make a public announcement of his sculpture gift to the museum and "clinch the deal," he said. The only hitch was that the Kramarskys were "very 'proper' people and they were not people to whose home you invite a Billy Rose."[24] His "reputation—with the tall roses and tall girls, the saloons and all the rest of it—he really did not belong in that society," Goldman said.[25] In 1949, Israel's government had had the same problem with Rose, and before the sculpture garden was completed, both orthodox Jews and Israel's writers and intellectuals also objected to him. This snobbery was a Jewish problem Philip Roth put his finger on when his Alexander Portnoy complained, "I am soiled, oh, I am impure—and also pretty fucking tired, my dear, of never being quite good enough for The Chosen People!"[26] Rose would also rage at his fellow Jews.

Still, Goldman was desperate to get Rose on the record and invited him to the gathering anyway, and Rose shared his sculpture garden plan, charmed everyone, and thrilled Goldman, who later said, "I was so exhilarated by the evening—meeting Billy Rose, and Billy Rose saying he was giving his sculpture—it was the biggest gift we could get for the Museum." The next day Rose had the Kramarskys visit his mansion to see his art, and that evening Rose told Goldman he needed Isamu Noguchi to design his sculpture garden and wanted to meet him the next day, a Sunday. Rose had purchased a Noguchi sculpture no later than 1955, and in 1958 Noguchi's fame grew because of the gardens he had created at UNESCO's Paris headquarters. Goldman did not know Noguchi so he contacted Baroness Bethsabée de Rothschild, who did, and on Sunday, Rose and Noguchi had lunch. "I wanted to show Billy Rose that if he does business with us, we deliver," Goldman said.[27]

Goldman next arranged to have Israel's ambassador to the United States, Avraham Harman, and Sam Rubin, president of the AICF, accept Rose's gift. They all met at Rose's home, where, according to Goldman, "one potentially dangerous moment" occurred. Rubin got carried away and rhapsodized that "such a gift may bring peace between Israel and Egypt and . . . how the nations would meet and governments would forget war." Goldman recalled that Rose responded with, "'Cut the bull____,' with all the dirty words associated. And that was of course very embarrassing to me."[28] But the meeting brought the deal closer to fruition, and on December 20 the Bezalel's Eytan wrote Rose, "We need not tell you how immensely grateful and enthusiastic we are about the prospect of receiving this extraordinary donation, which will no doubt be one of the most important individual contributions made to the development of our Museum."[29] Still, the dimensions of the gift were unknown, including to Rose, who had not thought through the details. He was just running on his obscure but powerful source of drive. "He was overflowing with vitality, [it] streamed out of him," said Stephen E. Weil, an art gallery executive. "Boundless energy."[30] Meanwhile, naysayers told Goldman, "Billy Rose is just a mirage—he'll never deliver."[31]

So Goldman decided to seize an upcoming event for an even more public announcement of Rose's gift. The annual AICF gala dinner and concert, featuring the New York Philharmonic, violinist Isaac Stern, and an audience of one thousand was set for January 6, 1960, at the Waldorf Astoria. The guest of honor was Spyros P. Skouras, president of 20th Century-Fox. The program was already printed, and Skouras's name was on the cover. Rose was not part of the organization, and his name was nowhere to be found. Nevertheless, Goldman decided this was the perfect venue for Rose to commit to his gift. "Then Billy Rose gets into the act," Goldman recalled. "He feels that if he's going to make a presentation of the gift at the Waldorf Astoria it has to be staged by him, because only Billy Rose knows [how] to stage!" Rose decided to transport Jacob Epstein's sculpture *The Annunciation* from his home to the Waldorf as a photo-op prop. At five feet, five inches, it was taller than Rose, and for the occasion he, Katz, and Goldman agreed to call the piece *Hannah,* since its true name denoted the moment the Virgin Mary learned from the angel Gabriel that she would give birth to the Son of God. The papers would have had a field day. "Anyway, at the dinner Billy Rose stole the show," Goldman said. The Rose magic that had averted an insurrection by the cast of *Jumbo* twenty-five years before was still operational. "His enthusiasm was such that whether [the AICF dinner guests] believed he would do what he was saying about donating the sculpture or not didn't matter. Everybody was ultimately taken in by him. And the meeting ran about three-and-a-half hours instead of the one-and-a-half that had been scheduled. . . . His enthusiasm was inspirational. It was everything."[32] Katz's assessment was the same: "Rose, true to form, stole the show with his surprise announcement. When it was his turn at the podium, he revealed that he would send his entire sculpture collection to Israel and fund the design and realization of a . . . sculpture garden designed by Isamu Noguchi."[33] The reaction of the audience at the Waldorf might have been bewilderment, rather than gasps. They had no reason to expect him there, and the Israel Museum project was little known. But over the previous quarter century the press had learned that Rose was good copy, and newspaper reports on the AICF dinner were all about Billy Rose.

TWO-TON KNICKKNACKS

The next day the news ran in all the New York dailies. The *Mirror, Herald-Tribune, Post, Times,* and more reported on his gift to Israel of fifty sculptures and a garden to display them, which together amounted to a grand $1 million gesture. It was Rose who made the story worth reporting, and the headlines made sure not to bury the lead, giving greatest prominence to his name in examples such as, "Billy Rose Gives His Art to Israel," "Rose Gives $1 Million Art Collection to Israel," and "Billy Rose Is Giving Israel Million in Art." The *Post* revisited the news three days later on Sunday, January 10, with a feature that included nine photographs of the works destined for Israel, but the topper was *Time* magazine's "Bonanza from Billy." The February 8 issue devoted four pages to Rose's gift, including three pages of photographs that introduced readers to the showman's art collection, including Antoine Bourdelle's massive *The Warrior,* Rodin's *Adam,* and Aristide Maillol's *Chained Liberty.* Most striking about the news coverage was Rose's open embrace of Israel. "I'm very close to these pieces, naturally, but I'm closer emotionally to the State of Israel," he told the *Herald-Tribune,* and to the *Times* he said, "If 2,000,000 people [of Israel] can gamble their flesh and blood, I can gamble a few tons of bronze and marble." Though he obscured his Jewish motivation in his interview with *Time*—"What was I going to do with these two-ton knickknacks—leave them to my sister Polly?"—his general openness regarding his feelings of loyalty and love toward the Jewish people signaled a change in the times that permitted him to express and enjoy such sentiments for the first time.[34]

In the years since Rose in 1944 told the *Washington Post* that he produced *We Will Never Die* only because it was a good show, the conditions of American Jewish life had shifted profoundly. The antisemitism of the war years had faded, and by 1962 an opinion poll found that just 1 percent of respondents felt Jews were a threat to America, a dramatic reduction from the 25 percent of 1944. The moment that the productions *Fun to Be Free, We Will Never Die,* and *A Flag Is Born* paved the way for had by 1960 largely arrived, and American Jews had not just the freedom to express Jewish identity alongside their American one but, with Israel, something new to express. Israel's birth, survival, and energy lifted American Jewish spirits well before its spectacular victory in the 1967 Six-Day War, and during the 1950s, whether by reading books about the country, participating in or watching Israeli folk dance performances, shopping in what by 1957 was a surge of Jewish gift shops stocked with Israeli products, or attending Israel Philharmonic Orchestra concerts when the musicians toured the United States in 1950–51 and again in 1960, Israel offered Jews a way to take "pride in the Jewish state and, by extension, the Jewish people as a whole," writes the historian Emily Alice Katz.[35] Popular culture took advantage of the buoyant mood with a hyperbolic expression of Jewish pride. "More tourists fly in to Tel Aviv with copies of Leon Uris' best-selling novel [*Exodus*] than with copies of the Bible," the Associated Press reported in November 1959.[36]

Rose had been waiting for this moment his whole life. He was now able to indulge his American and Jewish passions, his native patriotism and his love of Israel that were both equally part of him. In a January 1960 interview with a journalist for North American Jewish weeklies, he spoke of how his mother helped bring Jewish refugees to America. "[Rose] had learned early the universal and specific meaning of 'mitzvah' and he carried that heritage with him through the years. Over and again, Billy reverted to the treasure that was his legacy from his mother," reported Nathan Ziprin, who asked Rose two important questions. "'How does it feel to give away a collection to which one is so attached?' His reply was: 'Fine,'" wrote Ziprin. "'And how does it feel to give it to Israel?' I thought Billy would pour out a stream of sentimentality. Instead, he stunned me with a terse but highly tragic and meaningful answer: 'It provides the reason for my whole idiot existence.'"[37]

The clamor of publicity that greeted Rose's sculpture donation—all of it diligently seeded by Rose—was a boon to the obscure museum project. "For the first time the building of the Israel Museum became known not only to the Jewish world in the United States but also the American public," Goldman said. Katz agreed. "That was a shot in the arm that we really, really needed," he said. "No one knew about the Israel Museum, about the whole effort. All of a sudden there was this big article . . . in *Time*. . . . And so it was a huge shot in the arm for the project."[38]

On February 18 Noguchi signed a contract with the AICF to design the five-acre Billy Rose Sculpture Garden, as it was then called. Noguchi was at first reluctant to accept the assignment, apparently because he was not Jewish. "This [Rose] would not accept, contending that one who voluntarily incarcerated himself in a war relocation camp could not refuse such a challenge," Noguchi said. Rose's argument was direct and profound. He understood that the Japanese American artist's experience of exclusion and dislocation made him an ideal choice for the Israeli project, and Noguchi later decided Rose was right. "My going to Israel was in a way like going home and seeing people like myself," he said. "The Jew has always appealed to me as being the endless, continually expatriated person who really did not belong anywhere."[39] Few gave Rose credit for such insight, and he deliberately abjured anything resembling a sensitive artistic temperament, but he had a grasp of what artists were about. The paintings he collected were "very exciting because these painters almost invariably were wild hearts, desperate fellows," Rose said.[40]

The contract made it clear that Rose would donate his sculpture and funds to the AICF, a tax-exempt American organization, which would pay Noguchi the fee the two men agreed upon: $25,000 plus $30 per diem for expenses when Noguchi was in Israel, and first-class jet travel to and from that country. "In those days, that was already a considerable amount of money," Noguchi said.[41] In addition, Rose committed to spend an additional $100,000 to construct the garden. It was these amounts, when added to the value of the donated sculptures, that yielded the newsworthy $1 million gift.[42]

JERUSALEM OR BUST

Rose's enthusiasm and determination that his garden and the museum both be successful made him a determined foe of enemies and an indefatigable champion of the cause. Almost immediately after the contract was signed, he and Noguchi made their first trip together to Israel, where the pair were honored on March 1 at the Bezalel. When Rose returned home he organized for the middle of May a museum benefit at his mansion, where one hundred people viewed photographs of Jerusalem and the museum site and heard Max Abramovitz, the New York architect then at work on Lincoln Center's Avery Fisher Hall, speak "with great enthusiasm about the entire plan of the museum project."[43]

At the same time, Rose became incensed that Israel's orthodox Jews objected to his sculpture garden. During his Israel visit he met with Binyamin Mintz, who served in the nation's parliament as a member of the United Religious Front, and while the religious politician gave "the impression, after long conversations, that he would raise no great fuss about this matter," others did. The religious community viewed it as a direct contravention of the Jewish law against graven images and a project grossly ill suited to Jerusalem. Rose had no sympathy for this position. "As I see it, from where I sit, this is all so much poppycock," he wrote Teddy Kollek, a key originator and backer of the Israel Museum idea, who was then at work in the office of Prime Minister David Ben-Gurion. "No one will bow to these works, no one will worship them.... This seems like an easy way for a man to get his name in the papers."[44]

Secular Israelis also had qualms about the sculpture garden, as the eminent Hasidic rabbi Menachem Mendel Schneerson of Brooklyn stressed in May to the sculptor Jacques Lipchitz, whom Schneerson addressed as Chaim Yaakov Lipchitz. "I will cite the opinions of some prominent Jews on this project...and I bring only these as no one can accuse them of 'religious bias,'" Schneerson said. Several of the objections were principled. The poet Nathan Zach called on Jews to "display a little respect for our past." But others just did not like Rose. "The would-be benefactor should be told that not all gifts can be accepted unconditionally!" wrote the author David Zakkai, and Prof. Dov Sadan characterized the gift as "a collection of statues which had been assembled by the caprice of a pampered individual." Uri Avnery, editor of the sometimes racy *HaOlam Hazeh* (This World), which Schneerson called "a radically 'modernistic' publication," also found the idea in poor taste and castigated Rose as an "alien 'benefactor.'" Schneerson had no love for Rose either, and wrote Lipchitz, "You surely know that the whole project was started by one whose profession is associated with burlesque and night-show business, New York style."[45] Rose, however, would not budge, and he told Kollek that if the sculpture garden was "not set up in Jerusalem, my collection would not be set up anywhere in Israel."[46]

Initially there were reports of a compromise that would keep representative as opposed to abstract works out of the main display area, but it seems the real breakthrough was in the choice of the proper Hebrew word to describe the sculpture garden.[47] "I visited a number of rabbis, trying to understand the injunction and devise a solution," wrote Karl Katz. "If we directly translated Sculpture Garden, it would be *Gan Ha'pesalim*—literally 'garden of idols.' That clearly wouldn't work."[48] Instead, it was decided that the garden would be called an art garden and use the Hebrew word for art, which was not objectionable.

With this obstacle overcome, Rose assumed more responsibility for the museum. On November 30, 1960, Abba Eban congratulated and thanked him for becoming head of the finance committee, making him one of the most important players in the development not just of his sculpture garden, but of the museum as a whole.[49] Ralph Goldman later said, "And if you know anything about Billy Rose, you know that meant he also had to be the whole committee."[50] Rose soon undertook a world tour to collect money and art. In February 1961, he visited Rio de Janeiro and São Paulo, Brazil, to buy Mario Cravo sculptures, and upon his return planned additional major offensives: a June trip to London and an August visit to Scotland's Edinburgh Festival to view the sculptures of the late Sir Jacob Epstein, meet Lady Epstein, and land Epstein's works; a fundraising dinner for major donors at his New York home; a similar event in London at the home of Arthur Lourie, now Israel's ambassador to the United Kingdom, who had worked with Rose on the Israel public relations plan in 1949; and a meeting in Geneva with Baron Edmond de Rothschild.[51]

Rose succeeded everywhere. "There is a small amateur bandit at large in the art world today who is making the recent and spectacular hauls," wrote the syndicated columnist Inez Robb in an article that appeared in 140 newspapers on August 21, 1961. Rose had just announced two victories. Lipchitz donated to the museum 300 of his original plaster casts and Lady Epstein gave 250 of her husband's original casts. Israel sent Rose ecstatic congratulations. "The magnificent gifts of the two sculpture collections have received even more publicity here [in Israel] than in the States," wrote the future museum director, Yohanan Beham, "and if you continue in this manner some people might consider you a serious candidate for Prime Minister."[52] (Lipchitz later reneged on his deal with Rose and never donated the sculptures to the Israel Museum, probably because of Schneerson's disapproval.[53])

By November 19, Rose's plans were set for the December 7, 1961, fundraising dinner at his home, and he telegrammed invitations to the publishers Max Schuster and Bennett Cerf, his cartoonist friend Al Hirschfeld, the art collector Joe Hirschhorn, the film executive Jack Warner, and apparently Marlene Dietrich, who was among the fifty guests expected to donate at least $25,000 per person or couple "for the Jerusalem Museum now under construction on a hill in the Holy City," as Rose's invitation worded it.[54] The guest of honor was to have been Ambassador Adlai Stevenson, but Stevenson had to bow out. Rose replaced him with Nahum Goldmann.[55] The event was luxurious. Each diner had a dedicated waiter, and the chef Dione Lucas prepared the food. Dinner "began with 50 individual cheese soufflés. They all had to come out at the right time and in the right shape, and we had to take them upstairs quickly before they fell," Lucas said. Then came "baby trout with almonds, served with cucumber ice sherbert and then stuffed roast veal with chantrelles [sic], and covered with a mousseline sauce." A "tossed green salad with hot brioche and a pineapple filled with pineapple sherbert and fresh fruit" completed the feast.[56] The royal treatment apparently set a munificent tone—and perhaps induced a sense of indebtedness—that opened wallets. Ralph Goldman and Karl Katz were there, and on December 9 Goldman wired Israel with the good news. "A few minutes ago we received Ralph's cable informing us of the overwhelming success of your dinner," Beham wrote Rose. "Please accept my warmest congratulations and sincerest thanks. While I hope to see you in the not too distant future, I wanted to let you know that the fruits of your efforts are making my life considerably easier, because now we shall be able to continue the Bezalel [art] wing along the lines [of] the Archaeological wing [which] has expanded." As Beham indicated, the money was significant enough for the museum to realize grander ambitions. The dinner raised $600,000, Goldman said.[57]

By the time word of the New York dinner reached Israel, Rose was in London to work on last-minute details for the fundraiser there. "It's taken me the best part of a year to put this one together and if everyone shows up who has accepted, my chances of getting a good piece of money are excellent," he wrote Kollek.[58] He did not exaggerate his long devotion to the London fundraiser. Rose was already heavily invested in it by late June, when he wrote Lady Epstein's attorney that "Arthur Lurie [*sic*], Israel Ambassador to Great Britain, is holding dinner party for me at his home in London," then set for late September, and expected guests included Isaac Wolfson, owner of a retailing conglomerate, the financier Jack Lyons, and the wide-ranging businessman Charles Clore, as well as "a dozen other wealthy men and women who are interested in Art and, we hope, in a major art Museum in Israel."[59] The London dinner also was a success. Rose told Kollek about it on December 27, and the news that Rose had again triumphed and pulled off a New York–London fundraising double-header that together yielded more than $1 million elated museum officials and brought Rose more congratulations, but apparently not with the enthusiasm he desired.[60] On January 17, 1962, Jerusalem mayor Mordechai Ish-Shalom tried to appease an apparently sulking Rose: "I have already expressed in previous letters and cables our deep appreciation for your latest successes in New York and London and our admiration for everything you are doing . . . (but I never received any reply)." Rose may have felt he deserved more extravagant effusions of gratitude. His fundraising was crucially important, as Beham made clear on May 28 when he informed Rose that the museum decided to add yet more pavilions, after learning "of the success of your two dinners."[61]

As for Baron Edmond de Rothschild, in December 1961 Rose took time away from planning the London dinner to travel to Geneva to meet him and declare him—with a New Yorker's democratic informality—"a very nice fellow." The baron assured Rose he would keep the promise he made to Kollek to "act as Chairman of an International Art Committee for the Jerusalem Museum of Art." Rose further commended Rothschild to Kollek as "a warm first rate human being."[62]

MAKE BULLETS

The years 1960 and 1961, characterized by Rose's tenacious fundraising and his need for praise and control, continued through the museum's 1965 opening and established him, according to Kollek, as one of the Israel Museum's "greatest and most troublesome benefactors."[63] That formulation summed up

Rose's way of life. "Tough guys go further than sweet phonies," he reminded Kollek, whose characterization of Rose may have been spurred by a 1965 Rose letter that accused him of a double-cross.[64] "To welsh on this contract with my sculpture on your doorstep is too much. You all have a lesson to learn from the goyim," Rose wrote, venting some of the Jewish venom he had often been served.[65] Or Kollek may have had in mind a letter of August 3, 1964, in which Rose angrily complained about the planned arrangement of museum buildings, which he feared might obscure his garden. "What in the name of Christ does this mean," Rose demanded, with a particularly unsuitable choice of words for a project in Israel. "I sincerely hope that I misunderstood your paragraph. It's like telling me that you're going to build a building directly in front of the new Knesseth [*sic*]." Rose did misunderstand, Kollek told him. And the future Jerusalem mayor, who would himself emerge as one of the world's great showmen and personalities, composed just the sort of letter necessary to reassure Billy Rose. "We shall still have the nicest Museum Hill in the world," he said, "the most suitable and the most unspoiled site that anybody anywhere can imagine in the centre of any capital city in modern times."[66]

Ralph Goldman was exposed to the same volatile yet careful man and wrote Beham, "Billy will probably seek assurances until the day that the garden is completed and all the sculpture is there. Despite his show-business-like behavior, he is a calculating and extremely cautious individual." But the fact remained "that the museum in Jerusalem means a great, great deal to him. The garden will be great if the museum is great. He will be difficult, make demands and create problems—but if you and I did not have any problems, what would we do."[67] Jerusalem was Rose's chance at immortality—Jewish immortality. "Being the kind of practical man that he was, Rose knew that nowhere else in the world would his name be celebrated and perpetuated as much as it would be in a city like Jerusalem," Goldman said later.[68] However, this did not mean he trusted Jerusalem's tailors. When his luggage was lost by an airline, he did not buy new clothes in Israel but instead had the King David Hotel clean and press his suit every night. "He refused to shop in Israel," Katz said. "The goods would be inferior."[69]

Still, Rose was hardly insensible to Jerusalem's enticements and the excitement of being part of the ancient Jewish story and land. In a letter to Hillel Fefferman, the garden's prime contractor, Rose wrote, "Your executions of Noguchi's creations are dazzling and wonderful. The retaining walls you have built, judging by the photographs, look as if they were carved out of the Bible with Moses himself collecting and setting the stones. . . . Most sincerely, I am happy that you are doing this job, both for me and for Israel. Judging from the photographs, we are working on something which may be one of the genuine wonders of the Holy Land. If it tops the entire museum and the Shrine of the book well, that will be just too bad."[70] That chance of achieving a masterpiece persuaded Rose to spend five times his initial budget of $100,000. By March 1964, his expenditures exceeded half a million dollars. "That's as far as I want to go," Rose wrote Beham.[71]

But he went further. In April he visited Joe Hirschhorn in Connecticut. Rose was itching for him to make a big sculpture donation, and he longed to get the "zillionaire art collector up on the [Jerusalem] hill." The same month Rose traveled to Chicago, threw a big party at the Standard Club, and bagged sculptures by Henry Moore and Alberto Giacometti. On May 29, he held another "fancy black-tie" fundraiser at his New York mansion and in June was back in Chicago, where he landed "seven paintings worth half million or better including outstanding Cubist portrait Picasso large Kline magnificent [sic] Klees."[72] At the end of June he flew to Israel. Rose had finally persuaded Hirschhorn to visit Jerusalem, and during their stay together Rose won Hirschhorn's agreement to lend the museum thirty-seven sculptures, a victory Rose celebrated with a handwritten contract promising that on his eightieth birthday he would treat the Hirschhorns "to a beautiful party, anywhere in the world they want it (plus 1 share of att)." On November 9, 1964, Rose held yet another fundraising dinner at East Ninety-Third Street. It was a triumphant year, spoiled only when Hirschhorn's curator nixed the sculpture loan on November 11. He could not risk damage to the artworks during shipment.[73] But Rose never quit. In 1965 he was still campaigning for the museum, and on February 23 he invited Samuel Goldwyn to a fundraiser scheduled for March 2 at the Beverly Hills home of Edward G. Robinson. Rose flew to California for the event, and so did Teddy Kollek. Goldwyn refused to attend.[74]

As the May 11, 1965, opening day neared, Rose concentrated on publicity with the professionalism he first exhibited at his *Jumbo* pitch to Jock Whitney. On February 4 he appeared on the *Today Show*. For a half hour "Rose was poised, positive and superbly effective, and did not let two sentences pass without referring to Israel in some favourable light," the Israel Information Services office informed Kollek and Beham. "We had known in advance of this projected appearance, but I did not anticipate such a solid handling, with models, background, anecdotes and dignified salesmanship." Israeli ambassador Katriel Katz was also moved by Rose's performance, writing to him, "Believe me, Mr. Rose, it is not only the Israel National Museum, it is all of Israel, which owes you a debt we cannot repay."[75] It was the season for gratitude. The job was done. "It must be months since I even uttered the words 'Thank You' for all that you have done and are doing," Kollek wrote Rose. "Billy, you have been wonderful, utterly selfless and dedicated. . . . You have done a great thing for Israel and a great thing for our people. We are proud of your friendship and we shall prize it as long as we live."[76]

The feeling was mutual. "I love those two million loonies in Israel," Rose told a reporter. But a little bit of sentiment went a long way. So Rose continued: "They asked me, 'If the Arabs attack, what'll we do with your sculpture?' I told them, 'Melt it down and make bullets.'"[77]

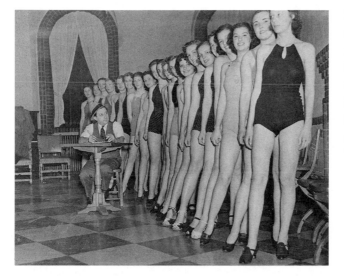

Billy Rose reviews swimmers for 1939 Aquacade. Billy Rose Theatre Division, The New York Public Library for the Performing Arts, Astor, Lenox and Tilden Foundations.

Aquacade's Aquabelle Number One, Eleanor Holm. New York World's Fair 1939–1940 records, Manuscripts and Archives Division, The New York Public Library. Photo by Murray Korman.

Rose, forty, marries the Aquacade
swimming star Eleanor Holm,
twenty-six. Courtesy of United
Press International.

Rose at his Roseholm estate in Mount Kisco, New York.
Arthur Rothstein (1915–1985) for *Look* magazine /
Museum of the City of New York. X2011.4.10548.47.

OPPOSITE PAGE Dramatic staircase with skylight at
Rose's five-story townhouse on Beekman Place. Samuel H.
(Samuel Herman) Gottscho (1875–1971) / Museum of the
City of New York. 88.1.1.373.

Kurt Weill, Rose, and Ben Hecht address the cast of *We Will Never Die*. Courtesy of the Weill-Lenya Research Center, Kurt Weill Foundation for Music, New York.

Rose, Hecht standing, and Peter Bergson at November 29, 1948, dinner marking the dissolution of the Bergson Group and Irgun. Photo by Larry Gordon. Courtesy of the Jabotinsky Institute in Israel.

Rose and Bernard Baruch at 1949 dinner for Baruch. With permission of the Princeton University Library.

ABOVE "Look at that beautiful building. Think of all the great stars who performed there. And I own it." Wurts Bros. (New York, NY) / Museum of the City of New York. X2010.7.2.84.

LEFT Abe Burrows with Rose and Eleanor at 1949 New Year's Eve party. Billy Rose Theatre Division, The New York Public Library for the Performing Arts.

ABOVE Rose and Joyce
Mathews during their first
marriage, in Harry's Bar in
Venice in 1958. © The Al
Hirschfeld Foundation. www.
AlHirschfeldFoundation.org.

RIGHT Rose with Joyce
Mathews and her daughter
Vicki after the couple married
for the second time on
December 29, 1961.

Rose's mansion on East Ninety-Third Street. Edmund Vincent Gillon / Museum of the City of New York. 2013.3.2.595.

In the living room of his mansion in 1964. AP Images/John Lindsay.

Rose and Isamu Noguchi fly to Israel to design the Billy Rose Art Garden. © 2017 The Isamu Noguchi Foundation and Garden Museum, New York / Artists Rights Society (ARS), New York.

Billy Rose shows David Ben-Gurion the sculptures for the art garden. Ben-Gurion Archives and Photography Department, Government Press Office, Israel.

Teddy Kollek promised Rose "the nicest Museum Hill in the world." Photo courtesy of the Eliot Elisofon Collection, Harry Ransom Center, University of Texas at Austin.

ABOVE TOP Billy Rose Art Garden shows sign in Hebrew reading "art garden." © 2017 The Isamu Noguchi Foundation and Garden Museum, New York / Artists Rights Society (ARS), New York.

ABOVE MIDDLE Israel Museum in Jerusalem. Photo courtesy of the Eliot Elisofon Collection, Harry Ransom Center, University of Texas at Austin.

Billy Rose Art Garden at the Israel Museum, Jerusalem. © 2017 The Isamu Noguchi Foundation and Garden Museum, New York / Artists Rights Society (ARS), New York.

Billy Rose with statue of Moses, a role model.
Photo by Eliot Elisofon, Courtesy of the Eliot Elisofon Collection.

epilogue

Rose's success with the Israel Museum was accompanied by his growing wealth in the United States, and the twin accomplishments were the fulfillment of his Jewish American life. His personal life during his last years was chaotic. On December 29, 1961, he married Joyce Mathews for the second time. This union lasted two years; they were divorced on February 10, 1964. Three weeks later, on March 1, Rose married for the fifth time. His new wife was Doris Warner Vidor, daughter of the film powerhouse Harry Warner and widow of the movie director Charles Vidor. At forty-eight, Warner Vidor was sixteen years younger than her sixty-four-year-old husband, but that was nothing new. Ever since Fanny Brice, Rose had married much younger women. What was novel was the wedding ceremony—the couple had a Jewish marriage. It was Rose's first. Rabbi Henry P. Silverman performed the service in Jamaica. He was the only Jewish clergyman on the Caribbean island where Rose in 1961 had purchased Elysium, a "palatial house," for £34,000, or $95,000. This marriage did not even survive the year, and the two were divorced in October.[1]

By then, Rose was involved with the actress Mercedes McCambridge, who was starring in Edward Albee's *Who's Afraid of Virginia Woolf* at the Billy Rose Theatre. Rose was imperious, and she adored it. One of his signature moves came after she and Rose had a fight and, as she later recalled,

I flew off to Los Angeles and hid. I got an unlisted number, and it hadn't been in service more than two hours when Billy called from New York. I was furious. I asked him how he got my number, and he said, 'My dear girl, you forget, I own the telephone company.' I said he didn't own that telephone company, and I shall never forget his soothing patient tone when he said, 'Mercy, don't you know that when you own one telephone company, you own them all?' And he roared with laughter. I have been revived so many times from the tawdriness of life by the exquisite arrogance of that one remark. To have heard a man say this is a great medicine!"[2]

By early 1965 this relationship had also ended, and Rose was again with Joyce. On April 9, she and her daughter Vicki accompanied Rose to Israel for the museum opening.[3] But in July he made the joke that comically revealed the kind of relationship with women he preferred. "Dear Members of the Harem," he wrote to the female staff at a talent agency. "This is your Pasha speaking."[4] However, it was women who held *him* in thrall. For the Israel Museum's opening show he suggested "'Women Through the Ages.' . . . This exhibition could combine great interest and great dignity. Under it all, of course, would be the greatest attraction of all—the female of the species." The museum instead opted for an exhibit of art "inspired by the Bible."[5]

The male friendships that outlasted his marriages were also lost, but to death instead of rancor. During his divorce from Eleanor in 1952 Rose wrote Baruch, "I'm again seeing some of the old cronies, whose company is always exhilarating: Ben Hecht, Ferenc Molnar and a half a dozen other worthies, whose words always tinkle."[6] Molnar died soon after Rose penned that note, and Hecht died in April 1964. "Ben is a great loss to me," Rose wrote Teddy Kollek.[7] Bernard Baruch died a year later in June 1965. "Mr. B dined often with Billy," said Baruch's nurse, Elizabeth Navarro. Rose's home "was one of the few places where Mr B did not leave at 10pm." Rose spoke at Baruch's funeral. "During the past 48 years . . . I have never known him to do a small or mean thing," he said. "Bernie has been the Mr. Big in my life."[8]

A JEWISH DISPLAY

During his last years the one constant of Rose's American life was money. By November 1961 he owned an acre of land on New York's Sixth Avenue adjacent to his Ziegfeld Theatre at Fifty-Fourth Street, and over the next four years he purchased additional buildings and assembled a lot suitable for an office building. The origin of the plan dated from 1955, when Rose briefly partnered with the New York developer William Zeckendorf on an unrealized idea to construct a "Palace of Progress" office building over Pennsylvania Station. He continued to study the stock market and in 1962 bought shares in the New York Central and Pennsylvania railroads. His 150,000 shares of Central in 1964 won him a seat on its board of directors, and that year AT&T shares split again, this time two for one, giving Rose 160,000 shares.[9] His wealth became a story when a public relations man calculated that between October 1963 and February 1964 Rose made $4 million, or $9,000 every hour the market was open. Rose determined that it was actually $8,733.[10] Such news sustained Rose's fame and popularity, and in 1963 Doubleday wanted to publish a biography of him. The sale of movie rights was a strong possibility, as there was "feverish interest" in a Rose film. The idea came and went, and in 1965 Rose's net worth approached $50 million. He dreamed of reaching $100 million. "I think if my luck holds out, by 1970 I will really be a rich fellow," he said.[11]

To this pursuit, Rose for the first time added traditional Jewish elements. The Israel Museum presented him with Jewish ceremonial works of art, including a cup for wine to welcome the Sabbath, two spice boxes used to mark the end of the Sabbath, and decorative silver objects that adorn the Torah scroll, including a breastplate and a pair of finials that top the scroll's wooden handles. These were for display, not use, and in September 1965 Rose wrote Kollek, "At long last, it all arrived and it looks mighty handsome."[12] As his friend Tex McCrary observed, these items were the only Jewish touches in his house. "He had begun to come back," McCrary said. "Come back to his roots."[13]

Some of his Jewish resentment and insecurity lingered. In 1965 when the Anti-Defamation League (ADL) completed its study of AT&T's underemployment of Jews, Rose arranged for ADL representatives to meet with AT&T's chairman, Frederick Kappel. "What's this idea on the telephone company discrimination. I own $11,000,000 worth of stock. I'll fire every one of them," Rose told ADL representatives. But when he traveled with them to the September 21 meeting, Rose became angry and nervous. "I know what they'll say," he said. "They'll say this little Jew sob [i.e., son of a bitch], this little Jew sob. I'll get rid of every one of them." Instead, Rose caved. He "talked much tougher to us how he would handle the people in the Bell company than he actually either handled them or pretended to handle them," said Arnold Forster, the ADL's top attorney. He behaved like "an insignificant Jew."[14]

ESTATE PLANNING

To be fair to the usually feisty Rose, he may not have been feeling well. In May 1965 he wrote of his return to New York from Israel, "I got back in one piece last Saturday evening and today, Wednesday, the blood is beginning to flow normally in my veins. I've done a lot of sound sleeping in the past few days. I didn't realize how tired I was." Even in poor health, he continued to correspond with Kollek about the museum's fundraising needs and paid attention to the care of his beloved garden—the olive trees, the light fixtures, and the fountain, which, Rose reminded Kollek, "should flow gently—not gush."[15] On November 22, he drew up a will, and two weeks later he traveled to Texas to have the pioneering heart surgeon Michael DeBakey cut him open and, the *Times* reported, "put a Dacron graft in the main trunk artery that supplies blood to most of the body. The graft connects the aorta with arteries of both legs." Rose kept the December 8 operation quiet. His sister Polly read about it in the newspapers.[16] Rose returned to New York on December 22, but it was not until January 25, 1966, when he seemed to be improving, that folks at the Israel Museum learned of his condition. "A miracle happened," wrote Rose's AICF secretary, Elaine Rosenfeld. "Something in Billy clicked; veins began to flow, blood began to circulate and Billy began to get well."[17] A few days later the sportswriter Jimmy Cannon saw a different Rose. He was, Cannon said, like a hawk "imprisoned in a sparrow's crippled body. He sat, diminished and clenched by pain."[18] On February 7, Rose added one last codicil to his will, and the next day he flew to his Jamaica home with his sister Polly. On the ninth he fell ill and was admitted to a hospital, where he died at three in the morning on February 10.

The next day Polly brought Rose's body to New York and the executors of his estate revealed that the usually meticulous Rose had made no provision for his burial. He apparently was more comfortable making businesslike plans for the disposition of his estate than handling details regarding his demise, so Polly and her sister Miriam conceived the idea that their brother should be buried on the grounds of the Billy Rose Art Garden. By February 12, this was already a problem. Kollek pointed out that in Israel "burial outside approved cemetery [is] impossible. Only exception was Israel's first president[.] None thereafter." But Kollek, by then mayor of Jerusalem, offered a substitute plan that he presented with a dose of Rose's own salesmanship. "On top of the highest of the Judean hills, on a spot from where all of Jerusalem and the ancient province of Judea can be seen, there is a cemetery. It is called 'Har Hamenuchot,' or the 'Mountain of Eternal Rest.' . . . If you agree, I will obtain the necessary permission of the Rabbinical authorities and . . . with my prerogative as Mayor, ask them to permit burying Billy in that special section, reserved for notable individuals."[19]

There is no record of Polly responding to this excellent and generous proposal. Instead, she and Miriam came up with their own plan, which apparently had the virtue that it would almost certainly be rejected by Rose's trustees and so give the sisters grounds to replace the trustees with themselves. The trustees did reject their $125,000 plan, telling the sisters, "Such a large amount might be questioned by the Attorney General on behalf of the Billy Rose Foundation, Inc." Citing this decision, the sisters in April sued for control of Rose's estate.[20] They did not prevail. They next tried a different tack and challenged the validity of Rose's will. A judge ruled against them. A year after Rose's death he was still unburied and stored in a "'waiting' vault in the Westchester Hills Cemetery."[21] His sisters then asked a court to give the Billy Rose Foundation $20 million, with the remainder to be shared by them. As their case progressed, Rose was finally buried on October 29, 1967, twenty months after his death, in "the largest mausoleum ever built in Westchester Hills Cemetery."[22] His sisters fought on, arguing now that Rose's charitable gift, by evading taxes, "was against public policy." Finally, an appeals court ruled against the sisters' dubious claim that they wanted to overturn Rose's will as a kind of public service, so that the American people, through imposition of the estate tax, would benefit from his wealth. In the end they were left with what their brother had provided them. Polly received $50,000 and the lifetime income of a $1 million trust estimated to yield $40,000 a year. In today's dollars, the bequest would be $375,000 and the annual income $300,000. Miriam Stern, who was estranged from her brother, received income from a $100,000 trust. Neither sister had children to inherit her wealth, and Rose's will called for both trusts to revert to his foundation after his sisters' deaths. Polly died in 1971 and Miriam in 1979.[23]

BELLA ROSA

"Now [Rose] has brought off—even if posthumously—one of his finest publicity coups. He is the subject of two biographies." In 1968, Maurice Zolotow, whose own biography of Rose was shut down by its subject, reviewed for the *Times* two new Rose biographies. *The Nine Lives of Billy Rose,* by Rose's sister Polly, was easily dispatched. "Her book teems with scandalous gossip about Rose's wives and mistresses and his sexual problems," Zolotow wrote. "But globs of erotical anecdotes, irrelevantly splashed on the canvas . . . strike me as having less to do with biography and more to do with writing pornography." As for Earl

Conrad's *Billy Rose: Manhattan Primitive,* according to Zolotow, it portrays Rose "as a power-driven, cruel, greedy, ruthless, lying, dishonest, conniving villain."[24]

What Zolotow did not and could not say was that Earl Conrad was born Earl Cohen and apparently suffered the discomfort many Jews still felt when presented with unflattering Jews. "I think he's a disgrace because he does all the things Jews are accused of doing," Rose's press agent Charles Samuels told Conrad after Rose's death. Such anxiety was not new. In 1945, when Rose got into a contract dispute with the scenic designer Norman Bel Geddes about a bill for *Seven Lively Arts,* Bert Lahr, the star comedian of the show, told Harold Ross of the *New Yorker,* "If Rose keeps on he will set the Jewish race back 2,000 years."[25] Though Conrad's new name protected him from being tarred with other Jews' supposed sins, his biography of Rose made it clear that he was still defensive, which was not unusual. In 1965, when the New York radio personality Long John Nebel, born John Zimmerman, interviewed Rose, he steered him away from Jewish subjects, at one point asking—as Rose spoke of the Israel Museum—about a trained seal act.[26]

The biographies were quickly forgotten, and another twenty years passed without much attention paid to the once ubiquitous shorthand expert; songwriter; nightclub owner; Broadway producer; fairgrounds impresario; master negotiator; newspaper columnist; theater owner; multimillionaire; secret Jewish rescuer, activist, and philanthropist; and frequently married and cheerfully self-described bastard. This résumé dazzled even him. "I can only refer to myself as my mother's son," he said in a 1965 radio interview. "I cannot compare myself to anybody because I am a little more mixed-up than anybody I can think of."[27] Then in 1989 Rose staged an unexpected but fitting comeback when his story was picked up by Saul Bellow, one of America's greatest writers, a heavyweight with the reputation and medals to win the showman his desired and deserved publicity. His novella *The Bellarosa Connection* is based on Rose's rescue of Kurt Schwarz but presented as fiction—what the *Times* called a tall tale about a "preposterous" episode.[28] In the story Rose is presented as a case, even as *the* case, of "the testing of Jewry by the American experience." He was certainly American. "There was a penny-arcade jingle about Billy, the popping of shooting galleries, the rattling of pinballs," writes Bellow. The fireworks, however, did double duty. They entertained his public and hid a treasure. "The God of his fathers still mattered," says *Bellarosa*'s narrator. "Billy was as spattered as a Jackson Pollock painting, and among the main trickles was his Jewishness."[29]

This book shares Bellow's verdict on Rose, which is hidden in the title of Bellow's story. Billy Rose, with all his flaws and pettiness and occasional brutality, is *Bellarosa,* or *bella rosa:* "beautiful rose." He met the challenges of American Jewish life on both fronts with all the intensity and joy and enthusiasm and caginess and wariness and toughness that his dual inheritances encouraged and required. As a savvy oddsmaker, Rose seems to have decided that the Jewish American project was a stacked deck. America is a huge country and the Jews are few, and even with all the ambition in the world, certain Jewish heights could be achieved only in Israel. Rose went there to scale those heights. But he came back, and he brought some Jewish artifacts with him to live, for the little time he had left, the mixed and rich and complex and confusing and thrilling experience of the American Jew. It is an identity he helped pioneer and invent, and it still can serve as a model for vital American citizenship.

acknowledgments

For some foolish reason I did not think researching the life of Billy Rose would take very great effort or digging. I was wrong, and the search for documents and photographs extended to Jamaica, Italy, Israel, Brazil, and Romania. There are many people to thank.

Relatives of Rose and others who knew him or knew his relations and shared their memories with me include Dorothy Rice Chase, Kathy DeAlmeida, Ethel Ferezy, Dorothy Field, Shirley Gatsik, Ralph Goldman, Stephen Gottlieb, Beverly Greenberg, Francine Helene, Dr. Francine Jacobs, Marcia Jacobs, Steve Jacobs, Evelyn Lishinsky, Gilbert Lloyd, Susan Loesser, Harris Millman, Zachary Rogow, Paul Thieberger, Nancy Turbeville, Jane Morgan Weintraub, Elaine Weitzen, Julie Wernick, Peter Wernick, and Martin Weyl. Patricia Klindienst kindly shared the interviews she had conducted with members of Rose's family.

Karl Katz forgave me my unpreparedness during the early days of my research. Vicki Walton was especially generous with her time and the sharing of information that only she possessed. John Wohlstetter was crucial to my research in Israel and continually sent me items of interest and importance that saved me much time and the embarrassment of missing important facts and stories. Fanny Brice's grandson, John Brice, provided the invaluable dictated notes for her unpublished biography. Judy Goetz Sanger graciously met with me in New York and shared stories of her friendship with Rose. Meeting her was one of the delights of my research. I am grateful to Charles McKay for introducing me to Ms. Sanger. Near the end of my research I was fortunate to speak with Miriam H. Weingarten.

Without the help of Idy Sherer, daughter of Kurt Schwarz, the Jewish refugee Billy Rose rescued from Europe in 1939, this book might not have come about. It was the generous help of Ms. Sherer, who kept her father's papers—including the telegrams he received from Rose—that filled me with the excitement and enthusiasm to tackle this project. I would not have found Ms. Sherer without the help of Janis Bellow Freedman, who provided me with a crucial excerpt from her personal journal regarding the origin of Saul Bellow's *The Bellarosa Connection*. Also critical to finding Sherer was Betty Hillman, the daughter of Herb Hillman, who told Bellow the story that became *Bellarosa*. Alfred Netter, the son of Kurt Schwarz's employer, provided me with the final piece of the puzzle. In my effort to learn everything possible about how Schwarz and Rose found each other, I tracked down Nina Turner, a Schwarz relation, and was helped by her friends Delia Joyce, Lorelei Goldman, and especially Charlotte Kaplan. However, I never unlocked that mystery.

Librarians, archivists, and fellow researchers endured my repeated phone calls and various forms of electronic pestering. I am grateful to Jeanne Abrams, Dr. Jillian Adams, Diana Alberghini, Erin Allsop, James Amemasor, Linnea Anderson, Tom Ankner, J. D. Arden, Ron Arons, James Auclair, Andreas Augustin, Richard Baker, Alice Baron, Giulia Barrera, Barbara Anne Beaucar, Ronald L. Becker, Anne-Marie Belinfante, Tad Bennicoff, Matthew Benz, Cara Setsu Bertram, Dr. Alice L. Birney, Lori Birrell, Sari Bitticks, Janine Biunno, Ray Bonis, Marisa Bourgoin, Richard Boursy, Ann Lind Bowers, Stella Breckenridge, Julia Brindisi, Jared Brown, Joyce Burner, Gale Burrow, Paola Busonero, Caitlin at Radcliffe's Schlesinger Library, Liz Campion, Beverly Carver, John Calhoun, Leslie Campbell, Dr. Raul Cârstocea, Robin Carroll-Mann, Anne Causey, Haley Chinn, Ilias Chrissochoidis, Susan Chung, Lucas Clawson, Christa Cleeton, Ken Cobb, Rose Lerer Cohen, Heidi Coleman, Ron Coleman, Jillian J. Collins, Tracie Conrad, Meghan R. Constantinou, Bea Crespo, David Crespy, Raffaella Crociani, Delores Culley, Katina Davis, Dana Dorman, Barry Dougherty, Jessika Drmacich-Flach, David Eifler, Garrett Eisler, Betsy Eisner, Tanya Elder, Ralf Engel, Bette M. Epstein, Bob Essman, Leanna Feldman, Emily Ferrigno, Karen J. Fishman, Moira Fitzgerald, William Fliss, Benjamin Formaker-Olivas, Eugenie Fortier, Richard Foster, Ilda Francois, Dennis Frank, David K. Frasier, Nancy Freeman, Elizabeth Frengel, Paul Friedman, Michael Frost, Sandra Garcia-Myers, Curt Gathje, Tina Genoves, Sacha Goldano, Sacha Goldgran, Ken Goldstein, Martin Gostanian, Carol Gould, Miriam Gray, Leo Greenbaum, Thomas Gressler, Grace Cohen Grossman, Atina Grossmann, Susan Halpert, Kasiya Halstead, Wayne G. Hammond, Grace Hansen, Will Hansen, Michelle Harvey, Nurit Harvey, Mahsa Hatam, Alexandra M. Henri, Ainsley Henriques, Peter Hermann, Alison Hinderliter, Micah Hoggat, Ellen Holt-Werle, Julia Huddleston, Mary K. Huelsbeck, Charlotte Infantino, Radu Ioanid, Cindy Jackson, Banmattie Jaideo, Julianna Jenkins, Emily Johnson, John C. Johnson, Christina V. Jones, Tanya Kato, Paul Keroack, Amalyah Keshet, Margaret Kieckhefer, Ginny L. Kilander, Tammy Kiter, Maurice Klapwald, Patricia Klindienst, Boni J. Koelliker, Christina Köstner, Laurence Kotler-Berkowitz, Kristine Krueger, James I. Lader, John Leavitt, Vince E. Lee, Amanda Leinberger, Marlea D. Leljedal, Julian Levinson, Susan Liberator, Thomas Lisanti, Dr. Martin Luchterhandt, Maureen Maryanski, Anna Massot, Christine McEvilly, Jeremy Megraw, Rachel Misrati, Misha Mitsel, Ilaria Della Monica, Leslie A. Morris, Francesca Moskowitz, Heike Müller, Roger Munsick, Simone O. Munson, Brandon Murray, Linda Briscoe Myers, Stephen C. Nelson, Tim Noakes, Joe Nuzzolo, David O. Olson, AnnaLee Pauls, Nicholas Pavlik, Derek J. Penslar, Chana Pollack, Josh Price, Mark Quigley, Penny R. Ramon, Rosalba Varallo Recchia, Jan Glier Reeder, Doug Reside, Prof. Ira Robinson, Lauren Robinson, Arieh Rochman-Halperin, Jenny Romero, Sharon Rork, David Rosado, Elaine Rosenberg, Rochelle Rubinstein, Nicole Ruby, Michele Sarfatti, Megan Malta Scauri, Elizabeth Schachter, Richard Schaffer, Deena M. Schwimmer, Leah Sugarman Siegel, David Sigler, Carrie Tallichet Smith, Tamar Soffer, Jeanne Solensky, Barbara Sontz, Miriam Spectre, Renato Spiegel, Cathy Spitzenberger, Dr. Hubert Steiner, Weatherly Stephan, Bruce Tabb, Kristen Tanaka, Deborah Turkewitz, Richard Tuske, Irvin Ungar, Huma Utka, Prof. Sydney Van Nort, Dr. Klaus Voigt, Kimberly Walen, Alexander L. Wallace, Sandy Wallace, Melinda Wallington, Sylvia Wang, Fred Wasserman, Lita Watson, Richard B. Watson, Joe Weber, Emily Wicks, Jocelyn K. Wilk, Jackie Willoughby, Christine Windheuser, Irma Wulz, Lewis Wyman, and Trina Yeckley.

Ned Comstock of the USC Archives of the Cinematic Arts came to my rescue once again. Miles Kreuger of the Institute of the American Musical allowed access to his unparalleled collection. I thank Jesse Harris, who shared his filmed interviews with former dancers at Billy Rose's Diamond Horseshoe. I am happy to thank Liraz Cohen at the Israel State Archives. I also owe much to Isabela Manelici, who went to great lengths to locate files in Romania that might show whether Billy Rose helped two sisters—relatives of Theodor Herzl—escape captivity in that country and immigrate to Israel. Margalit Bejarano shared with me her work on the Jews of Cuba. Ainsley Henriques was my lifeline in Jamaica. Judy Baumgold was especially patient and industrious in helping me locate papers and film and audio interviews conducted with her late father, Ralph Goldman, of the American Jewish Joint Distribution Committee, concerning Billy Rose and the Israel Museum. Irvin Ungar opened his amazing Arthur Szyk archive to me. It now belongs to the Magnes Collection of Jewish Art and Life at the University of California, Berkeley.

Alessandro Cassin, Natalia Indrimi, Daniela Marinkovic, and Anna Pizzuti helped me find key documents in Rome's archives. In Brazil, Dr. Lina Gorenstein, Edgard Leite, and Dr. Dina Lida helped me locate press coverage of Rose's visit there. John Calhoun at the Billy Rose Theatre Division uncovered treasures. Amanda Seigel at the New York Public Library Dorot Jewish Division translated items from the Yiddish newspaper *Forverts*. Chris Hart was kind enough to look for relevant papers that belonged to his father, Moss Hart. Jared Brown provided me with an introduction to Mr. Hart. Hagai Shvadron did all he could to track down the Israeli artist Baruch Klinger, who painted a portrait of Rose. Megan Savage at the America-Israel Cultural Foundation helped me locate and get permission to view AICF papers at a storage facility in New Jersey. Francesca M. Moskowitz of New Jersey's Pascack Valley Historical Society did me a great favor in researching the home Rose bought for his mother.

I am happy to offer special thanks to the owners of Tavern Island for allowing me to visit the property formerly owned by Billy Rose.

Elin Elisofon provided me with images of the photographs taken by her father, Eliot Elisofon, of the opening of the Billy Rose Art Garden in Jerusalem and allowed me to license a wonderful photo. Joan Fullerton exhibited extraordinary patience as I attempted to locate her father's photographs of Rose's mansion on East Ninety-Third Street, an effort that was unfortunately unsuccessful. Matthew R. Ivler kindly provided me with a photograph of Rose's mother's tombstone at Mount Lebanon Cemetery. David Leopold of the Al Hirschfeld Foundation very generously helped me license two Hirschfeld cartoons. Dr. Adi Portugez helped me track down the photograph of Rose with David Ben-Gurion, and Israel's Government Press Office allowed me to feature it in this book. Sincere thanks to Derek Zasky and the Abe Burrows Estate for allowing me to publish photographs found in the Abe Burrows Papers at the New York Public Library. David Stein at the Kurt Weill Foundation allowed me to publish images of documents and photographs from the collection. Thank you to the Jabotinsky Institute in Israel for permission to use a photograph from its collection. Judith Cohen at the US Holocaust Memorial Museum went out of her way to obtain scans of the *We Will Never Die* brochure. Clyde Adams reached out to the

Murray Korman heir Leslie Greaves, who granted permission to use Korman's photograph of Eleanor Holm.

Kerstin Ullrich allowed me to see her interview notes and other research material relating to her intended biography of Billy Rose's chef Annemarie Huste. I reached Ullrich thanks to the help of Huste's daughter, Bea Huste-Petersen. Andrea A. Sinn translated German documents and offered many useful suggestions and good counsel. Gilad Tocatly sent his documentary film, *Teddy's Museum*. Bret Primack sent copies of his privately held audio recordings of the Ben Hecht television show, which contained gems, and I am grateful to the Grolier Club, which allowed me to view the Ben Grauer collection. Friends who offered help included John M. Efron for translations from the Yiddish; Philip Simon, who found for me an otherwise impossible-to-locate e-mail; Eric Lipsitt, who brought to my attention a song that mentions Billy Rose; and Michael Gillis, who translated a Hebrew document.

James S. Snyder, former director of the Israel Museum, cleared the way for me to view and quote from the Billy Rose papers kept in the museum's archives. Haim Haran wrote on my behalf to the Romanian Consiliul National pentru Studierea Arhivelor Securitatii to allow me to see records relating to his mother and aunt. Cathy at Temple Beth Sholom provided an important document.

Family help was also essential during research trips, and I thank my nephew Ben and sister-in-law Jackie for the use of the apartment in New York, and my cousins Anat and Ziv and brother-in-law David for accommodations in Los Angeles. In DC, I bunked with good friends Lisa and David. I even pressed my daughter Rebecca into research service while she was in Israel. She and her sister Ilana listened to too much about Billy Rose.

But the gold medal goes once again to my wife, Danielle.

abbreviations

AB	Abe Burrows Papers, Billy Rose Theatre Division, New York Public Library
ACS	Archivio Centrale dello Stato, Rome, Italy
AJJDC	American Jewish Joint Distribution Committee, Archives, Center for Jewish History, New York
ASA	Arthur Szyk Archive, Magnes Collection, University of California, Berkeley
BGRI	Ben-Gurion Research Institute, Ben-Gurion University, Sede Boker, Israel
BHP	Ben Hecht Papers, Newberry Public Library, Chicago
BMB	Bernard M. Baruch Papers, Princeton University Library, Princeton, NJ
BRAB	Billy Rose, ABC file, Israel Museum Archives, Jerusalem
BRDF	Billy Rose Donor Files, Israel Museum Archives, Jerusalem
BRP	Billy Rose Papers, 8-MWEZ + n.c. 26,289, Billy Rose Theatre Division, New York Public Library
BRTD	Billy Rose Theatre Division, New York Public Library
COP	Clifford Odets Papers, Lilly Library, Indiana University, Bloomington
CUL	Department of Manuscripts and Archives, Columbia University, New York
DLP	Dione Lucas Papers, Schlesinger Library, Radcliffe Institute, Harvard University, Cambridge, MA
ECP	Earl Conrad Papers, University of Oregon Libraries, Eugene
FBM	Fanny Brice Material (working title of "278 pages of rough notes dictated by Miss Brice" to Goddard Lieberson). Property of John Brice.
HB	Harper & Bros. Papers, Princeton University Library, Princeton, NJ
INP	Isamu Noguchi Papers, Isamu Noguchi Museum, New York
JBF	Janis Bellow-Friedman papers. Privately held.
JEB	Joseph E. Beck Papers, Historical Society of Pennsylvania, Philadelphia
JDC	Joint Distribution Committee Archives, Jerusalem
JSR	Jacques Seligmann & Co. Records, Archives of American Art, Smithsonian, Washington, DC
KSP	Kurt Schwarz Papers, United States Holocaust Memorial Museum, Washington, DC
LOC	Library of Congress, Washington, DC
LSP	Lee Strasberg Papers, Manuscript Division, Library of Congress, Washington, DC

MHC	Mark Hellinger Collection, Friedsam Memorial Library Archives, St. Bonaventure University, St. Bonaventure, NY
MHL	Margaret Herrick Library, Beverly Hills, CA
MLS	Max Lincoln Schuster Papers, Columbia University Libraries, New York
MZP	Maurice Zolotow Papers, unpublished *Billy Rose of Broadway* manuscript and interview notes, 8-MWEZ + n.c. 25,518, boxes 1 and 2, Billy Rose Theatre Division, New York Public Library
NYPL	New York Public Library
NYWF	New York World's Fair Papers, Manuscripts and Archives, New York Public Library
RAG	Ruth and Augustus Goetz Papers, Billy Rose Theatre Division, New York Public Library
SGP	Samuel Goldwyn Papers, Margaret Herrick Library, Beverly Hills, CA
TEA	Temple Emanu-El, Archives, New York
TGA	Theatre Guild Archive, Yale Collection of American Literature, Yale University, New Haven, CT
TKP	Teddy Kollek Papers, Israel State Archives, Jerusalem
UNRRA	United Nations Relief and Rehabilitation Administration, Archives, United Nations, New York
USCCAL	Cinematic Arts Library, University of Southern California, Los Angeles
USCIS	United States Citizenship and Immigration Services, Washington, DC
UTA	Harry Ransom Center, University of Texas at Austin
WPP	William Pahlmann Papers, Hagley Museum and Library, Wilmington, DE
WHS	Wisconsin Historical Society, Madison
WFP	John Hay Whitney and Betsey Cushing Whitney Family Papers, Manuscripts and Archives, Yale University Library, New Haven, CT
WWP	Walter Winchell Papers, Billy Rose Theatre Division, New York Public Library

Introduction

1. NYWF, box 510, folder 15, anonymous ("A Friend") to Mr. Whalen, March 28, 1929 [*sic*]. Stamped with the date April 7, 1939.

2. "Billy Rose Puts On Two Shows," *Life*, July 19, 1937, 36.

3. S. J. Woolf, "Broadway Barnum," *New York Times Magazine*, April 23, 1939, 7.

4. ECP, research folder 3, Jack Alexander, "Million-Dollar-a-Year Ego," *Saturday Evening Post*, December 21, 1940, 38.

5. MHC, Mark Hellinger, "All in a Day," n.d. [1931].

6. "Press Stunt Raided in Times Sq.," *Variety*, March 29, 1939, 25; "Blind to 'See' Fair through Models," *New York Times*, March 28, 1939, 25.

7. Quoted in Michael Kammen, *People of Paradox: An Inquiry concerning the Origins of American Civilization* (Ithaca, NY: Cornell University Press, 1990), 266.

8. ECP, interview folder 2, "Helen Schrank," June 22, 1966, 6.

9. Saul Bellow, "Cousins," in Saul Bellow, *Collected Stories* (New York: Viking, 2001), 206.

ONE Illustrious Ancestors

1. MZP, interview notes, "Childhood and Youth," 1.

2. Fannie's brother Abraham Wernick arrived in New York in 1900 at age twenty-seven. See "Supplement to Manifest of Alien Passengers" for the SS *Southwark*, arrived in New York on July 18, 1900, line 19, Abraham Wirniak. In 1900, Fannie said she was twenty-three, though even if she was twenty-five she was younger than Abraham. See "Twelfth Census of the United States," Schedule no. 1—Population, New York City, Borough of Manhattan, Enumeration District 77, Sheet no. 14, line 9. Fannie's father, Israel Wernick, was buried in New York by the Twersky burial society. See Mount Lebanon Cemetery at www.mountlebanoncemetery.com.

3. Steven J. Zipperstein, *The Jews of Odessa: A Cultural History, 1794–1881* (Stanford, CA: Stanford University Press, 1986), 104–5; Paul Ira Radensky, "Hasidism in the Age of Reform: A Biography of Rabbi Duvid ben Mordkhe Twersky" (PhD diss., Jewish Theological Seminary, 2001), 82–83, 113.

4. MZP, "Childhood," 1; Radensky, "Hasidism," 69.

5. New York County Clerk Archives, Certificate of Incorporation of S.R. & F.R. Washquick Co., filed and recorded on June 13, 1908; Proceedings of the Board of Estimate and Apportionment of the City of New York, Vol. 10 (1915), entry for S.R. & F.R. Washquick Co.

6. MZP, "Childhood," 1, and "On Billy Rose," 4.

7. Radensky, "Hasidism," 214.

8. MZP, "Childhood," 1; Radensky, "Hasidism," 69.

9. MZP, "On Billy Rose," 1.

10. MZP, "Childhood," 1.

11. Timothy J. Gilfoyle, "Anthony Comstock," in *The Encyclopedia of New York City*, ed. Kenneth T. Jackson (New Haven, CT: Yale University Press, 1995), 271.

12. Michael Meerson and Peter Schäfe, eds., *Toledot Yeshu: The Life Story of Jesus*, vol. 1, Introduction and Translation (Tübingen: Mohr Siebeck, 2014), 3, 5; Michael Wex, *Born to Kvetch: Yiddish Language and Culture in All Its Moods* (London: Souvenir Press, 2011), 18.

13. "For Selling 'Massa Tolo,'" *New York Sun,* September 30, 1897, 5.

14. The author is grateful to Prof. John Efron for his translation of the Yiddish title, which can be found in the catalogue of the New York Public Library under author S. Rosenthal.

15. MZP, "Childhood," 1.

16. Rebecca Leung, "The World's Most Competitive Man," CBS News, February 23, 2004, www.cbsnews.com/news/the-worlds-most-competitive-man/.

17. "List or Manifest of Alien Immigrants," SS *Rhynland*, arrived in Philadelphia on September 22, 1895, line 6. Regarding Rosenberg's hometown, Zolotow says he was from the "city of Podolsk," which was not a city but a province. On the ship manifest documenting the arrival of Rosenberg's sister, Udel Ginsberg, the town of origin is Zurin, often spelled Dzhurin. It was in Podolsk. See "List or Manifest of Alien Immigrants," SS *Rhynland*, arrived in Philadelphia on June 6, 1898, line 8.

18. MZP, *Billy Rose of Broadway,* 31.

19. Saul Bellow, *It All Adds Up: From the Dim Past to the Uncertain Future* (New York: Penguin, 1995), 296.

20. MZP, "Childhood," 2.

21. MZP, *Billy Rose,* 32.

22. New York City Department of Records, marriage certificate of David Rosenberg and Fannie Wernick, November 13, 1896.

23. "Sossnitz, Jos. L.," in *Trow's New York City Directory for the Year Ending July 1, 1898* (New York: Trow Directory, 1898), 1229.

24. Annie Polland and Daniel Soyer, *Emerging Metropolis: New York Jews in the Age of Immigrations, 1840–1920* (New York: NYU Press, 2013), 120.

25. MZP, "Childhood," 3; "Rose, Billy," in *Current Biography 1940* (New York: H. W. Wilson, 1940), 695.

26. BRTD, "Interview with Billy Rose on the Long John Nebel radio show, Aug. 5, 1965," audio disc 1.

27. New York City Department of Records, Manhattan births, cert. no. 33537, Samuel Wolf Rosenberg.

28. Radensky, "Hasidism," 14, 181–82.

29. For Velvel Wernick see New York City Department of Records, certificate of death, Israel Vernick, May 9, 1930.

30. New York State census, 1905, Borough of Manhattan, Election District 13, Block E, Assembly District 4, page 22, line 11; student records of Community School 44, Bronx, NY, for "William Rosenberg (09-06-99)." For Rose's name in high school, see "Commerce Student Shorthand Champion of Manhattan," Commerce High School *Caravel,* April 1916, 449.

31. Polly Rose Gottlieb, *The Nine Lives of Billy Rose* (New York: Crown, 1968), 57.

32. Moses Rischin, *The Promised City: New York's Jews, 1870–1914* (Cambridge, MA: Harvard University Press, 1977), 79.

33. Arnold Bennett, "The Book of the Month—Your United States," *Hearst's Magazine,* March 1913, 498.

34. John H. Lienhard, "Tenement Houses," accessed December 8, 2017, www.uh.edu/engines/epi2137.htm; Polland and Soyer, *Emerging Metropolis,* 123.

35. Polland and Soyer, *Emerging Metropolis,* 122.

36. Supplement to Manifest of Alien Passengers, SS *Southwark,* arrived on July 18, 1900, line 19, "Abraham Wirniak"; New York certificate of birth, no. 16844, Marjam Rosenberg.

37. List or Manifest of Alien Immigrants, SS *Rotterdam,* arrived on November 4, 1901, lines 9 and 10. See "Record of Aliens Held for Special Inquiry" for arrival date and entry number 46 for the name Schmuel.

38. List or Manifest of Alien Immigrants, SS *Rijndam,* arrived on September 15, 1903, lines 16–19.

39. Naomi Pasachoff and Robert J. Littman, *A Concise History of the Jewish People* (Lanham, MD: Rowman and Littlefield, 2005), 236.

40. MZP, "Childhood," 1.

41. US census, 1900, Charles and Ida Ginsburg [*sic*], 232 Rivington Street.

42. Shirley Gatsik, interview with the author, May 9, 2014.

43. BRP, box 2, "Correspondence 1953–1964," folder 1, Gatsik to Rose, July 19, 1960, and Rose to Gatsik, July 20, 1960.

44. MZP, "Childhood," 2.

TWO   Clever Isaac

1. MZP, *Billy Rose of Broadway,* 28.

2. New York State census, 1905, Borough of Manhattan, Election District 13, Block E, Assembly District 4, page 22, line 13. Maurice Wernick identifies himself as a phar-

macist on his June 25, 1914, Declaration of Intention to naturalize as an American citizen. Solomon Wernick is listed as a druggist on the 1920 US census, Passaic, NJ, District 5, Second Ward, Enumeration District 37, Sheet 3B, line 72.

3. Jacob A. Riis, *How the Other Half Lives: Studies among the Tenements of New York* (New York: Charles Scribner's Sons, 1914), 217, 224.

4. Richard Maney, *Fanfare: The Confessions of a Press Agent* (New York: Harper, 1957), 169.

5. MZP, *Billy Rose,* 28; Polly Rose Gottlieb, *The Nine Lives of Billy Rose* (New York: Crown, 1968), 43.

6. New York Municipal Archives, Paula Rosenberg birth certificate, no. 49548.

7. MZP, *Billy Rose,* 38; *Trow's General Directory of the Boroughs of Manhattan and Bronx, City of New York* (New York: Trow Directory, 1910), 513.

8. Gil Ribak, *Gentile New York: The Images of Non-Jews among Jewish Immigrants* (New Brunswick, NJ: Rutgers University Press, 2012), 79, 160; Ted Merwin, *In Their Own Image: New York Jews in Jazz Age Popular Culture* (New Brunswick, NJ: Rutgers University Press, 2006), 102–4.

9. MZP, interview notes, "Childhood and Youth," 6.

10. Community School 44, Bronx, NY, William Rosenberg school records.

11. "The Airship 'America' of 1910: The First Attempt to Fly the Atlantic," Airships. net, accessed April 16, 2017, www.airships.net.

12. David Rosenberg's occupation is illegible because a word appears to be written over an earlier entry. It seems that there was confusion or perhaps a family argument over his occupation or lack thereof. See US census, 1910, Borough of Manhattan, Enumeration District 63, Sheet 2B, line 88.

13. MZP, *Billy Rose,* 39.

14. Patricia Klindienst, interview with Gertrude Cohen Friedberg, January 7, 2011. Provided to the author by Klindienst.

15. "Wellman, on Trent, Is Delayed off Hook," *Standard Union,* October 19, 1910, 1.

16. "Wellman Is Anxious to Try Again," *Brooklyn Daily Times,* October 19, 1910, 1; "Fog Holds Up Steamer with Wellman Aboard; Plans New Sea Flight," *Brooklyn Daily Eagle,* October 19, 1910, 1.

17. "Residents of Graham avenue," *Standard Union,* October 21, 1910, 11.

18. MZP, *Billy Rose,* 40.

19. Gail Fenske, *The Skyscraper and the City: The Woolworth Building and the Making of Modern New York* (Chicago: University of Chicago Press, 2008), 46, 52, 54.

20. Henry James, *The American Scene* (Bloomington: Indiana University Press, 1968), 74.

21. Francis J. Oppenheimer, "Louis J. Horowitz, Master Builder," *Magazine of Wall Street,* January 24, 1920, 351.

22. "An Immigrant Who Became One of Our Greatest Builders," *Literary Digest,* February 28, 1920, 49.

23. David Nasaw, *Going Out: The Rise and Fall of Public Amusements* (Cambridge, MA: Harvard University Press, 1999), 83, 85.

24. Rem Koolhaas, *Delirious New York: A Retroactive Manifesto for Manhattan* (New York: Monacelli, 1994), 10, 29–30.

25. Quoted in Eli Lederhendler, *New York Jews and the Decline of Urban Ethnicity* (Syracuse, NY: Syracuse University Press, 2001), 1.

26. James, *American Scene,* 86.

27. Ben Hecht, *A Child of the Century* (New York: Simon and Schuster, 1954), 398.

28. ECP, interview folder 2, "Tex McCrary," June 23, 1966, 9; AB, box 106, folder 2, funeral oration for Billy Rose, dated February 13, 1966, 2.

29. "Landmarks Preservation Commission report on (Former) Public School 64, June 20, 2006," www.nyc.gov/html/lpc/downloads/pdf/reports/ps64.pdf.

30. *The Official Year-Book of the Public Schools Athletic League of the City of New York, 1914* (New York: Public Schools Athletic League, 1914), 24.

31. MZP, *Billy Rose,* 43; Alva Johnston, "Profiles, Mass Entertainment," *New Yorker,* April 27, 1935, 23.

32. *The Official Year-Book of the Public Schools Athletic League and the Girls' Branch of the Public Schools Athletic League of the City of New York, 1915* (New York: Public Schools Athletic League, 1915), 22, 25. Rose graduated from PS 44 on January 30, 1914, per student records of Community School 44, Bronx, NY, for "William Rosenberg (09-06-99)."

33. *Official Year-Book,* 1914, 75–76.

34. Ibid., 20, 22.

35. *High Schools of New York City: A Hand-book of Procedure & Personnel* (New York: High School Teachers' Association of New York City, 1921), 29.

36. Deborah Dash Moore, *At Home in America: Second Generation New York Jews* (New York: Columbia University Press, 1981), 103.

37. New York State census, 1915, New York, NY, Election District 58, Assembly District 23, Block no. 1, page 5, line 48.

38. For Rose's grades see Community School 44 records for William Rosenberg (note 32). For new address, see David Rosenberg's 1915 census record (note 37).

39. Samuel Wernick's World War I draft registration, 1918, shows his father, Israel Wernick, living "c/o David Rosenberg"; for Abraham Wernick, see *Trow General Directory of New York City* (New York: R. L. Polk, 1916), 1761; for Abraham Taffel, see *Trow General Directory of New York City* (New York: R. L. Polk, 1917), 1898 (all above accessed February 5, 2018, www.ancestry.com); for Maurice Wernick, see *American Druggist and Pharmaceutical Record* 63 (1915): 46.

40. ECP, interview folder 2, "Morris Permut," n.d., 4; Jeffrey S. Gurock, *When Harlem Was Jewish, 1870–1930* (New York: Columbia University Press, 1979), 100.

41. ECP, interview folder 2, "Helen Schrank," June 22, 1966, 13.

42. ECP, interview folder 2, "Charles Samuels," June 2, 1966, 9, and interview

folder 1, "Arnold Forster," June 30, 1966, 1; Vicki Walton, interview with the author, August 7, 2014.

43. Mercedes McCambridge, *The Quality of Mercy* (New York: Times Books, 1981), 236.

44. US census, 1920, New York, NY, Enumeration District 1500, sheet 6A, lines 47–50, and sheet 6B, lines 51–53. The lodgers Clara Belinsky and the other, whose name is illegible, share Fannie's mother's maiden name of Belenkies. See New York City Department of Records, death certificate of Fannie Rosenberg, December 9, 1936.

45. MZP, interview notes, "Shorthand," 1.

46. *Commerce Caravel,* Autumn 1916, 27.

47. *Commerce Caravel,* April 1915, 288, 276–77; October 1915, 25–27; and January 1916, 189; *The Handbook: Commerce 1919* (New York: High School of Commerce, 1919), 24–25.

48. *Commerce Caravel,* January 1916, 214.

49. High School of Commerce 1915 yearbook, 67; "Success Formula," *Caravel,* April 1915, 271.

50. "Isaac Cleverly Turns a Loss into Profit," *Commerce Caravel,* April 1915, 272–73.

51. MZP, "Shorthand," 5.

52. ECP, interview folder 1, "Ray Henderson," June 21, 1966, 5.

53. ECP, interview folder 1, "Louis Leslie," June 8, 1966, 5.

54. ECP, research folder 2, "Shorthand Not for Billy Rose," *New York Sun,* December 30, 1939.

55. Elizabeth Alice Clement, *Love for Sale: Courting, Treating, and Prostitution in New York City, 1900–1945* (Chapel Hill: University of North Carolina Press, 2006), 101, 149.

56. Julius Moskowitz, "Isaac's Scheme," *Commerce Caravel,* October 1915, 10–11.

57. Gilbert King, "The Smoothest Con Man That Ever Lived," *Smithsonian,* August 22, 2012, www.smithsonianmag.com.

58. S. Litzky, "Never Again," *Commerce Caravel,* February 1916, 291–93.

59. Robert Kimball and Linda Emmet, eds., *The Complete Lyrics of Irving Berlin* (New York: Applause Theatre and Cinema Books, 2005), 130.

60. *Commerce Caravel,* April 1916, 449.

61. *Gregg Writer,* June 1915, 568.

62. MZP, "Shorthand," 1, and "On Billy Rose," 5.

63. *Commerce Caravel,* April 1916, 461.

64. MZP, "Shorthand," 1.

65. Nathaniel C. Fowler Jr., "Stenography as a Profession," *Commerce Caravel,* April 1915, 308–12.

66. High School of Commerce 1915 yearbook, 5.

67. Frank Rutherford, "The Late Rabbi Schindler," *Gregg Writer,* July 1915, 606.

68. CUL, Charles Swem, "Shimko-Howell-Swem Interview," John Robert Gregg Oral History, 30, 37.

69. MZP, "Shorthand," 3.

70. "Shorthand School Champion of Manhattan," *Gregg Writer,* March 15, 1916, 396.

71. "High School of Commerce Wins New York Shorthand Championship," *Gregg Writer,* March 1917, 351.

72. Richard Barr, quoted in David A. Crespy, *Richard Barr: The Playwright's Producer* (Carbondale: Southern Illinois University Press, 2013), 120.

73. "A New Typewriting Star," *Gregg Writer,* December 1916, 191–92.

74. "Gregg Shorthand Team Wins New York Championship," *Stenographer and Phonographic World,* April 1917, 120.

75. MZP, "Shorthand," 2; ECP, "Louis Leslie," 5, 16–17.

76. "The High School of Commerce New York City Wins the School Shorthand Championship," *Gregg Writer,* April 1918, 342.

77. MZP, "Shorthand," 2.

78. Earl Conrad, *Billy Rose: Manhattan Primitive* (New York: World, 1968), 8; Cahan, *The Rise of David Levinsky* (New York: Harper and Row, 1966), 529.

79. Louis J. Horowitz and Boyden Sparkes, *The Towers of New York: The Memoirs of a Master Builder* (New York: Simon and Schuster, 1937), 173; ECP, research correspondence folder 1, "War Industries Board Personal History Statement by William Rosenberg."

80. William S. Rosenberg, "The Yaphank Cantonment," *Commerce Caravel,* December 1917, 110.

81. BRTD, "Interview with Billy Rose on the Long John Nebel radio show, Aug. 5, 1965," audio disc 1; ECP, interview folder 1, "Dave Dreyer," June 6, 1966, 1.

82. CUL 6, "Reminiscences of Nita Naldi: Oral History, 1958," 5.

83. Judy Goetz Sanger, interview with the author, September 18, 2014.

84. Rupert P. SoRelle, "Some of Our Readers Who Are 'Doing Their Bit' Stenographically for Uncle Sam," *Gregg Writer,* October 1917, 50.

85. "Editorial Brevities," *Gregg Writer,* November 1918, 118–19.

THREE Not Bad for Delancey Street

1. National Archives and Records Administration, Washington, DC, War Industries Board, box 108, "Chairman's Office, 1-F1 Organization Charts of W.I.B. & Agencies"; "Baruch: Life and Letters," *Fortune,* October 1933, 38.

2. Margaret L. Coit, *Mr. Baruch* (Boston: Houghton Mifflin, 1957), 42–43, 95.

3. James Grant, *Bernard M. Baruch: The Adventures of a Wall Street Legend* (New York: John Wiley and Sons, 1997), 15, 20.

4. John Milton Cooper Jr., *Woodrow Wilson: A Biography* (New York: Vintage Books, 2011), 392, 427.

5. CUL, oral history interview with Kitty Carlisle Hart, 1979, 3:428–30.

6. WWP, box 1, folder 3, Rose to Winchell, November 1, 1940.

7. ECP, interview folder 2, "Tape—July 9, 1965 11:15–11:30 P.M. Tex McCrary WOR," 9.

8. MZP, interview notes, "Shorthand," 4; Earl Conrad, *Manhattan Primitive: Billy Rose* (Cleveland: World, 1968), 19.

9. ECP, interview folder 2, "Helen Schrank," June 22, 1966, 10; Grant, *Bernard M. Baruch,* 5.

10. MZP, interview notes, "Songwriting," 10. See also Charles Hamm, *Irving Berlin: Songs from the Melting Pot; The Formative Years, 1907–1914* (New York: Oxford University Press, 1997), 95–96.

11. Jordan A. Schwarz, *The Speculator: Bernard M. Baruch in Washington, 1917–1965* (Chapel Hill: University of North Carolina Press, 1981), 9.

12. ECP, "Tape—July 9, 1965," 9.

13. *Press Time: A Book of Post Classics* (New York: Books, 1936), 55.

14. Bernard M. Baruch, *Baruch: The Public Years* (New York: Holt, Rinehart and Winston, 1960), 81.

15. Coit, *Mr. Baruch,* 177.

16. Woodrow Wilson Collection, Princeton University Library, box 56, folder 19, "Printed Matter Newspaper Clipping from 'Pitching Horseshoes'"; "What Makes Billy Run?," *Time,* June 2, 1947, 47.

17. ECP, research correspondence folder 1, Charles W. Burtyk Jr., to Earl Conrad, June 21, 1966; Application for Employment, July 25, 1918; Personal History Statement, numbers 5 and 24.

18. "National Shorthand Reporters' Association Convention," *Gregg Writer,* October 1919, 85; "N.S.R.A. Notes," *Gregg Writer,* August 1917, 609.

19. ECP, interview folder 1, "Louis Leslie," June 8, 1966, 5–7.

20. Charles G. Reigner, "Sidelights on the Speed Contest," *Stenographer and Phonographic World,* October 1919, 297; *The Bulletin: Published by the National Shorthand Reporters' Association,* November 1919, 4.

21. MZP, "Shorthand," 8; ECP, "Louis Leslie," 8.

22. BRTD, "Interview with Billy Rose on the Long John Nebel radio show, Aug. 5, 1965," audio disc 2.

23. ECP, interview folder 2, "Mrs. Jack Rosenthal (Frayre)," June 1, 1966; MZP, "On Billy Rose," 1.

24. Manhattan City Register Office, Liber 3124, 469–70; Matthew A. Postal, *Hamilton Heights / Sugar Hill Historic District Designation Report* (New York: New York City Landmarks Preservation Commission, 2000), 11, 17, www.nyc.gov.

25. Polly Rose Gottlieb, *The Nine Lives of Billy Rose* (New York: Crown, 1968), 287.

26. Christopher Gray, "Built with the Ladies in Mind," *New York Times,* October 25, 2012, RE6.

27. US census, 1920, New York, NY, Enumeration District 1444, Sheet 8.

28. Manhattan City Register Office, Liber 3104, 282–84; Liber 3111, 453–54; and Liber 3117, 395–97.

29. CUL, Charles Swem, "Shimko-Howell-Swem Interview," John Robert Gregg Oral History, 29.

30. MZP, interview notes, "On Billy Rose," 4.

31. Harold H. Messner and Samuel N. Leiterman, "Come to Think of It," *Commerce Caravel,* November 1915, 72–75.

32. MZP, "Shorthand," 7.

33. MZP, "Shorthand," 6; "Our Successful Alumni," *Commerce Caravel,* October 1920, 29.

34. MZP, "Shorthand," 6–8; BRP, box 5, folder 3, "Billy Rose Explains Plans to Governor," *Fort Worth Star Telegram,* n.d.

35. "Wood Appears Favorite of Texas G.O.P.; Party Splits," *Fort Worth Star-Telegram,* May 26, 1920, 4; MZP, "Shorthand," 7–8.

36. Steven A. Riess, "Billiards," in *Sports in America from Colonial Times to the Twenty-First Century: An Encyclopedia,* ed. Steven A. Riess (London: Routledge, 2011), 1:167.

37. ECP, interview folder 2, "Gilbert Lloyd," June 9, 1966, 4, and "Charles Samuels," June 2, 1966, 11.

38. Lewis Yablonsky, *George Raft* (New York: McGraw-Hill, 1974), 13.

39. Quoted in Michael Adams, *Slang: The People's Poetry* (Oxford: Oxford University Press, 2009), 33.

40. MZP, "Songwriting," 10; ECP, interview folder 1, "Hilda (Wiener) Brozen," May 3, [1966], n.p. [3].

41. WWP, box 1, folder 3, Rose to Winchell, November 12, 1947.

42. ECP, research folder 3, Jack Alexander, "Million-Dollar-a-Year Ego," *Saturday Evening Post,* December 21, 1940, 41.

43. ECP, interview folder 1, "Chester Conn," n.d., 10.

44. "What Makes Billy Run?," 47.

45. Alistair Cooke, "Mr. Broadway," *Listener,* December 9, 1948, 888.

46. ECP, "Chester Conn," 8.

47. MZP, "Shorthand," 9.

48. BRDF, Bezalel folder, Rose to Daniel Gelmond, August 5, 1965.

49. Manhattan City Register Office, Liber 3177, page 299. Fannie's interest in 767 St. Nicholas Avenue resurfaced briefly in May 1921. On May 5, Clurman sold the property back to Fannie, who then turned around and sold it on May 17 to one Dora Wolper for $100. By then the three mortgages on the property, totaling $14,850, had become liens due to nonpayment. See Liber 3207, 457–58, and Liber 3224, 281–82.

50. MZP, interview notes, "Childhood and Youth," 2.

51. Tom Nicholas and Ann Scherbina, "Real Estate Prices during the Roaring Twenties and the Great Depression," *Real Estate Economics: Journal of the American Real Estate and Urban Economics Association* 41, no. 2 (2013): 296.

52. US census, 1920, New York, NY, Enumeration District no. 444, Ward 5, Sheet no. 14B, line 95.

53. ECP, research correspondence folder 1, Warren to Earl Conrad, July 18, 1966.

54. ECP, "Louis Leslie," 9.

55. MZP, "Songwriting," 1.

56. Isaac Goldberg, *Tin Pan Alley: A Chronicle of the American Popular Music Racket* (New York: John Day, 1930). Quotations are from the 1961 edition: Isaac Goldberg, *Tin Pan Alley: A Chronicle of American Popular Music* (New York: Frederick Ungar, 1961), 225, 9.

57. Ted Merwin, *In Their Own Image: New York Jews in Jazz Age Popular Culture* (New Brunswick, NJ: Rutgers University Press, 2006), 8.

58. Goldberg, *Tin Pan Alley,* 108.

59. ECP, interview folder 2, "Richard Maney," June 10, [1966], 7.

60. ECP, interview folder 2, "Charles Samuels," June 2, 1966, 2.

61. Goldberg, *Tin Pan Alley,* 231.

62. Edward Eliscu, *With or without a Song* (Lanham, MD: Scarecrow, 2001), 93.

63. ECP, interview folder 1, "Ray Henderson," June 21, 1966, 1.

64. Laurence Bergreen, *As Thousands Cheer: The Life of Irving Berlin* (New York: Da Capo, 1996), 168.

65. MZP, "Songwriting," 1.

66. ECP, interview folder 1, "Walter Hirsch," June 23, 1966, 1–2; MZP, "Songwriting," 3.

67. "Harlem Opera House," *New York Clipper,* August 18, 1920, 11.

68. Gary Marmorstein, *A Ship without a Sail: The Life of Lorenz Hart* (New York: Simon and Schuster, 2012), 70; Frederick Nolan, *The Sound of Their Music: The Story of Rodgers & Hammerstein* (New York: Applause Theatre and Cinema Books, 2002), 88.

69. Frederick Nolan, *Lorenz Hart: A Poet on Broadway* (New York: Oxford University Press, 1994), 50; Bergreen, *As Thousands Cheer,* 335.

70. LSP, Rose to Strasberg, September 25, 1959.

71. Mercedes McCambridge, *The Quality of Mercy* (New York: Times Books, 1981), 238.

72. MZP, "Songwriting," 9–10.

73. Elizabeth Alice Clement, *Love for Sale: Courting, Treating, and Prostitution in New York City, 1900–1945* (Chapel Hill: University of North Carolina Press, 2006), 17.

74. "Billy Rose Admits Marriage," *Clipper,* June 28, 1924, 18. For *The Melody Man* cast see www.playbill.com/vault, accessed April 18, 2017.

75. MZP, "Songwriting," 5.

76. Brian Walker, *Barney Google and Snuffy Smith: 75 Years of an American Legend* (n.p.: Ace Books, 1983), 77.

77. Gilbert Seldes, *The 7 Lively Arts* (Mineola, NY: Dover, 2001), 224.

78. Stephen J. Monchak, "Billy De Beck [*sic*] Marks 20th Year with King," *Editor & Publisher,* October 7, 1939, 29.

79. MZP, "Songwriting," 8.

80. ECP, "Walter Hirsch," 1.

81. ECP, interview folder 1, "Dave Dreyer," June 6, 1966, 1.

82. Quoted in Nolan, *Lorenz Hart*, 51.

83. ECP, "Walter Hirsch," 1.

84. ECP, "Ray Henderson," 3.

85. Eliscu, *With or without a Song*, 93.

86. Quoted in Nolan, *Lorenz Hart*, 51.

87. Michael Feinstein, "It Went a Little Something Like This," review of *The B Side: The Death of Tin Pan Alley and the Rebirth of the Great American Song*, by Ben Yagoda, *New York Times*, February 15, 2015, Sunday Book Review, 11.

88. Nolan, *Lorenz Hart*, 49.

89. Vicki Walton, interview with the author, August 5, 2014.

90. Charlotte Chandler, *Hello, I Must Be Going: Groucho and His Friends* (New York: Simon and Schuster, 2007), 495.

91. MZP, "Childhood and Youth," 2.

92. Abraham Cahan, *Yekl and the Imported Bridegroom, and Other Stories of the New York Ghetto* (New York: Dover, 1970); Clement, *Love for Sale*, 34.

93. "List or Manifest of Alien Passengers for the United States Immigration Officer at Port of Arrival," SS *Carmania*, Liverpool to Boston, arrived on November 1, 1923, list 30, line 8.

94. Frances A. Johnson Westervelt, *History of Bergen County, New Jersey, 1630–1923* (New York: Lewis Historical, 1923), 222–23.

95. Certificate of Incorporation of Park Ridge Hebrew Community Center, provided to the author by Temple Beth Sholom, Park Ridge, NJ.

96. New York City Department of Records, marriage certificate of Joseph Berenstein and Miriam Rosenberg, no. 25326.

97. MZP, "Childhood and Youth," 2–3.

98. A. J. Liebling, *Back Where I Came From* (New York: North Point, 1993), 274.

99. Cecil Beaton, *Cecil Beaton's New York* (Philadelphia: Lippincott, 1938), 161.

FOUR "Since Henry Ford Apologized to Me"

1. FBM, 132.

2. Arthur Garfield Hays, *City Lawyer: The Autobiography of a Law Practice* (New York: Simon and Schuster, 1942), 137.

3. John Murray Anderson, *Out without My Rubbers: The Memoirs of John Murray Anderson* (New York: Library, 1954), 146.

4. Richard Rodgers, *Musical Stages: An Autobiography* (New York: Da Capo, 1995), 79.

5. MZP, interview notes, "Night Clubs," 6.

6. ECP, research folder 3, Jack Burton, "The Honor Roll of Popular Songwriters, No. 81—Billy Rose," *Billboard*, December 16, 1950.

7. MZP, interview notes, "Songwriting," 6–7; Isabella Arden, "Matchbox Furniture to Mansions—Melanie Kahane Designed All," *Palm Beach Daily News,* December 23, 1985.

8. Burton W. Peretti, *Nightclub City: Politics and Amusement in Manhattan* (Philadelphia: University of Pennsylvania Press, 2007), ix, 3, 5.

9. Frederick Nolan, *The Sound of Their Music: The Story of Rodgers & Hammerstein* (New York: Applause Theatre and Cinema Books, 2002), 96; Stanley Walker, *The Night Club Era* (New York: Frederick A. Stokes, 1933), 35.

10. MZP, "Songwriting," 6–7.

11. ECP, research folder 3, Billy Rose, "I'm a Sucker for Screwballs," *Collier's,* November 20, 1948, 20.

12. MZP, "Songwriting," 7.

13. Sam Kashner and Nancy Schoenberger, *A Talent for Genius: The Life and Times of Oscar Levant* (Los Angeles: Silman-James, 1994), 43.

14. "Rose Knocks Double-Crossing Publishers," *Billboard,* April 5, 1924, 13.

15. Abel Green, "Abel's Comment," *Clipper,* May 1, 1924, 17.

16. "Publishers Who Erred Will Please Rise and Take a Bow," *Billboard,* November 20, 1926, 24.

17. Advertisement, Irving Berlin, Inc., *Variety,* August 6, 1924, 49.

18. Nathan Miller, *New World Coming: The 1920s and the Making of Modern America* (New York: Scribner, 2003), 205.

19. Moses Rischin, introduction to *Grandma Never Lived in America*, ed. Moses Rischin (Bloomington: Indiana University Press, 1985), xxvi.

20. George J. Lankevich, *Postcards from Times Square* (Garden City Park, NY: Square One, 2001), 70–71.

21. Advertisement, I & Y Cigars, *Variety,* February 7, 1924, 47; A. J. Liebling, *The Jollity Building* (New York: Ballantine, 1962), 7–15.

22. Abel Green, "Abel's Comment," *Clipper,* June 14, 1924, 18.

23. "Convention Closed More Shows than Equity: Gigantic Democratic Flop Cost Legits $100,000," *Variety,* July 2, 1924, 13.

24. Rodgers, *Musical Stages,* 78.

25. Frederick Nolan, *Lorenz Hart: A Poet on Broadway* (New York: Oxford University Press, 1994), 56–57.

26. Armond Fields and L. Marc Fields, *From Bowery to Broadway: Lew Fields and the Roots of American Popular Theater* (New York: Oxford University Press, 1993), xiii; photograph insert shows the Lew Fields Theatre.

27. "'Melody Man' Libel on Composers," *Clipper,* May 15, 1924, 18; John Corbin, "Among the New Plays," *New York Times,* May 18, 1924, section 7, 1.

28. "Summer's First Bump," *Variety,* May 21, 1924, 40.

29. Abel Green, "Abel's Comment," *Clipper,* May 24, 1924, 18.

30. "Nine Shows Posted Notices with Convention's Opening," *Variety,* June 25, 1924, 12.

31. "New Productions?," *Variety,* May 28, 1924, 39; "Failures of the Season," *Variety,* June 4, 1924, 13.

32. "Shows in N.Y. and Comment," *Variety,* June 18, 1924, 11.

33. "Marks in Operetta Field," *Talking Machine World,* July 15, 1924, 134; "Sketch for Miss Moscovitz," *Variety,* July 2, 1924, 13; "No Welch-Jordan Act," *Variety,* September 24, 1924, 6.

34. Harold Clurman, *The Fervent Years: The Story of the Group Theatre and the Thirties* (New York: Hill and Wang, 1957), 158.

35. Guy Logsdon, *The Whorehouse Bells Were Ringing, and Other Songs Cowboys Sing* (Urbana: University of Illinois Press, 1995), 145.

36. "New York City," *Clipper,* November 9, 1901, 796; "New Plays," *Clipper,* October 5, 1901, 680.

37. Val., review of *The Fatal Wedding,* by Theodore Kremer, *Variety,* June 11, 1924, 39–40.

38. Unsigned review of *The Fatal Wedding, New York Times,* June 3, 1924, 22.

39. Val., review of *The Fatal Wedding,* 40.

40. ECP, research folder 3, Jack Alexander, "Million-Dollar-a-Year Ego," *Saturday Evening Post,* December 21, 1940, 17.

41. Quoted in ECP, research correspondence folder 2, J. Grayson to Earl Conrad, n.d., 2.

42. A. Wilfred May, Observations . . . , *Commercial and Financial Chronicle,* September 14, 1961, 4.

43. Mel Gussow, *Conversations with Miller* (London: Nick Hern Books, 2015), 28.

44. ECP, interview folder 2, "Charles Samuels," May 31, 1966, 1.

45. Peretti, *Nightclub City,* 8.

46. BRTD, "Interview with Billy Rose on the Long John Nebel radio show, Aug. 5, 1965," audio disc 3.

47. Peretti, *Nightclub City,* xi–xii.

48. Peretti, *Nightclub City,* 74.

49. Liebling, *Jollity Building,* 17.

50. MZP, interview notes, "Night Clubs," 1, and *Billy Rose of Broadway,* 168.

51. "'Sawdust'—At Last!," *Variety,* March 25, 1925, 50.

52. "Sally's Double Wedding and $20,000," *Variety,* January 10, 1924, 10.

53. Gilbert Maxwell, *Helen Morgan: Her Life and Legend* (New York: Charles Scribner's Sons, 1997), quoted in Amy Lawrence, "Bruised and Confused: Helen Morgan and the Limits of Pathos," *Film History: An International Journal* 25, no. 3 (2013): 5.

54. "Helen Morgan among Features at Palace," *New York Times,* January 25, 1927, 18.

55. Lawrence, "Bruised and Confused," 5.

56. Accounts of the first Rose-Brice meeting are found in FBM, 126–27; Herbert G. Goldman, *Fanny Brice: The Original Funny Girl* (New York: Oxford University Press, 1992), 133; MZP, "Night Clubs," 5.

57. MZP, "Night Clubs," 1–3; "Jerry Hitchcock," *Variety*, May 27, 1925, 48; "The Back-Stage," *Variety*, October 14, 1925, 48.

58. Jonathan Eig, *Get Capone: The Secret Plot That Captured America's Most Wanted Gangster* (New York: Simon and Schuster, 2010), 27.

59. Billy Rose, *Wine, Women and Words* (New York: Pocketbook, 1950), 75.

60. "'The Yes Man' for Los Angeles," *Billboard*, July 11, 1925, 23.

61. "Billy Rose's School for Songwriters," *Billboard*, July 4, 1925, 21.

62. "Friedman to Produce," *Billboard*, September 19, 1925, 23.

63. Arnold Shaw, *The Jazz Age: Popular Music in the 1920s* (New York: Oxford University Press, 1989), 163.

64. Edward Eliscu, *With or without a Song* (Lanham, MD: Scarecrow, 2001), 94.

65. "$5 Cover Night Club," *Variety*, November 25, 1925, 1; Rose, *Wine*, 83.

66. "City Brevities," *New York Times*, December 28, 1925, 28.

67. Stephen Nelson, *"Only a Paper Moon": The Theatre of Billy Rose* (Ann Arbor, MI: UMI Research Press, 1987), 46.

68. "Cabaret and Orchestra Reviews, Fifth Avenue Club, N.Y.," *Billboard*, February 6, 1926, 23.

69. "'There Is No Bridge between Washington and Pinsk,'" *American Hebrew and Jewish Messenger*, September 2, 1921, 365–66.

70. "Active Week for New York Resorts," *Billboard*, December 5, 1925, 22.

71. "Raze Criterion Club for 12-Story Project," *New York Times*, April 29, 1928, 16.

72. Peretti, *Nightclub City*, 13.

73. "Cabaret Reviews, 5th Ave. Club," *Variety*, February 3, 1926, 46.

74. "Young Kahn's Cabaret, 5th Ave. Club," *Variety*, February 3, 1926, 46.

75. "Cabaret and Orchestra," *Billboard*, February 6, 1926, 23.

76. "Cabaret Reviews," *Billboard*, March 13, 1926, 22.

77. Clara Tice Papers, Pennsylvania State University Libraries, 1988–004R Vault/21.01, "Unpublished Typescript of Clara Tice Autobiography/Memoir," 1/4–1/5.

78. *City of Promises: A History of the Jews of New York*, ed. Deborah Dash Moore, vol. 3, *Jews in Gotham*, by Jeffrey S. Gurock (New York: NYU Press, 2012), 74, 76–77.

79. "Joe Newman's 5th Ave. Club," *Variety*, August 25, 1926, 54.

80. MZP, "Night Clubs," 5, 7.

81. "Society Card Meant Nothing at 5th Ave. Club," *Variety*, March 10, 1926, 10.

82. "Caravan, N. Y.," *Variety*, March 24, 1926, 45; Rodgers, *Musical Stages*, 79.

83. Victoria Saker Woeste, *Henry Ford's War on Jews and the Legal Battle against Hate Speech* (Stanford, CA: Stanford University Press, 2012), 3, 50, 52, 53.

84. "Since Ma Is Playing Mah Jong," *Variety*, January 31, 1924, 51.

85. "Dance Teachers Hold a 'Henry Ford' Night," *New York Times*, August 26, 1926, 10.

86. "Joe Frisco," *Variety*, April 7, 1926, 12.

87. Woeste, *Henry Ford's War,* 50; "Land o' Melody," *Billboard,* September 18, 1926, 21.

88. Woeste, *Henry Ford's War,* 179, 267–69, 271–72.

89. N. T. G. [Nils T. Granlund], Joys and Glooms of Broadway, *Variety,* July 27, 1927, 2.

90. Reprinted in David L. Lewis, *The Public Image of Henry Ford: An American Folk Hero and His Company* (Detroit: Wayne State University Press, 1976), 147.

FIVE Crazy Quilt

1. Quoted in Herbert G. Goldman, *Fanny Brice: The Original Funny Girl* (New York: Oxford University Press, 1992), 52–53.

2. "Profiles, Fire Sign," *New Yorker,* April 20, 1929, 25.

3. J. Brooks Atkinson, "Miss Brice Enlists in the Drama," The Play, *New York Times,* September 22, 1926, 30.

4. Rose, quoted in Goldman, *Fanny Brice,* 133.

5. Barbara Wallace Grossman, *Funny Woman: The Life and Times of Fanny Brice* (Bloomington: Indiana University Press, 1991), 149–50, 160, 162, 164, 167–69.

6. N. T. G. [Nils T. Granlund], Joys and Glooms of Broadway, *Variety,* September 14, 1927, 2.

7. "Land o' Melody," *Billboard,* July 17, 1926, 21; "Publishers Who Erred Will Please Rise and Take a Bow," *Billboard,* November 20, 1926, 24; "Music Biz in Lent Not as Bad as Expected," *Variety,* March 16, 1927, 47.

8. Earl Conrad, *Billy Rose: Manhattan Primitive* (New York: World, 1968), 52–53; ECP, interview folder 1, "Dave Dreyer," June 6, 1966, 1, 3.

9. Goldman, *Fanny Brice,* 134–35; FBM, 127.

10. Grossman, *Funny Woman,* 171.

11. Ibid., 170; FBM, 127.

12. "Billy Rose Flew to L.A. in Planes," *Variety,* February 1, 1928, 29.

13. "Melody Mart Notes," *Billboard,* July 28, 1928, 27; MZP, *Billy Rose of Broadway,* 213.

14. ECP, research correspondence folder 1, Wolfe [Kaufman] to Earl Conrad, n.d.

15. Goldman, *Fanny Brice,* 139.

16. FBM, 128–29.

17. "Fannie Brice Wed to Rose by Mayor," *New York Times,* February 9, 1929, 15.

18. New Jersey property records, book 2045, page 318, Arthur P. West to William Rosenberg.

19. MHL, Richard Wallace Papers, Scrapbook #2 1928–1934, Rose to Wallace, April 29, 1929.

20. ECP, interview folder 2, "Maurice Zolotow," June 14, 1966, 2.

21. MZP, *Billy Rose,* 212.

22. FBM, 78, 88.

23. TEA, Marion R. Altenberg, Sec'y to Miss Fannie [*sic*] Brice, to Cong. Emanu-El, October 25, 1933; James I. Lader, archivist, Temple Emanu-El, e-mail to author, April 20, 2016; FBM, 127.

24. Noralee Frankel, *Stripping Gypsy: The Life of Gypsy Rose Lee* (Oxford: Oxford University Press, 2009), 42.

25. ECP, interview folder 1, "Chester Conn," n.d., 5–6.

26. John Murray Anderson, *Out without My Rubbers: The Memoirs of John Murray Anderson* (New York: Library, 1954), 197.

27. Goldman, *Fanny Brice,* 153.

28. MZP, "On Billy Rose," n.p. [1].

29. MZP, interview notes, "Songwriting," 9–10.

30. Goddard Lieberson Papers, Houghton Library, Harvard University, MS Thr 851, folder marked "Correspondence Arranged by Jonathan," Brice to Lieberson, April 28, 1951, and Lieberson to Miss Fanny Strassman, postmarked May 11, 1933. "Der Schlemiel" is the return address on the envelope.

31. Gilbert Seldes, "Stage-Door Johnny, Pro Tem.," *Esquire,* September 1934, 137.

32. MZP, *Billy Rose,* 209.

33. FBM, 137.

34. Goldman, *Fanny Brice,* 6.

35. FBM, 137.

36. "Joseph Schenck Signs Fannie [*sic*] Brice to Be Star of All-Audien," *Exhibitors Herald-World,* March 23, 1929, 26. This article claims it was a three-picture deal, but a later lawsuit reveals it was for two films. For this and for Brice's fee see New York Supreme Court, Billy Rose against Art Cinema Corp., Index Number 9672, Year 1930, Exhibit 7—Annexed to Foregoing Affidavit, 122–23. For Rose's fee see Exhibit A—Annexed to Foregoing Affidavit, 97–99.

37. Mordaunt Hall, "Miss Brice's Screen Debut," The Screen, *New York Times,* December 22, 1928, 14.

38. Grossman, *Funny Woman,* 179.

39. Goldman, *Fanny Brice,* 140, 143.

40. MZP, "On Billy Rose," n.p. [1].

41. "Two Actors Are Now M-G-M Short Directors," *Variety,* November 21, 1928, 3; "Jolson Didn't Write," *Variety,* November 28, 1928, 16; "'Show Boat' Film Songs," *Variety,* December 12, 1928, 55; MZP, *Billy Rose,* 153–54.

42. "Whiteman Film, Revue in Form, Is Now Set," *Variety,* July 17, 1929, 5; Larry Neill, quoted in Don Rayno, *Paul Whiteman, Pioneer in American Music, Volume II: 1930–1967* (Lanham, MD: Scarecrow, 2009), xv, 32, 238.

43. "Billy Rose to Do Shows," *Billboard,* September 14, 1929, 27; "Billy Rose on Show," *Variety,* August 7, 1929, 227; F. Scott Fitzgerald, *The Great Gatsby* (New York: Scribner's, 1953), 136.

44. Clef [pseud.], "Musical Notes," *Film Daily,* November 6, 1929, 10; "'Great Day!' Arrives with Youmans Tunes," *New York Times,* October 18, 1929, 24.

45. "13 Shows Out," *Variety,* November 13, 1929, 66; Krystyn R. Moon, *Yellowface: Creating the Chinese in American Popular Music and Performance, 1850s–1920s* (New Brunswick, NJ: Rutgers University Press, 2005), 127.

46. Harold Clurman, *The Fervent Years: The Story of the Group Theatre and the Thirties* (New York: Hill and Wang, 1957), 106.

47. US census, 1930, New York, NY, Enumeration District 31–562, enumerated April 23, 1930, Sheet 13B, lines 53–57; FBM, 136–37.

48. Lader, e-mail to author, April 20, 2016. Religious school records show the Brice children at 1111 Park Avenue in the fall of 1930. For 1111 Park Avenue, see James Trager, *The New York Chronology: The Ultimate Compendium of Events, People, and Anecdotes from the Dutch to the Present* (New York: Harper Resource, 2003), 417. For Jews on Park Avenue, see Anne Roiphe, *1185 Park Avenue: A Memoir* (New York: Free Press, 1999), 4. An online search of the *New York Times* turns up many Jewish wedding and death announcements at 1111 Park Avenue.

49. ECP, interview folder 2, "Helen Schrank," June 22, 1966, 1; FBM, 114, 144.

50. "Silo's Fifth Avenue Art Galleries," Frick Collection, accessed May 25, 2016, research.frick.org; ECP, interview folder 2, "Maurice Zolotow," June 14, 1966, 2.

51. FBM, 131.

52. "Jed Harris' Long Rest," *Variety,* May 15, 1929, 57; "Film People Return," *Film Daily,* December 5, 1929, 2; Moss Hart, *Act One* (New York: Random House, 1959), 243, 256.

53. James Zeiger, "Broadway, the Elements of Success: Jed Harris's 1926 Production," in *Art, Glitter, and Glitz: Mainstream Playwrights and Popular Theatre in 1920s America,* ed. Arthur Gewirtz and James J. Kolb (Westport, CT: Praeger, 2004), 95–96.

54. MZP, *Billy Rose,* 222–23.

55. "Billy Rose's Show with Jed Harris In," *Variety,* May 14, 1930, 63; "Inside Stuff—Legit," *Variety,* May 22, 1929, 55; "Keeping Score on Smash Hits of B'way Stage," *Chicago Tribune,* September 28, 1930, part 7, 3.

56. Martin Gottfried, *Jed Harris: The Curse of Genius* (Boston: Little, Brown, 1984), 78; MZP, *Billy Rose,* 224; "Harris Sues Rose, Says 'Quilt' Made $100,000; Asks an Accounting," *Variety,* September 6, 1932, 36.

57. ECP, interview folder 2, "Richard Maney," June 10, [1966], 1.

58. "The Effendi Billy Rose," *Literary Digest,* July 7, 1934, 19; Seldes, "Stage-Door Johnny," 154.

59. ECP, "Richard Maney," 1.

60. George Jessel, *The World I Lived In* (Chicago: Henry Regnery, 1975), 98–100.

61. "Out-of-Town Reviews, Corned Beef and Roses," *Variety,* October 22, 1930, 71.

62. George Jean Nathan, *The Theatre Book of the Year, 1950–1951* (New York: Knopf, 1951), 51.

63. "Out-of-Town Reviews," 71; Goldman, *Fanny Brice,* 148.

64. Richard Maney, *Fanfare: The Confessions of a Press Agent* (New York: Harper, 1957), 147–48; MHC, Mark Hellinger, "All in a Day," n.d., from scrapbook labeled "Hellinger Daily 10/17/30."

65. "'Sweet and Low' Has Audacious Fun," *New York Times,* November 18, 1930, 28.

66. Goldman, *Fanny Brice,* 149–50; Anthony Slide, *The Encyclopedia of Vaudeville* (Jackson: University Press of Mississippi, 2012), 348.

67. Goldman, *Fanny Brice,* 150; MHC, Hellinger, "All in a Day."

68. Quoted in Norman Katkov, *The Fabulous Fanny: The Story of Fanny Brice* (New York: Knopf, 1953), 228.

69. "Hello, Broadway," *Clipper,* January 2, 1915, 6; Trav S.D., *No Applause—Just Throw Money: The Book That Made Vaudeville Famous* (New York: Faber and Faber, 2005), 7.

70. E. Y. Harburg Collection, Irving S. Gilmore Music Library, Yale University, MSS 83, box 24, folder 198, clippings from scrapbook, "Billy Rose's Crazy Quilt," Gilbert W. Gabriel, "Sweeter, Lower, and Baker," *New York American,* n.d. [May 1931].

71. Seldes, "Stage-Door Johnny," 154.

72. MHC, Hellinger, "All in a Day."

73. "Barnstorming Extraordinary," *Stage,* May 1932, 13.

74. "New York—Inside Out, Bits of Philosophy about Theater Ads and Ballyhoo— And How It Works," *Pittsburgh Press,* May 19, 1932, 28.

75. Arthur Pollock, "The Theatres," *Brooklyn Daily Eagle,* March 19, 1932, 8; ECP, research folder 3, Richard Maney, "Billy Rose Gives the Formula for a Successful Road Show," September 10, 1933.

76. FBM, 133.

77. ECP, research correspondence folder 2, Ned Alvord letter, May 7, 1968.

78. Anderson, *Out without My Rubbers,* 145.

79. ECP, interview folder 2, "Richard Maney," June 10, [1966], 2, 4; Thomas Vinciguerra, ed., *Backward Ran Sentences: The Best of Wolcott Gibbs from the New Yorker* (New York: Bloomsbury, 2011), 176, 180.

80. Vicki Walton, interview with the author, August 7, 2014.

81. "Barnstorming Extraordinary," *Stage,* 13.

82. Seldes, "Stage-Door Johnny," 154.

83. For Rose in the Wurlitzer, see Rosse Papers Correspondence, Herman and S. Helena Rosse Archive, Chapin Library, Williams College, box 1, Rosse Corres. 1932, January–September, "Estimate, for Mr. William Rose, Att: Mr. Herman Rosse," August 25, 1932. For William Rose, Inc., see *City Directory of New York 1933,* 2801, accessed January 25, 2018, www.ancestry.com; for office space, see Ross Laird, *Brunswick Records: A Discography of Recordings, 1916–1931,* vol. 1, *New York Sessions, 1916–1926* (Westport, CT: Greenwood, 2001), 11, and "Brunswick Radio Rents Floors," *New York Times,* May 8, 1930, 50. The radio company's space on the fourteenth and fifteenth floors totaled twenty-two thousand square feet, so Rose's fifteenth-floor office was about half that size.

84. Maney, *Fanfare,* 149; FBM, 132–33.

85. "Billy Rose," *Stage,* September 1934, 22.

86. Maney, *Fanfare,* 149.

87. "Effendi Billy Rose," 19.

88. Seldes, "Stage-Door Johnny," 154.

89. Marilyn Backus, "1932 Duesenberg 8, J-182 Dual Cowl Phaeton by LeBaron," *TORQUE,* March–April 2005, 8; Dennis Adler, *Duesenberg* (Cincinnati: F+W Media, 2004), 7–8, 107, 108, 110; Donald L. Miller, *Supreme City: How Jazz Age Manhattan Gave Birth to Modern America* (New York: Simon and Schuster, 2014), 92; Jon Bill, "Duesenberg Model J Dual Cowl Phaeton," Auburn Cord Duesenberg Museum, Auburn, Indiana.

90. Office of the City Clerk, New York, marriage license for Frederick Stern and Miriam Rosenberg, no. 7506, April 21, 1931.

91. Stephen Gottlieb, interview with the author, October 27, 2015.

92. ECP, "Helen Schrank," 2.

93. ECP, interview folder 1, "Hilda (Wiener) Brozen," May 3, [1966], 1–3.

94. "Reverting to Type," *Brooklyn Daily Eagle,* January 31, 1933, 13.

95. ECP, "Helen Schrank," 2.

96. New York County Clerk's Office, Billy Rose against Art Cinema Corp., Index Number 9672, Year 1930, motion filed August 17, 1931.

97. Arthur Garfield Hays, *City Lawyer: The Autobiography of a Law Practice* (New York: Simon and Schuster, 1942), 140.

98. CUL, "Reminiscences of Ray Henderson, 1958," 5–6.

99. Hays, *City Lawyer,* 137–38.

100. ECP, research folder 2, "Billy Rose (1899–1966)," *American Guild of Authors and Composers Bulletin* 3, no. 2 (May 1966): 1.

101. "What Makes Billy Run?," *Time,* June 2, 1947, 44.

102. ECP, Interview folder 1, Chester Conn, 5; ECP, interview folder 2, "Jean Kennedy Taylor," May 9, [1966], 8.

103. Quoted in Ron Lackman, *Mercedes McCambridge: A Biography and Career Record* (Jefferson, NC: McFarland, 2005), 105.

six   A Cosmic Scale

1. H. Allen Smith, *The Life and Legend of Gene Fowler* (New York: William Morrow, 1977), 215.

2. Richard Maney, *Fanfare: The Confessions of a Press Agent* (New York: Harper, 1957), 150.

3. Ben Hecht and Gene Fowler, *The Great Magoo* (New York: Covici-Friede, 1933), 190.

4. ECP, interview folder 2, "Richard Maney," June 10, [1966], 4.

5. Maney, *Fanfare,* 150; George Abbott, *"Mister Abbott"* (New York: Random House, 1963), 159.

6. Jeffrey Brown Martin, *Ben Hecht, Hollywood Screenwriter* (Ann Arbor, MI: UMI Research Press, 1985), 2, 10.

7. Leslie A. Fiedler, "Genesis: The American Jewish Novel through the Twenties," in *Jewish-American Literature: An Anthology*, ed. Abraham Chapman (New York: Mentor, 1974), 584.

8. Hecht and Fowler, *Great Magoo,* 201.

9. Unsigned review of *The Great Magoo,* by Ben Hecht and Gene Fowler, *Variety,* December 6, 1932, 47.

10. Maney, *Fanfare,* 151.

11. "Albert Lewis" [advertisement], *Hollywood Filmograph,* December 23, 1933, 28.

12. Herman Rosse, "Designs for *The Great Magoo,*" *Theatre Arts Monthly,* January 1933, 8–9.

13. Quoted in Harriet Hyman Alonso, *Yip Harburg: Legendary Lyricist and Human Rights Activist* (Middletown, CT: Wesleyan University Press, 2012), 43.

14. Daniel Okrent, *Last Call: The Rise and Fall of Prohibition* (New York: Scribner, 2010), 351.

15. Gilbert Seldes, "Stage-Door Johnny, Pro Tem.," *Esquire,* September 1934, 137.

16. "Casino de Paree Blends Continental Café and American Show Features," *Variety,* December 19, 1933, 46.

17. Seldes, "Stage-Door Johnny," 137.

18. Lewis Erenberg, "Impresarios of Broadway Nightlife," in *Inventing Times Square: Commerce and Culture at the Crossroads of the World,* ed. William R. Taylor (New York: Russell Sage Foundation, 1991), 172.

19. Inside Stuff—Vaude, *Variety,* July 3, 1934, 59; Inside Stuff—Vaude, *Variety,* December 19, 1933, 46; "B'way Cabaret Grosses 40G Weekly," *Variety,* February 13, 1934, 1.

20. "Casino de Paree," *Variety,* December 19, 1933, 46; Steven Brower, "Father of Macy's Thanksgiving Day Parade Balloons Revealed," *Print,* November 27, 2013, www.printmag.com/environmental/parade-balloons.

21. ECP, research folder 3, Lucius Beebe, "Billy Rose Revives a Tradition, but Isn't 'Over-Elegant' about It," February 18, 1934.

22. Seldes, "Stage-Door Johnny," 137.

23. Ibid.

24. Edith J. R. Isaacs, "Good Playing A-Plenty: Broadway in Review," *Theatre Arts Monthly,* January 1934, 12.

25. Erenberg, "Impresarios," 171.

26. "The Night-Club Comes Alive Again," *Stage,* January 1934, 5–6.

27. Erenberg, "Impresarios," 170.

28. ECP, research folder 3, A. J. Liebling, "Master of His Own House," *New York World-Telegram,* May 19, 1934.

29. Lipstick, "Tables for Two," *New Yorker,* January 20, 1934, 53.

30. Bennett Cerf, *Try and Stop Me* (New York: Simon and Schuster, 1945), 144.

31. Seldes, "Stage-Door Johnny," 137.

32. "Charities to Benefit by 3 Supper Parties," *New York Times,* March 14, 1934, 16; "Two Social Events to Help Infirmary," *New York Times,* April 15, 1934, section 2, 5; "Benefit for Dramatists," *New York Times,* May 23, 1934, 22.

33. "Re-Title Jolson-Keeler Film," *Film Daily,* November 21, 1934, 2.

34. "B'way Cabaret," *Variety,* February 13, 1934, 1; Seldes, "Stage-Door Johnny," 137.

35. ECP, interview folder 1, "Irving Hoffman," June 17, 1966, 3; MZP, interview notes, "Casino de Paree," 1.

36. Herbert G. Goldman, *Fanny Brice: The Original Funny Girl* (New York: Oxford University Press, 1992), 154–56; MZP, "Casino de Paree," 1.

37. Alan Block, *East Side, West Side: Organizing Crime in New York, 1930–1950* (Cardiff: University College Cardiff Press, 1980), 134–37.

38. Maurice Zolotow, "You Think You Know How to Drink Beer?" in *Best Articles 1953,* ed. Rudolf Flesch (New York: Hermitage House, 1953), 139; ECP, research correspondence folder 1, Washburn to Earl Conrad, November 6, 1966.

39. Craig Thompson and Allen Raymond, *Gang Rule in New York: The Story of a Lawless Era* (New York: Dial, 1940), 66, 284, 382–84, 393.

40. ECP, interview folder 1, "Dave Dreyer," June 6, 1966, 6.

41. ECP, interview folder 2, "Richard Maney," June 10, [1966], 2.

42. Quoted in Burton W. Peretti, *Nightclub City: Politics and Amusement in Manhattan* (Philadelphia: University of Pennsylvania Press, 2007), 4.

43. ECP, interview folder 1, "Irving Hoffman," June 27, 1966.

44. ECP, research folder 3, Thomas MacCabe, ["Billy Rose profile"], *New York World-Telegram,* [1961].

45. Quoted in Sidney Zion, *Read All about It!* (New York: Penguin, 1984), 143.

46. Stephen Nelson, *"Only a Paper Moon": The Theatre of Billy Rose* (Ann Arbor, MI: UMI Research Press, 1987), 25.

47. "New Hammerstein Theatre Dedicated," *New York Times,* December 1, 1927, 32.

48. Liebling, "Master."

49. ECP, research folder 3, Lucius Beebe, "Out of the Sticks to Make a Broadway Riot," *New York World-Telegram,* July 18, 1934.

50. Art Arthur, Reverting to Type, *Brooklyn Daily Eagle,* June 25, 1934, 12.

51. "Billy Rose's Music Hall Has Premiere Tonight," *Brooklyn Daily Eagle,* June 21, 1934, 21; Art Arthur, Reverting to Type, *Brooklyn Daily Eagle,* June 25, 1934, 12.

52. Abel Green, "Billy Rose's Music Hall Is Another New Phase of Show Biz," *Variety,* June 26, 1934, 48; Art Arthur, Reverting to Type, *Brooklyn Daily Eagle,* July 2, 1934, 11.

53. MZP, "Casino de Paree," 4.

54. Burns Mantle, "Restaurant with Vaudeville Now the Rage in N.Y.," *Chicago Daily Tribune,* July 1, 1934, E2.

55. "Night Club Reviews," *Variety,* June 26, 1934, 59; MZP, "Casino de Paree," 4.

56. BRTD, "Interview with Billy Rose on the Long John Nebel radio show, Aug. 5, 1965," audio disc 4.

57. Art Arthur, Reverting to Type, *Brooklyn Daily Eagle,* September 8, 1934, 4; Mantle, "Restaurant with Vaudeville."

58. MZP, "Casino," 4; "What Price Sentiment," *Variety,* July 24, 1934, 59.

59. BRTD, "Interview with Billy Rose," audio disc 4.

60. *Stage,* January 1934, 3, 26–27.

61. Robert Benchley, "The Theatre, the Follies and Others," *New Yorker,* January 13, 1934, 25.

62. Barbara Wallace Grossman, *Funny Woman: The Life and Times of Fanny Brice* (Bloomington: Indiana University Press, 1991), 201.

63. BRTD, "Interview with Billy Rose," audio disc 2.

64. Grossman, *Funny Woman,* 201.

65. H. L. Mencken, "Individualism Cheats the Coroner," *Vanity Fair,* June 1934, 35, 65.

66. Jefferson Chase, "The Lost Art of Magnificence," *Vanity Fair,* June 1934, 25, 68.

67. Information on Rose's passport was provided in US Department of State, letter to the author, December 18, 2015. The *Majestic* arrived in Southampton on August 2, 1934, and the trip took five-plus days, so it appears to have sailed on July 28. See William H. Miller, *Picture History of British Ocean Liners, 1900 to the Present* (Mineola, NY: Dover, 2001), 24.

68. "Rosoff to Help Kings Brewery Reorganization," *Brooklyn Daily Eagle,* July 31, 1934, 3.

69. "Night Club Reviews, Tabarin, Paris," *Variety,* March 20, 1934, 44.

70. George Jean Nathan, "Ferenc Molnar (1878–1952)," in *A George Jean Nathan Reader,* ed. A. L. Lazarus (Rutherford, NJ: Fairleigh Dickinson University Press), 126.

71. "'The Play's the Thing' in Musical Version," *New York Times,* July 13, 1931, 12; Mordaunt Hall, "John Barrymore in '20th Century,'" *New York Times,* May 13, 1934, X3.

72. Art Arthur, Reverting to Type, *Brooklyn Daily Eagle,* June 25, 1934, 12, and July 2, 1934, 11.

73. MZP, "Casino de Paree," 5; Maney, *Fanfare,* 155; May Birkhead, "European Shoots Lure Americans," *New York Times,* August 12, 1934, section 2, 4. Rose's description matches information found in BMB, box 743, Game Book, entry dated August 20.

74. "Foreign Review, Star of the Circus," *Variety,* July 10, 1934, 48.

75. "'Broadway Circus' Planned for Spring, Billy Rose Would Include 1,800 Dancers and Show Girls in Huge Human Spectacle," *New York Times,* July 26, 1934, 14; "Two Seasoned New Yorkers Lay Plans for the Ensuing Season," *Washington Post,* July 29, 1934, S1.

76. "'Circus Queen' for U.S., to Play under Canvas; Maybe with Lil Harvey," *Variety,* September 4, 1934, 2.

77. "Without an Elephant," *New York Times,* September 2, 1934, X2.

78. Ibid.

79. Rem Koolhaas, *Delirious New York: A Retroactive Manifesto for Manhattan* (New York: Monacelli, 1994), 10, 41.

80. ECP, research folder 1, typewritten notes dated August 28, 1934; MZP, "Casino de Paree," 7.

81. MZP, "Casino de Paree," 7.

82. BMB, box 259, Rose to Baruch, April 17, 1936.

83. Neal Gabler, *Winchell: Gossip, Power and the Culture of Celebrity* (New York: Vantage Books, 1995), 197; *Walter Winchell/Federal Bureau of Investigation* (Washington, DC: Federal Bureau of Investigation, 1999[?]), September 7, 1934, letter from Frank [Fay] to J. Edgar Hoover, [n.p.].

84. "Rose Wins Point," *Variety,* December 25, 1934, 40.

85. TEA, letter of September 14, 1933, on Brice's personal stationery; the letter shows a home address of 32 East Sixty-Fourth Street.

86. Goldman, *Fanny Brice,* 162.

87. MZP, "On Billy Rose," 4.

88. Saul Bellow, *Humboldt's Gift* (New York: Avon Books, 1976), 38.

SEVEN **Jumbo**

1. Geoffrey Block, "'Bigger than a Show—Better than a Circus': The Broadway Musical, Radio, and Billy Rose's *Jumbo*," *Musical Quarterly* 89, no. 2–3 (Summer–Fall 2006): 165; "Arcadia May Get Rose Spec," *Variety,* September 11, 1934, 55.

2. WFP, MS 1938, series 1, box 132, folder 2, "Accuse Billy Rose and 'Jumbo' Aids of Stealing Show," *New York Daily News,* May 5, [1938].

3. ECP, interview folder 1, "Rose Hecht," n.d.

4. "Inside Stuff—Legit," *Variety,* September 25, 1934, 54; Saul Bellow, "Cousins," in *Him with His Foot in His Mouth, and Other Stories* (New York: Penguin, 1998), 237.

5. Joseph McBride, *Hawks on Hawks* (Lexington: University Press of Kentucky, 2013), chap. 12, 1.

6. Will Morrissey, *On a Shoestring* (Santa Barbara, CA: Willdon Paul, 1955), 206–7; UTA, William A. Bradley Literary Agency Records, MS-0491, box 53.5, Alan Brock, "'Jumbo Rose.'"

7. Benjamin Welles, "Raoul Pène Du Bois, a Note or Two on the Scene and Costume Designer Extraordinary," *New York Times,* September 8, 1940, section 9, 1–2.

8. Morrissey, *On a Shoestring,* 206.

9. Foster Hirsch, *The Boys from Syracuse: The Shuberts' Theatrical Empire* (New York: Cooper Square, 1998), 310.

10. Hugh Fordin, *Getting to Know Him: A Biography of Oscar Hammerstein II* (Boston: Da Capo, 1995), 145–46; "Four Musicals in the Works," *Variety,* March 13, 1935, 54; Frederick Nolan, *The Sound of Their Music: The Story of Rodgers & Hammerstein* (New York: Applause Theatre and Cinema Books, 2002), 125–27.

11. Sidney Zion, *Read All about It!* (New York: Penguin, 1984), 12.

12. Morrissey, *On a Shoestring,* 207; Bella C. Landauer, "Jumbo's Influence on Ad-

vertising or Some *Jumbo* Trade-Cards," *New-York Historical Society Quarterly Bulletin* 18, no. 3 (October 1934): 43–52.

13. "Books," *Stage,* June 1932, 46–47; "Theatre Asides, Circus," *Stage,* April 1933, 24.

14. "Fairs Dropping Circus Acts as Customers Ask for Girly Revues," *Variety,* August 7, 1934, 55; "Two Men from a Gun," *Stage,* June 1935, 40–41; USCCAL, *Hollywood Reporter* Collection, Jum Jumbo, "'Jumbo' or 'Twenty Thousand Leagues under the Hippodrome,'" *Hollywood Reporter,* December 30, 1935, 141.

15. MZP, interview notes, "Jumbo," 3–4; WFP, John C. Pinto to John F. Wharton, June 8, 1935, "Jumbo Estimated Production & Preliminary Costs, Schedule 1," item 12, "Expenses to Date."

16. MZP, "Jumbo," 3.

17. Michael Maslin, *Peter Arno: The Mad, Mad World of the New Yorker's Greatest Cartoonist* (New York: Regan Arts, 2016), 79–81; "John Hay Whitney," *Stage,* July 1935, 61.

18. The date of the pitch seems to have been May 2, 1935, per WFP, John C. Pinto to John F. Wharton, "Jumbo Estimated Production & Preliminary Costs, Schedule 1," summary below item 12, "Expenses to Date."

19. John Murray Anderson, *Out without My Rubbers: The Memoirs of John Murray Anderson* (New York: Library, 1954), 146; Stephen Nelson, *"Only a Paper Moon": The Theatre of Billy Rose* (Ann Arbor, MI: UMI Research Press, 1987), 34–35, 41.

20. Morrissey, *On a Shoestring,* 207–8; WFP, Cohen Cole Weiss Wharton to John Hay Whitney, August 29, 1935.

21. Anderson, *Out without My Rubbers,* 146.

22. Block, "'Bigger than a Show," 175–79.

23. "Schnozzola Due for Hipp Circus; Opening in May," *Variety,* February 20, 1935, 53; "News from the Dailies," *Variety,* May 8, 1935, 74; "Irked at 'Jumbo' Delay, Durante May Bow Out 100%; See Equity's 'Circus' OK," *Variety,* July 31, 1935, 53.

24. "Whiteman in 'Jumbo,'" *Variety,* June 19, 1935, 71.

25. "Irked at 'Jumbo' Delay," 53; "'Jumbo' a Circus, Equity Rules; Rose Points for Sept. 15," *Variety,* August 7, 1935, 56.

26. WFP, John F. Wharton to John Hay Whitney, June 10, 1935; M. D. Merwin to John Hay Whitney, August 19, 1935; Cohen Cole Weiss Wharton to John Hay Whitney, August 29, 1935.

27. CUL, Richard Rodgers oral history, 164.

28. Nelson, *"Only a Paper Moon,"* 33–34, 38, 40.

29. Ibid., 38.

30. "Asides," *Stage,* November 1935, 42.

31. Richard Maney, *Fanfare: The Confessions of a Press Agent* (New York: Harper, 1957), 156–57, 160.

32. ECP, interview folder 2, "Richard Maney," June 10, [1966], 2.

33. ECP, interview folder 2, "Morris Permut," n.d., 2.

34. CUL, Richard Rodgers oral history, 164.

35. Polly Rose Gottlieb, *The Nine Lives of Billy Rose* (New York: Crown, 1968), 101; MZP, *Billy Rose of Broadway*, 343.

36. "Bluebloods, Rubbernecks and Autos Jam 6th Ave. for 'Jumbo's' Debut," *Variety*, November 20, 1935, 59.

37. MZP, *Billy Rose*, 358.

38. Edith J. R. Isaacs, "Distance Lends Enchantment, Broadway in Review," *Theatre Arts Monthly*, January 1936, 15–16; "Personae Gratae," *Theatre Arts Monthly*, January 1936, 49; Andre La Tersa, [Photograph of *Jumbo*], *Theatre Arts Monthly*, January 1936, 83.

39. Block, "'Bigger than a Show,'" 168, 170, 172, 179.

40. Brooks Atkinson, "'Jumbo' Finally Gets Under Way at the Hippodrome, with Actors, Acrobats and Animals," The Play, *New York Times*, November 18, 1935, 20. For all other *Jumbo* reviews, see WHS, Albert R. Johnson Papers, 1910–1967, Theatre and Live Dramatic Performances, box 7, folder 1.

41. Frederick Nolan, *Lorenz Hart: A Poet on Broadway* (New York: Oxford University Press, 1994), 206.

42. Nelson, "'*Only a Paper Moon*,'" 45.

43. For attendance figures see NYWF, box 510, folder 15, "Memorandum, To: The President, From: Technical Adviser," March 15, 1938, 4.

44. WFP, John C. Pinto to John F. Wharton, "Jumbo Estimated Weekly Operating Expense Based on Receipts of $40,000, Schedule 2," June 8, 1935.

45. "'Jumbo' Folds with Much Dissension and Way in Red; Jock Whitney Lost $160,000; Creditors Offered 50%," *Variety*, April 22, 1936, 59.

46. Block, "'Bigger than a Show,'" 191, 182, 168, 178; Maney, *Fanfare*, 156, 160.

47. Maney, *Fanfare*, 160.

48. ECP, interview folder 2, "Abner Silver," June 14, 1966, 1.

49. Betsy Blair, *The Memory of All That: Love and Politics in New York, Hollywood, and Paris* (New York: Alfred A. Knopf, 2003), 9.

50. Mercedes McCambridge, *The Quality of Mercy* (New York: Times Books, 1981), 228.

51. Jane Morgan Weintraub, interview with the author, April 25, 2014.

52. ECP, interview folder 2, "Helen Schrank," June 22, 1966, 11.

53. ECP, interview folder 2, "Charles Samuels," June 2, 1966, 5.

54. AB, box 106, folder 2, funeral oration for Billy Rose, dated February 13, 1966, 1–2.

55. ECP, interview folder 1, "Mrs. Lee Rogow," June 8, 1966.

56. ECP, interview folder 2, "Tex McCrary," June 23, 1966, 9.

57. ECP, interview folder 1, "Burton Lane," June 27, 1966, 3.

58. Meredith Willson, *"But He Doesn't Know the Territory"* (Minneapolis: University of Minnesota Press, 2009), 95; MZP, "On Billy Rose," 1.

59. ECP, interview folder 2, "Gloria Safier," June 13, 1966, 1–2.

60. CUL, Richard Rodgers oral history, 161. Audio recording of *The Ben Hecht Show* (television series), episode of October 7, 1958, courtesy of Bret Primack.

61. "What Makes Billy Run?," *Time,* June 2, 1947, 44.

62. WHS, Albert R. Johnson Papers, 1910–1967, Theatre and Live Dramatic Performances, box 7, folder 1, John Mason Brown, "Billy Rose's 'Jumbo' at the Hippodrome," *New York Post,* [date illegible].

63. BRTD, "Interview with Billy Rose on the Long John Nebel radio show, Aug. 5, 1965," audio disc 3.

EIGHT It Can't Happen Here

1. Dr. Robert G. Waite, "'Raise My Voice against Intolerance': The Anti-Nazi Rally in Madison Square Garden, March 27, 1933, and the American Public's Outrage over the Nazi Persecution of Jews," *New York History Review Annual* (2013): 188–89, 192, 207–8.

2. Otto D. Tolischus, "Reich Jews Plead for Haven Abroad," *New York Times,* November 27, 1935, 11.

3. Quoted in Leonard Dinnerstein, "Antisemitism in Crisis Times in the United States: The 1920s and 1930s," in *Anti-Semitism in Times of Crisis,* ed. Sander L. Gilman and Steven T. Katz (New York: NYU Press, 1991), 217.

4. Dinnerstein, "Antisemitism in Crisis Times," 219.

5. MZP, interview notes, "Fort Worth," 3.

6. "'Jumbo,' Costing $340,000, Tremendous Stage Offering," *Los Angeles Times,* November 28, 1935, 18; USCCAL, *Hollywood Reporter* Collection, Jum Jumbo, "'Jumbo' or 'Twenty Thousand Leagues under the Hippodrome," *Hollywood Reporter,* December 30, 1935, 141.

7. Jan Jones, *Billy Rose Presents . . . Casa Mañana* (Fort Worth: Texas Christian University Press, 1999), 23.

8. Jerry Flemmons, *Amon, the Texan Who Played Cowboy for America* (Lubbock: Texas Tech University Press, 1998), 18–19, 26.

9. Will Morrissey, *On a Shoestring* (Santa Barbara, CA: Willdon Paul, 1955), 212; "News from the Dailies," *Variety,* March 4, 1936, 78; Jones, *Billy Rose Presents,* 8, 16, 23, 166.

10. MZP, "Fort Worth," 1–3.

11. James V. Allred Collection, 1921–1970, University of Houston Libraries, Special Collections, box 143, folder 17, Billy Rose to Governor Allred, April 13, 1936.

12. MZP, "Fort Worth," 1–3; Jones, *Billy Rose Presents,* 25.

13. Jones, *Billy Rose Presents,* 51.

14. ECP, research folder 3, S. J. Woolf, "Broadway Barnum," *New York Times Magazine,* April 23, 1939, 17.

15. Rachel Shteir, *Striptease: The Untold History of the Girlie Show* (Oxford: Oxford University Press, 2004), 4, 130.

16. Burns Mantle, "Restaurant with Vaudeville Now the Rage in N.Y.," *Chicago Daily Tribune,* July 1, 1934, E2; Marco Duranti, "Utopia, Nostalgia and World War at

the 1939–40 New York World's Fair," *Journal of Contemporary History* 41, no. 4 (October 2006): 665.

17. Jones, *Billy Rose Presents,* 30–31.

18. Stephen Nelson, *"Only a Paper Moon": The Theatre of Billy Rose* (Ann Arbor, MI: UMI Research Press, 1987), 55.

19. Jones, *Billy Rose Presents,* 33–36, 46, 70–72, 85–86; Nelson, *"Only a Paper Moon,"* 53, 56–57, 60; WHS, Albert R. Johnson Papers, 1910–1967, box 5, folder 18, "Casa Mañana Program."

20. BRTD, box 5, folder 3, Richard Watts Jr., "Sight and Sound," *New York Herald Tribune,* July 26, 1936.

21. BRTD, box 5, folder 3, "That Mr. Rose Again," *New York Times,* July 26, 1936.

22. John Harkins, "Texas Centennial Rose Field Day in Production Ideas," *New York American,* July 21, 1936.

23. Quoted in Jones, *Billy Rose Presents,* 1.

24. BRTD, box 5, folder 3, Robert Garland, "Texas Offers Visitor Real Entertainment," *New York World-Telegram,* July 22, 1936.

25. Agnes de Mille, *Portrait Gallery* (Boston: Houghton Mifflin, 1990), 111–12.

26. BRTD, box 5, folder 3, Ward Morehouse, "Fort Worth after Dark," *New York Sun,* [August 5, 1936].

27. Lotos Club Papers, New York Historical Society, "Dinner in Honor of Grace George and William A. Brady, The Lotos Club, Sunday, April 26, 1942."

28. NYWF 1939/40, box 510, folder 14 (Pl. 6, Rose, Billy, 2 of 3 [1939]), Rose to Moses, August 5, 1936, and Moses to Rose, August 8, 1936. The Moses letter appears to be signed by assistant Maurice Mermey, but Mermey's letter to Rose of August 13 attributes the August 8 response to Moses.

29. WHS, Albert R. Johnson Papers, box 5, folder 18, "Casa Mañana Crowds Amaze 'Maytime' Star and Architect."

30. NYWF, box 510, folder 14, Billy Rose telegram to Earl [*sic*] Andrews, August 14, 1936.

31. NYWF, box 510, folder 14, W. Earle Andrews telegram to Billy Rose, August 14, 1936.

32. "Then, Where?" *Variety,* September 23, 1936, 47; "Billy Rose, Hank Ford at Cleveland in '37," *Variety,* October 21, 1936, 71; "Texas Expos' B. O. Blues," *Variety,* September 16, 1936, 63.

33. "Fannie [*sic*] Brice Set for 'Great Ziegfeld,'" *Variety,* August 28, 1935, 2; "Brice East for 'Follies' after 'Ziegfeld' Filming," *Variety,* October 16, 1935, 58.

34. Barbara Wallace Grossman, *Funny Woman: The Life and Times of Fanny Brice* (Bloomington: Indiana University Press, 1991), 219; Herbert G. Goldman, *Fanny Brice: The Original Funny Girl* (New York: Oxford University Press, 1992), 168.

35. MZP, interview notes, "Jumbo," 1.

36. BRTD, box 5, folder 3, "Frontier Show Director Is Honored," n.d. [November 3, 1936].

37. MZP, "Jumbo," 1.

38. "Fanny Rosenberg," *Forverts* [Jewish Daily Forward], December 10, 1936, 14 (translated from the Yiddish by Amanda Seigel, librarian, Dorot Jewish Division, New York Public Library); "Mother of Billy Rose Dies," *New York Times,* December 10, 1936, 27; "Milestones," *Time,* December 21, 1936, 47.

39. Department of Health of the City of New York, standard certificate of death, register no. 26492, "Fannie Rosenberg"; photograph of Fannie Rosenberg's headstone courtesy of Matthew R. Ivler, Lebanon Cemetery Association of Queens, Inc., Glendale, NY.

40. MZP, interview notes, "Childhood and Youth," 3.

41. Arthur Garfield Hays, *City Lawyer: The Autobiography of a Law Practice* (New York: Simon and Schuster, 1942), 142.

42. Jones, *Billy Rose Presents,* 103.

43. "Billy Rose, Hank Ford," *Variety,* October 21, 1936, 71.

44. Dawn Pawson Bean, *Synchronized Swimming: An American History* (Jefferson, NC: McFarland, 2005), 7–11.

45. "Noted Swimmers to Tour as Pros," *Brooklyn Daily Eagle,* October 22, 1936, 21; "Olympic Dive Champ Turns Professional," *Brooklyn Daily Eagle,* October 27, 1936, 18.

46. "Crime Doesn't Pay at Cleve. Expo, So Mrs. Castle Makes It a Rumba; Snake Show Tops," *Variety,* July 15, 1936, 87; "Fanner Sans Fans Beats Toto's Draw at Cleveland Expo; Specials a Pull," *Variety,* September 2, 1936, 63.

47. "National Swim Champion Wins Medley Crown," *Brooklyn Daily Eagle,* July 10, 1927, 28; "Miss Lambert Breaks Record for Backstroke," *Brooklyn Daily Eagle,* July 24, 1927, 28; "Mermaids Create New Records in L. I. Swim Meet," *Brooklyn Daily Eagle,* August 7, 1927, 30; "Holiday Sport Results," *Brooklyn Daily Eagle,* February 23, 1928, 27.

48. Harold C. Burr, "Eleanor Holm Thrills Mother, but Shocks Dad with Her Aquatic Feats," *Brooklyn Daily Eagle,* February 24, 1928, 26.

49. "Eleanor Holm Grabs Second Olympic Title; Salica Is on His Way," *Brooklyn Daily Eagle,* August 12, 1932, 16.

50. "Movies Sign Eleanor Holm," *New York Times,* August 23, 1932, 17; Arthur Forde, "As Seen and Heard," *Hollywood Filmograph,* August 27, 1932, 8.

51. "Eleanor Holm Will Defend Her Title," *Brooklyn Daily Eagle,* January 19, 1933, 20; Lew Zeidler, "Eleanor Jarrett Confides She Will Turn Pro after Olympics," *Brooklyn Daily Eagle,* July 13, 1936, 6.

52. Avery Brundage Papers, University Archives, University of Illinois Urbana-Champaign, RS 26/20/37, box 263, folder "Eleanor Holm Jarrett," "Statement of Ada Taylor Sackett," "Statement of Jas. G. Driver, August 12, 1936," "Statement of Mary Lou Petty," "Statement of J. Herbert Lawson, M.D."

53. Ben Hecht, *Charlie: The Improbable Life and Times of Charles MacArthur* (New York: Harper and Brothers, 1957), 149.

54. "Jarrett Is Disappointed," *New York Times,* July 25, 1936, 7; "Officials Disgraced Selves on Ship, Says Eleanor Holm Jarrett," *Brooklyn Daily Eagle,* July 26, 1936, 3.

55. "Brundage Scores 'Alien Agitators,'" *New York Times,* December 4, 1935, 26.

56. William Weer, "To Whom It May Concern," *Brooklyn Daily Eagle,* July 27, 1936, 14.

57. "U.S. Athletes Fight Ban in Olympics of Eleanor Holm Jarrett," *Brooklyn Daily Eagle,* July 24, 1936, 7.

58. William Weer, "'I'll Never Be Happy Again,' Says Mrs. Jarrett, Arriving Home," *Brooklyn Daily Eagle,* August 20, 1936, 1.

59. "Mrs. Jarrett Sees Swim Stars Ready to Turn Pro," *Brooklyn Daily Eagle,* October 21, 1936, 23; "Variety House Reviews, Chicago," *Variety,* September 9, 1936, 58; "Cleve. Decides Dick-Joan Marriage NSG B.O; 'Girls'-Jarretts Strong 18G," *Variety,* January 13, 1937, 10.

60. "Holm Goes Pro in Rose Dunk," *Variety,* March 3, 1937, 49.

61. MZP, interview notes, "Aquacade," 2.

62. Bean, *Synchronized Swimming,* 12.

63. "Swim Tours Loses Injunction Suit vs. Eleanor Holm Jarrett," *Variety,* December 9, 1936, 43; Nelson, *"Only a Paper Moon,"* 68.

64. FBM, 183.

65. ECP, research folder 3, Jack Alexander, "Million-Dollar-a-Year Ego," *Saturday Evening Post,* December 21, 1940, 41; ECP, research correspondence folder 2, Wolfe Kaufman to Earl Conrad ("dear earl"), n.d., 2.

66. "Hitler in 'Hall of Horrors' at the Fair Is Mayor's Idea," *New York Herald Tribune,* March 4, 1937; "Feature Story," *New York Post,* March 8, 1937, Biblion, New York Public Library, http://exhibitions.nypl.org/biblion/worldsfair/moment-time -brink-war/story/story-germany.

67. TKP, Billy Rose correspondence, box 87/23, "Excerpt from Letter from Monica Dehn to I. L. Kenen, March 31, 1949."

68. Quoted in Nelson, *"Only a Paper Moon,"* 68.

69. ECP, correspondence folder 1, Wolfe Kaufman to Earl Conrad, n.d.

70. MZP, *Billy Rose of Broadway,* 400–401.

71. ECP, interview folder 1, "Ben Gordon," May 17, [1966], 4.

72. Jones, *Billy Rose Presents,* 108; John Vacha, *Meet Me on Lake Erie, Dearie! Cleveland's Great Lakes Exposition, 1936–1937* (Kent, OH: Kent State University Press, 2011), 169.

73. ECP, interview folder 1, "Richard Barstow," June 20, 1966, 4.

74. ECP, interview folder 2, "Helen Schrank," June 22, 1966, 12.

75. ECP, interview folder 1, "Walter Hirsch," June 23, 1966, 3.

76. de Mille, *Portrait Gallery,* 112.

77. ECP, "Helen Schrank," 9.

78. ECP, Alexander, "Million-Dollar-a-Year Ego," 41.

79. ECP, interview folder 1, "Dave Dreyer," June 6, 1966, 6; ECP, Alexander, "Million-Dollar-a-Year Ego," 16.

80. Vicki Walton, interview with the author, August 6, 2014.

81. ECP, interview folder 1, "Burton Lane," July 27, 1966, 1.

82. ECP, "Walter Hirsch," 3.

83. ECP, interview folder 1, "Hilda (Wiener) Brozen," May 3, [1966], 2.

84. BRTD, box 5, folder 3, "Billy Rose Picked as 'Man of Year' in Show Business," *Fort Worth Star-Telegram,* December 30, 1936.

85. MZP, *Billy Rose,* 401–3.

86. Jones, *Billy Rose Presents,* 107.

87. Nelson, *"Only a Paper Moon,"* 69–71, 74.

88. Billy Rose, *Wine, Women and Words* (New York: Pocketbook, 1950), 37.

89. Ibid., 156.

90. "WPA Finds 'New Audience,'" *Variety,* November 4, 1936, 53; Angela Sweigart-Gallagher, "Performing the Promise of Democracy: The Federal Theatre Project's (Re)Imaginings of American National Community" (PhD diss., University of Wisconsin-Madison, 2008), 47, 57.

91. Brooks Atkinson, The Play, *New York Times,* October 28, 1936, 30.

92. Nelson, *"Only a Paper Moon,"* 61.

93. Jones, *Billy Rose Presents,* 119.

94. Ibid., 115, 119.

95. Quoted in ibid., 119.

96. Garrett Eisler, "'This Theatre Is a Battlefield': Political Performance and Jewish-American Identity, 1933–1948" (PhD diss., City University of New York, 2012), 17.

97. Erika Fischer-Lichte, *Theatre, Sacrifice, Ritual: Exploring Forms of Political Theatre* (New York: Routledge, 2005), 171–72.

NINE Let's Play Fair

1. Jan Jones, *Billy Rose Presents . . . Casa Mañana* (Fort Worth: Texas Christian University Press, 1999), 94, 119–20, 115; John Vacha, *Meet Me on Lake Erie, Dearie! Cleveland's Great Lakes Exposition, 1936–1937* (Kent, OH: Kent State University Press, 2011), 176, 178; "Billy Rose Puts On Two Shows," *Life,* July 19, 1937, 36–39. Jones mistakenly dates the MGM short from 1936; it was released in 1938. For more information on the film, see IMDb, accessed January 31, 2018, http://www.imdb.com/title/tt0029914.

2. Jones, *Billy Rose Presents,* 116, 134, 138.

3. "Cleve's Rose-Holm Romance Rumor Jazzes Expo Biz, Despite Denials," *Variety,* July 28, 1937, 60; Los Angeles Superior Court, Archives & Records Center, Fannie Rosenberg vs. William Rosenberg, no. D172840, 1.

4. ECP, interview folder 2, "Gloria Safier," June 13, 1966, 1–2.

5. Mercedes McCambridge, *The Quality of Mercy* (New York: Times Books, 1981), 228.

6. ECP, interview folder 1, "Doris Julian," May 12, [1966], 2.

7. BRTD, "Interview with Billy Rose on the Long John Nebel radio show, Aug. 5, 1965," audio disc 2.

8. Billy Rose, *Wine, Women and Words* (New York: Pocketbook, 1950), 23; Earl Wilson Collection, Jerome Lawrence and Robert E. Lee Theatre Research Institute, Thompson Library, The Ohio State University, "Celebrities: Articles, Letters, Notes; Billy Rose," SPEC.TRI.EW.64.8, Herb Stein, "On the Hollywood Scene," February 18, 1952.

9. NYWF, box 510, folder 15, John Krimsky to the General Manager, August 24, 1937.

10. "Billy Rose Too Tough on His Terms, Geo. White Says Nix, French Casino Reorg-Reopening Still Under Way," *Variety*, December 1, 1937, 49; "Manhattan Night Life," *Fortune*, March 1936, 94; "Rose Gets French Casino," *New York Times*, December 6, 1937, 19.

11. BRTD, John Golden Papers, box 34, folder 65 (Whalen, Grover A., 1919–51), Golden to Grover Whalen, October 15, 1937, and list with subheads: Play, Producers, Dramatists, Events, Song Writers, etc., and "World's Fair (phoned from Mr. Krimsky's office—Nov. 18, 1937)."

12. Richard Maney, *Fanfare: The Confessions of a Press Agent* (New York: Harper, 1957), 168.

13. Philip Roth, *Portnoy's Complaint* (New York: Vintage International, 1994), 26.

14. ECP, research folder 3, Jack Alexander, "Million-Dollar-a-Year Ego," *Saturday Evening Post*, December 21, 1940, 16.

15. Rem Koolhaas, *Delirious New York: A Retroactive Manifesto for Manhattan* (New York. Monacelli, 1994), 70, 79.

16. NYWF, box 510, folder 15, William G. Morrissey to the President, March 8, 1937.

17. Quoted in Marco Duranti, "Utopia, Nostalgia and World War at the 1939–40 New York World's Fair," *Journal of Contemporary History* 41, no. 4 (2006): 668.

18. "Amusement Area Offers Freaks, Peeks and Rides," *Life*, July 3, 1939, 64.

19. Rachel Shteir, *Striptease: The Untold History of the Girlie Show* (Oxford: Oxford University Press, 2004), 207.

20. NYWF, box 510, folder 15, Billy Rose to Grover Whalen, n.d. Whalen's telegrammed reply of December 23 seems immediate, and Rose's telegram was probably sent the same day.

21. NYWF, box 510, folder 15, Whalen to Rose, December 23, 1937.

22. Maney, *Fanfare*, 167.

23. NYWF, box 1943, folder 8, R. M., "Billy Rose to Spoof Coming World's Fair," *New York World-Telegram*, January 15, 1938 (news clippings also in this folder); WHS, National Broadcasting Company records, 1921–1976, Subseries: Correspondence, 1921–1942, Rose to John Royal, January 11, 1938.

24. NYWF, box 1943, folder 8, "Broadway Turns Out for Rose's Club Show," *Daily Mirror,* January 19, 1938; Mary Van Rensselaer Thayer, "Park Avenue Throng at Billy Rose Show," *New York World-Telegram,* January 19, 1938.

25. Stephen Nelson, *"Only a Paper Moon": The Theatre of Billy Rose* (Ann Arbor, MI: UMI Research Press, 1987), 84; Shteir, *Striptease,* 208.

26. Don Marquis, "The Golden Egg," *Stage,* May 1935, 32.

27. E. E. Cummings, "Burlesque: I Love It," *Stage,* March 1936, 61.

28. NYWF, box 1943, folder 8, Robert Coleman, "Casa Manana Show Proves a Delight," *Daily Mirror,* January 20, 1938, and "Billy Rose Launches His Glittering Extravaganza at Casa Manana," *New York World-Telegram,* January 19, 1938; "Billy Rose Opens Night Club, Showing Whalen How to Spend Millions on Fair," *New York Journal and American,* January 19, 1938.

29. NYWF, box 510, folder 14, Billy Rose to Grover Whalen, February 4, [1938].

30. NYWF, box 510, folder 15, Technical Adviser to the President, "Billy Rose Proposal," March 16, 1938, 1, 6.

31. NYWF, box 510, folder 15, Commander Flanigan to the President, "Discussion with Mr. Billy Rose regarding Participation in the Fair," April 4, 1938, 2, and box 1378, folder 6, H. B. Jr., "Memorandum of Conference with Mr. Billy Rose," May 18, 1938.

32. NYWF, box 1378, folder 6, Lee Shubert to W. Earle Andrews, May 14, 1938, 1; box 1378, folder 6, Fortune Gallo to Earle Andrews, May 27, 1938; and box 9, folder 9, W. Earle Andrews to Director of Entertainment, June 7, 1938.

33. NYWF, box 1421, folder 5, "The People of the State of New York, Plaintiff, against New York World's Fair 1939 Incorporated, Gotham Productions, Inc. and Billy Rose's Exposition Spectacles, Inc., Defendants," Testimony of Mary L. Jorzick, Exhibit "B," 2. The document reveals the original deadline dates of December 1, 1938, for a synopsis (later postponed to February 1, 1939), and January 15, 1939, for the deposit of $100,000 (later postponed to January 24).

34. AJJDC, Oral History Collection, Isamo [*sic*] Noguchi interviewed by Elaine Weitzen, December 11, 1984, 7.

35. "Billy Rose to Give Big Show at Fair," *New York Times,* July 2, 1938, 28.

36. NYWF, box 1552, folder 9, Mr. Fife to Mr. Boone, "Memo on a meeting . . . [of] June 27, 1938," 2.

37. "This Is an Advertisement," *Variety,* August 3, 1938, 56.

38. NYWF, box 540, folder 16, Memorandum from George P. Smith Jr. to Director of Concessions, July 14, 1938, 2.

39. NYWF, box 510, folder 15, George P. Smith Jr. to Director of Concessions, July 20, 1938, 1–2; folder 14, Rose to Whalen, August 4, 1938, and Rose to Whalen, August 15, 1938, and Rose to John Krimsky, August 15, 1938.

40. NYWF, box 510, folder 14, Maurice Mermey to the Amusements Area Board, September 22, 1938.

41. Ibid.

42. "Chatter, Broadway," *Variety,* October 19, 1938, 53.

43. Theodore Strauss, "News and Notes of Night Clubs," *New York Times,* November 13, 1938, section 9, 2.

44. "Rialto Gossip," *New York Times,* October 9, 1938, section 10, 1; NYWF, box 1943, folder 8, "Dickey to Head Rose Projects at New York's Fair," *Billboard,* November 2, 1938; Phil M. Daly, "Along the Rialto," *Film Daily,* November 4, 1938, 3.

45. BHP, MMS Hecht, box 61, folder 1586, Rose to Hecht, April 1, 1944, 1.

46. "A Rose by Any Name You Like," *New York Times,* March 26, 1939, section 10, 2.

47. NYWF, box 510, folder 14, Memorandum from Mr. Cobb to Mr. Whalen, November 14, 1938.

48. NYWF, box 510, folder 14, Memorandum from Mr. Brownell to Messrs. Pach, Flanigan, Bardell, Krimsky, November 17, 1938, and attached signed contract letter from Whalen to Rose of November 16, 1938, 1. Also see letter with contract amendments from Whalen to Rose, November 21, 1938; John Krimsky to Herbert Brownell, November 17, 1938.

49. NYWF, box 1943, Folder 8, Frank T. Farrell, "Eleanor Holm," *New York World-Telegram*, November 17, 1938.

50. John Murray Anderson, *Out without My Rubbers: The Memoirs of John Murray Anderson* (New York: Library, 1954), 182.

51. Brooks McNamara, "The Entertainment District at the End of the 1930s," in *Inventing Times Square: Commerce and Culture at the Crossroads of the World,* ed. William R. Taylor (New York: Russell Sage Foundation, 1991), 188.

52. ECP, Alexander, "Million-Dollar-a-Year Ego," 38.

53. "One observer," quoted in Lewis Erenberg, "Impresarios of Broadway Nightlife," in Taylor, *Inventing Times Square,* 175.

54. F. Scott Fitzgerald, *The Great Gatsby* (New York: Scribner's, 1953), 1.

55. Erenberg, "Impresarios," 173–75.

56. Louis Sobol, *The Longest Street: A Memoir* (New York: Crown, 1968), 178.

57. "The Effendi Billy Rose," *Literary Digest,* July 7, 1934, 19.

58. McNamara, "Entertainment District," 187; Erenberg, "Impresarios," 172.

59. CUL, Rare Book and Manuscript Library, Popular Arts Project, Nita Naldi interview (1958), 5; George Lang, *Nobody Knows the Truffles I've Seen* (New York: Alfred A. Knopf, 1998), 113; private papers of Kerstin Ullrich, Doris Lilly, "Funny Guy: Broadway Billy Rose Was a Showman and a Bore," *Avenue,* June–July 1991, 76.

60. Lys Symonette and Kim H. Kowalke, eds., *Speak Low (When You Speak Love): The Letters of Kurt Weill and Lotte Lenya* (Berkeley: University of California Press, 1996), 291.

61. Saul Bellow, letter to the author, September 3, 1983.

62. Stephen J. Whitfield, *In Search of American Jewish Culture* (Hanover, NH: Brandeis University Press, 1999), 51–53.

63. Saul Bellow, *Humboldt's Gift* (New York: Penguin Books, 1996), 389.

64. Whitfield, *In Search,* 51, 53.

65. MZP, interview notes, "Diamond Horseshoe Notes—Mainly," 1.

66. MZP, *Billy Rose of Broadway*, 523.

67. WHS, Albert R. Johnson Papers, box 10, folder 11, "Advertisement," *New York Mirror*, December 18, 1938.

68. McNamara, "Entertainment District," 188.

69. Theodore Strauss, "News Notes of the Night Clubs," *New York Times*, January 1, 1939, section 9, 2; "Night Club Reviews, Diamond Horseshoe," *Variety*, December 28, 1938, 36; WHS, Albert R. Johnson Papers, box 10, folder 11, "Billy Rose's Diamond Horseshoe, New York," *Billboard*, January 7, 1939, 18.

70. Betsy Blair, *The Memory of All That: Love and Politics in New York, Hollywood, and Paris* (New York: Alfred A. Knopf, 2003), 8–9.

71. "Night Club Reviews, Diamond Horseshoe," 36.

72. Strauss, "News Notes of the Night Clubs"; WHS, "Billy Rose's Diamond Horseshoe," 18.

73. BRTD, Billy Rose Clipping File, Candide, "Only Human, Billy Rose, Chapter One," *New York Daily News*, n.d.

74. "Girls, Girls, Girls," *Fortune*, July 1939, 120–21, 178.

75. ECP, interview folder 2, "Charles Samuels," June 2, 1966, 6.

76. ECP, interview folder 1, "Sal Imbimbo," June 3, 1966, 1–2.

77. Blair, *Memory of All That*, 10, 12–13, 22.

78. ECP, "Sal Imbimbo," 3.

79. Dorothy Rice Chase, interview with the author, May 14, 2015.

80. Lewis Erenberg, "Impresarios of Broadway Nightlife," in *Inventing Times Square: Commerce and Culture at the Crossroads of the World*, ed. William R. Taylor (New York: Russell Sage Foundation, 1991), 175.

81. ECP, research folder 3, S. J. Woolf, "Broadway Barnum," *New York Times Magazine*, April 23, 1939, 7.

82. "Girls, Girls, Girls," 178.

83. WHS, Billy Rose Clippings File, Jimmy Cannon, "Sports Today, Last Visit with Billy Rose," *New York Journal American*, February 14, 1966.

84. NYWF, box 510, folder 15, Technical Adviser to the President ("Dear Mr. Whalen"), May 8, 1939.

85. WHS, Albert R. Johnson Papers, box 4, folder 4, Robert Coleman, "'Aquacade' Triumphs at Worlds Fair; Beauty, Thrills," *New York Mirror*, May 5, 1939.

86. WHS, Albert R. Johnson Papers, box 4, folder 4, John Anderson, "Billy Rose's Aquacade Opens with a Splash," *New York Journal American*, May 5, 1939.

87. Brooks Atkinson, The Play, *New York Times*, May 5, 1939, 28.

88. W. G., "The Theatre in Flushing," *New Yorker*, May 20, 1939, 51.

89. Lavinia, "Around the Fair," *New Yorker*, June 17, 1939, 71.

90. Abel Green, "Billy Rose's Aquacade with $30,000 Weekly Nut Looks No. 1 N.Y. Fair Show," *Variety*, May 10, 1939, 55.

91. NYWF, box 510, folder 16, Billy Rose telegram to Grover Whalen, February 20,

1939, and box 1943, folder 8, Carl Warren, "Fair Decides to Go Girlie in Fun Zone," *Sunday News,* February 19, 1939, 88.

92. MZP, interview notes, "Aquacade," 9.

93. A. J. Liebling, *The Telephone Booth Indian* (New York: Broadway Books, 2004), 47–48.

94. Warren Susman, "'Personality' and the Making of Twentieth-Century Culture," in *New Directions in American Intellectual History,* ed. John Higham and Paul K. Conkin (Baltimore: Johns Hopkins University Press, 1980), 217–19.

95. NYWF, box 1378, folder 6, Mr. Brownell to Commander Flanigan, January 17, 1939, and H. A. Flanigan to Mr. John J. Shubert, January 17, 1939.

96. NYWF, box 1421, folder 5, "The People of the State of New York, Plaintiff, against New York World's Fair 1939 Incorporated, Gotham Productions, Inc. and Billy Rose's Exposition Spectacles, Inc., Defendants," Testimony of Grover A. Whalen, 2.

97. NYWF, Box 510, folder 16, Maurice Mermey to the Vice-President, Jan. 25, 1939.

98. NYWF, box 9, folder 8, "AGREEMENT made this 13th day of April, 1940 [1940 contract between Rose and Fair]," 1 (this contains the only mention of the April 18, 1939, contract); NYWF, box 9, folder 9, "AGREEMENT made this ___ day of June, 1938," 10; NYWF, box 1421, folder 5, "The People of the State of New York, Plaintiff, vs. New York World's Fair 1939 Incorporated, Gotham Productions, Inc. and Billy Rose's Exposition Spectacles, Inc., Defendants," by Lockwood J., January 4, 1940, 3; NYWF, box 1421, folder 5, "People of the State of New York, Plaintiff, against New York World's Fair, Affidavit of G.V. Pach," 3.

99. NYWF, box 9, folder 9, testimony of G. V. Pach, 3.

100. MZP, "Aquacade," 7. Zolotow is the only source that states the $1.6 million exemption from fair participation, and it does explain why the 10 percent participation figure yielded only $4,280 through September 5. If the Aquacade brought in more than $100,000 a week, then it would have realized about $1.65 million through September 5 ($110,000 less than the $1.76 million it made through September 12). A total of $1.65 million, minus the $1.6 million exemption, would have left $50,000 subject to the 10 percent participation rate. This would have given the fair $5,000, which would not be far off from the $4,280 recorded.

101. Agnes de Mille, *Portrait Gallery* (Boston: Houghton Mifflin, 1990), 109.

102. Jessica Weglein, Wendy Scheir, Jill Peterson, Susan Malsbury, and Michelle Schwartz, *New York World's Fair 1939 and 1940 Incorporated Records* (New York: New York Public Library Manuscripts and Archives Division, 2008), ix; "N.Y. Fair's Midway Ops Can't See How They'll Get Even," *Variety,* September 13, 1939, 47; MZP, *Billy Rose,* 438; Green, "Billy Rose's Aquacade"; BRTD, Billy Rose Clipping File, Earl Wilson, "Billy Rose Counts His Aquacade Million While Rest of the Fair Counts Its Debts," *New York Post,* October 26, 1939.

103. MZP, "Aquacade," 9.

104. NYWF, box 1421, folder 5, "People of the State of New York, Plaintiff, vs. New York World's Fair," 5–6.

105. MZP, "Diamond Horseshoe Notes—Mainly," 2.

106. ECP, research correspondence folder 2, J. Grayson to Earl Conrad ("Dear Earl"), n.d., 1.

107. DLP, folder 2.2, typescript page begins, "For about one year I was housekeeper."

108. "N.Y. Fair's Midway Ops," 47.

109. MZP, *Billy Rose,* 438.

110. Weglein et al., *New York World's Fair,* ix.

111. BRTD, Billy Rose Clipping File, Wilson, "Billy Rose Counts His Aquacade Million."

112. "Rose Netted over $1,000,000 in 1939; Wants No Competition for Next Fair," *Variety,* November 22, 1939, 1.

113. ECP, Alexander, "Million-Dollar-a-Year Ego," 17; BRTD, Billy Rose Clipping File, "Rose Made Million, Bids for Coast Fair," *Daily Mirror,* November 23, 1939.

114. "Eleanor Holm Wed to Rose," *New York Times,* November 15, 1939, 19; BRTD, Billy Rose Clipping File, "Miss Holm Wed to Billy Rose at Pecora's Office," *New York Herald Tribune,* n.d. [November 15, 1939].

115. "Two Ballrooms," *Variety,* March 13, 1940, 84.

116. Sobol, *Longest Street,* 269.

117. MZP, "Aquacade," 13; Burton W. Peretti, *Nightclub City: Politics and Amusement in Manhattan* (Philadelphia: University of Pennsylvania Press, 2007), 208.

118. Nelson, *"Only a Paper Moon,"* 118.

119. ECP, interview folder 2, "Helen Schrank," June 22, 1966, 5.

120. ECP, research folder 1, Leonard Lyons, The Lyons Den, October 20, 1966.

121. MZP, *Billy Rose,* 530.

TEN Saving Kurt Schwarz

1. BRTD, Billy Rose Clipping File, Candide, "Only Human, Billy Rose, Chapter One," *New York Daily News,* n.d.

2. Robert M. Fells, *George Arliss: The Man Who Played God* (Lanham, MD: Scarecrow, 2004), 2, 9, 42, 211; Arliss Archives, accessed April 25, 2017, arlissarchives .com/category/radio/disraeli-radio. The radio play aired on January 17, and Rose named Disraeli his hero on January 20.

3. BMB, box 259, Rose to Baruch, October 23, 1936, and Baruch to Rose, November 2, 1936.

4. Irving Howe, quoted in Deborah Dash Moore, *At Home in America: Second Generation New York Jews* (New York: Columbia University Press, 1981), 9.

5. Eli Lederhendler, *New York Jews and the Decline of Urban Ethnicity* (Syracuse, NY: Syracuse University Press, 2001), 13.

6. Steven Bayme, *Jewish Arguments and Counterarguments: Essays and Addresses* (Hoboken, NJ: Ktav, 2002), 195.

7. Stephen J. Whitfield, *In Search of American Jewish Culture* (Hanover, NH: Brandeis University Press, 1999), 92–96.

8. Neal Gabler, *Winchell: Gossip, Power and the Culture of Celebrity* (New York: Vantage Books, 1995), 195, 589.

9. WWP, box 1, folder 3, Rose to Winchell, January 22, 1944.

10. MZP, interview notes, "Casino de Paree," 5.

11. BHP, box 31, folder 790, Walter Winchell [Ben Hecht], On Broadway, *Daily Mirror,* July 31, 1935.

12. Louis Sobol, *The Longest Street: A Memoir* (New York: Crown, 1968), 175–76; MZP, interview notes, "Lyons," 7.

13. "Germans at Rally Felicitate Hitler," *New York Times,* October 4, 1937, 16.

14. Martin Gilbert, *Kristallnacht: Prelude to Destruction* (New York: Harper Perennial, 2006), 13–14.

15. ECP, research folder 2, Frank T. Farrell, "Token of Affection: One $60,000 Pool," *New York World-Telegram,* November 17, 1938.

16. KSP, Rose to Sekretaer Mayestic Hotel Rome [Kurt Schwarz], December 6, 1938.

17. "Billy Rose, Classed in 1-A, Is Eager to Go; Angered by Report He Claimed 61 Dependents," *New York Times,* July 18, 1942, 5.

18. MZP, "On Billy Rose," 4.

19. USCIS, Kurt Schwarz naturalization documents, File Series C-File, Number C-5772388, and File Series AR-2 Form, Number A-1621628; KSP, Helene Schwarz to Kurt, dated Easter Sunday.

20. USCIS, Kurt Schwarz, "Petition for Naturalization"; Stephen McClatchie, ed., *The Mahler Family Letters* (Oxford: Oxford University Press, 2006), 312; Hotel Bristol Vienna, accessed December 25, 2017, www.bristolvienna.com.

21. For Schwarz's arrival in Italy on February 8, 1938, see ACS, Ministero dell'Interno, Direzione Generale della Pubblica Sicurezza, AAA.GG.RR. A16, box 116, f. Schwarz kurt, "Regia Questura di Roma," May 29, 1938.

22. Mary Felstiner, "Refuge and Persecution in Italy, 1933–1945," Museum of Tolerance Online Multimedia Learning Center, 19–20, accessed September 20, 2016, motlc .wiesenthal.com/site/pp.asp?c=gvKVLcMVIuG&b=395073. According to Felstiner, the category of persons most likely to be arrested prior to Hitler's state visit included Jews and "ex-Austrians," making Schwarz's arrest likely. In addition, according to Herb Hillman, the man who told Schwarz's story to Saul Bellow, Schwarz was arrested twice in Italy (JBF, journal entry dated May 24, 1989). Schwarz's arrest in February 1939 for illegal currency dealing is documented. The other arrest must have been in 1938 during Hitler's visit. Finally, in a letter from Helene Schwarz to her son on May 22, 1938, she wonders why he did not receive her letter of April 4 until May 5. Schwarz may have been imprisoned during those weeks and released on May 5, when Hitler had left Rome for Naples. For Schwarz on Italian list of foreign Jews, see "Rubrica speciale degli ebrei stranieri," November 10, 1938, 133. That page lists 67 names, and multiplying this number by

130 yields 8,700 names without the additional pages that list last names starting with T through Z. The author thanks Anna Pizzuti for this document. A census of August 1938 found 9,445 foreign Jews in Italy. See Michele Sarfatti, *The Jews in Mussolini's Italy: From Equality to Persecution* (Madison: University of Wisconsin Press, 2006), 127. Another historian puts the number at 10,173. See Susan Zuccotti, "The Italian Racial Laws, 1938–1943: A Reevaluation," in *Studies in Contemporary Jewry,* vol. 13, *The Fate of the European Jews, 1939–1945: Continuity or Contingency?,* ed. Jonathan Frankel (New York: Oxford University Press, 1997), 135.

23. Zuccotti, "Italian Racial Laws," 143.

24. KSP, Helene Schwarz to Kurt, March 4, 1939; Elizabeth Schachter, "Carlo Alberto Viterbo: A Neglected Figure of Italian Judaism," *Italianist* 33, no. 3 (October 2013): 510–11.

25. Richard Pankhurst, "Plans for Mass Jewish Settlement in Ethiopia (1936–1943)," *Tezeta, a Collection of Articles Published on 'Ethiopia Observer' in the 60s and 70s,* April 20, 2005, tezetaethiopia.wordpress.com. Schwarz partnered with the German Jewish journalist Karl Marx in a scheme to obtain foreign currency to help them escape Italy. Marx planned to go to Ethiopia. ACS, Ministero dell'Interno, Divis. Poliz. Politica, fasc. Personali (1927–1944), Faccon 105, Bender, Trude, 2 (of 3).

26. JBF, journal entry dated May 24, 1989.

27. "Italy Exiles Jews Entering since '19," *New York Times,* September 2, 1938, 1.

28. S. N. Behrman Papers, Manuscripts and Archives Division, New York Public Library, box 21, folder 2, Manfred Furst to S. N. Behrman, November 3, 1938, 2.

29. Al Hirschfeld Papers, Archives of American Art, Smithsonian Institution, Letters, 1939, Vazsonyi Hirschfeld Gizella to Hirschfeld, April 11, 1939, 1, www.aaa.si.edu /collections.

30. "Radio Personals," *Motion Picture Daily,* January 12, 1939, 8.

31. Rose's Refugee Show for N.Y. May Switch," *Variety,* January 11, 1939, 41; "Chatter, Broadway," *Variety,* February 1, 1939, 53; United Press, "Billy Rose Stages 'All-Refugee' Show," *Pittsburgh Press,* January 30, 1939, 4.

32. Theodore Strauss, "Notes of Night Clubs," *New York Times,* January 29, 1939, section 9, 2; "Benefit for Refugees," *New York Times,* February 24, 1939, 21.

33. Michele Sarfatti, "Characteristics and Objectives of the Anti-Jewish Racial Laws in Fascist Italy, 1938–1943," in *Jews in Italy under Fascist and Nazi Rule, 1922–1945,* ed. Joshua D. Zimmerman (Cambridge: Cambridge University Press, 2005), 75.

34. Zuccotti, "Italian Racial Laws," 143. Emigrants were allowed to take only 2,500 lira. The historian Klaus Voigt, letter to the author, November 3, 2014; Nuno Valero, "National States and Central Banks in the Mediterranean World in the Interwar Period," in *Banking and Finance in the Mediterranean: A Historical Perspective,* ed. John A. Consiglio, Juan Carlos Martinez Oliva, and Gabriel Tortella (Farnham, UK: Ashgate, 2012), 207.

35. For Karl Marx, see Margarete Myers Feinstein, "Jewish Observance in Amalek's Shadow: Mourning, Marriage, and Birth Rituals among Displaced Persons in

Germany," in *"We Are Here": New Approaches to Jewish Displaced Persons in Postwar Germany,* ed. Avinoam J. Patt and Michael Berkowitz (Detroit: Wayne State University Press, 2010), 261.

36. National Archives, United Kingdom, KV 2/3266, "Carl Marx, alias Auguste: German," Statement by Karl MARX—Translation of "Appendix 3, Rome," 5. Marx was arrested on January 26, 1939, and since he and Schwarz worked together the latter must have been arrested the same day. Marx admitted he "helped Jews who had to leave the country on account of the new laws to get money out." For the imprisonment of Marx and Schwarz as conspirators, see ACS, MI, DGPS, AAA.GG.RR. A16, b.116, f. Schwarz kurt, Direzione Generale della P.S __ Divisione Polizia Politica, N. 500/4219, February 9, 1939.

37. KSP, Rose telegram to Schwarz, January 29, 1939.

38. KSP, Schwarz passport; "List or Manifest of Alien Passengers for the United States Immigrant Inspector at Port of Call," SS *Rex,* arriving at Port of New York, March 23, 1939, list 20, line 6, Schwarz, Kurt, accessed February 5, 2018, www.ancestry.com.

39. KSP, Rose telegram to Schwarz, February 22, 1939, and "Mein geliebtes Alles!" [Helene Schwarz to Kurt Schwarz], March 4, 1939. I assume Helene Schwarz wrote her son the day she received his letter.

40. KSP, Helene Schwarz to Billy Rose, March 16, 1939. She mailed the letter to Rose at his Casa Mañana club.

41. KSP, Rose telegram to Schwarz, care of commissioner of immigration and naturalization, Ellis Island, NY, n.d.

42. "List or Manifest," SS *Rex,* line 6, Schwarz, Kurt; "Record of Aliens Held for Special Inquiry," SS *Rex* (Italian Lines), arrived on March 23, 1939, accessed February 5, 2018, www.ancestry.com.

43. "Press Stunt Raided in Times Sq.," *Variety,* March 29, 1939, 25.

44. KSP, "Mein geliebtes teures Alles!" [Helene Schwarz to Kurt Schwarz], May 7, 1939, 1; Helene Schwarz ("Mama") to Kurt Schwarz, May 14, 1939, 3; and "Mein unsagbar geliebtes" [Helene Schwarz ("Mama") to Kurt Schwarz], May 17, 1939, 6.

45. KSP, Billy Rose to Kurt Schwarz, June 21, 1939; USCIS, Kurt Schwarz, "Petition for Naturalization."

46. Guy Jean Forgue, *Letters of H.L. Mencken* (New York: Knopf, 1961), 203.

47. Leonard Dinnerstein, *Antisemitism in America* (New York: Oxford University Press, 1994), 114.

48. Ibid., 115–19.

49. Jane Morgan Weintraub, interview with the author, April 25, 2014; Miriam H. Weingarten, interview with the author, September 11, 2017.

50. Quoted in Erik Lee Preminger, *Gypsy & Me* (Boston: Little, Brown, 1984), 168.

51. MZP, interview notes, "Shorthand," 9.

52. Lee Grant, *I Said Yes to Everything* (New York: Penguin, 2014), 166–68.

ELEVEN We Will Never Die

1. Garrett Eisler, "'This Theatre Is a Battlefield': Political Performance and Jewish-American Identity, 1933–1948" (PhD diss., City University of New York, 2012), 1.

2. Lindbergh, quoted in ibid., 76.

3. Michael Denning, *The Cultural Front: The Laboring of American Culture in the Twentieth Century* (London: Verso, 1998), 4–5, 9–10.

4. Eisler, "'This Theatre,'" v.

5. Ichiro Takayoshi, *American Writers and the Approach of World War II, 1935–1941* (New York: Cambridge University Press, 2015), 80, 91.

6. "Topics of the Times," *New York Times,* January 2, 1940, 8.

7. Brooks Atkinson, "Melancholy Time of Year," *New York Times,* March 10, 1940, section 11, 1.

8. Brooks Atkinson, The Play, *New York Times,* March 7, 1940, 18.

9. Brooks Atkinson, "'The Fifth Column,'" *New York Times,* March 17, 1940, section 10, 1.

10. "Hemingway Play 'The Fifth Column' Brings Madrid Bombing to Broadway," *Life,* March 25, 1940, 100; Wolcott Gibbs, "The Theatre, Saint Dorothy," *New Yorker,* March 16, 1940, 44.

11. Verna Kale, "The Fifth Column: A Play by Ernest Hemingway," *Hemingway Review* 27, no. 2 (Spring 2008): 132.

12. TGA, MSS 436, Series 1, Correspondence and Subject Files, box 188, folder 4809, Rose to Lawrence Langner, April 22, 1940.

13. SGP, Robert E. Sherwood correspondence, folder 3816, Sherwood telegram to Samuel Goldwyn, April 18, 1941.

14. Brooks Atkinson, "Billy Rose Gives Show at Fort Dix," *New York Times,* May 29, 1941, 14.

15. Brooks Atkinson, "Trouping at Fort Dix," *New York Times,* June 8, 1941, section 9, 1.

16. BRTD, George S. Kaufman Papers, *ZC-264, reel 3, Henry L. Stimson, secretary of war, to George Kaufman, February 15, 1941.

17. Scott Meredith, *George S. Kaufman and His Friends* (New York: Doubleday, 1974), 181.

18. Mark Shechner, "Dear Mr. Einstein: Jewish Comedy and the Contradictions of Culture," in *Jewish Wry: Essays on Jewish Culture,* ed. Sarah Blacher Cohen (Detroit: Wayne State University Press, 1987), 144–45.

19. Michael Galchinsky, "Beatrice Kaufman, 1895–1945," *Jewish Women's Archive Encyclopedia,* accessed November 8, 2016, jwa.org/encyclopedia/article/kaufman-beatrice.

20. Stephen J. Whitfield, *In Search of American Jewish Culture* (Hanover, NH: Brandeis University Press, 1999), 62.

21. Ralph Ingersoll to Ben Hecht, December 19, 1940, 2 (letter held by author); Denning, *Cultural Front,* 95.

22. Ben Hecht, *1001 Afternoons in New York* (New York: Viking, 1941), 165.

23. Ibid., 166–67.

24. Michael A. Meyer, *The Origins of the Modern Jew* (Detroit: Wayne State University Press, 1967), 8.

25. Quoted in Eisler, "'This Theatre,'" 78.

26. "Freedom Rally Thrills 17,000," *New York Times,* October 6, 1941, 1.

27. BRTD, Helen Hayes Papers, box 5, folder 13, Ben Hecht and Charles MacArthur, "Fun to Be Free," in *It's Fun to Be Free* (New York: Stage, Screen, Radio and Arts Division, Fight For Freedom, 1941), n.p.

28. Eisler, "'This Theatre,'" 81.

29. Ibid., 93, 79.

30. Monty Noam Penkower, "In Dramatic Dissent: The Bergson Boys," in *The Nazi Holocaust: Historical Articles on the Destruction of European Jew,* ed. Michael R. Marrus, part 8, *Bystanders to the Holocaust* (Westport, CT: Meckler, 1989), 2:827.

31. Ibid., 2:826.

32. Hecht, *1001 Afternoons,* 364.

33. BHP, box 55, folder 1069, Bergson to Hecht, August 28, 1941, and Bergson to Hecht, September 12, 1941.

34. Ben Hecht, *Child of the Century* (New York: Simon and Schuster, 1954), 516–17, 522.

35. Nina S. Spiegel, *Embodying Hebrew Culture: Aesthetics, Athletics, and Dance in the Jewish Community of Mandate Palestine* (Detroit: Wayne State University Press, 2013), 59, 9, 19–20.

36. Rafael Medoff and Chaim I. Waxman, *The A to Z of Zionism* (Lanham, MD: Scarecrow, 2009), 41.

37. Jonathan D. Sarna, "A Projection of America as It Ought to Be: Zion in the Mind's Eye of American Jews," in *Envisioning Israel: The Changing Ideals and Images of North American Jews,* ed. Allon Gal (Detroit: Wayne State University Press, 1996), 57–59.

38. Yitshaq Ben-Ami, "The Irgun and the Destruction of European Jewry," in *Perspectives on the Holocaust,* ed. Randolph L. Braham (Boston: Kluwer-Nijhoff, 1983), 82.

39. ECP, interview folder 2, "Helen Schrank," June 22, 1966, 7.

40. Quoted in Sidney Zion, *Read All about It!* (New York: Penguin, 1984), 142.

41. Henry L. Feingold, "Stephen Wise and the Holocaust," in Marrus, *Nazi Holocaust,* part 8, *Bystanders,* 2:756.

42. BHP, box 61, folder 1586, Rose to Hecht, May 2, 1944.

43. Walter Laqueur, *The Terrible Secret: Suppression of the Truth about Hitler's "Final Solution"* (New York: Henry Holt, 1998), 68, 76.

44. "Nazi Punishment Seen by Roosevelt," *New York Times,* July 22, 1942, 1, 4.

45. Associated Press, "Wise Gets Confirmations," *New York Times,* November 25, 1942, 10; Penkower, "In Dramatic Dissent," 824.

46. Ben Hecht, "The Extermination of the Jews," *American Mercury,* February 1943, 194, 196.

47. Hecht, *Child of the Century,* 551–52.

48. Eisler, "'This Theatre,'" 118, 120.

49. Stephen J. Whitfield, "The Politics of Pageantry, 1936–1946," *American Jewish History* 84, no. 3 (September 1996): 237.

50. Quoted in Kitty Carlisle Hart, *Kitty: An Autobiography* (New York: Doubleday, 1988), 148–49.

51. Hecht, *Child of the Century,* 553.

52. ASA, *We Will Never Die,* official souvenir program, Hollywood Bowl, n.p.; Whitfield, "Politics of Pageantry," 238.

53. Whitfield, "Politics of Pageantry," 221–22.

54. Plans for productions in Philadelphia, Washington, DC, and Chicago were in place when the New York show opened. See "40,000 Here View Memorial to Jews," *New York Times,* March 10, 1943, 12.

55. Monty Noam Penkower, *The Holocaust and Israel Reborn: From Catastrophe to Sovereignty* (Urbana: University of Illinois Press, 1994), 83.

56. Erika Fischer-Lichte, *Theatre, Sacrifice, Ritual: Exploring Forms of Political Theatre* (London: Routledge, 2005), 163, 165–66, 174; Robert Skloot, *"We Will Never Die:* The Success and Failure of a Holocaust Pageant," *Theatre Journal* 37, no. 2 (May 1985): 175.

57. Whitfield, "Politics of Pageantry," 240–41.

58. USCCAL, Edward G. Robinson Collection, box 42, folder 20, "Proclamation."

59. Whitfield, "Politics of Pageantry," 239.

60. David S. Wyman Institute for Holocaust Studies, "Shattering the Silence: We Will Never Die," photograph of Billy Rose at Yeshiva College, accessed November 22, 2016, wymaninstitute.org/special/bergsonexhibit/we-will-never-die.php.

61. Skloot, *"We Will Never Die,"* 175.

62. BGRI, Hillel Kook Collection, group 690, series no. 2, box 4, folder 8, Leonard Lyons, The Lyons Den, *New York Post,* March 3, 1943.

63. LOC, George and Ira Gershwin Collection, Correspondence, box 66, Van–Z, Weill to Gershwin, April 5, 1943.

64. Rafael Medoff, *Militant Zionism in America: The Rise and Impact of the Jabotinsky Movement in the United States, 1926–1948* (Tuscaloosa: University of Alabama Press, 2002), 85.

65. BRTD, John Golden Papers, 1874–1971, 8-MWEZ + n.c. 25,780, 27.27, Rose, Billy [1944], Siegel to Rose, February 23, 1943.

66. BGRI, Hillel Kook Collection, "Memo from the National Headquarters of the Committee for a Jewish Army," February 5, 1943, 6, and "Broadway Greets 'Harriet' Tonight," *New York Times,* March 3, 1943.

67. "Radio Preview of 'We Will Never Die,'" *Brooklyn Daily Eagle,* March 6, 1943, 14.

68. Whitfield, "Politics of Pageantry," 240.

69. "40,000 Here," 12.

70. Whitfield, "Politics of Pageantry," 242.

71. Arthur Pollock, The Theater, *Brooklyn Daily Eagle,* March 10, 1943, 9.

72. Skloot, *"We Will Never Die,"* 176–77.

73. Whitfield, "Politics of Pageantry," 241.

74. "Washington to See Pageant of Jewish Race at Constitution Hall April 12," *Washington Post,* March 28, 1943, 8.

75. BRTD, Howard Bay Papers, box 40, folder "Correspondence, 1939–1956," Rose to Howard Bay, April 8, 1943.

76. Penkower, "In Dramatic Dissent," 832; ASA, invitation to *We Will Never Die* in Washington, DC

77. BHP, box 31, folder 794, "'Narrator's Pitch' written for Washington."

78. FDR Presidential Library and Museum, Digital Collections, Holocaust/Refugee Collection, Additional Materials from the ER Papers, My Day column, April 14, 1943, www.fdrlibrary.marist.edu/_resources/images/hol/ho100439.pdf.

79. Jewish Federation Council of Greater Los Angeles, Community Relations Committee Collection 2, box 7, folder 21, Harry Maizlish to Leon Lewis, July 26, 1943.

80. BRTD, "Interview with Billy Rose on the Long John Nebel radio show, Aug. 5, 1965," audio disc 3.

TWELVE Abracadabra

1. SGP, Mayo, Virginia, folder 3600, Rose to Goldwyn, January 5, 1943; Ralph Blumenthal, *Stork Club: America's Most Famous Nightspot and the Lost World of Café Society* (Boston: Little, Brown, 2000), 2; ECP, research folder 3, Alice Davidson, "Rembrandts and Roast Beef," *New York Post,* December 13, 1943, daily magazine and comic section; Michael Korda, *Another Life: A Memoir of Other People* (New York: Random House, 1999), 66.

2. Rare Books and Special Collections, Princeton University Libraries, Harper & Bros. records, box 26, folder 1, George T. Bye to Cass Canfield at Harper, July 15, 1940; Robert Mankoff, ed., *The Complete Cartoons of the "New Yorker"* (New York: Black Dog and Leventhal, 2004), disc 1, 184; "Billy Rose Buys Benton," *Art Digest,* November 15, 1940, 11; CUL, Columbia Center for Oral History, *Thomas Hart Benton Memoir,* 155; Justin Wolff, *Thomas Hart Benton: A Life* (New York: Farrar, Straus and Giroux, 2012), 266.

3. Clifford Odets, *The Time Is Ripe: The 1940 Journal of Clifford Odets* (New York: Grove, 1988), 121, 204–5, 210.

4. ECP, interview folder 1, "Dave Dreyer," June 6, 1966, 3.

5. Lee E. Cooper, "Billy Rose Buys Home in Beekman Place; Pays Cash for Former Reynolds Residence," *New York Times,* December 28, 1939, 38; Jeremy Gerard, "William S. Paley, Builder of CBS, Dies at 89," *New York Times,* October 27, 1990.

6. WPP, Billy Rose, Acc 2388, Ser. 10, box 31, "Rooms with Imagination" [unidentified article], and "By Agnes" [fragment of a news article dating from the spring of 1940].

7. "Life Calls on Billy Rose & Wife," *Life,* May 13, 1940, 112–17.

8. HML, "By Agnes."

9. Ibid.

10. Quoted in John Murray Anderson, *Out without My Rubbers: The Memoirs of John Murray Anderson* (New York: Library, 1954), 187.

11. Ferenc Molnar, *Companion in Exile* (New York: Gaer Associates, 1950), 202, 176.

12. Gabriel Miller, introduction to Odets, *Time Is Ripe,* 1.

13. Odets, *Time Is Ripe,* 65, 225, 232.

14. Ibid., 192.

15. Margaret Brenman-Gibson, *Clifford Odets, American Playwright* (New York: Atheneum, 1981), 296.

16. Odets, *Time Is Ripe,* 209.

17. Harold Clurman, *The Fervent Years: The Story of the Group Theatre and the Thirties* (New York: Hill and Wang, 1957), 260.

18. BRTD, John Anderson Papers, MWEZ + n.c. 16,210, John Anderson, "'In Time to Come' and 'Clash by Night' Open on Broadway," *New York Evening Journal,* December 29, 1941; Gerald Weales, *Clifford Odets, Playwright* (New York: Pegasus, 1971), 150; Gilbert Miller, *Clifford Odets* (New York: Continuum, 1989), 126, 134, 136.

19. ECP, research correspondence folder 2, Wolfe Kaufman to Earl Conrad, n.d.

20. Houghton Library, Harvard University, Modern Books and Manuscripts, John Mason Brown Papers, 1922–1967, Series I, Letters to John Mason Brown, 4488, Rose, Billy, Rose to Brown, January 30, 1942.

21. COP, Box 8, Series: Diaries and Calendars, folder 4, Rose to Odets, November 27, 1950, 1.

22. Billy Rose, *Wine, Women and Words* (New York: Pocketbook, 1950), 91, 108–9.

23. "So What . . . ?," *New Castle Tribune,* May 7, 1943, 4.

24. Alva Johnston, "The Wahoo Boy—II," *New Yorker,* November 17, 1934, 29.

25. "Club Man Buys Bedford Farm," *New Castle Tribune,* January 14, 1949, 4; "Art Treasures May Have Burned in Fire," *New Castle Tribune,* April 5, 1956, 1.

26. ECP, interview folder 1, "Advanced Music Corporation" (Chester Conn), June 1, 1966, 2.

27. Rose, *Wine,* 109.

28. ECP, research correspondence folder 2, Wolfe Kaufman to Earl Conrad, n.d. ["dear oil"].

29. Sally Guard, "Still Very Much in the Swim," *Sports Illustrated,* June 15, 1992. According to Gemma Cook at the Churchill Archives Centre, during Churchill's visit to the States in March 1946 he had "time for socializing" and a dinner scheduled for March 18 with a few millionaires. E-mail correspondence held by author.

30. Bennett Cerf, *Try and Stop Me* (New York: Simon and Schuster, 1945), 60.

31. SGP, Correspondence, folder 243, Lynn Farnol to Goldwyn, November 19, 1947.

32. RAG, box 22, folder 12, Ruth Goetz, "My Life as a Wife," 6, 8.

33. Ibid., 6.

34. "Billy Rose to Take Charge of Rally Features," *New Castle Tribune*, April 9, 1943, 1; "Eleanor Holm Will Take Part in Rally; Sales over $250,000," *New Castle Tribune*, April 16, 1943, 1.

35. Antoine Gilly, "Pots and Pans," *New Castle News*, August 31, 1951, 6.

36. Karl Katz, interview with the author, April 4, 2014.

37. LOC, Manuscript Division, Lee Strasberg Papers, Rose to Strasberg, December 23, 1955.

38. "Diamond Horseshoe," *Life*, July 26, 1943, 75–78.

39. NYPL, Schomburg Center, "An Interview with Dick Campbell," disc 3.

40. ECP, interview folder 2, "Charles Samuels," May 31, 1966, n.p. [2].

41. Lewis Nichols, The Play, *New York Times*, December 3, 1943, 26; ECP, research folder 3, Alice Davidson, "Rembrandts and Roast Beef," *New York Post*, December 13, 1943.

42. Marilyn Nissenson, *The Lady Upstairs: Dorothy Schiff and the New York Post* (New York: St. Martin's Griffin, 2007), 135–36.

43. ASA, Gloria Lubar and Edward F. van der Veen, "Bergson Admits His Committee Has No Right to Collect Funds," *Washington Post*, October 4, 1944, 15.

44. Arnold Aronson, "Architect of Dreams: The Theatrical Vision of Joseph Urban," Columbia University Web Resources, accessed October 8, 2017, www.columbia.edu/cu/lweb/eresources/archives/rbml/urban/architectOfDreams/text.html.

45. Christopher Innes, *Designing Modern America: Broadway to Main Street* (New Haven, CT: Yale University Press, 2005), 60–61; Murray Schumach, "About the Ziegfeld and How It Got to Be 21 Years Old Today," *New York Times*, February 1, 1948, section 10, 3; Sam Zolotow, "Premiere Tonight of 'South Pacific,'" *New York Times*, December 29, 1943, 15; BHP, box 61, folder 1586, Rose to Hecht, April 1, 1944. Apparently New York's city comptroller, Lazarus Joseph, gave Rose inside information on the Ziegfeld auction. See ECP, research correspondence folder 2, Wolfe [Kaufman] to Earl Conrad, n.d., and Wolfe to Conrad, October 26, [1966].

46. For the September 1, 1944, party at the Ziegfeld, see TGA, box 188 f. 4808, Wolfe Kaufman to Theresa Hellburn [*sic*], August 31, 1944.

47. Louis Rapoport, *Shake Heaven & Earth: Peter Bergson and the Struggle to Rescue the Jews of Europe* (Jerusalem: Gefen, 1999), 75; Rafael Medoff, *Militant Zionism in America: The Rise and Impact of the Jabotinsky Movement in the United States, 1926–1948* (Tuscaloosa: University of Alabama Press, 2002), 87.

48. Edward David Pinsky, "Cooperation among American Jewish Organizations in Their Efforts to Rescue European Jewry during the Holocaust, 1939–1945" (PhD diss., New York University, 1980), 393, 410, 413, 416–17, 421.

49. BHP, box 61, folder 1586, Rose to Hecht, April 1, 1944.

50. BHP, box 61, folder 1586, Rose to Hecht, January 30, 1944.

51. Franklin D. Roosevelt, *Public Papers of the Presidents of the United States: F. D. Roosevelt, 1944–45* (Washington, DC: US Government Printing Office, 1950), 48–50.

52. Richard Breitman and Allan J. Lichtman, *FDR and the Jews* (Cambridge, MA: Belknap Press of Harvard University Press, 2013), 262.

53. BHP, box 61, folder 1586, Rose to Hecht, January 30, 1944.

54. BHP, box 55, folder 1069, Bergson to Hecht, March 10, 1944; WWP, box 1, folder 3, Rose to Winchell, January 22, 1944.

55. BHP, box 61, folder 1533, Perkins to Hecht, January 25, 1944.

56. BHP, box 61, folder 1586, Rose to Hecht, March 6, 1944.

57. BHP, box 61, folder 1586, Rose to Hecht, April 27, 1944, and March 29, 1944.

58. BHP, box 61, folder 1586, Rose to Hecht, March 29, 1944, and April 1, 1944.

59. BHP, box 61, folder 1586, Rose to Hecht, April 19, 1944.

60. BHP, box 61, folder 1586, Rose to Hecht, April 17, 1944.

61. BHP, box 55, folder 1069, Bergson to Hecht, March 28, 1944; BHP, box 61, folder 1586, Rose to Hecht, April 6, 1944.

62. BHP, box 61, folder 1586, Rose to Hecht, April 25, 1944.

63. BHP, box 61, folder 1586, Rose to Hecht, May 9, 1944.

64. BHP, box 61, folder 1586, Rose to Hecht, June 12, 1944.

65. BHP, box 61, folder 1586, Rose to Hecht, June 27, 1944.

66. BHP, box 61, folder 1586, Rose to Hecht, March 25, 1944.

67. BHP, box 61, folder 1586, Rose to Hecht, May 2, 1944.

68. LOC, Maurice Rosenblatt Papers, box 79, folder 11, Wise to Ickes, December 22, 1943.

69. Quoted in Medoff, *Militant Zionism*, 187.

70. ASA, "Announcement of the Formation of a Hebrew Committee"; LOC, Maurice Rosenblatt Papers, box 79, folder 11, Wise to Ickes, December 22, 1943, and American Zionist Emergency Council to [deleted name], October 24, 1944. The letter references earlier letters of July 6 and August 31.

71. NYPL, Dorothy Schiff Papers, box 24, folder "Hebrew Committee for National Liberation, 1944, Jan. 5–Dec. 30; 1945, Feb. 16–Aug. 11," Peter Bergson to Theodore Thackery, July 9, 1944, 2.

72. Rapoport, *Shake Heaven & Earth,* 75; "Hebrew Committee for National Liberation Established; Attacked by Jewish Groups," Jewish Telegraphic Agency, May 19, 1944, www.jta.org/archive.

73. LOC, Maurice Rosenblatt Papers, box 79, folder 2, "Memoir," chap. 3, 1.

74. NYPL MA, Dorothy Schiff Papers, box 24, folder "Hebrew Committee," Gloria Lubar and Edward F. van der Veen, "Bergson Admits $1,000,000 Fund Raised, Vague on Its Use," *Washington Post,* October 3, 1944, 1, B-1, and Bergson to Theodore Thackery, October 10, 1944, and Lubar, "Bergson Admits His Committee Has No Right to Collect Funds," *Washington Post,* October 4, 1944, 1, 15.

75. BHP, box 61, folder 1586, Rose to Hecht, April 1, 1944, 1. On the other hand, despite Bergson's 1944 claim that Rose gave him money, in a much later interview he said, "Billy Rose was a terribly stingy bastard, but he never took a penny. He was a very fabulously wealthy man, and he never gave [us] a nickel. But he did a lot of work, he did a lot of work, and very good work." David Wyman, "'Confronting the Holocaust': Historian David Wyman Interviews Hillel Kook, Who Led the Effort in the U.S. to Push American Leaders to Rescue European Jews," in *A People's History of World War II,* ed. Marc Favreau (New York: New Press, 2011), 151.

76. UTA, Morris Ernst Collection, 53.1, Rose to Ernst, October 21, 1944.

77. "David Dubinsky, 90, Dies; Led Garment Union," *New York Times,* September 18, 1982; Fred Rodell, "Morris Ernst," *Life,* February 21, 1944, 97.

78. Ira M. Beck Memorial Archives, University of Denver, Owen Chariton, "Max Goldberg of Denver: Philanthropist, Fundraiser and Rose Hospital Founder," *Rocky Mountain Jewish Historical Notes,* Winter/Spring 2000, 3–4.

79. LOC, Irving Berlin Collection, Correspondence, box 354, Rose to Berlin, May 4, 1945.

80. "'Black Book of Polish Jewry' Estimates 1,000,000 Polish Jews Killed by Nazis," Jewish Telegraphic Agency, December 15, 1943, www.jta.org/archive; Michael Fleming, *Auschwitz, the Allies and Censorship of the Holocaust* (Cambridge: Cambridge University Press, 2014), 193, 191; BRTD, "Interview with Billy Rose on the Long John Nebel radio show, Aug. 5, 1965," audio disc 3.

81. "$30,000 for Rose Memorial," *New York Times,* August 30, 1945, 19.

82. "The Origin of the Rose Medical Center, Denver, Colorado," accessed October 3, 2017, coloradohealthcarehistory.com.

83. Bertram D. Hulen, "President Orders Eisenhower to End New Abuse of Jews," *New York Times,* September 30, 1945, 1.

84. BMB, Series 1B: Selected Correspondence, 1912–1965, vol. 117, folder 96, Rose to Baruch, October 31, 1945.

85. BRTD, "Interview with Billy Rose," audio disc 3.

86. AJJDC, NY AR45–54 00034 00925-Zeilsheim, Koppel S. Pinson, "Education Report for Zeilsheim," 1; UNRRA, Record Number S-1303–0000–1940, folder "U.S. Zone—Team 503—Zeilsheim, 2/9/1945—15/7/1946," "week ended 16. 11. 45," 1, no. 31; UNRRA, Record Number S-1301–0000–1086, folder 060, Rose, Billy, "Incoming Telegram," December 2, 1945.

87. Hebrew University, Institute of Contemporary Jewry, Oral History Division, "The Role of the American Jewish Chaplains in Assisting the Remnants of European Jewry," interview with Eli Heimberg, tape no. c/861, entry dated December 8, 1945. The Heimberg folder contains Heimberg's letters to his wife.

88. General Mark W. Clark Collection, The Citadel Archives and Museum, Charleston, SC, box 66, vol. 10, Diaries, December 8, 1945, 100, 105.

89. "Billy Rose Reports Polish Jewish Abused; Suggests UNRRA Force a House-cleaning," *New York Times,* December 17, 1945, 5.

90. General Mark W. Clark Collection, box 5, folder 8, Rose to Clark, December 21, 1945.

THIRTEEN A Flag Is Born

1. UNRRA, Record Number S-0436–0042–06, folder "U.S. Zone—Team 311—Landsberg, 11/8/1945–15/10/1946," Assistant District Medical Officer (Dr. A. Sainz de la Pena) to Files, November 24, 1945; AJJDC, NY AR45–54 00034 00925-Zeilsheim, Koppel S. Pinson, "Education Report for Zeilsheim," 3.

2. "Billy Rose Reports Polish Jewish Abused; Suggests UNRRA Force a House-cleaning," *New York Times,* December 17, 1945, 5.

3. LOC, Manuscript Division, Lee Strasberg Papers, Rose to Strasberg, September 25, 1959.

4. "Lehman Warns of Moral Decay Unless Palestine Opens to Jews," *New York Times,* June 21, 1946, 6; I. F. Stone, *Underground to Palestine* (New York: Boni and Gaer, 1946), xiii.

5. Rafael Medoff, "When Leonard Bernstein 'Dug' the Irgun," *Forward,* September 4, 2008, forward.com/opinion/14142/when-leonard-bernstein-dug-the-irgun-02473; Erika Fischer-Lichte, *Theatre, Sacrifice, Ritual: Exploring Forms of Political Theatre* (New York: Routledge, 2005), 195; Arthur A. Goren, "A 'Golden Decade' for American Jews: 1945–1955," in *American Jewish History,* ed. Jeffrey S. Gurock, vol. 4, *American Jewish Life, 1920–1990* (New York: Routledge, 1998), 19.

6. AJJDC, NY AR45–54 00179 00022, "Meeting of the Emergency Administration Committee," April 2, 1946, "Remarks by the Chairman," no. 5, n.p., and NY AR45–54 00179 00016, "Meeting of the Emergency Administration Committee," April 9, 1946, "Remarks by the Chairman," no. 5, 1; Frank Emerson Andrews, *Philanthropic Giving* (New York: Russell Sage Foundation, 1950), 177.

7. NYPL, Schomburg Center, "An Interview with Dick Campbell," disc 3; "Billy Rose Has a Big First Night," *Life,* December 25, 1944, 24–26; William Du Bois, "Erstwhile Mahout Captures Sixth Avenue," *New York Times,* December 10, 1944, section 2, 1; "Closing on Feb. 10 for 'Carmen Jones,'" *New York Times*, February 2, 1945, 16.

8. CUL, oral history interview with Kitty Carlisle Hart, 1979, 5:692–93.

9. Bosley Crowther, "Between the Eyes," *New York Times,* May 6, 1945, section 2, 1; Agnes de Mille, *Portrait Gallery* (Boston: Houghton Mifflin, 1990), 113.

10. "$75,000 for a Rembrandt," *New York Times,* October 26, 1945, 21; "Auction News," in *The New International Year Book: A Compendium of the World's Progress for the Year 1946,* ed. Charles Earle Funk (New York: Funk and Wagnalls, 1947), 63; BRTD, Billy Rose Clipping File, Walter Winchell, "New York," n.d.

11. Sidney Skolsky, "Movie Gossip from Hollywood," *New Castle News,* February 21, 1946, 12; MHL, Paramount Pictures contract summaries, subject files, 15-f. 1422, Rose, Billy 1946.

12. AJJDC, "Meeting of the Emergency Administration Committee," April 2,

1946, "Remarks by the Chairman," n.p., and "Meeting of the Emergency Administration Committee," April 9, 1946, "Remarks by the Chairman," 1.

13. "Film Leaders Pledge a Million to the UJA," *Motion Picture Daily,* April 16, 1946, 1, 6.

14. Theatre Guild Archive, Yale Collection of American Literature, Beinecke Rare Book and Manuscript Library, Yale University, box 188, folder 4809, Rose to Lawrence Langner, April 9, 1946, and Rose to Helburn, April 22, 1946; "Mrs. Roosevelt to Address UJA Dinner April 30," *Film Daily,* April 16, 1946, 1, 4; "Trade's $1,000,000 N.Y.-UJA Quota," *Billboard,* April 27, 2016, 52.

15. "ITOA Meet Yields $80,000 for UJA," *Motion Picture Daily,* April 26, 1946, 7; "$80,000 for UJA Pledged at ITOA Meet," *Film Daily,* April 26, 1946, 1; Eleanor Roosevelt, My Day, May 3, 1946, www2.gwu.edu/~erpapers/myday.

16. "UJA Raises Half of Industry Quota," *Film Daily,* May 1, 1946, 1; "Raise $501,000 at N.Y. Dinner for Fund," *Showmen's Trade Review,* May 4, 1946, 18.

17. LOC, Irving Berlin Collection, Correspondence, box 354, Berlin to Rose, July 24, 1946, and Rose to Berlin, July 26, 1946.

18. Howard Morley Sachar, *A History of the Jews in America* (New York: Vintage Books, 1993), 559; Edward S. Shapiro, *A Time for Healing: American Jewry since World War II* (Baltimore: Johns Hopkins University Press, 1992), 63.

19. "200 Honor Rose," *Motion Picture Daily,* December 13, 1946, 4; "Baruch to Present Rose Award at FJP Dinner," *Film Daily,* December 10, 1946, 1, 4.

20. AJJDC, NY AR45–54 00189 0353, Bergson to Rose, May 10, 1946; NY AR45–54 00189 0352, Rose to Henry C. Bernstein, July 26, 1946; NY AR45–54 00189 0351, Myrtle Horowitz to Edward M. M. Warburg, August 9, 1946.

21. Atay Citron, "Ben Hecht's Pageant-Drama: *A Flag Is Born,*" in *Staging the Holocaust: The Shoah in Drama and Performance,* ed. Claude Schumacher (Cambridge: Cambridge University Press, 1998), 78; Rafael Medoff, "Ben Hecht's 'A Flag Is Born': A Play That Changed History," David S. Wyman Institute for Holocaust Studies, April 2004, new.wymaninstitute.org.

22. Palestine Statehood Committee Records, HM 53, reel 8, group 690, series 3, box 10, folder 9, "Repatriation Fund," 2.

23. Fischer-Lichte, *Theatre, Sacrifice, Ritual,* 193; Stephen Nelson, *"Only a Paper Moon": The Theatre of Billy Rose* (Ann Arbor, MI: UMI Research Press, 1987), 126. Nelson says Rose "backed the show . . . but requested that his name not appear in the program credits."

24. Garrett Eisler, "'This Theatre Is a Battlefield': Political Performance and Jewish-American Identity, 1933–1948" (PhD diss., City University of New York, 2012), 10, 157.

25. Citron, "Ben Hecht's Pageant-Drama," 70–71.

26. Eisler, "'This Theatre,'" 10.

27. Ibid., 9.

28. "Leading U.S. Jews Denounce Bombing," *New York Times,* July 25, 1946, 9.

29. Quoted in Stephen J. Whitfield, "The Politics of Pageantry, 1936–1946," *American Jewish History* 84, no. 3 (September 1996): 245.

30. Nelson, *"Only a Paper Moon,"* 126; BHP, box 61, folder 1586, Rose to Hecht, July 25, 1944.

31. Citron, "Ben Hecht's Pageant-Drama," 80–81.

32. Ibid., 92–93.

33. Westchester County Property Records, Liber 4425, 447, August 5, 1946.

34. "Harry S. Truman, Statement and Directive by the President on Immigration to the United States of Certain Displaced Persons and Refugees in Europe," American Presidency Project, December 22, 1945, www.presidency.ucsb.edu /ws/?pid=12253.

35. "Refugee Arrivals Put at 6,213 in Year," *New York Times,* December 24, 1946, 8; Michael Joseph Cohen, *Truman and Israel* (Berkeley: University of California Press, 1990), 112, 115; Shira Klein, "Displaced Persons Act," in *Anti-immigration in the United States: A Historical Encyclopedia,* ed. Kathleen R. Arnold (Santa Barbara, CA: Greenwood, 2011), 1:162.

36. BBP, vol. 117, Rose, Billy, 1946, folder 96, Rose to Baruch, October 21, 1946, and Joseph Birstein to Edward Warburg, October 18, 1946; Billy Rose, "Sweet Music and Torture," *PM,* November 12, 1946, reprinted *Euclid Ave. Temple Bulletin* (Cleveland, Ohio), November 22, 1946, 5–6, collections.americanjewisharchives.org.

37. Will Morrissey, *On a Shoestring* (Santa Barbara, CA: Willdon Paul, 1955), 208; Polly Rose Gottlieb, *The Nine Lives of Billy Rose* (New York: Crown, 1968), 44. According to affidavits filed by one Gordon D. Novel and his son, Sur, in New York's Westchester County on October 24, 2011, and October 21, 2011, respectively, Gordon Novel claimed he spoke with Billy Rose in 1965 to discuss whether Rose was Novel's biological father. Rose said that Novel's mother, Sybil Nolan, "caused [him] to get a vasectomy." (A Sybil Nolan did live in Dallas in July 1937, per "Obituary of Walter Earnest Nolan," *Valley Morning Star* [Harlingen, TX], July 23, 1937, 4.) Novel also said he visited Rose's sister Polly and that she confirmed that she had heard about his existence. The Novel family tried to get the courts to exhume Rose's body for DNA testing to discover whether Gordon Novel was Rose's son, but the request was denied. Novel family papers held by the author; information about Novel family provided in an e-mail to the author from Sur Novel, October 16, 2013.

38. "Billy Rose Plans to Bring 25 Orphans from Europe's Camps and Rear Them Here," *New York Times*, March 21, 1947, 8; Beth B. Cohen, "Face to Face: American Jews and Holocaust Survivors, 1946–54," in *"We Are Here": New Approaches to Jewish Displaced Persons in Postwar Germany*, ed. Avinoam J. Patt and Michael Berkowitz (Detroit: Wayne State University Press, 2010), 138; AJJDC, NY AR45–54 00114 00190, Beck to Louis Novins, March 19, 1947; JEB, #3083, box 2, folder 5, "Vignettes of famous people (ca. 1950–ca. 1970)," 3.

39. AJJDC, NY AR45–54 00114 00062, Carl Stern to Edward M. M. Warburg, August 12, 1947.

40. UNRRA, S-0125, box 64, file 1, Heise to UNRRA Displaced Persons Hq, March 24, 1947, and UNRRA US Zone Headquarters, Inter-Office Memo, Subject "Attached letter."

41. UNRRA, S-0401, box 1, file 1, "Adoptions—Unaccompanied Children 7/8/1945–9/5/1947," Molly Flynn to Myer Cohen, May 9, 1947.

42. MLS, box 123, "Wine Women and Song, Billy Rose, MLS Working Folder 2," memo from HWS to JAG, July 31, 1946; John Wheeler, *I've Got News for You* (New York: Dutton, 1961), 172.

43. "A Rose Is a Columnist," *Time,* June 24, 1946, 72; "Rose Cuffo Colyum [*sic*] Makes Grade; Goes Commercial Jan. 1," *Billboard,* August 24, 1947, 38.

44. Billy Rose, Pitching Horseshoes, *Nashua Telegraph,* June 13, 1947, 11.

45. AJJDC, Pinson, "Education Report for Zeilsheim," 3; UNRRA S-0436, box 42, file 6, "U.S. Zone—Team 311—Landsberg," memorandum from O. A. Nelson to Brigadier General Walter J. Muller, December 10, 1945, 1; AJJDC, Stern to Warburg, August 12, 1947.

46. Julian Levinson, "Roth in the Archives: 'Eli, the Fanatic' and the Nitra Yeshiva Controversy of 1948," provided by Levinson to the author in manuscript.

47. "70 Refugee Orphans to Farm and Study on Million-Dollar Estate in Westchester," *New York Times,* March 16, 1948, 29.

48. *In Memoriam, Rabbi Dr. Leo Jung, 1892–1987* (New York, 1988), n.p. [Reminiscence of Mr. Moses Feuerstein]; Walter Bennett, "Yeshiva Case Is Unsettled," *New Castle Tribune,* October 29, 1948, 1, 9; "Rabbinical Students Wed, Babies Toddle at Yeshiva," *New Castle Tribune,* August 11, 1950; Mrs. Hanson W. Baldwin, "Kisco Yeshiva Lists Major Debts Paid Off," *New Castle Tribune,* April 27, 1951, 4.

49. JEB, #3083, box 2, folder 5, 3; Billy Rose, "Billy Rose Writes Chaim Weizmann," *Euclid Ave. Temple Bulletin* (Cleveland, OH), January 2, 1948, 3–4; S. Ilan Troen, "American Experts in the Design of Zionist Society: The Reports of Elwood Mead and Robert Nathan," in *Envisioning Israel: The Changing Ideals and Images of North American Jews,* ed. Allon Gal (Detroit: Wayne State University Press, 1996), 207, 209, 211–12.

50. Michael Scammell, *Koestler* (New York: Random House, 2009), 335; TKP, Billy Rose correspondence, box 87/23, Arthur Lourie to Walter Eytan, December 28, 1948.

51. Clifford Odets, *The Time Is Ripe: The 1940 Journal of Clifford Odets* (New York: Grove, 1988), 121 (Odets misspelled the name as Stretsin); Judith Tydor Baumel, *The "Bergson Boys" and the Origins of Contemporary Zionist Militancy,* trans. Dena Ordan (Syracuse, NY: Syracuse University Press, 2005), 94; Meyer Weisgal, . . . *So Far: An Autobiography* (New York: Random House, 1971), 127. For Strelsin in Israel in October, see "Social & Personal," *Palestine Post,* October 26, 1948, 2. Strelsin's conversations with Rose took place before the trip, so likely in September.

52. Israel State Archives, Jerusalem, Lourie to Eytan, December 28, 1948.

53. WWP, box 1, folder 3, Rose to Winchell, November 12, 1947; BMB, vol. 117,

"Mr. and Mrs. Billy Rose [Itinerary]," January 5, 1949; TKP, Billy Rose correspondence, box 87/23, Lourie to [Arthur] Liverhant, December 30, 1948, and Eliahu Epstein to Ben-Gurion, December 31, 1948.

54. TKP, Billy Rose correspondence, box 87/23, Strelsin to Ben-Gurion, February 28, 1949.

55. Maurcie Zolotow, "The Fabulous Billy Rose," *Collier's,* February 15, 1947, 11; Blair Howell, "Romanticism of Composers Lerner and Loewe First Seen in 'Brigadoon,'" *Deseret News,* October 5, 2013, www.deseretnews.com; HB, box 26, folder 2, Rose, Billy & Stanley Walker, 1942–1945, CC [Cass Canfield] to BWH, July 31, 1945, and Billy Rose to Canfield, August 11, 1945.

56. HB, box 26, folder 2, George T. Bye to Cass Canfield, December 14, 1943; MLS, box 123, folder 2, memo from HWS to JAG, July 31, 1946, and Rose to Schuster, August 27, 1946, Cerf to Rose, August 24, 1946, and Schuster to Rose, August 28, 1946.

57. ECP, research folder 1, Maurice Zolotow, "Zolotow, Et Al., Also on Billy Rose Biogs," *Variety,* n.d.

58. MZP, *Billy Rose of Broadway,* 1.

59. Billy Rose, *Wine, Women and Words* (New York: Pocketbook, 1950), 270–71.

60. Hugh Trevor-Roper, *The Last Days of Hitler* (Chicago: University of Chicago Press, 1992), 210.

61. Rose, *Wine,* 143, 270–72. Some of Rose's story is verifiable. In July 1941, columnist John Truesdell ran news of Rose's correspondence with Halifax and the idea for exhibiting Nazis, but searches of the *Beobachter* newspaper failed to unearth an article or cartoon about Rose. See "John Truesdell in Hollywood," *Cincinnati Enquirer,* July 17, 1941, 6.

62. MLS, box 123, folder 1, "Guess who's written a book!," advertisement, *New York Times,* October 25, 1948, "Move over, De Maupassant," advertisement, *New York Times Book Review,* November 7, 1948, and "BILLY ROSE'S HILARIOUS NEW BOOK," advertisement for *Look* magazine serial, *New York Herald Tribune,* June 22, 1948; MLS, box 123, folder 2, "List of Papers Taking BILLY ROSE," October 14, 1948, and Annenberg to Rose, September 3, 1947; WHS, Mss 208, Sloan papers, box 15, folder 1, Billy Rose, Pitching Horseshoes, *New York Herald Tribune,* August 27, 1948, and accompanying articles about opera proposal. For radio program, see Billy Rose to Bob Stephan of the *Cleveland Plain-Dealer,* November 25, 1947. Author has screenshot of this item featured on eBay on March 13, 2017.

63. ECP, research correspondence folder 2, Wolfe to Earl Conrad, September 20, 1966; ECP, interview folder 2, "Charles Samuels," June 1, 1966, n.p. [1], and "Mrs. Lee Rogow," June 15, 1966, 3, 5.

64. BHP, box 61, folder 1586, Rose to Ben Hecht, July 2, 1948, 2; MLS, folder 2, MLS memo, "LS session with Rose 11/11/47," and memo from LS to MLS, RLS, JAG, November 12, 1947; Michael Korda, *Making the List: A Cultural History of the American Bestseller, 1900–1999* (New York: Barnes and Noble, 2001), 96.

65. TKP, Billy Rose correspondence, box 87/23, Lourie to Walter Eytan, January 3, 1949.

66. TKP, Billy Rose correspondence, box 87/23, Rose to Lourie, January 6, 1949; Lourie to Rose, January 10, 1949; Ascher Moissis to Lourie, January 14, 1949; Strelsin to Ben-Gurion, February 28, 1949, 2.

67. TKP, Billy Rose correspondence, box 87/23, "Excerpt from Letter from Monica Dehn to I. L. Kenen, March 31, 1949"; "Social & Personal," *Palestine Post,* March 16, 1949, 2.

68. Gottlieb, *Nine Lives,* 216; JDC, recording of Ralph Goldman dictating notes regarding Billy Rose, tape of reels 1, 2, and 3. Quote found at 27:15–27:25. This recording was obtained with the very generous help of Goldman's daughter, Judy Baumgold. (Goldman says Rose was in Israel in 1949 for Independence Day, but the celebrations were for Purim.)

69. BGRI, David Ben-Gurion diary, entry dated March 16, 1949, 81–82.

70. TKP, Billy Rose correspondence, box 87/23, Moshe Pearlman to Zeev Sherf, April 7, 1949, and Arthur Lourie to Reuven Dafni, December 20, 1949.

71. Billy Rose, foreword to *Israel Revisited,* by Ralph McGill (Atlanta: Tupper and Love, 1950), vii.

72. TKP, Billy Rose correspondence, box 87/23, Louric to Shoham HaMisrad, Tel Aviv, April 22, 1949.

73. TKP, Billy Rose correspondence, box 87/23, Lourie to Rose, May 2, 1949, and Lourie to Herlitz, May 31, 1949.

74. TKP, Billy Rose correspondence, box 87/23, Moshe Pearlman to Zeev Sherf, April 7, 1949.

75. TKP, Billy Rose correspondence, box 87/23, Eliahu Elath to Arthur [Lourie], March 14, 1949; Lourie, "Minute of Talk with Billy Rose (Wednesday afternoon, July 27, 1949)."

76. TKP, "Excerpt from Letter."

FOURTEEN Uncaged Tiger

1. BMB, Subseries 1B: Selected Correspondence, v. 135, Rose to Baruch, December 16, 1949.

2. Ernest Samuels and Jayne Samuels, *Bernard Berenson: The Making of a Legend* (Cambridge, MA: Belknap Press of Harvard University Press, 1987), 442.

3. Bernard Berenson Papers, Villa I Tatti, Harvard University Center for Italian Renaissance Studies, Cambridge, MA, *Diary,* March 28, 1949, 33, and Rose to Berenson, April 26, 1949; Jerry Tallmer, "Pitching Horseshoes and Column Ideas with Billy Rose," *Villager,* May 10, 2014, thevillager.com/2014/01/23/pitching-horseshoes-and -column-ideas-with-billy-rose.

4. BMB, Subseries 1B, v. 128, Baruch to Rose, November 12, 1948.

5. BMB, box 743, Williamsburg Settlement album, n.p.; BMB, Subseries 1B, v. 135, Billy Rose, "Billy Rose on Baruch, Ex-Boss, at 79," *Anderson Daily Mail,* n.d.

6. BMB, Subseries 1B, v. 128, Baruch to Rose, November 22, 1949.

7. BMB, Rose to Baruch, December 16, 1949.

8. BMB, Rose to Baruch, December 16, 1949, and Rose to Baruch, January 7, 1949.

9. MHL, Adolph Zukor correspondence, Subject Files-General, 2-f. 18, Correspondence 1945–1949, Rose to Zukor, December 21, 1949.

10. Louis Sobol, *The Longest Street: A Memoir* (New York: Crown, 1968), 193–94.

11. BHP, box 61, folder 1586, Rose to Hecht, May 9, 1944, 2.

12. TGA, MSS 436, box 188, folder 4808, Rose to William Fitelson, March 17, 1950.

13. WPP, Billy Rose, Acc 2388, Ser. 1, box 72, Rose to Pahlmann, August 25, 1950.

14. BMB, box 138, Abba Eban file, Eban to Baruch, July 6, 1950.

15. Peter L. Hahn, *Caught in the Middle East: U.S. Policy toward the Arab-Israeli Conflict, 1945–1961* (Chapel Hill: University of North Carolina Press, 2004), 75.

16. BGRI, letters folder "July 1950," item 147401, Ben-Gurion to Lourie for Goldenberg, July 2, 1950, and item 147456, Goldenberg to Ben-Gurion, July 14, 1950.

17. BGRI, letters folder "July 1950," v. 141, Rose to Baruch, September 5, 1950. The weapons lists seem to have been sent to Rose by someone other than Goldenberg, as the attached note to Rose is signed with another, illegible name.

18. COP, Correspondence, 1921–1963, box 4, Rose to Odets, November 27, 1950.

19. "Rose Goes NBC, Shutters 'Shoe," *Billboard,* January 13, 1951, 1, 42; Stephen Nelson, *"Only a Paper Moon": The Theatre of Billy Rose* (Ann Arbor, MI: UMI Research Press, 1987), 94; ECP, research folder 3, Thomas MacCabe, [no title], *New York World-Telegram,* [1962].

20. ECP, interview folder 1, "Chester Conn," n.d., 12, 17.

21. "Joyce Mathews Attempts Suicide," *New York Times,* July 16, 1951, 22; Vicki Walton, interviews with the author, August 4 and 5, 2014.

22. ECP, research folder 3, "What Did Rose Tell Joyce before She Cut Her Wrists?," *New York Post,* July 16, 1951, and research folder 2, *American Weekly,* November 25, 1951.

23. Tom Wolfe, *The Bonfire of the Vanities* (New York: Picador, 1987), 68; ECP, "What Did Rose," ECP, interview folder 1, "Doris Julian," May 12, [1966], 2.

24. ECP, research correspondence folder 2, Wolfe Kaufman to Earl Conrad ("dear earl")," n.d., 2, and interview folder 1, "Chester Conn," 16.

25. ECP, interview folder 2, "Helen Schrank," June 22, 1966, 1.

26. Louis Nizer, *My Life in Court* (New York: Pyramid, 1977), 188–89; Barbara Wallace Grossman, *Funny Woman: The Life and Times of Fanny Brice* (Bloomington: Indiana University Press, 1991), 230.

27. "Eleanor Holm, Plantiff," US Court of Appeals for the Second Circuit, January 5, 1968, Justia US Law, law.justia.com; "Modigliani, Barnes and Billy Rose," Henry and Rose Pearlman Collection, accessed October 11, 2017, www
.pearlmancollection.org/reminiscence/modigliani-barnes-and-billy-rose; Albert

Barnes Foundation archives, Merion, PA, Billy Rose, AR.ABC.1951.373, Barnes to Rose, May 28, 1951, 1.

28. Ed Hosten, "32,000 Pay Homage at Israel Bond Rally," *Brooklyn Eagle,* May 1, 1952, 1; "Brooklyn Hails Israel's Fourth Anniversary," *Brooklyn Eagle,* May 1, 1952, 12.

29. JSR, General Correspondence, box 82, folder 15, Jacques Seligmann to Rose, June 7, 1954; Rolls-Royce Foundation, Schoellkopf/Inskip Cards, LBLW 35.

30. Quoted in Erik Lee Preminger, *Gypsy & Me* (Boston: Little, Brown, 1984), 149.

31. BMB, v. 171, Rose to Baruch, February 12, 1954 (letter is misdated as February 12, 1953).

32. BMB, v. 163, Rose to Baruch, March 24, 1952.

33. BMB, v. 163, Rose to Baruch, March 25, 1953, and Rose to Baruch, "Holiday Greeting," n.d.

34. BMB, v. 157, Baruch to Rose, December 28, 1953, and Baruch to Rose, January 20, 1955.

35. "Art Treasures May Have Burned in Fire," *Chappaqua Sun,* April 5, 1956, 1.

36. JSR, box 82, folder 15, Germain Seligman to Rose, May 1, 1956; "Art Treasures," 1; photograph caption, *New Castle Tribune,* April 5, 1956, 3.

37. RAG, box 22, folder 12, Ruth Goetz, "My Life as a Wife," 12–13.

38. Judy Goetz Sanger, interview with the author, September 18, 2014.

39. Ethel Ferezy, interview with the author, September 17, 2014.

40. Sanger, interview, September 18, 2014.

41. Ibid.

42. Polly Rose Gottlieb, *The Nine Lives of Billy Rose* (New York: Crown, 1968), 44.

43. Sanger, interview, September 18, 2014.

44. "Art Treasures," 6; Alexander King Papers, Library of Congress, Rose to Alexander King, April 13, 1956.

45. ECP, research folder 3, Norman Katkov, "Billy Rose," *New York Post,* n.d.

46. RAG, Goetz, "My Life," 15–16.

47. New York Landmarks Commission, 56 East 93 St. House, L.P. no. 0437, Richard R. Scherer to Hon. Harmon H. Goldstone, Chairman, February 21, 1970, and Irwin Fruchtman to Frank Gilbert, May 11, 1972; Edith Crouch, *Walker & Gillette: American Architects; From Classicism through Modernism (1900s–1950s)* (Atglen, PA: Schiffer, 2013), 100, 104.

48. ECP, research folder 2, Douglas Watt, "Drop That Loot, Billy, and Get Back to Work," *New York Daily News,* October 22, 1959.

49. New York State Supreme Court, Billy Rose against Pierre Gustvae Bader, index no. 6162, May 15, 1956; WPP, Billy Rose, Acc 2388, Ser. 1, box 72, "Denies Home-Sale Deal, Hits Billy Rose Motives," [unknown newspaper], n.d.; "Deeds," Register, New York County, Abstract Index, Block 1504, lot no. *NOW P 0 47 (formerly P 0 55); Lee Grant, *I Said Yes to Everything* (New York: Penguin, 2014), 168.

50. "Island off Norwalk Purchased by Billy Rose as Summer Home," *Bridgeport Post,* September 23, 1957, 32; Preminger, *Gypsy & Me,* 149.

51. ECP, interview folder 1, "Richard Barstow," June 20, 1966, 5.

52. Sanger, interview, September 18, 2014; Grant, *I Said Yes,* 166–68; Vicki Walton, interview with the author, August 6, 2014; Murray Schumach, "Billy Rose's Isle of Passionate Peacocks for Sale in Connecticut," *New York Times,* July 27, 1967, 37.

53. ECP, interview folder 2, "Tex McCrary," June 23, 1966, 3, 7. Photographs of animal skins on the floor appear in Schumach, "Billy Rose's Isle."

54. Sobol, *Longest Street,* 269.

55. New York State Dept. of State, Division of Corporations, Entity Information, Billy Rose Foundation, Inc., DOS ID# 113701.

FIFTEEN Israel Museum

1. ECP, research folder 2, Douglas Watt, "Drop That Loot, Billy, and Get Back to Work," *New York Daily News,* October 22, 1959.

2. "Joyce Mathews Sues," *New York Times,* July 23, 1959, 33.

3. Melanie Kahane, "Billy Rose's House," *Interiors,* August 1960, 66–71.

4. Lewis Funke, "News and Gossip of the Rialto," *New York Times,* June 22, 1958, section 2, 1; Gerald Schoenfeld, *Mr. Broadway: The Inside Story of the Shuberts, the Shows, and the Stars* (Milwaukee, WI: Applause Theatre and Cinema Books, 2012), 41–42; Sir Roy Strong, "Tribute," in *Oliver Messel: In the Theatre of Design,* ed. Thomas Messel (New York: Rizzoli, 2011), 52; Oliver Messel Papers, Victoria and Albert Museum, London, Rose to Messell [*sic*], July 9, 1958; Ken Bloom, *Routledge Guide to Broadway* (New York: Routledge, 2007), 184.

5. ECP, research folder 1, A. Wilfred May, Observations . . . , *Commercial and Financial Chronicle,* September 14, 1961, and February 17, 1966; Martin S. Fridson, *It Was a Very Good Year: Extraordinary Moments in Stock Market History* (New York: John Wiley and Sons, 1998), 164.

6. Leonard Lyons, The Lyons Den, *Reading Eagle,* July 23, 1959, n.p.

7. ECP, research folder 2, Robert Coleman, "Fabulous Is Word for Billy Rose," *New York Mirror,* n.d., and research folder 3, Thomas MacCabe, *New York World-Telegram,* n.d. [late 1961].

8. JDC, file NY_OH_194, "Transcript—Interview with Ralph Goldman," August 22, 1994, 6–8, and file NY_OH_195, October 25, 1994, 13; "U.S. Ambassador, Jerusalem Mayor Sign U.S. Museum Grant," *B'nai B'rith Messenger,* March 14, 1958, 5.

9. Central Zionist Archives, zionistarchives.org.il, Z6\1471–1t, Goldmann to Rose, March 19, 1959.

10. JDC, file NY_OH_195, "Transcript—Interview with Ralph Goldman," October 25, 1994, 13.

11. Karl Katz, interview with the author, April 4, 2014. For timing of Eytan's first contact with Rose, see BRAB, Katz to Rose, October 21, 1959. Katz's letter refers to Eytan's letter to Rose of "several months ago."

12. LSP, Rose to Strasberg, September 25, 1959.

13. Miriam H. Weingarten, interview with the author, September 11, 2017, and Weingarten, e-mails to the author, September 12 and 14, 2017.

14. BRAB, Katz to Rose, October 21, 1959.

15. BRAB, Katz to Rose, November 6, 1959.

16. Katz, interview, April 4, 2014.

17. Ibid.

18. ECP, Watt, "Drop That Loot."

19. CUL, oral history interview with Kitty Carlisle Hart, 1979, 5:693.

20. JDC, file NY_OH_225, "Transcript—Interview with Karl Katz," October 20, 1994, 15.

21. Katz, interview, April 4, 2014.

22. JDC, "Transcript—Interview with Karl Katz," 16.

23. JDC, file NY_OH_195, "Transcript—Interview with Ralph Goldman," October 25, 1994, 14.

24. Ibid.

25. JDC, file NY_OH_196, "Transcript—Interview with Ralph Goldman," October 27, 1994, 1–2.

26. Philip Roth, *Portnoy's Complaint* (New York: Vintage Books, 1994), 266.

27. JDC, file NY_OH_196, "Transcript—Interview with Ralph Goldman," October 27, 1994, 2–5.

28. Ibid., 13.

29. BRAB, Eytan to Rose, December 20, 1959.

30. ECP, interview folder 1, "Mr. Weil," June 6, 1966, 1–2.

31. JDC, file NY_OH_196, "Transcript—Interview with Ralph Goldman," October 27, 1994, 5.

32. Ibid., 8–9, 10.

33. Karl Katz, *The Exhibitionist: Living Museums, Loving Museums* (New York: Overlook, 2016), 153.

34. BMB, vol. 202, Rose to Baruch, January 13, 1960. All clippings are found here.

35. Emily Alice Katz, *Bringing Zion Home: Israel in American Jewish Culture, 1948–1967* (Albany, NY: SUNY Press, 2015), 20, 71, 108, 129–30, 138.

36. John Higham, *Send These to Me: Immigrants in Urban America* (Baltimore: Johns Hopkins University Press, 1984), 171–72; Arthur A. Goren, "A 'Golden Decade' for American Jews: 1945–1955," in *American Jewish History*, ed. Jeffrey S. Gurock, vol. 4, *American Jewish Life, 1920–1990* (New York: Routledge, 1998), 3, 8–9; Associated Press, "'Exodus' Is Pulling Tourists to Israel," *Lakeland Ledger*, November 15, 1959, 8-C.

37. Nathan Ziprin, Off the Record, *Canadian Jewish Chronicle*, January 15, 1960, 10.

38. JDC, file NY_OH_196, "Transcript—Interview with Ralph Goldman," October 27, 1994, 17; JDC, "Transcript—Interview with Karl Katz," 17.

39. Quoted in Ana Maria Torres, *Isamu Noguchi: A Study of Space* (New York: Monacelli, 2000), 128.

40. BRTD, "Interview with Billy Rose on the Long John Nebel radio show, Aug. 5, 1965," audio disc 4.

41. JDC, file NY_OH_116, "Transcript—Interview with Isamu Noguchi," December 11, 1984, 2.

42. America-Israel Cultural Foundation, Archives, Dolphin Express, Inc. (shipping facility and warehouse), Hillside, NJ, box 8, Israel Museum Bequests-Correspondence 1971–1975, "Dear Mr. Noguchi," February 18, 1960 (this is the original contract signed by Ralph Goldman and Noguchi); INP, MS-Proj 102, "List 1, Donations of Mr. Billy Rose to the National Museum of Israel." The numbers don't quite add up. The estimated value of the forty-four sculptures on this undated list is $739,500.

43. INP, MS_Proj_099, "Reception" invitation, and MS_PROJ_098, Ralph Goldman to Noguchi, June 3, 1960.

44. BRDF, folder 45–01, no. 1, Rose to Kollek, April 14, 1960.

45. Jacques Lipchitz Papers, Archives of American Art, Smithsonian Institution, box 4, folder 13, Schneerson to Lipchitz, 28 of Iyar, 5720 [May 25, 1960], and Schneerson to Lipchitz, 23 of Adar I, 5722 [February 27, 1962].

46. BRDF, folder 45–01, no. 1, Rose to Kollek, April 14, 1960.

47. "Compromise Reached on Billy Rose's Sculpture Garden in Israel," *Jewish Telegraphic Agency*, March 11, 1960, www.jta.org/archive.

48. Katz, *Exhibitionist,* 171–72.

49. BRAB, Eban to Rose, November 30, 1960.

50. JDC, file NY_OH_195, "Transcript—Interview with Ralph Goldman," 12.

51. "Compositor Billy Rose veio comprar esculturas do baiano Mário Cravo," *Jornal do Brasil,* February 11, 1961; "'Show man' dos EU veio ao Brasil para comprar esculturas," *O Estado de São Paulo,* February 16, 1961, 9. First article provided to the author by Edgard Leite, director, Centro de Historia e Cultura Judaica, Rio de Janeiro; second provided by Prof. Lina Gorenstein, São Paulo University.

52. Inez Robb, "Rose Heists Art," *Warren County Observer* (Warren, PA), August 21, 1961, 7; BRDF, folder 45–01, no. 1, Beham to Rose, August 30, 1961.

53. Maya Balakirsky Katz, *The Visual Culture of Chabad* (New York: Cambridge University Press, 2010), 193.

54. MLS, Series 1: Catalogued Correspondence, box 5, Rose to Mr. & Mrs. M. Lincoln Schuster, November 19, 1961.

55. BRDF, folder 45–01, no. 1, Rose to Teddy Kollek, December 1, 1961.

56. Katz, interview, April 4, 2014; Erik Lee Preminger, *Gypsy & Me* (Boston: Little, Brown, 1984), 146–47; "Blue Ribbon Cook," *Life,* April 4, 1949, 98–103; DLP, MC 601, box 2, folder 2, "Draft 'Commentaries,'" article begins, "For about one year I was . . ."; Jeanne Schinto, "Remembering Dione Lucas," *Gastronomica,* Winter 2011, 34–45.

57. BRDF, folder 45–01, no. 1, Beham to Rose, December 10, 1961 (it is likely that Goldman sent word from New York on December 9 and that the time difference re-

sulted in a reply on the tenth); JDC, file NY_OH_197, "Transcript—Interview with Ralph Goldman," December 5, 1994, 6.

58. BRDF, folder 45–01, no. 1, Rose to Kollek, December 1, 1961.

59. BRDF, folder 45–01, no. 1, Rose to Lousada, June 28, 1961, 3.

60. TKP, Kollek to Rose, January 3, 1962 (Kollek refers to Rose's "letter of December 27"); Leonard Lyons, The Lyons Den, *San Mateo Times,* January 8, 1962, 18.

61. BRAB, Ish-Shalom to Rose, January 17, 1962, 1; BRDF, 45–01, no. 1, Y. Beham to Rose, May 28, 1962.

62. TKP, Kollek to Rose, January 3, 1962, 3. This letter indicated that the Rothschild meeting had taken place in December. Rose confirms the Geneva meeting in BRDF, 45–01, no. 1, Rose to Y. Beham, June 15, 1962, 2.

63. BRDF, folder 45–01, no. 3, Kollek to Danny Gelmond, June 9, 1965.

64. BRDF, Bezalel folder, 1963–1965, Rose to Kollek, September 17, 1965.

65. BRDF, folder 45–01, no. 1, Rose to Kollek, n.d. ["King David Hotel, Jerusalem. Wednesday"].

66. TKP, box 11889/16, Rose to Kollek, August 3, 1964, and Kollek to Rose, August 11, 1964.

67. BRDF, folder 45–01, no. 1, Goldman to Beham, January 11, 1962.

68. JDC, file NY_OH_196, "Transcript—Interview with Ralph Goldman," 18.

69. Katz, interview, April 4, 2014.

70. BRDF, folder 45–01, no. 1, Rose to Fefferman, December 3, 1962, 1–2.

71. BRDF, folder 45–01, no. 2, Rose to Beham, March 10, 1964

72. TKP, Rose to Teddy Kollek, April 23, 1964, and Rose to Kollek, June 23, 1964.

73. BRDF, 45–01, no. 2, Rose to Y[ohanan] Beham, April 29, 1964; Joseph H. Hirschhorn Papers, Archives of American Art, Smithsonian Institution, Collection 7449, box 20, folder "Rose, Billy," [contract], June 30, 1964; "Sculpture under Consideration to Billie [*sic*] Rose Sculpture Garden," November 1, 1964; [Hirschhorn] to Billie [*sic*], November 3, 1964; and Abram Lerner to Rose, November 11, 1964.

74. SGP, Invitations 1965–69, folder 3519, Rose to Goldwyn, February 23, 1965.

75. BRDF, folder 45–01, no. 2, Yosef Yaakov to Kollek and Beham, February 8, 1965, and Katz to Rose, February 4, 1965.

76. BRDF, Bezalel folder, Kollek to Rose, March 16, 1965.

77. BRTD, Billy Rose Clipping File, Norton Mockridge, "Billy Sees a Less-Than-Rosy Future," *New York World-Telegram,* March 3, 1965.

Epilogue

1. "U.S. Producer Here," *Kingston Gleaner,* July 17, 1961, 6; "Land Sales," *Kingston Gleaner,* January 31, 1962, 2; Registrar General's Department, St. Catherine, Jamaica, Marriage Register, no. 58, Billy Rose and Doris Warner Vidor, March 1, 1964.

2. Mercedes McCambridge, *The Quality of Mercy* (New York: Times Books, 1981), 226–27.

3. BRDF, 45–01, no. 2, Rose to Yohanan Beham, April 8, 1965.

4. UTA, Audrey Wood Collection 27.1, Rose to Audrey Wood, Miriam Howell, and Kay Brown, July 2, 1965.

5. BRDF, folder 45–01, no. 1, Rose to Teddy Kollek, August 16, 1962, 1; W. Granger Blair, "Israel Museum Will Open Tomorrow atop a Stony Judean Hill in Jerusalem," *New York Times,* May 10, 1965, 35.

6. BMB, vol. 157, Rose to Baruch, February 15, 1952.

7. TKP, box 11889/16, Rose to Kollek, April 23, 1964.

8. ECP, research correspondence folder 2, Navarro to Earl Conrad, July 2, [1966]; "Billy Rose Lauds Baruch," *New York Times,* June 21, 1965, 17.

9. BRTD, Billy Rose Clipping File, John Wheeler, "The Rags to Riches Tale of Billy Rose," *Milwaukee Journal Green Sheet,* November 15, 1961, 1, and Associated Press, "Billy Rose Calculates Wealth by Height," n.d.; "News of Realty: Rose Seeks Club," *New York Times,* May 6, 1965, 64; "News of Realty: Deal on 6th Ave.," *New York Times,* November 25, 1965, 79; "Palace Is Slated for Penn Station," *New York Times,* June 8, 1955, 1.

10. A. Wilfred May, Observations . . . , *Commercial and Financial Chronicle,* February 17, 1966, 4; ECP, research folder 3, Albin Krebs, "$9,000 an Hour," *New York Herald Tribune,* n.d.

11. UTA, Margaret Cousins Collection, box/folder 26.6, Margaret Cousins to Roger Kahn, n.d.; BRTD, Billy Rose Clipping File, Associated Press, "Billy Rose Calculates Wealth."

12. BRAB, Karl Katz to Rose, June 10, 1965; BRDF, Bezalel folder, Rose to Teddy Kollek, September 13, 1965; Vicki Walton, interview with the author, August 5, 2014.

13. ECP, interview folder 2, "Tex McCrary," June 23, 1966, 9.

14. ECP, interview folder 1, "Arnold Forster," June 30, 1966, 1; WHS, Dore Schary Papers, ca. 1920–1980, Series: 1977 Additions, Subseries: Anti-Defamation League Files, box 153, folder 5, Harold Braverman to Forster, September 30, 1965, 1.

15. BRDF, Bezalel folder, Rose to William [*sic;* Willem] Sandberg, May 27, 1965; Kollek and Sandberg to Rose, January 5, 1966; Daniel Gelmond to Rose, January 25, 1966; and Rose to Kollek, May 27, 1965.

16. "Billy Rose Is Recuperating after Surgery in Houston," *New York Times,* December 10, 1965, 58.

17. BRDF, 45–01, no. 3, Rosenfeld to Teddy Kollek, January 26, 1966.

18. BRTD, Billy Rose Clipping File, Jimmy Cannon, "Last Visit with Billy Rose," *New York Journal-American,* February 14, 1966.

19. BRDF, folder 45–01, no. 3, Teddy [Kollek] to [Elaine] Rosenfeld, February 12, 1966; Elaine [Rosenfeld] to Kollek, February 13, 1966, and February 14, 1966.

20. Polly Rose Gottlieb, *The Nine Lives of Billy Rose* (New York: Crown, 1968), 253–55; "Billy Rose's Sisters Ask Control of Brother's $30-Million Estate," *New York Times,* April 2, 1966, 31; "Billy Rose's Sisters Lose Request on His Estate," *New York Times,* May 7, 1966, 32.

21. "Billy Rose's Sisters Lose Legal Attempt to Contest His Will," *New York Times,* October 20, 1966, 33; "Billy Rose Estate Is Still in Dispute," *New York Times,* January 30, 1967, 31.

22. Irving Spiegel, "Billy Rose Entombed in Westchester Mausoleum after 20 Months of Litigation," *New York Times,* October 30, 1967, 37.

23. Robert E. Tomasson, "Rose Sisters Fail to Break His Will," *New York Times,* December 25, 1967, 21.

24. Maurice Zolotow, "Lots of Barnum, a Little Napoleon," review of *The Nine Lives of Billy Rose,* by Polly Rose Gottlieb, and *Billy Rose: Manhattan Primitive,* by Earl Conrad, *New York Times,* March 17, 1968, Sunday Book Review, 8.

25. ECP, interview folder 2, "Charles Samuels," June 2, 1966, 9; UTA, Norman Bel Geddes Collection, box 213, folders 1–3, Correspondence and Contracts with Billy Rose, Bel Geddes to Miss Bugel, January 29, 1945 (includes Lahr statement, reported by Bel Geddes).

26. BRTD, "Interview with Billy Rose on the Long John Nebel radio show, Aug. 5, 1965," audio disc 3.

27. ECP, interview folder 2, Tex McCrary interview with Billy Rose, July 9, 1965 (transcript typed June 27, 1966), 9–10.

28. William H. Pritchard, "Blackmailing Billy Rose," *New York Times,* October 1, 1989.

29. Saul Bellow, *The Bellarosa Connection* (New York: Penguin, 1989), 74, 47, 41.

index

Hirschhorn, Joe, 222, 225

Hitchcock, Joe, 46, 47

Hitler, Adolf, 80, 97, 139, 141, 154, 167, 173, 196, 279n22

Holm, Eleanor (wife): antisemitism of, 109–10, 146, 200, 205, 206; in Aquacades, 105–6, 109, 111–12, 115, 123, 130; at beautiful legs contest, 144; divorce from Rose, 204, 206, 207, 209, 228; divorce of first husband, 115, 206; homes shared with Rose, 162–63, 165; images of, *226 figs.;* to Israel with Rose, 193, 198; marriage of Rose to, 135, 138, *226 fig.;* New Year's party (1949), 201, 202, *226 fig.;* Olympic difficulties, 106–9; orphanage proposal and, 186, 190; relationship with Rose, 146, 162–63, 164; Rose's premarital involvement with, 105–6, 110–12, 115, 116; topaz bracelet, 182; in war bonds rally at Mt. Kisco, 167

Holocaust. *See* Nazi Germany, Holocaust, and World War II

Hoover, J. Edgar, 83, 84

Horowitz, Louis J., 12, 21

"I Hold Her Hand and She Holds Mine: Ain't Nature Grand?" (Rose song), 32, 53, 57, *152 fig.*

Imbimbo, Sal, 129–30

Irgun, 152, 174, 180, 181, 184, 185, *226 fig.*

Israel, State of: American support for, 181, 218; Balfour Declaration, 19; ceasefire of 1949, 213; *A Flag Is Born* (Hecht play), xv, *152 fig.,* 184–86, 218; Haganah, 152, 181, 184; Irgun, 152, 174, 180, 181, 184, 185, *226 fig.;* Jewish immigration to Palestine, Rose support for, xv, 180–81, 184–86; King David Hotel, bombing of, 185; proposed burial of Rose in, 230; Rose support for, 110, 192–94, 197–200, 203–4,

206; Rose's trips to, 193–94, 197–99, 224, 228; Six-Day War (1967), 218; toughness, culture of, 153, 199; UJA "Campaign for Survival" and, 181, 185; UN partition of Palestine, 192

Israel Museum, Jerusalem, and Billy Rose Art Garden, xv, 212–26; art collecting by Rose for, 221–22, 225; exterior images, *226 figs.;* Hillel Fefferman, Rose's letter to, 224–25; fundraising by Rose, 220–23, 225, 230; Goldmann's inquiry about Rose's sculpture collection, 213–14; Jewish ceremonial artworks presented to Rose, 229; Katz interview with Rose, 214–15; maintenance of garden, 30, 230; naming of art garden, 221; negotiation of Rose gift, 215–17, 219–20; Isamu Noguchi and, 216, 217, 219, 220, 224, *226 fig.;* opening day, 225–26, 228; Orthodox and secular Jewish objections to Rose gift, 215, 220–21; press coverage, 217–19, 221–22, 225–26; volatility of Rose as benefactor of, 223–24

It Can't Happen Here: Sinclair Lewis novel, 113; Rose's version, at Fort Worth Fair and Cleveland Aquacade, *70 fig.,* 113–14, 139, 156; Works Progress Administration Federal Theatre Project, 113

"It's Only a Paper Moon" (Rose song), 72

James, Henry, 11–12, 166

James, William, xiv

Jarrett, Arthur, 107, 108, 115

Javits, Jacob, 210

The Jazz Singer (stage production), 63

Jessel, George, 32, 63–65, 120, 144, 151, 163, 166

Jewish Agency, 152, 198

Jewish identity: American versus European Jewish culture, 126; of Fanny

Brice, 53, 57; Criterion Club, New York City, 48–49; emotional traits of Rose and, 33, 85; enjoyment, Jewish capacity for, 38; Gregg shorthand and, 19; Hecht on, 150–51; intermarriage, 138; New York City, Jewish infatuation with, 12–13, 42; *New York Post* on, 169; Rose's sense of, 14–15, 57, 138–40, 150–51, 169–71, 206, 218–19, 229, 232–33; songwriting and entertainment as Jewish pursuits, 31–32, 34; World War II as changing, 147–48, 155; Yiddish theater, influence of, xiv, 32, 74, 157, 162

Jewish immigration: mother's backing of, xiv, 2, 7, 137–38, 173, 218–19; to Palestine/Israel, Rose support of, xv, 180–81, 184–86; Kurt Schwarz, rescue of, 140–46, *152 fig.,* 169, 186, 232, 279–80n22; to United States after war, 187, 190

Jewish philanthropist, Rose as: development of, xiv–xv, 137–40; Federation of Jewish Philanthropies award for Rose, 184; Herzl sisters in Romania and, 213; mother's influence on, xiv, 2, 7, 137–38, 173, 218–19; orphanage proposal, 186–91, 195; press [non] coverage of, 167–69, 195, 218, 232; "Refugee Review," Casa Mañana, NYC, 142; Roosevelt election fund, contributions to, 174–75; Maurice Rose hospital fundraising, 175–76; Kurt Schwarz, rescue of, 140–46, *152 fig.,* 169, 186, 232, 279–80n22; UJA "Campaign for Survival," 181–84; Yeshiva Farm Settlement, Mt. Kisco, New York, 191. *See also* Israel, State of; Israel Museum; Jewish refugees/displaced persons; Nazi Germany, Holocaust, and World War II

Jewish refugees/displaced persons (DPs):

in *A Flag Is Born,* 186; immigration to Palestine, 180, 185, 186; immigration to United States, 187, 190; orphanage proposal, 186–91, 195; postwar management of, 176–79; "Refugee Review," Casa Mañana, NYC, 142, 151; Rose visiting DP camps, 177–78, 180, 187, 195; UJA "Campaign for Survival" and, 181, 182; UNRRA, 177–79, 180, 184, 189; USNA, 188, 191; WRB, 170–71

Jolson, Al, 32, 54, 75

Jumbo (1935), 86–96; Actor's Equity show, not regarded as, 91, 92; branding formula of Rose and, xiii; Catholic response, 132; financial backing, 89–90, 91; financial success, 94, 121, 128; Fort Worth Centennial festivities, Texas, enlistment of Rose for, 98–99; giant clown, *70 fig.,* 93; *The Great Magoo* and, 72; at Hippodrome, NYC, 91–92, 93, 94; Al Hirschfeld cartoon, *70 fig.;* New York attractions as ancestors of, 12; origins of concept, 81, 86, 90, 122; popular and critical success, 92–95; rehearsals and publicity, 91–92, 158; RKO interest in acts from, 98, 104; storyline, 90–91; Paul Whiteman and, 60, 91; writing of, 87–89

Kahane, Melanie, 40, 212

Kahn, Otto, 48, 51, 55

Kahn, Roger Wolfe, 48–49

Katz, Karl, 214–15, 217, 219, 221, 222

Katz, Katriel, 225–26

Kaufman, Beatrice, 150, 155

Kaufman, George S., 114, 150, 155, 163, 182

Kaufman, Wolfe, 55, 164, 166, 197

Kelly, Gene, 95, 130

Kern, Jerome, 60, 87–88

King of Jazz (movie), 60